"Careful thought in bioethics is impossible without a well-grounded concept of persons. In public discourse, however, the nature of a human being is rarely considered. In a similar way, academic discussion of personhood sometimes leaves the questions of bio-ethics unexplored. *Taking Persons Seriously* brings these two crucial areas into rigorous conversation. The essays in this collection are academically rigorous, and they provide a sweeping engagement with the most important questions of our day."

—GREGORY E. GANSSLE, CHAIR OF PHILOSOPHY, TALBOT SCHOOL OF THEOLOGY, BIOLA UNIVERSITY

"*Taking Persons Seriously* is a deep dive into the ontological foundations of what it means to be a human person. Yet the various authors don't leave the philosophical question of human nature as an abstraction; rather, they apply their conclusions to pressing contemporary bioethical issues, arguing (rightly in my opinion) that ontology provides the starting point for discussions about bioethics."

—SEAN MCDOWELL, ASSOCIATE PROFESSOR OF CHRISTIAN APOLOGETICS, TALBOT SCHOOL OF THEOLOGY, BIOLA UNIVERSITY

"At nearly every level of our culture—intellectual, social, technological, medical, philosophical, ethical, legal—we have been witnessing a steady erosion of a robust understanding of human personhood. So I am heartened by the appearance of *Taking Persons Seriously*. It offers a powerful, rich, and cutting-edge cross-disciplinary defense of robust personhood, extending from the womb to personhood at the end of life. I highly recommend this excellent and important volume."

—PAUL COPAN, CHAIR OF PHILOSOPHY AND ETHICS, PALM BEACH ATLANTIC UNIVERSITY

"Although intent on serving the good of humanity, bioethics largely ignores the fundamental nature of human persons. In this impressive volume, Mihretu Guta and Scott Rae assemble a diverse group of experts to correct this ontological neglect to preserve the priority of persons. This book can't be ignored!"

—Brandon Rickabaugh, assistant professor of philosophy, Palm Beach Atlantic University

"To reach sound conclusions about bioethical issues, we need a proper understanding of the nature of human persons. This collection of essays will be helpful to anyone who wants to deepen their understanding of what human persons are, why they matter, and the ways such an understanding should guide our approach to theory and practice in bioethics."

—Michael W. Austin, professor of philosophy, Eastern Kentucky University

Taking Persons Seriously

Taking Persons Seriously

Where Philosophy and Bioethics Intersect

EDITED BY
MIHRETU P. GUTA
SCOTT B. RAE

◥PICKWICK *Publications* · Eugene, Oregon

TAKING PERSONS SERIOUSLY
Where Philosophy and Bioethics Intersect

Copyright © 2024 Wipf and Stock Publishers. All rights reserved. Except for brief quotations in critical publications or reviews, no part of this book may be reproduced in any manner without prior written permission from the publisher. Write: Permissions, Wipf and Stock Publishers, 199 W. 8th Ave., Suite 3, Eugene, OR 97401.

Pickwick Publications
An Imprint of Wipf and Stock Publishers
199 W. 8th Ave., Suite 3
Eugene, OR 97401

www.wipfandstock.com

PAPERBACK ISBN: 978-1-6667-3722-6
HARDCOVER ISBN: 978-1-6667-9645-2
EBOOK ISBN: 978-1-6667-9646-9

Cataloguing-in-Publication data:

Names: Guta, Mihretu P., editor. | Rae, Scott B., editor.

Title: Taking persons seriously : where philosophy and bioethics intersect / edited by Mihretu P. Guta and Scott B. Rae.

Description: Eugene, OR : Pickwick Publications, 2024 | Includes bibliographical references and index.

Identifiers: ISBN 978-1-6667-3722-6 (paperback) | ISBN 978-1-6667-9645-2 (hardcover) | ISBN 978-1-6667-9646-9 (ebook)

Subjects: LCSH: Theological anthropology. | Bioethics—Religious aspects. | Medical ethics—Religious aspects. | Christian ethics.

Classification: BX1795.H4 T34 2024 (paperback) | BX1795.H4 T34 (ebook)

06/04/24

Scripture quotation taken from the (NASB®) New American Standard Bible® is copyright © 2020 by The Lockman Foundation. Used by permission. All rights reserved. www.lockman.org.

Scripture marked NIV is from the Holy Bible, New International Version®, copyright ©1973, 1978, 1984, 2011 by Biblica, Inc.® Used by permission. All rights reserved worldwide.

We dedicate this volume to our families in gratitude for their love and support for all our academic projects:
Angie and Pete Guta
Sally, Taylor, Cameron, and Austin Rae

Contents

Figures	ix
Permissions	xi
Contributors	xiii
Acknowledgments	xix
Abbreviations	xxi
Introduction MIHRETU P. GUTA AND SCOTT B. RAE	1

PART I | ONTOLOGY AND PERSONHOOD

1. Concrete but Not Crystalline: The Metaphysics of Human Persons   15
   TIMOTHY HOUK AND RUSSELL DISILVESTRO

2. Modal Arguments for Generic Substance Dualism and Why the Soul Matters for Bioethics   49
   J. P. MORELAND

3. Aristotelian-Thomistic Framework for Detecting Covert Consciousness in Unresponsive Persons   93
   MATTHEW OWEN, ARYN D. OWEN, ANTHONY G. HUDETZ

4. Consciousness and the Self without Reductionism: Touching Churchland's Nerve   126
   ERIC LAROCK AND MOSTYN JONES

5. Does Personhood Come in Degrees?   149
   MIHRETU P. GUTA

6	Ethics and the Generous Ontology ERIC T. OLSON	181

PART II | BIOETHICS AND PERSONHOOD

7	Taking Persons Seriously: Applications to Bioethics SCOTT B. RAE	199
8	The Permanent (?) Vegetative (?) State ERIK M. CLARY	220
9	Will Posthumans Be Persons? Taking the Transhumanist Goal Seriously MATTHEW EPPINETTE	256
10	On Gene Editing LUMAN R. WING	293
11	In Technology's Shadow: Technological Non-Neutrality and Ethical Considerations Regarding Human Enhancements E. A. STEVENS	315
12	Stories from Palliative Care MICHAEL D. BACON	338
	Index	361

Figures

Figure 1: Mind-Body Powers and the Full NCC (ch. 3)   116
Figure 2: Square of Personhood Opposition (ch. 5)   160
Figure 3: CRISPR-Cas9 Mediated Gene-Editing Mechanisms (ch. 10)   299

Permissions

The editors gratefully acknowledge permission from:

Appraisal: The Journal of the British Personalist Forum, to replicate part of "Objects, Dispositions and Lockean Person-Making Properties," by Mihretu P. Guta (*Appraisal* 11 [Spring 2016] 4–11)

Adam Cribbs, to reprint figure 3, *CRISPR-Cas9 Mediated Gene-Editing Mechanisms*

Springer Science and Business Media to adapt part of *Human Capacities and Moral Status*, by Russell DiSilvestro (Dordrecht: Springer, 2010)

Theoretical Medicine and Bioethics to reprint "Ethics and the Generous Ontology," by Eric T. Olson (31 [2010] 259–70)

Contributors

MICHAEL D. BACON holds a BA in history from Princeton University and an MDiv from Fuller Theological Seminary, and received his clinical pastoral training at Methodist Hospital of Southern California. He is the Advance Care Planning Facilitator at Memorial Care Long Beach Medical Center in Long Beach, California, where he guides patients, staff, and community members through the advance care planning process. He is passionate about helping individuals reflect on how to live according to their values and empowering them with tools to do so. He sees advance care planning not only as a means by which patients can explore their own values but also as a way to protect at-risk patients from coercion and exploitation. He is also a chaplain in the US Army Reserve, where he has served in combat engineer and combat stress control units. He currently lives in Signal Hill with his wife, daughter, and dog.

ERIK M. CLARY, DVM, MDiv, PhD, is Associate Professor of Surgery and Bioethics at Oklahoma State University (OSU) College of Veterinary Medicine in Stillwater, Oklahoma. Upon completing a residency in veterinary surgery, Erik was recruited to Duke University Medical Center as a researcher working in the developing field of minimally invasive surgery. After a decade of service directing the laboratory efforts of one of the nation's premiere endosurgical research programs, he undertook postgraduate studies in theology and ethics that culminated in a PhD (Southeastern Baptist Theological Seminary). Erik wrote his dissertation addressing the issue of indefinite life support for people diagnosed as being in a permanent vegetative state. Erik has lectured and published widely on this issue. Before joining the faculty at OSU in 2018, his service in the field of bioethics included a post-doctoral fellowship (L. Russ Bush Center for Faith and

CONTRIBUTORS

Culture, Wake Forest, NC) working chiefly on the issue of physician-assisted suicide, and six years as a bioethics consultant to California state senator Bob Huff. On the national scene, Erik is a regular contributor to bioethics-focused meetings with recent papers delivered to the American Society for Bioethics and Humanities, the Center for Bioethics & Human Dignity, and the Evangelical Theological Society. As a bioethicist, Erik brings to bear in his analyses the uncommon combination of formal training in comparative medicine and research, theology, and ethics.

RUSSELL DISILVESTRO, PhD, is Professor and Chair of the Department of Philosophy at California State University Sacramento. He holds philosophy degrees from Indiana University (BA), Biola University/Talbot School of Theology (MA), and Bowling Green State University (MA, PhD). After earning his PhD, he began teaching at Sacramento State in 2006, and from 2012 to 2016 he served as Director of the CSUS Center for Practical and Professional Ethics; his teaching and research helped support their Philosophy Department's major concentration in ethics, politics, and law. He works on the intersection between metaphysics and ethics, especially as it relates to contemporary bioethical issues involving the nature and moral status of human beings. In 2010 he published a book in Springer's Philosophy and Medicine series titled *Human Capacities and Moral Status*, which argued that the moral status of individual human persons can be grounded in their capacities without embracing inegalitarian consequences for disabled, elderly, and immature human persons.

MATTHEW EPPINETTE, MBA, PhD, is Executive Director of The Center for Bioethics & Human Dignity (CBHD). He has two decades of experience in the field of bioethics, including having served CBHD from 2002 to 2007. In addition to being the author of a number of academic papers and book chapters, he serves as Editor of *Dignitas*, an online, open-access, peer-reviewed publication. He has also cowritten and coproduced six documentary films addressing bioethics issues. His current research interests include transhumanism, Alasdair MacIntyre's ethics and epistemology, and the intersection of fiction, film, and other areas of popular culture that raise or address bioethics issues.

MIHRETU P. GUTA completed his PhD in philosophy at Durham University (UK) under the supervision of Professors E. J. Lowe and Sophie Gibb. He subsequently worked as a postdoctoral research fellow within the Durham Emergence Project (funded by the John Templeton Foundation).

He specialized in metaphysics, philosophy of mind, and the philosophy of neuroscience, with special emphasis on the emergence of consciousness and its relation to the brain. His other research interests include the philosophy of physics, moral philosophy, and applied ethics, particularly bioethics. His published work includes: *Consciousness and the Ontology of Properties*, ed. (2019); *Insights into the First-Person Perspective and the Self: An Interdisciplinary Approach*, Journal of Consciousness Studies, special issue, coedited with Sophie Gibb (2015); a book version of this special issue, published under a new title, *Selfhood, Autism and Thought Insertion* (2021); a special issue on *E. J. Lowe's Metaphysics and Analytic Theology*, coedited with Eric LaRock (2021); and papers and book reviews in many academic journals such as *Philosophia Christi*, *Journal of Consciousness*, *TheoLogica*, the journal of the *British Personalist Forum*, *Analysis*, *Philosophical Quarterly*, the journal of the *American Scientific Affiliation*, and *Frontiers in Systems Neuroscience*. He is working on a single written research monograph entitled *The Metaphysics of Substance and Personhood: A Non-Theory Laden Approach*. Currently, Guta teaches philosophy and bioethics at both Biola University and Azusa Pacific University. In the past Guta taught philosophy at Durham University in the UK. He was also an Assistant to the Academic Dean and Lecturer at the Evangelical Theological College in Addis Ababa, Ethiopia, where he taught academic theology, philosophy, and ethics. He lectured at numerous academic institutions, including supervision of PhD philosophy students at Addis Ababa University.

TIMOTHY HOUK, PhD, is Associate Professor of Philosophy at College of the Sequoias in Visalia, CA. He holds a BA in philosophy from California State University, Sacramento; an MA in philosophy of religion and ethics from Biola University; and a PhD in philosophy from the University of California, Davis. From 2018 to 2019 he served as a postdoctoral fellow at the University of Texas Health Science Center at Houston where he taught medical ethics and consulted with members of hospital ethics boards and committees. His research is in metaphysics and ethics—primarily in the areas of free will, agency, autonomy, and manipulation.

ANTHONY G. HUDETZ, DBM, PhD, is Professor of Anesthesiology, Biomedical Engineering, and Director of Laboratory Science in the Department of Anesthesiology, University of Michigan, Ann Arbor. He is also the Director of the Center for Consciousness Science at the University of Michigan. Dr. Hudetz received his higher education in Budapest. He first studied physics at

CONTRIBUTORS

the Eötvös Loránd University, receiving his MS in 1974. He obtained a Doctor of Biologiae Medicinalis (DBM) degree from the Semmelweis University of Medicine in 1979, and a PhD in the field of medical science from the Hungarian Academy of Sciences in 1985. Dr. Hudetz held previous faculty appointments in the Experimental Research Institute and Second Department of Physiology, Semmelweis University of Medicine, in the Department of Biomedical Engineering, Louisiana Tech University, and in the Departments of Physiology and Anesthesiology at the Medical College of Wisconsin. Dr. Hudetz's primary research interest is in discovering the mechanisms by which anesthetics produce loss of consciousness and the mechanism by which consciousness recovers after anesthesia. His research group led pioneering work in experimental brain electrophysiology, providing the first preclinical evidence for directed anterior-posterior cortical functional disconnection under anesthesia. They performed novel pharmacological reanimation studies to understand the mechanism of regaining consciousness during anesthesia. Using functional magnetic resonance imaging in humans, they demonstrated the differential effect of anesthesia on various cortical networks and discovered the preferential suppression of nonspecific thalamocortical connectivity. Recent investigations from the Hudetz laboratory revealed the important effect of anesthesia on the temporal dynamics of cortical states, both in local circuits and in large-scale networks, supporting Dr. Hudetz's hypothesis of general cortical disintegration as the principal mechanism of anesthetic-induced unconsciousness. Dr. Hudetz has edited multiple books, and he has over 190 research articles and chapter publications, principally in the areas of neuroscience, anesthesiology, and the neurobiology of consciousness. His work has been funded by the National Institute of General Medical Sciences for over twenty-five years. He has presented keynote lectures at numerous scientific meetings, and his work has been featured in the media.

MOSTYN JONES has taught philosophy at various mid-Atlantic universities and colleges in the US. His writing has focused on topics in neurophilosophy and the philosophy of mind such as imagination, consciousness, free will, and human nature.

ERIC LAROCK, PhD, is Associate Professor of Philosophy at Oakland University and Affiliate Faculty at the Center for Consciousness Science, University of Michigan. His primary research areas are philosophy of mind, philosophy of neuroscience, and metaphysics. He has published in such venues as Cambridge University Press, *Consciousness and Cognition*,

Frontiers in Human Neuroscience, *Kant Studies*, *Philosophia Christi*, Routledge, and *Theory & Psychology*.

ERIC T. OLSON, PhD, is Professor of Philosophy at a British university. He was previously Senior Lecturer at the University of Cambridge. He is the author of *The Human Animal* (1997), *What Are We?* (2007), and (with Aaron Segal) *Do We Have a Soul?* (2024), as well as many articles on metaphysics and the philosophy of mind.

ARYN D. OWEN is the Eastern Washington Educator at Airlift Northwest, the medevac branch of UW Medicine, where she also serves as a flight nurse.

MATTHEW OWEN, PhD, teaches philosophy at Yakima Valley College in Washington State and is an affiliate faculty member at the Center for Consciousness Science at the University of Michigan Medical School. After completing his PhD at the University of Birmingham, England, he was the inaugural Elizabeth R. Koch Research Fellow for Tiny Blue Dot Consciousness Studies at Gonzaga University, under the supervision of Drs. Christof Koch and Brian Clayton. He has published articles in a variety of research journals including *Synthese*, *Frontiers in Systems Neuroscience*, *Entropy*, and *TheoLogica*. His first monograph, *Measuring the Immeasurable Mind: Where Contemporary Neuroscience Meets the Aristotelian Tradition* was published in 2021.

J. P. MORELAND, PhD, is Distinguished Professor of Philosophy at Talbot School of Theology at Biola University. He received a BS in physical chemistry from the University of Missouri, a ThM in theology from Dallas Theological Seminary, an MA in philosophy from the University of California at Riverside, and a PhD in philosophy from the University of Southern California. He has authored, edited, or contributed papers to ninety-five books, including *Does God Exist?*, *Universals*, *Consciousness and the Existence of God*, *The Blackwell Companion to Natural Theology*, *The Blackwell Companion to Substance Dualism*, and *Debating Christian Theism*. He has also published over ninety articles in journals such as *Philosophy and Phenomenological Research*, *American Philosophical Quarterly*, *Australasian Journal of Philosophy*, *MetaPhilosophy*, *Philosophia Christi*, *Religious Studies*, and *Faith and Philosophy*. In August 2016, Moreland was selected by The Best Schools as one of the fifty most influential living philosophers in the world.

SCOTT B. RAE is Senior Advisor to the President, Biola University; Dean of Faculty; and Professor of Christian Ethics at Talbot School of Theology, Biola University. He has a BS in Economics from Southern Methodist University,

CONTRIBUTORS

a ThM from Dallas Theological Seminary, and a PhD from the University of Southern California. His primary interests are in bioethics and business ethics, dealing with the application of Christian ethics to medicine and the marketplace. He is the author of fourteen books, including *Moral Choices: An Introduction to Ethics* (2009); *Biotechnology and the Human Good*, with C. Ben Mitchell et al. (2007); *Outside the Womb: Moral Guidance for Assisted Reproduction*, with D. Joy Riley (2010); *Business for the Common Good: A Christian Vision for the Marketplace*, with Kenman L. Wong (2010); *Body and Soul: Human Nature and the Crisis in Ethics*, with J. P. Moreland (2000); *Beyond Integrity: A Judeo-Christian Approach to Business Ethics* (2012); and *Doing the Right Thing* (2013), a companion book to the film series written and produced by the late Chuck Colson. He has articles in various journals, including *Linacre Quarterly*, *National Catholic Bioethics Quarterly*, *Southern California Review of Law and Women's Studies*, and the *Southern Baptist Journal of Theology*. He has consulted with several Southern California hospitals in ethics for fifteen years. He is a fellow of the Center for Bioethics and Human Dignity and the Wilberforce Forum. He is married to Sally, with three grown sons, Taylor, Cameron, and Austin.

E. A. STEVENS received a master's degree in philosophy from Talbot School of Theology, Biola University. She completed her PhD at the University of Aberdeen, Scotland, in philosophy with an emphasis on the philosophy of technology and bioethics. Her research considers bioethics from the standpoint of enhancement technologies and the philosophy of Don Ihde in particular. Her focus is on Ihde's conception of enchantment in conversation with Charles Taylor's understanding of the premodern enchanted world, both of which work with and further develop Merleau-Ponty's phenomenology. She has presented papers on the topics of mind uploading and radical life extension. Her further research interests include transhumanism, philosophical aesthetics, beauty, and modern and contemporary art.

LUMAN R. WING received an MA in theology and a PhD in biochemistry from the University of Aberdeen, Scotland, and has over twenty-five years of experience in the biopharmaceutical industry as a toxicologist. He also worked as Adjunct Professor at the University of San Diego, Azusa Pacific University, and Trinity International University, where he taught undergraduate courses in microbiology and graduate courses in bioethics. Lu is currently a pharmaceutical consultant, an active member of the American Society of Pharmaceutical Scientists, and a consultant with the BIOCOM interdisciplinary research team in cell and gene therapy.

Acknowledgments

Many people played crucial roles for this volume to finally be where it is now. We would like to thank our contributors for their time, interest, and commitment to be part of this project. This volume would not have been possible without their contributions! We also would like to thank the anonymous reviewers of the chapters for their time and invaluable help that led to the improvement of this volume.

Our thanks also go to Talbot School of Theology at Biola University for supporting us in many ways that allowed us to complete this volume.

We especially want to recognize the incredible support we received from Laurissa Kuch (Talbot Philosophy Department) throughout the preparation of this manuscript. Laurissa formatted all of the chapters for us. She did it with joy and passion. We couldn't have done it without her help. We thank you so much, Laurissa!

I (Mihretu) would like to express my sincerest thanks to my former professor of bioethics, Dr. Scott Rae, for collaborating with me on this project. It was back in my graduate student years that I asked Dr. Rae if he would consider one day doing something together on bioethics. Without hesitation, his response was an enthusiastic yes. After so many years, we finally joined hands on this project. Thank you, Dr. Rae, for keeping your promise!

We thank our families for their understanding and encouragement as we worked on this time-consuming project.

Finally, special thanks go to Matthew Wimer, George Callihan, Rebecca Abbott and Savanah N. Landerholm at Wipf and Stock Publishers.

Abbreviations

ANH	artificial nutrition and hydration
Cas9	CRISPR-associated protein 9
CIMT	constraint-induced movement therapy
CNS	central nervous system
CPR	cardiopulmonary resuscitation
CRISPR	clustered regularly interspaced short palindromic repeats
DA	Aristotle. *On the Soul*. In *The Complete Works of Aristotle: The Revised Oxford Translation*, edited by Jonathan Barnes, translated by J. A. Smith, 1:641–92. Princeton, NJ: Princeton University Press, 1984
DAN	dorsal attention network
DFT	dualist field theory
DMN	default mode network
DNA	deoxyribonucleic acid
DNR/AND	Do not resuscitate/allow natural death
DOC	disorders of consciousness
EM	electromagnetic
ESH	emergent subject hypothesis
GSD	generic substance dualism
IEET	Institute for Ethics and Emerging Technologies
IVF	in vitro fertilization

ABBREVIATIONS

LIS	locked-in syndrome
Meta	Aristotle. *Metaphysics*. In *The Complete Works of Aristotle: The Revised Oxford Translation*, edited by Jonathan Barnes, translated by W. D. Ross, 2:1552–728. Princeton, NJ: Princeton University Press, 1984
MCS	minimally conscious state
MSTF	Multi-Society Task Force on PVS
NCC	neural correlates of consciousness
PAM	proto-spacer adjacent motif
PAS	physician-assisted suicide
PGD	preimplantation genetic diagnosis
PVS	persistent vegetative state
RNA	ribonucleic acid
QDA	Aquinas, Thomas. *Questions on the Soul*. Translated by James H. Robb. Milwaukee: Marquette University Press, 1984
SD	substance dualism
SP	standard physicalism
ST	Aquinas, Thomas. *Summa Theologica*. Translated by Fathers of the English Dominican Province. New York: Benziger, 1947
TCH	temporal circuit hypothesis
VS	vegetative state
UWS	unresponsive wakefulness syndrome
WTA	World Transhumanist Association (now Humanity+)

Introduction

Mihretu P. Guta and Scott B. Rae

This book aims to show why a proper ontology of human personhood has paramount importance for issues in bioethics. The field of bioethics deals with diverse topics such as medical ethics, animal ethics, environmental ethics, and technology ethics.[1] Such multifaceted aspects of bioethics often bring up questions that are practical in nature. In this regard, bioethics is said to belong to one of the branches of ethics known as *applied ethics*. This is the branch of ethics that mainly focuses on applying the principles, the rules, and the norms of ethics (moral philosophy) to bioethical issues. But what is ethics (morality)? In simple terms, ethics is the study of what constitutes morally right and wrong actions and behaviors. In this regard, ethical norms or standards provide us with the framework that allows us to make value judgments regarding diverse human activities. In short, at the heart of ethics lies the age-old question: *How ought we to live*?

Different ethical theories (e.g., Kantian ethics, consequentialism, virtue ethics) propose different answers for this age-old question.[2] These answers are developed (broadly speaking) along two lines, namely, *moral realism* and *moral irrealism*. According to moral realism, there is mind-independent moral reality (property) that determines whether our moral beliefs are true or false. In contrast, moral irrealism denies moral reality. In the absence of moral reality, there cannot be moral beliefs that can be evaluated as true or false. Hence, given moral irrealism, one can make up

---

1. See, e.g., Vaughn, *Doing Ethics*, pt. 4; Kass, *Life, Liberty and Defense*.
2. See Shafer-Landau, *Concise Introduction to Ethics*.

one's own moral values as one sees fit.³ There can also be a sense in which one could defend a hybrid position, thereby embracing moral realism in certain situations and moral irrealism in others. As interesting as these issues sound, for present purposes, this volume will not delve into them. But the bioethical discussions advanced in this volume strongly presuppose in one way or another a realist conception of morality as it relates to human personhood.

Contemporary discussions on bioethics often focus on seeking solutions for a wide range of issues that revolve around persons. The issues in question are multilayered, involving such diverse aspects as the metaphysical/ontological, personal, medical, moral, legal, cultural, social, political, religious, and environmental. In navigating through such a complex web of issues, it has been said that the central problems philosophers and bioethicists face are ethical in nature. In this regard, biomedical sciences and technological breakthroughs take a leading role in terms of shaping the sorts of questions that give rise to ethical problems. For example:

- Is it ethical to keep terminally ill patients alive on dialysis machines or artificial ventilators?
- Is it ethical to take someone's vital organs upon death and transplant them into another person's body without any prior consent from a deceased person?

Reproductive techniques also raise complicated ethical issues involving in vitro fertilization, contraceptives, prenatal testing, abortions, and genetic enhancements. Moreover, biomedical issues raise ethical problems in regard to research on human subjects, stem cell research, and enhancement biotechnology. The beginning- and end-of-life issues bring up their own complicated ethical conundrums, involving, among other things, terminating life support and euthanasia.

Over the past two decades, excellent interdisciplinary work addressing multifaceted ethical problems had been produced.⁴ Nevertheless, some philosophers argue that debates about ethical problems in bioethics cannot adequately be tackled without bringing metaphysical reflections to bear on

---

3. See, e.g., McNaughton, *Moral Vision*.

4. Arras et al., *Routledge Companion to Bioethics*; Kuhse et al., *Bioethics*; Kuhse and Singer, *Companion to Bioethics*; Pierce and Randels, *Contemporary Bioethics*; Savulescu and Bostrom, *Human Enhancement*; Singer and Viens, *Cambridge Textbook of Bioethics*; Steinbock, *Oxford Handbook of Bioethics*; Beckwith, *Do the Right Thing*.

human personhood.⁵ Others claim that whatever problems that surface in bioethics, which also include the nature of human personhood, can be given proper treatment within the framework of utilitarian or consequentialist ethics.⁶ Still other philosophers appeal to individual rights or autonomy and mental capacity as a basis to tackle complex bioethical issues that are linked to human persons.⁷ But debates about multifaceted ethical problems in bioethics cannot be divorced from ontological questions. Within the current conceptual framework of the debate, there is a serious lack of emphasis on the ontology of persons as a starting point for discussions that underlie bioethical issues. In this volume, we hope to provide such a starting point.

But what is ontology? Contemporary philosophers propose widely divergent answers for this question.⁸ Yet, historically, the most influential answer for this question traces its roots back to Aristotelian metaphysics. For example, within the framework of Aristotelian tradition, E. J. Lowe defines ontology as "the study of what categories of entities there are and how they are related to one another."⁹ Similarly, Michael Loux and Thomas Crisp characterize ontology as a philosophical inventory of things that are.¹⁰ In a recent work dedicated to the study of ontology, Peter van Inwagen distinguishes between ontology and meta-ontology. An ontology, as Van Inwagen characterizes it, is an attempt to generate a detailed and systematic answer to the "ontological question": "What is there?" Meta-ontology is a reflective answer to the question "What are we asking when we ask the ontological question and how shall we go about answering it?"¹¹ The essays in the first part of this volume focus on tackling both ontological and meta-ontological questions.

Utilizing progress from ontology to bear on the debate on human personhood might open up new ways to tackle complex ethical problems in bioethics. In most cases, the existing discussions and debates on bioethics take place along predictable lines, namely, addressing both traditional issues such as abortion, euthanasia, biotechnology, and whatever new issues

---

5. Oderberg, "Metaphysical Status of Embryo"; Moreland and Rae, *Body & Soul*.

6. Singer, *Practical Ethics*; *Writings on Ethical Life*.

7. Thomson, "Defense of Abortion"; Tooley, "Abortion and Infanticide"; Dennett, "Conditions of Personhood."

8. See, e.g., Quine, "On What There Is?"

9. Lowe, *Survey of Metaphysics*, 14; see also Lowe, *Possibility of Metaphysics*.

10. Loux and Crisp, *Metaphysics*, 13.

11. Van Inwagen, *Being*, xv.

come up from time to time. There is no agreement among both philosophers and bioethicists as to what the best approach is in dealing with disputes over ethical problems in bioethics. As things stand, it is difficult to say with confidence what solution could be forthcoming. There is a need for a clear, defensible account of the ontological status of human personhood which can serve as a framework within which questions regarding the ever-growing complex ethical problems in bioethics can be properly pursued. One way forward is to think systematically about what the issues are, hence engaging with the ontology of human personhood. This book tries to make a significant contribution in this regard, thereby also filling the gap in the current literature.

The contributors of essays for this book are experts in the fields of metaphysics and bioethics, as well as emerging scholars. The main themes of the book are summed up in two parts. In part 1, the chapters mainly focus on issues related to the ontology of human personhood, whereas the chapters in the second part focus on bioethical issues and their implications for human personhood. Taken together, the objective of these themes concerns the importance and centrality of having a proper ontology of human personhood for our understanding of the nature of complex ethical problems in bioethics, both on nonempirical as well as empirical grounds. This means that we need to engage in ground-level debates about the ontology of persons. This is a nonnegotiable first step in taking steps forward in seeking a plausible solution(s) for the complex ethical problems in bioethics. Although the contributors in this book advance their arguments in their own ways, they all agree on one central methodological point: the importance of taking the ontology of persons for bioethics seriously. This is the spirit that brings the contributors of this book together as they seek to build their case(s) concerning the nature of persons.

In their essay, "Concrete but Not Crystalline: The Metaphysics of Human Persons," Timothy Houk and Russell DiSilvestro advance their discussion of the metaphysics of human personhood against the backdrop of a realist metaphysics, which takes, among other things, human persons as concrete particulars (individual substances) that persist through time while undergoing various sorts of changes. Houk and DiSilvestro illustrate some of the ways metaphysical distinctions in philosophy impact bioethics. They lay out different accounts of the metaphysics of person-making properties. They show how these accounts lead to different conclusions about ethical requirements concerning, for instance, how to treat human individuals at early stages of a normal human lifespan. They argue that focusing on the phenomenon of abnormal conditions in the middle of a human lifespan can be used to decide between such accounts. They also consider some objections against this sort of methodology. They particularly address the issue of whether ethics and bioethics depend on metaphysics. They argue that a strong case can be made to show that ethics is dependent on metaphysics. Houk and DiSilvestro conclude that, given the important role metaphysics plays in our ethical reasoning and thinking, we should always pay attention to the sorts of metaphysical assumptions we entertain. If we do this, we will have a better chance to clarify and improve our own assumptions.

In his essay entitled "Modal Arguments for Generic Substance Dualism and Why the Soul Matters for Bioethics," J. P. Moreland makes a case for how and why the human soul is essential for grounding high, equal value to human persons. Moreland thinks that there is a very good argument for what he calls generic substance dualism (GSD). Moreland argues that the strict physicalist views of human persons fail to ground value for human persons. For Moreland, GSD has great advantage over that of a strict physicalist view of human persons in solving the problem of grounding value for human persons. Moreland also gives several reasons for why the body has significant value on a GSD view. Moreland also presents a specific modal argument for GSD. Moreland clarifies each premise in the argument and explains why each is more reasonable than its negation. In doing so, Moreland's goal is to analyze and apply modal epistemology to modal arguments in defense of a GSD. Moreland also analyzes and evaluates the modal epistemology of Timothy O'Connor, George Bealer, and Edmund Husserl. Moreland also considers and provides defeaters for several of the most prominent objections raised against modal arguments. Moreland concludes that the modal argument succeeds in providing strong reasons for a cumulative case for GSD.

In their essay, "Aristotelian-Thomistic Framework for Detecting Covert Consciousness in Unresponsive Persons," Matthew Owen, Aryn D. Owen, and Anthony G. Hudetz set out to show that physicalism is not the only view that provides a philosophical foundation for the science of consciousness as well as empirically detecting consciousness. They argue that the mind-body powers model of neural correlates of consciousness provides a metaphysical framework that is needed to tackle this issue. They argue that the mind-body powers model of neural correlates of consciousness could underlie the theoretical possibility of empirically detecting consciousness. The model in question is informed by an Aristotelian-Thomistic hylomorphic ontology as opposed to a physicalist ontology. As they see it, the mind-body powers model provides a philosophical foundation for the science of consciousness. They claim that the model plays a critical role in our effort to empirically detect consciousness. But the sort of advantage that the mind-body powers model has is lacking in an alternative physicalist approach. In making such a claim, however, Owen, Owen, and Hudetz are not implying that the mind-body powers model provides the only alternative. Rather, their claim is that the model in question provides a sufficient ground to explore the possibility of empirically detecting and scientifically studying consciousness. In light of such considerations, they conclude that if the philosophical foundation of physicalism continues to falter, that will not be a good justification for the research field to experience instability.

In their essay, "Consciousness and the Self without Reductionism: Touching Churchland's Nerve," Eric LaRock and Mostyn Jones challenge the views of some neuroscientists and philosophers who believe that neurobiological facts alone are relevant to answering fundamental ontological questions such as: What am I? What is consciousness? They advance their discussion by focusing on Patricia Churchland's view. In her recent book, *Touching a Nerve*, Churchland argues that naturalism provides a better account of human personhood and consciousness than dualism. LaRock and Jones examine Churchland's identification of human persons with brain stuff. They also examine Churchland's naturalistic account of consciousness. LaRock and Jones argue that even if it may be the case that Cartesian dualism fails to account for the phenomena of neural dependence, nothing follows from this that no other brand of dualism could do the job. They argue that Cartesian dualism is not the only dualist theoretical model available. They introduce non-Cartesian brands of dualism that have greater consilience than naturalism with respect to the deliverances of neuroscience regarding the nature of consciousness and persons. They argue that some of those brands of non-Cartesian dualism count as testable hypotheses. LaRock and Jones forcefully argue that Churchland's purported common neurobiological mechanism of consciousness fails on empirical grounds. For example, they argue that contrary to Churchland's claim, neuronal synchrony strengthens during anesthetic-induced unconsciousness. They also sketch out a new non-Cartesian hypothesis of dualism and indicate how it is testable and fits better the recent data obtained from neuroanesthesia.

LaRock and Jones also reflect on the implications of their discussion for bioethics and show how it rebuts Churchland's bioethical claim that our "moral nature" reduces to our brains. For LaRock and Jones, the bearers of our moral nature are not brains but persons. If the bearers of our moral nature are persons, then LaRock and Jones conclude that persons are not brains.

In his essay, "Does Personhood Come in Degrees?," Mihretu P. Guta discusses what it would take to establish an ontological basis of human personhood. Guta examines the views of human personhood advocated by three influential contemporary philosophers, namely, Michael Tooley, Peter Singer, and Daniel Dennett. After a detailed analysis of the logical structure of the views of human personhood advanced by these philosophers, Guta finds their conception of personhood wanting. Guta then discusses the contemporary powers ontology advanced and defended by philosophers such as John Heil and C. B. Martin. Guta shows how the powers ontology can be used to address currently the most controversial issue of whether personhood is something that can be lost, say due to the malfunctioning of cognitive faculties which results in various sorts of cognitive disabilities. Guta argues that given the explanatory advantage that the powers ontology gives us, there are excellent reasons to think that the disruption of the normal operation of a person's cognitive faculties does not indicate the loss of the capacities in question. Rather the malfunctioning of cognitive faculties and the ensuing inability to exercise the capacities in question is only indicative of instances of a different sort of dispositional manifestations. For Guta, the manifestation of disposition is not a one-way street in the sense of stimulus-response mechanism. Rather the manifestation of dispositions tracks multiple paths (multidirectional). Guta argues that the apparent loss of certain personhood grounding properties is only an instance of a different kind of dispositional manifestation at work. Guta argues that personhood is not something that can be lost. Based on such considerations, Guta draws a conclusion that human personhood does not come in degrees at all.

In his essay, "Ethics and the Generous Ontology," Eric Olson discusses the way in which metaphysics impinges on ethics. Olson examines the temporal parts ontology, which he calls "generous ontology." Olson discusses the implications of this ontology for issues related to personal identity and also asks, among other things, whether short-lived entities, which he calls "subpeople," have moral status. Olson explores the issue of whether the interests of subpeople clash with ours, if the interests of sub- and crosspeople (combination of several people) differ from our own. Olson also discusses the Parfitian proposal that postulates that the primary interest bearers or moral people are said to be maximal aggregates of R-interrelated person-stages. However, for Olson, without generous ontology, there would be no sub- or crosspeople. Olson argues that every human organism starts out as an embryo with no need for psychological continuity as a condition for personal identity and persistence. Olson argues that a being's having full moral status seems to be contingent on the truth of the generous ontology. If this turns out to be true, then a being in question might have to always be R-related to itself in order to have a moral status. But if this is not the case, then the conditions for full moral status can be said to be less demanding. For Olson, all of this shows the impact of metaphysics upon ethics.

Building upon the discussions advanced in the first part of this volume, the essays in the second part focus on bioethics and personhood:

In his essay, "Taking Persons Seriously: Applications to Bioethics," Scott B. Rae points out that current bioethical discussions often sideline the centrality of metaphysics. However, Rae points out that even though metaphysical considerations are not explicitly embraced in broader academic environment, their presence is implicit in the arguments and debates advanced by mainstream views on bioethical issues. After giving a nice summary of the essays discussed in part 1, Rae turns his attention to important bioethical issues such as abortion, infanticide, embryo research, reproductive technologies, biotechnology, genetic testing, gene editing, and human persons at the end of life—removing treatments and physician-assisted suicide/euthanasia. Rae discusses these issues within the framework of the arguments developed by other contributors in this volume. He shows how each chapter contributed to this volume is interconnected in the sense of showing the centrality of metaphysical basis for a proper conception of human personhood. Rae's discussion shows what is lacking in current bioethical discussions and why, without a proper ontological/metaphysical framework, establishing an adequate conception of human personhood is not possible. That means that, as Rae points out, some of the popular conceptions of human personhood that imply that personhood is something that can be gained and lost depending on retaining certain psychological capacities are deeply implausible. Rae nicely shows how the themes of the twelve chapters in this volume make a coherent whole.

INTRODUCTION

In his essay, "The Permanent (?) Vegetative (?) State," Erik M. Clary discusses one of the challenging issues in medical ethics which concerns vegetative-state patients. The term "persistent vegetative state" was introduced by neuro-specialists Bryan Jennett and Fred Plum. Clary points out that Jennett and Plum described that affected individuals are insensate and uninterruptedly unconscious due to a cerebrum that has ceased to function. But if the brainstem is preserved, people in the persistent vegetative state are said to experience wakefulness. People in such state are said to be capable of breathing independently, that is, without ventilatory assistance. They are also said to be capable of responding to a variety of stimuli. Clary pulls together various threads of contemporary controversies on vegetative-state patients and underscores the need to resist drawing hasty conclusions regarding the extent to which the situation of the vegetative-state patients is irreversible. Clary argues that the phenomenon of vegetative state continues to be perplexing even though it has been known for nearly fifty years. Clary shows why the broad depiction of mindless patients cannot be sustained in the face of medical data. Clary presents a wide range of data on vegetative patients and argues that there are lots of things we cannot confidently assert as to the condition of people in the vegetative state. Clary finalizes his discussion with some theological reflections on the complex and, often, less clear situations surrounding people who are in a vegetative state. Clary shows why this phenomenon should be handled in an ethically sensitive manner since our knowledge in this area is far from perfect.

In his essay, "Will Posthumans Be Persons? Taking the Transhumanist Goal Seriously," Matthew Eppinette discusses a hotly debated issue of transhumanism. Eppinette claims that the transhuman movement actively aims at moving beyond current ideas of what it is to be human. Transhumanists set out to figure out the next phase of evolution after or beyond human beings. Eppinette shows in what way the next phase of transhumanist evolution is taken to culminate in becoming posthuman. Eppinette tries to answer the key question of how Christians are supposed to think about the idea of posthuman and its alleged possibility. Eppinette argues why transhumanism inevitably leads us to raise central questions as to what to make of the personhood of various imagined forms of post humanity. Eppinette develops his discussion with an overview of transhumanism. He outlines some of transhumanism's key terms. He engages with important literature that deal with transhumanism including some of its leading proponents and organizations that promote it. Eppinette concludes his discussion by examining posthuman views of personhood and shows how to evaluate it from a Christian standpoint.

In his essay, "On Gene Editing," Luman R. Wing examines the science and the ethical implications of gene editing. This is a fairly recent biotechnological advancement. Luman begins his discussion with an overview of the biology of gene editing, referred to as the CRISPR-Cas9 (clustered regularly interspaced short palindromic repeats–CRISPR-associated protein 9) technology. Luman discusses how gene editing technology has recently emerged as a new methodology that is taken to be very promising to treat and prevent disease. However, as Luman shows, technology can also be used to alter traits unrelated to medical needs. Luman argues that when gene editing technology is used for medically unrelated reasons, say, to change the human genome, it could result in unwanted genetic consequences, such as tumor formation. Luman points out that abusing this technology could cause serious harm to human beings. Luman concludes his discussion by showing how true biologists recognize that the study of the complex human biology must be a science that should aim at understanding human nature holistically.

In her essay "In Technology's Shadow: Technological Non-Neutrality and Ethical Considerations Regarding Human Enhancements," E. A. Stevens forcefully argues why contrary to some popular perceptions, technology is far from neutral. Such perception of technology, as Stevens, shows is widespread within the field of bioethics. Stevens's essay ably demonstrates that while technology has many positive benefits, we should not lose sight of the fact that it can also be misused. For Stevens, technological neutrality is untenable. Stevens focuses on enhancement technologies as a test case to establish her conclusion as to why technology is not neutral. Stevens develops her discussion by using examples of specific bioethicists who see technology as neutral. For Stevens, commitment to neutrality results in a user's autonomy which she claims factors into the conversation. She also discusses the work of the philosopher of technology Don Ihde. She concludes her chapters by drawing some of the implications of her views on non-neutrality of technology for human personhood.

In the final essay, entitled "Stories from Palliative Care," Michael D. Bacon discusses the issue of palliative care. He discusses some really very challenging life situations based on his own firsthand experience as the advance care planning facilitator at Memorial Care Long Beach Medical Center in Long Beach, California. Bacon guides patients, staff, and community members through the advance care planning process. In his essay, he presents practical aspect of what palliative care looks like. He shows how the palliative care teams work to help patients manage serious and life-limiting illnesses while maximizing their quality of life. Bacon made observations working on an adult inpatient palliative care team at an acute-care hospital in Southern California. Bacon's essay shows why answering the question of what constitutes a good quality of life proves to be harder than many of us would like to admit. His essay points out how the practical life situation is very different from largely conceptual matters discussed in the previous eleven chapters of this volume.

BIBLIOGRAPHY

Arras, John D., et al. *The Routledge Companion to Bioethics*. New York: Routledge, 2015.
Beckwith, Francis J., ed. *Do the Right Thing: Readings in Applied Ethics and Social Philosophy*. 2nd ed. Belmont, CA: Wadsworth, 2002.
Dennett, Daniel. "Conditions of Personhood." In *The Identities of Persons*, edited by Amélie Oksenberg Rorty, 175–96. Topics in Philosophy 3. Berkeley: University of California Press, 1976.
Eberl, Jason T. *The Nature of Human Persons: Metaphysics and Bioethics*. Notre Dame Studies in Medical Ethics and Bioethics. Notre Dame, IN: University of Notre Dame Press, 2020.
Locke, John. *An Essay Concerning Human Understanding*. Edited by Roger Woolhouse. Penguin Classics. New York: Penguin Classics, 1997.
Loux, Michael J., and Thomas M. Crisp. *Metaphysics: A Contemporary Introduction*. 4th ed. Routledge Contemporary Introductions to Philosophy. New York: Routledge, 2017.
Lowe, E. J. *The Possibility of Metaphysics: Substance, Identity, and Time*. Oxford: Clarendon, 1998.
———. *A Survey of Metaphysics*. Oxford: Oxford University Press, 2002.
Kass, Leon R. *Life, Liberty and the Defense of Dignity: The Challenge for Bioethics*. San Francisco: Encounter, 2002.
Kuhse, Helga, and Peter Singer, eds. *A Companion to Bioethics*. 2nd ed. Blackwell Companions to Philosophy. Oxford: Wiley-Blackwell, 2009.
Kuhse, Helga, et al. *Bioethics: An Anthology*. 3rd ed. Blackwell Philosophy Anthologies. Oxford: Wiley-Blackwell, 2016.
McNaughton, David. *Moral Vision: An Introduction to Ethics*. Oxford: Blackwell, 1988.
Moreland, J. P., and Scott B. Rae. *Body & Soul: Human Nature & the Crisis in Ethics*. Downers Grove, IL: IVP Academic, 2000.
Oderberg, David. "The Metaphysical Status of the Embryo: Some Arguments Revisited." *Journal of Applied Philosophy* 25 (2008) 263–76.
Pierce, Jessica, and George Randels, eds. *Contemporary Bioethics: A Reader with Cases*. Oxford: Oxford University Press, 2009.
Quine, Willard Van Orman. "On What There Is?" *Review of Metaphysics* 2 (1948) 21–38.

INTRODUCTION

Savulescu, Julian, and Nick Bostrom, eds. *Human Enhancement*. Oxford: Oxford University Press, 2009.
Shafer-Landau, Russ. *A Concise Introduction to Ethics*. Oxford: Oxford University Press, 2020.
Singer, Peter. *Practical Ethics*. 2nd ed. Cambridge: Cambridge University Press, 1993.
———. *Writings on an Ethical Life*. New York: Harper Perennial, 2000.
Singer, Peter, and A. M. Viens, eds. *The Cambridge Textbook of Bioethics*. Cambridge: Cambridge University Press, 2008.
Steinbock, Bonnie, ed. *The Oxford Handbook of Bioethics*. Oxford Handbooks. Oxford: Oxford University Press, 2007.
Strawson, Galen. *Locke on Personal Identity: Consciousness and Concernment*. Princeton, NJ: Princeton University Press, 2011.
Taylor, Stacey, J., ed. *The Metaphysics and Ethics of Death: New Essays*. Oxford: Oxford University Press, 2013.
Thomson, Judith J. "A Defense of Abortion." *Philosophy & Public Affairs* 1 (1971) 47–66.
Tooley, Michael. "Abortion and Infanticide." *Philosophy & Public Affairs* 2 (1972) 37–65.
Van Inwagen, Peter. *Being: A Study in Ontology*. Oxford: Oxford University Press, 2023.
Vaughn, Lewis. *Doing Ethics: Moral Reasoning, Theory, and Contemporary Issues*. 6th ed. New York: Norton, 2022.

PART I

Ontology and Personhood

1

Concrete but Not Crystalline
The Metaphysics of Human Persons

Timothy Houk and Russell DiSilvestro[1]

1. INTRODUCTION

The goal of this paper is to illustrate some of the ways that practical and knowable metaphysical distinctions in philosophy impact bioethics. After we set the stage in this introductory section, in section 2, we rehearse how different accounts of the metaphysics of person-making properties lead to different conclusions about ethical requirements for how to treat human individuals at early stages of a normal human lifespan (e.g., infancy), and we argue that attending carefully to the phenomenon of abnormal conditions in the middle of a human lifespan (e.g., teenagers who are temporarily brain damaged) is helpful for deciding between such accounts. In section 3, we consider some objections about this kind of methodology. For example, some might object that ethics generally, and bioethics specifically, needn't concern itself with metaphysics because (a) ethics does not actually depend on metaphysics or (b) even if it does, we can practice and theorize about the latter without the former—but we argue such objections are misguided. We conclude that, given the impact metaphysics has on ethics, we should be

---

1. Order of authorship was determined by a coin flip.

PART I | ONTOLOGY AND PERSONHOOD

alert to metaphysical assumptions we and others inevitably make in thinking about bioethics, and should seek to clarify and improve our own such assumptions when we can.

Today, one of us typed "metaphysics" on the Barnes & Noble online search engine and noticed that two of the first eight hits were books on New Age spirituality.[2] This online mini-experiment confirms earlier in-person experiences of seeing "metaphysics" signs in bookstores that direct customers not to the "Philosophy" section but to the "New Age & Alternative Beliefs" section.[3] If bookstores were our only guide, we might think metaphysics typically involves things like astral projection, plant consciousness, and crystals.

But historically, metaphysics is foundational to the practice and discipline of philosophy—and thankfully, even Barnes & Noble still reflects this.[4] Typing "metaphysics" into Google brings this dictionary definition: "The branch of philosophy that deals with the first principles of things, including abstract concepts such as being, knowing, substance, cause, identity, time, and space." It is of particular interest that this dictionary accents "abstract" concepts, and this accent is more emphatic with the second definition: "Abstract theory with no basis in reality; this concept of society as an organic entity is, for market liberals, simply metaphysics." Metaphysics, whether about crystals or not, is apparently something "abstract" in some deep, and potentially debilitating, way.

We aim to carefully push back against these characterizations of metaphysics, especially as they relate to human persons like us and you. But there are different ways of pushing back here, and not all of them are equally helpful. Any adequate pushback needs to balance the pictures from bookstores and dictionaries while still acknowledging why they are there to begin with.

One might push back by noting that, since the academic discipline of physics studies reality, perhaps metaphysics is a related discipline still capable of being rooted in reality. But this connection would be too hasty for several reasons, as philosopher Peter van Inwagen reminds us:

---

2. The titles were Ashby, *Kemetic Tree of Life*; Lindsey-Billingsley, *Black Consciousness*.

3. I picked those categories directly from today's B&N interface: https://www.barnesandnoble.com/h/books/browse.

4. Five of the first eight hits were on Immanuel Kant, followed by Arthur Schopenhauer, Martin Heiddeger, and—finally!—Aristotle.

Certain twentieth-century coinages like "metaphilosophy" and "metapsychology" encourage the impression that metaphysics is a study that somehow "goes beyond" physics. In reality, however, the Greek phrase "ta meta ta phusica," from which our word "metaphysics" is derived, is the term that the early editors of Aristotle's corpus used to refer to his book (from their point of view, his "books") on what he called first philosophy. And this phrase means only "the ones [sc. books] that come after the ones about nature." As is often the case, etymology is no guide to meaning.[5]

Likewise, one might push back by noting that Aristotle himself, in those books his editors titled *Ta meta ta phusica*, did not focus only on abstract questions (much less crystals!). However, focusing too closely on Aristotle's own choice of topics is too limiting, as philosopher Michael Rea notes:

> Aristotle famously characterized metaphysics as the study of being qua being, or of being as such. But this characterization is almost certain to be useless to anyone who is not already well versed in philosophy generally and in the history of metaphysics in particular. Indeed, I suspect that few professional metaphysicians have any clear idea what this characterization means; and I think that even fewer would be inclined to think of themselves as studying "being as such" in pursuing their various research projects.[6]

Fortunately, we can recognize that Aristotle's methods and topics in *Ta meta ta phusica* are representative of an influential strand of metaphysics, and even foundational to later strands of it, without requiring that his methods or topics are exhaustive of all strands of it. Typical contemporary collections on metaphysics recognize this, and focus not only on topics like (to echo the earlier definition above) being, time, and space but also on topics like human beings (e.g., what is a human being?), human relations with time and space (e.g., when, if ever, are you the same individual now that you were several years ago?), and human freedom (e.g., when are

---

5. Van Inwagen, "Introduction," 1. We might update Van Inwagen's point: in some hyper-specialized academic subcultures, for any subject *x*, "meta-*x*" is that pseudo-subject for those without enough intelligence, skill, self-discipline or grit to hack it studying *x*, but who still have the aspiration (and chutzpah!) to comment on subjects within *x*. So perhaps metaphysics is for those who failed at physics but still want to criticize how physicists do their job?

6. Rea, *Arguing about Metaphysics*, 1. For a more robust discussion here, see Rea, *Metaphysics*, ch. 1 ("Introduction"), sect. 1 ("The Nature of Metaphysics").

my thoughts and actions free?). For example, while Van Inwagen and Rea reach slightly different preferred characterizations of metaphysics,[7] they agree that it can be one of the most personally important and existentially relevant practices we do.

For an example of how metaphysics can have personally far-reaching implications, consider how Michael Rea introduces a book on a topic in metaphysics by rehearsing the ancient "debtor's paradox":

> Imagine calling on a friend to collect a debt and receiving, instead of your money, the following philosophical argument: "As we all know, a human being is just a collection of particles. But, as we also know, if you add particles to or subtract particles from a collection of particles, you get a new collection. Now, this debt was contracted several weeks ago, and many of the particles that composed the person who contracted the debt have long since passed into the environment. So I am a different collection of particles from the one that contracted the debt. Thus, since a human being is just a collection of particles, I am a different human being from the one who contracted the debt. Therefore, I do not owe you any money!"[8]

Rea later recounts an ancient if humorous approach to this puzzle:

> The Debtor's Paradox is the oldest, first appearing in the writings of the comic playwright Epicharmus in the fifth century B.C. Of course, Epicharmus did not give the puzzle any sort of sophisticated philosophical treatment. In the scene in which it appears, the debtor's friend apparently decides that the best way to respond to the argument is simply to strike the debtor. The debtor becomes enraged, at which point the friend points out that, by the debtor's own reasoning, he cannot be held responsible for delivering the blow.[9]

---

7. "Perhaps in the end, all we can say is this: some 'categories' or 'concepts' are sufficiently 'general' that a statement will count as a 'metaphysical statement' if—given that it is made in a context in which no restrictions of intended reference are in force, and given that the person who makes it is making a serious effort to say what is strictly and literally true—it employs only these categories" (Van Inwagen, "Introduction," 4). "Thus, in short: Metaphysics is the attempt to provide rigorously developed answers to non-scientific questions about what exists and about the necessary connections among such concepts, properties, and relations as pertain to things other than reasons, values, and mathematical objects" (Rea, *Arguing about Metaphysics*, 3).

8. Rea, *Material Constitution*, xv.

9. Rea, *Material Constitution*, xviii. Rea himself notes: "My information about Ephicharmus's play comes from Sedley 1982, 255–56" (Rea, *Material Constitution*, xviiin5, referring to Sedley, "Stoic Criterion of Identity").

This nicely illustrates how metaphysics can be as practical as a punch in the face. It's not, of course, that metaphysics necessarily leads to blows! Instead, what we might call "applied" metaphysics involves living out the consequences of our metaphysical assumptions about ourselves and our place in the world. The example of the debtor's paradox shows the absurdity of certain "physical" accounts of what makes a person (as a responsible agent) survive from one time to another, and the debtor's friend in the comedy rubs in the impracticality of such accounts.

In this chapter, we aim to illustrate the practicality of metaphysics through some topics about human persons where metaphysical distinctions are central. In section 2 we examine how different metaphysical views may result in different moral conclusions, and in section 3 we examine two methodological objections to using metaphysical distinctions this way. Our goal is not to be comprehensive or decisive, but illustrative and suggestive.

2. HOW DIFFERENT METAPHYSICAL VIEWS MAY RESULT IN DIFFERENT MORAL CONCLUSIONS

In this section we rehearse how different accounts of the metaphysics of person-making properties lead to different conclusions about ethical requirements for how to treat human individuals at early stages of a normal human lifespan (e.g., infancy). We also argue that attending carefully to the phenomenon of abnormal conditions in the middle of a human lifespan (e.g., teenagers who are temporarily brain damaged) is helpful for deciding between such accounts.

Persons are individuals that possess certain kinds of properties, which we might call "person-making properties" since they make an individual a person rather than a nonperson like a rock or a tree.[10] Different accounts of such person-making properties abound. For example, John Locke, in one of his discussions, said a person is "a thinking intelligent Being, that has reason and reflection, and can consider it self as itself, the same thinking thing in different times and places."[11] And Mary Anne Warren suggested "the traits which are most central to the concept of personhood" include (1)

---

10. In defining person-making properties this way, I am not claiming that there are certain properties that make a given individual person (like me) that individual person rather than another individual person (like my brother)—or even that there are such properties. Such claims are possible, but would require further argument.

11. Locke, *Essay Concerning Human Understanding*, 2.27.9.

"consciousness ... and in particular the capacity to feel pain"; (2) "reasoning"; (3) "self-motivated activity"; (4) "the capacity to communicate"; and (5) "the presence of self-concepts and self-awareness."[12]

One of us has argued elsewhere that whichever account of the person-making properties we choose to focus on, it is important to formulate those properties so that they include not merely what might be called "immediate" capacities (for example, the capacity to think right now), but "higher-order" capacities as well (for example, the capacity to develop the capacity to think).[13] The idea is that if we employ the concept of "capacity" or "power" or "disposition" or "potential" in the best ways, this can help us articulate how (for example) human infants are "persons with potential" rather than "potential persons."[14]

To illustrate this, let us now consider part of a standard debate about "potential persons," and then examine how metaphysical distinctions about person-making properties lead to diverse moral conclusions, and then notice how certain cases help us choose between rival accounts of person-making properties.

In discussions of the early stages of human life (such as infancy), the somewhat vague claim that "an individual's potential is relevant to its moral status" is sometimes made more precise in the following way:[15]

---

12. Warren, "On Moral and Legal Status," 55.

13. DiSilvestro, "Reproductive Autonomy," 67.

14. A closely related discussion (which we do not have space to unpack in this chapter) is the persistence of persons through time. There are two main approaches to persistence: endurance and perdurance. Something endures if it is wholly present at each moment of its existence. For example, if there are such things as indivisible simple particles (like what ancient Greek philosophers called "atoms"), perhaps they endure: perhaps a particle is wholly present at each moment it exists, and it endures from one moment of its existence to the next. Something perdures if it is only partly present at each moment of its existence. For example, if there are such things as baseball games, perhaps they perdure: perhaps a game is not wholly present in the first inning, but is spread out in time over nine innings. Indeed, some clarify perdurance by talk of a "space-time-worm" whose segments are the temporal slices—like each inning of a nine-inning baseball game. If you think that even simple particles perdure rather than endure, you will treat each time slice of the persisting particle like an inning of a baseball game: even though the particle is simple and indivisible spatially (having no spatial parts), it nevertheless is complex and divisible temporally (having any number of distinct temporal stages). So, an important question that connects with discussions about dispositional properties of persons is this: Do persons persist by enduring or perduring?

15. Some of what follows in this section is adapted from DiSilvestro, *Human Capacities and Moral Status*, 131–42.

> The fact that an individual is a potential person is sufficient for it to possess a right to life.

Let's call this the key claim. The key claim is often opposed by the example of the potential president, which got its first statement by Australian philosopher Stanley Benn:

> [My argument] is not the argument that infants are potential persons, and have rights as such. For if A has rights only because he satisfies some condition P, it doesn't follow that B has the same rights now because he could have property P at some time in the future. It only follows that he will have rights when he has P. He is a potential bearer of rights, as he is a potential bearer of P. A potential president of the United States is not on that account Commander-in-Chief.[16]

Benn's example has garnered a fair amount of attention over the last four decades, and variations on it abound—for example, Peter Singer used a British version, noting that "Prince Charles is a potential King of England, but he does not now have the rights of a king."[17]

Let us examine several distinctions that help us understand this example, a problem this example illustrates, and three ways of responding to the problem.

2.1 Normative vs. Descriptive Senses of "Person"

It is helpful to have a clearer understanding of the concept of a person that appears both in the key claim above and in the example of the potential president.[18] We think one of the most important distinctions in the way the word "person" is used is what Joel Feinberg calls the distinction between normative (or moral) personhood on the one hand and descriptive (or commonsense) personhood on the other:

> To be a person in the normative sense is to have rights, or rights and duties, or at least to be the sort of being who could have rights

---

16. Benn, "Abortion, Infanticide, and Respect," 143.
17. Singer, *Practical Ethics*, 153.
18. We believe the claim relies upon an inadequate concept of a person. The concept of a person in the claim, even when interpreted charitably, is still somewhat technical, narrow, and apt to mislead. Still, it is worth investigating whether the potential president example really does count against the claim, as stated, before moving on. And the first step in this investigation is getting clear on what might be meant by "person" and "potential person" in the claim.

and duties without conceptual absurdity . . . when we attribute personhood in a purely normative way to any kind of being, we are attributing such moral qualities as rights or duties, but not (necessarily) any observable characteristics of any kind—for example, having flesh or blood, or belonging to a particular species.[19]

There are certain characteristics that are fixed by a rather firm convention of our language such that the general term for any being who possesses them is "person." . . . I shall call the idea defined by these characteristics "the commonsense concept of personhood." When we use the word "person" in this wholly descriptive way we are not attributing rights, duties, eligibility for rights and duties, or any other normative characteristics to the being so described. At most we are attributing characteristics that may be a ground for ascribing rights and duties.[20]

There is nothing incoherent about claiming that an individual is a person in some descriptive sense while denying that it is a person in some normative sense. But as Feinberg's last sentence indicates, there are many examples of substantive proposals for the relationship between an individual's descriptive personhood and its normative personhood. Indeed, it's easy to see why there are at least as many accounts of the relationship between descriptive and normative personhood as there are accounts of those two types of personhood themselves. For example, the statement "a person's a person, no matter how small"—from the famous children's book *Horton Hears a Who!*[21]—could mean one of four things:

1. A normative person is a normative person, no matter how small.
2. A descriptive person is a descriptive person, no matter how small.
3. A normative person is a descriptive person, no matter how small.
4. A descriptive person is a normative person, no matter how small.[22]

---

19. Feinberg, "Abortion," 186 (emphasis added). A similar point is made by Locke and by Warren.

20. Feinberg, "Abortion," 187 (first two emphases added). Again, Locke and Warren make similar points.

21. Seuss, *Horton Hears a Who!*

22. One reviewer requested clarification here. Given the story of the children's book and because of the phrase "no matter how small," we do not think (1) and (2) are mere tautologies (like "N is N" or "D is D"). (1) is basically saying: "Smallness cannot cancel normative personhood; the claim that something is small can never defeat the claim that something is a normative person; while it may be an open question precisely what

We think Seuss was making point (4), for what it's worth. But notice that each of these four claims, when filled out with exactly one of the many accounts of descriptive personhood ("thinking thing"), and with exactly one of the many accounts of normative personhood ("individual with right to life"), becomes a claim that does not explicitly mention the word "person" at all despite being doubly and deeply personal:

1* An individual with a right to life is an individual with a right to life, no matter how small.

2* A thinking thing is a thinking thing, no matter how small.

3* An individual with a right to life is a thinking thing, no matter how small.

4* A thinking thing is an individual with a right to life, no matter how small.

---

the normative person-making properties are, smallness or bigness are not among those properties." Likewise for (2): "Smallness cannot cancel descriptive personhood; the claim that something is small can never defeat the claim that something is a descriptive person; while it may be an open question precisely what the descriptive person-making properties are, smallness or bigness are not among those properties." On the other hand, we do not think (3) and (4) are mere identity statements (like "Peter Parker is Spider-man" or "The property of being even is the property of being divisible by two without remainder"). Rather, (3) and (4) are statements about a relation between two properties, and assert that such a relation cannot be cancelled by smallness. But here we should be careful, since the precise relation is open to at least two charitable readings of (3) and (4). Either (3) and (4) may state when a first property must be inferred from a second property (this is a weaker, epistemic reading), or they may state when a first property is the basis or ground of a second property (this is a stronger, metaphysical reading). (3) On a weaker epistemic reading: "If something is a normative person, then we may infer that it is a descriptive person (and smallness cannot block that inference)." (3) On a stronger metaphysical reading: "If something is a normative person, then we may infer that it is a descriptive person, and this is because the property of being a normative person is a basis or ground of being a descriptive person; the property of being a normative person makes something a descriptive person; being a normative person is a descriptive person-making property, and smallness cannot block that relation between the two properties." (4) On a weaker epistemic reading: "If something is a descriptive person, then we may infer that it is a normative person (and smallness cannot block that inference)." (4) On a stronger metaphysical reading: "If something is a descriptive person, then we may infer that it is a normative person, and this is because the property of being a descriptive person is a basis or ground of being a normative person; the property of being a descriptive person makes something a normative person; being a descriptive person is a normative person-making property, and smallness cannot block that relation between the two properties."

Again, we think Seuss himself was making something like point (4*), but it's worth noting that (4*) is only one of many interesting sorts of claims that seeks to make a characteristic of descriptive personhood into a ground of normative personhood in precisely the way that Feinberg notices. Indeed, that is why some "pro-life" advocates wear T-shirts with the original Seuss quote on the front, while some "pro-choice" advocates reject such shirts.

The key claim above, when interpreted charitably, uses the word "person" in the two-word phrase "potential person" in a descriptive sense, not a normative sense. That key claim was:

> (Q) the fact that an individual is a potential person is sufficient for it to possess a right to life.

So, interpreted charitably, the key claim is not:

> (QN) the fact that an individual is a potential (normative) person is sufficient for it to possess a right to life.

Rather, the key claim is that:

> (QD) the fact that an individual is a potential (descriptive) person is sufficient for it to possess a right to life.

The key claim leaves completely open the question of precisely which characteristics—reason and/or consciousness, etc.—are constitutive of being a "person" in a descriptive sense. That is, the key claim, as stated, leaves completely open what the "person-making properties" are, and whether they include some, all, or none of the ones Locke mentioned.

The example of the potential president also uses the word "person" in a descriptive sense, not a normative sense. As Benn originally put it:

> I characterize a person . . . as someone aware of himself, not just as process or happening, but as agent, as making decisions that make a difference to the way the world goes, as having projects that constitute certain existing or possible states as "important" and "unimportant," as capable, therefore, of assessing his own performances as successful or unsuccessful.[23]

One need not be committed to Benn's particular proposal regarding the characteristics constitutive of being a descriptive "person" in order to rely upon his example of the potential president. (That is, one need not agree with him on what the person-making properties are.) However, one

---

23. Benn, "Abortion, Infanticide, and Respect," 141.

certainly does need to keep to some descriptive use of the word "person"—and to stay away from all normative uses of the word "person"—in order to rely upon Benn's example. Otherwise, the entire structure of the example, and its relevance to the key claim above, falls apart.

2.2. A Standard Response vs. Another Way

One of the standard responses to Benn's example of the potential president is to claim that, although Benn is correct both in his description of the example and in the general principle he extracts from the example, Benn is mistaken in thinking that either the general principle or the example are relevant to the key claim. According to this standard response, Benn has simply misunderstood the defender of the key claim. We believe this standard response is correct, but of limited importance.

First, consider why the standard response is correct. Benn imagines the defender of the key claim arguing as follows (for the sake of clarity, we will drop Benn's use of the letters *a*, *b*, and *p*, but will insert several phrases about times):

1. An individual has the right to life at a given time only because that individual is a person at that time.

Therefore,

2. An individual has the right to life at a given time because that individual could be a person at some time after that time.

If the defender of the key claim really were arguing from (1) to (2), then the example of the potential president would be an appropriate criticism. As Joel Feinberg put it,

> It is a logical error ... to deduce actual rights from merely potential (but not yet actual) qualification for those rights. What follows from potential qualification ... is potential, not actual, rights; what entails actual rights is actual, not potential, qualification. As the Australian philosopher Stanley Benn puts it, "A potential president of the United States is not on that account Commander-in-Chief [of the US Army and Navy]." This simple point can be called "the logical point about potentiality."[24]

---

24. Feinberg, "Abortion," 194.

However, a standard response to Benn's example is that Benn has misunderstood the defender of the key claim. "After all," this standard response goes, "the defender of the key claim would not accept (1) in the first place. Still less would she attempt to argue for (2) on the basis of (1)." As Michael J. Wreen notes,

> Proponents of [the view that all potential persons have a right to life] would agree that mere potential possession of the qualifications for a right is not sufficient for actual possession of that right. But the question, they would add, is what the actual qualifications for possession of a right to life are. They hold that potential personhood is that—or, better, one such—actual qualification, or sufficient condition, and so quite correctly claim that the "logical point about potentiality" that Feinberg mentions counts nought against them.[25]

As we said above, we believe this standard response is correct. However, we recognize that there is another way of employing Benn's example that might appear to cause problems. In particular, the example of the potential president does more than merely illustrate the fallacy of reasoning from (1) to (2), or "the logical point about potentiality." In addition, as we shall now explain, the example of the potential president subtly advances a certain way of thinking about persons in the first place, and it is this way of thinking about persons that might appear to cause problems.

2.3 Fine vs. Tricky Assumptions

To see why, notice Benn's example of the potential president relies upon two assumptions about presidents and two parallel assumptions about persons. While the assumptions about presidents are fine, the assumptions about persons are tricky. Let us state them before explaining and evaluating them:

Fine assumptions:

(F1) The term "president" is a phase sortal.

(F2) Having the right to command the military at a given time requires being an actual president at that time.

Tricky assumptions:

(T1) The term "person" is a phase sortal.

25. Wreen, "Possibility of Potentiality," 138.

(T2) Having the right to life at a given time requires being an actual person at that time.

2.4 Phase vs. Substance Sortals

(F1) says that the term "president" is what logic teachers call a phase sortal rather than a substance sortal. This assumption is rarely made explicit, but it is important to make it so. Briefly, sortals are types of nouns that serve as concepts for classifying and describing the world, and they can be divided up into substance sortals and phase sortals. British philosopher David Wiggins notes that the difference between substance sortals and phase sortals is

> between sortal concepts which present-tensedly apply to an individual x at every moment throughout x's existence, e.g. human being, and those which do not, e.g. boy, or cabinet minister.[26]

Part of the logic of phase sortals is illustrated by Wiggins's example of "boy": there is nothing incoherent about an individual falling under a phase sortal P during one period of time, and yet failing to fall under P during a later period of time. Another part of the logic of phase sortals is illustrated by Wiggins's example of "cabinet minister": there is nothing incoherent about an individual failing to fall under a phase sortal P during one period of time, and then coming to fall under P during a later period of time. These two parts of the logic of phase sortals illustrate why it is fine, and makes perfect sense, to treat the term "president" as a phase sortal. There is nothing incoherent about an individual failing to be a president during one period of time, and then being a president during a later period of time: George Washington read John Locke before Washington became president. And there is nothing incoherent about an individual being a president during one period of time, and then failing to be a president during a later period of time: Washington enjoyed a well-deserved retirement after he was president.

(F2) says that having the right to command the military at a given time requires being an actual president at that time. When (F1) and (F2) are combined, the result is that whenever an individual does not fall under the phase sortal "president," that individual does not have the right to command the military. (This, too, is fine and makes perfect sense: George

---

26. Wiggins, *Identity and Spatio-Temporal Continuity*, 7. See also his *Sameness and Substance* and *Sameness and Substance Renewed*.

Washington did not have the right to command the military before he was president or after he was president, but only while he was president.) And since, when an individual is merely a potential president, that individual does not fall under the phase sortal "president," it follows that, when an individual is merely a potential president, that individual does not have the right to command the military.

Now then. There are two tricky assumptions that must be accepted in order to make the example of the potential president relevant to discussions about potential persons. These two tricky assumptions are worded almost exactly the same as the two unobjectionable assumptions just considered, with the only differences being the substitution of the word "person" for the word "president" and the substitution of the phrase "right to life" for the phrase "right to command the military" in the relevant places:

(T1) The term "person" is a phase sortal.

(T2) Having the right to life at a given time requires being an actual person at that time.

When (T1) and (T2) are combined, the result is that whenever an individual does not fall under the phase sortal "person," that individual does not have the right to life. And since, when an individual is merely a potential person, that individual does not fall under the phase sortal "person," it follows that, when an individual is merely a potential person, that individual does not have the right to life. If (T1) and (T2) are true, then the key claim above must be rejected as false.

But are (T1) and (T2) true? Some philosophers have attacked (T1) by arguing that the term "person" is not a phase sortal at all, but is rather a substance sortal. This attack often takes the form of a complaint that there is something fundamentally incoherent in talking about a "potential person," or that to speak of a "potential person" is to make some kind of category mistake.

We are rather sympathetic with this line of attack. However, there are two reasons why, for the sake of the present discussion, we are willing to grant (T1). The first reason is simply a matter of usage: it seems to us that the term "person" is sometimes used as a phase sortal, sometimes used as a substance sortal, and sometimes used with no clear commitment either way. Among philosophers and non-philosophers alike, these different uses of "person" often pass one another unnoticed. While this variety of uses may be regrettable, it is no good to deny that it goes on.

The second reason for granting (T1) is simply a matter of consistency: it would be self-defeating for a defender of the key claim above to complain that Benn uses "person" as a phase sortal. After all, the key claim above uses "person" as a phase sortal too. Those philosophers who insist that "person" is a substance sortal can profitably argue, we believe, that this is an excellent reason to prefer the key claim above (Q: "The fact that an individual is a potential person is sufficient for it to possess a right to life") far less than a more philosophically sophisticated version of the original vague claim above ("An individual's potential is relevant to its moral status"). Still, we are willing for the sake of discussion to pretend that "person" is a phase sortal, like "president." The question we intend to investigate is this: Once (T1) is granted, how plausible is (T2)?

2.5 Innocent Implication vs. Embarrassing Entailment.

We believe this question can be investigated by focusing on a specific feature of the American presidency: an individual can be a president during one period of time; can cease being a president during a second period of time; and then can become a president, again, during a third period of time.

One source of this feature of the American presidency is the provision in the American constitution that allows for presidents to run for reelection to a second term of office. Since nearly all first-term presidents have attempted to get reelected for a second term, and since these reelection attempts are very much in the public view, it is somewhat surprising that philosophers have not spent more time examining this aspect of the presidency in discussions of potential presidents and potential persons.

However, there may be an explanation for why philosophers have not spent more time on this characteristic of the presidency: it is very unusual for a first-term president to even make the attempt at reelection for a second term after having taken a break from the presidency, and it is even more unusual for such an attempt at reelection after having taken a break to succeed. This is not surprising, since the reasons why a first-term president would take a break from the presidency to begin with—illness, age, unpopularity, scandal, defeat, and death—are often excellent reasons for not running for the office in a future election.

Still, there is nothing incoherent about this feature of the American presidency. This facet of the American presidency illustrates how there is nothing incoherent about an individual falling under a phase sortal P during one period of time, failing to fall under P during a second period of time, and then falling under P again during a third period of time. (Indeed, this merely combines the two parts of the logic of phase sortals noted above after what David Wiggins said about "boy" and "cabinet minister.")

Imagine the following case: Grover is president from 3000 to 3004, ceases being president in 3005, and then gets reelected to be president from 3009 to 3012. (Recall that the historical Grover Cleveland was president from 1885 to 1889 and 1893 to 1897.) Put differently, Grover is an actual president from 3000 to 3004, a potential president from 3005 to 3008, and an actual president from 3009 to 3012. The important point for us is that from 3005 to 3008, Grover is not an actual president but a potential president. Now enter (F2). Since having the right to command the military at a given time requires being an actual president at that time, and from 3005 to 3008 Grover is not an actual president, it follows that from 3005 to 3008 Grover does not have the right to command the military. The result illustrated by Grover's case may be called the innocent implication: if an individual temporarily fails to fall under the phase sortal "president" at a given time, then that individual loses the right to command the military at that time.

In order to see how this example of reelecting the potential president has a parallel in the case of persons, we need only combine (T1) with the truth, mentioned just a moment ago, that there is nothing incoherent about an individual falling under a phase sortal P during one period of time, failing to fall under P during a second period of time, and then falling under P again during a third period of time.

Imagine the following case of a teenager who is temporarily brain damaged: Frodo possesses the properties that constitute being a person from 3000 to 3004, loses those properties in 3005, and then regains those properties from 3009 to 3012. (Recall that a fictional Frodo was unconscious and mistaken for dead after a nasty bite for a period of time in *The Lord of the Rings*.[27]) Put differently, Frodo is an actual person from 3000 to 3004, a potential person from 3005 to 3008, and an actual person from 3009 to 3012. The important point for us is that from 3005 to 3008 Frodo was not an actual person but a potential person. Now enter (T2). Since having the right to life at a given time requires being an actual person at that time, and since from 3005 to 3008 Frodo is not an actual person, it follows that from 3005 to 3008 Frodo does not have the right to life. The result

---

27. Tolkien, *Two Towers*, 709, 723.

illustrated by Frodo's case may be called the embarrassing entailment: if an individual temporarily fails to fall under the phase sortal "person" at a given time, then that individual loses the right to life at that time.

To see why this entailment is embarrassing, take any given definition of "person" in a descriptive sense: for example, a definition that claims that an individual is a person just in case that individual has consciousness. Now imagine that Frodo has consciousness from 3000 to 3004, loses his consciousness from 3005 to 3008 due to a brain injury or temporary coma, and gets his consciousness back again in 3009. (T1) and (T2), when combined, entail that Frodo does not have the right to life from 3005 to 3008.

Frodo's lapse in personhood is just as detrimental to Frodo's right to life whether it lasts for four years, four days, or four minutes. Imagine Frodo goes in for surgery and is given a general anesthetic that makes him completely unconscious during the surgery. (T1) and (T2) entail that Frodo does not have the right to life during the time of this surgery.

There are at least three approaches for avoiding the embarrassing entailment.

1. Actual or potential person? The first approach for avoiding the embarrassing entailment is to claim that, even though Frodo is not actually a person from 3005 to 3008, Frodo still retains his right to life from 3005 to 3008, since Frodo is a potential person during this time. According to this first approach, an individual has the right to life at a given time as long as it is either an actual person at that time or a potential person at that time.

But this first approach completely abandons (T2), which said "Having the right to life at a given time requires being an actual person at that time." Indeed, this first approach is tantamount to endorsing the key claim above: "The fact that an individual is a potential person is sufficient for it to possess a right to life."

2. Actual or past person? A second approach for avoiding the embarrassing entailment is to claim that, even though Frodo is not actually a person from 3005 to 3008, Frodo still retains his right to life from 3005 to 3008 because he already was a person from 3000 to 3004. According to this second approach, an individual has the right to life at a given time as long as it is either an actual person at that time or was an actual person at some previous time.

This second approach, unlike the first, is not tantamount to endorsing the key claim above ("The fact that an individual is a potential person is sufficient for it to possess a right to life"). But this second approach, just like the first, must abandon (T2) ("Having the right to life at a given time requires being an actual person at that time"). The example of reelecting the potential president shows why. Grover did not have the right to command the military from 3005 to 3008, even though Grover already was a president from 3000 to 3004. If (T1) ("The term 'person' is a phase sortal") and (T2) are correct, then there is no reason to think that the situation is any different for Frodo and the right to life than it is for Grover and the right to command the military. Once (T2) is abandoned, the alleged parallel between presidents and persons falls apart, and the example of the potential president does not give us any reason for rejecting the key claim.

Since we think the argument of the previous paragraph is an important one, we want to restate it by echoing an anonymous reviewer who summarized the argument as follows: "Accepting past person as sufficient for grounding right to life is tantamount to rejecting (T2). But, if (T2) is to be rejected, then we must also reject (F2). However, then we get a problematic result for the supposedly analogous case (the president case) where an individual who was a past president but who is not currently an actual president has all the presidential rights. This can't be an acceptable outcome. So if (T2) is rejected in favor of this strategy (appealing to past person) for avoiding the embarrassing entailment, then the analogy between persons and presidents will have broken down. But if the analogy no longer holds, then the president analogy can give us no reason for rejecting the key claim."

3. Actual persons have potential? A third approach for avoiding the embarrassing entailment is to claim that Frodo does not cease being a person from 3005 to 3008, since the properties constitutive of being a person include various types of capacities, dispositions, and powers. For example, if we focus on a definition of a person which emphasizes reason, then, according to this approach, something is a person at a given time as long as it has either the immediate power to reason at that time or a deeper latent disposition to reason at that time. The deeper latent disposition to reason is just the ability to acquire the immediate power to reason. According to this approach, even though Frodo does not have the immediate power to reason from 3005 to 3008, he still has the deeper latent disposition to reason from 3005 to 3008. Therefore, Frodo is still a person from 3005 to 3008.

This third approach, unlike the first two, does not require abandoning (T2). However, this third approach has an interesting result: without explicitly endorsing the key claim, this third approach ends up generating a right to life for precisely the same entities as the key claim. This is because the talk about "a deeper latent disposition to reason" and "the ability to acquire the immediate power to reason" are simply other ways of talking about potential. Saying that Frodo has, from 3005 to 3008, the deeper latent disposition to reason, is the same as saying that Frodo has, from 3005 to 3008, the potential to reason.

Once it is recognized that this third approach depends upon potentiality in this way, it becomes clear that this third approach is a mere notational variant on the first approach. The first approach combined two claims (focusing again, for the sake of illustration, on a reason-based definition of person):

- X has the right to life only if x is a person or a potential person.
- X is a person just in case x has reason.

The third approach takes these same two claims and simply relocates the concept of potential (which it calls a deeper latent disposition) from the first claim to the second claim:

- X has the right to life only if x is a person.
- X is a person just in case x has reason or the potential to have reason.

This third approach, then, is merely a slightly different way of fleshing out the vague claim introduced above, which we can now label (P):

(P) An individual's potential is relevant to its moral status.

The key claim is one way of fleshing out (P), which we can now label (Q):

(Q) The fact that an individual is a potential person is sufficient for it to possess a right to life.

But this third approach for avoiding the embarrassing entailment suggests another way of fleshing out (P), which we can label (R):

(R) The fact that an individual is a person* (an individual with reason or the potential to have reason) is sufficient for it to possess a right to life.

(Q) and (R) are related in the following way: any individual that has a right to life according to one principle will also have a right to life according to the other principle.[28]

---

28. A fourth approach might seek to combine some features of the second and third approaches as follows: What if one affirms (T1) ("The term 'person' is a phase sortal"),

PART I | ONTOLOGY AND PERSONHOOD

To sum up: we have just examined three ways of avoiding (Q) ("The fact that an individual is a potential person is sufficient for it to possess a right to life") while retaining a commitment to (T1) ("The term 'person' is a phase sortal"). Each of these ways involves either abandoning (T2) ("Having the right to life at a given time requires being an actual person at that time") or packing potentiality into the concept of a person to begin with. If (T2) is abandoned, the alleged parallel between persons and presidents falls apart, and the example of the potential president does not give us any reason for rejecting (Q). If potentiality is packed into the concept of a person to begin with, then there will be no difference in the range of entities that have a right to life according to (Q) and the range of entities that have a right to life according to (R).

There are three general lessons to be learned from this discussion of Benn's example of the potential president, and these lessons apply whenever an account of moral status uses the term "person." First, as Feinberg taught us, it is important to be clear on whether "person" is being used in a normative sense or in a descriptive sense. Second, as Wiggins taught us, it is important to be clear on whether "person" is to be taken as a phase sortal or a substance sortal. Third, and perhaps most importantly: whenever an account of moral status uses the term "person" in the descriptive sense as

---

but views "person" as a phase sortal such that once x is sorted into 'person,' x can never be sorted out of it? That is, what if gaining certain properties is sufficient for becoming a person, but not necessary for remaining a person? Such a view might preserve (T2) ("Having the right to life at a given time requires being an actual person at that time"), because those like Frodo would still be actual persons even while "out of commission." But such a view might not preserve the personhood of typical human embryos and fetuses, unless and until they crossed the relevant threshold for obtaining the personmaking properties for the first (decisive) time. While it would take us farther afield to fully evaluate this fourth approach, it strikes us as coherent, but in need of further defense. It's coherent because it treats "person" like "king or queen in Narnia" in Lewis, *Lion, Witch, and Wardrobe*, ch. 17. As the lion Aslan says to Peter, Edmund, Susan, and Lucy in the coronation scene: "Once a king or queen in Narnia, always a king or queen. Bear it well, Sons of Adam. Bear it well, Daughters of Eve!" Likewise, perhaps this fourth view says to all of us: "Once a person, always a person." But such a view would need to be defended on grounds that are different than the potential president example. For recall, the president does not continue to be president once his or her time in office is done. We noted above that he or she does not continue having the right to command the military after in office. But we recognize he or she does still get some secret service detail, and the honorific title Mr. President or Madame President at speaking engagements. A fuller defense would need to carefully consider both post-office "presidential" rights and pre-office "presidential" rights (e.g., those of a president-elect) to see if there are comparable "personal" rights.

a phase sortal, it is important to be clear on whether x being a potential descriptive person is sufficient for x being an actual normative person.

In the example above, this third general lesson asks: If an account claims that x is a person just in case x has reason, does the account also claim that x being a potential person is sufficient for x having the right to life? But this third general lesson can be used whenever there are accounts of descriptive personhood (like "reason") linked to accounts of normative personhood (like "the right to life"). This third lesson applies the final sentence from Joel Feinberg, and examples of the boy and the cabinet minister from David Wiggins, and the famous quote from *Horton Hears a Who!* by Dr. Seuss.

If being a potential descriptive person is sufficient for being an actual normative person, then one should expect the account of moral status in question to not be vulnerable to the problem of the embarrassing entailment. If not, then one should expect the account of moral status in question to be vulnerable to the problem of the embarrassing entailment, unless it escapes this entailment by being clear that x having certain potentials (i.e., dispositions, capacities, latent powers) is itself sufficient for x being both an actual descriptive person and an actual normative person too.

Finally, two meta-lessons from our discussion here can be suggested. First, we should be alert to metaphysical assumptions we and others inevitably make in thinking about bioethics. Second, we should seek to clarify and improve our own such assumptions whenever we can.

3. ON THE RELATION BETWEEN METAPHYSICS AND ETHICS

We have illustrated how one's metaphysics impacts one's ethics. However, some might object to this and suggest that, contrary to what we have argued, metaphysics is ultimately distinct from ethics, and ethics is autonomous with respect to metaphysical truths. There are two ways this objection could go.

First, one could object that ethical truths are not grounded in metaphysical truths in the way that we have suggested above. For example, we argued that whether an individual is a potential descriptive person (a metaphysical matter) determines whether they are a normative person (an ethical matter). So one could object here and suggest that descriptive personhood is not only distinct from normative personhood, it is entirely unrelated such that the former is neither necessary nor sufficient for the latter. If this is correct, then investigating the metaphysics of persons is ultimately unhelpful for determining the moral status of individuals. Call this the ontological objection. In response to this, we explore the various ways in which a thing can have a particular moral status and we argue that, especially when personhood is considered, a thing's descriptive properties (a metaphysical matter) are essential to grounding its moral status (a normative matter).

Second, one could object on methodological grounds. One could grant that perhaps ethics is grounded in metaphysics such that truths about normative personhood are true in virtue of metaphysical truths, but still object that we do not need to know about or do metaphysics in order to know or do ethics. The idea would be that we could treat ethics as an autonomous subdiscipline of philosophy such that we do not need to consider the metaphysics of personhood before making judgments about ethics. Call this the methodological objection. In response to this we argue that, although it is possible to know some ethical truths without a robust metaphysics, this does not mean that metaphysics cannot, or ought not, inform our ethics. Rather, we argue for a "reflective equilibrium" model where one can both use justified beliefs about ethics to inform one's metaphysics and also use justified beliefs about metaphysics to inform one's ethics. On this model, doing metaphysics still plays a crucial role in doing ethics because the two domains are importantly related to each other.

3.1 The Ontological Objection

We first consider the objection that ethics is not grounded in metaphysics. We argued that different views about the metaphysics of descriptive persons impacts who counts as normative persons. In response, one could object that ethical truths do not depend on descriptive truths in this way.

One way to make this objection would involve appealing to David Hume's famous argument that we cannot derive "ought" from "is" (Hume's law).[29] This means that no amount of descriptive claims about metaphysics will ever logically entail a normative moral claim.[30] So one might suggest that our argument runs afoul of Hume's law because when we claim

---

29. Hume, *Treatise of Human Nature*, 1:3.1.1.27.

30. Philosophers differ on their interpretation of Hume on this point. For example, Annette C. Baier notes that Hume says that inferring an "ought" from an "is" only "seems altogether inconceivable" and that he actually argues that, on his account of moral sentiments, such an inference can be justified (Baier, *Progress of Sentiments*, 177).

descriptive personhood determines normative personhood, we appear to be inferring normative moral truths from descriptive metaphysical truths.

In response to this it is important to note the limitations of Hume's law. We grant that, as a matter of logical entailment, descriptive claims do not entail normative claims. As such, the claim

- *X* is a potential (descriptive) person

  does not, by itself, logically entail the claim

- *X* has a right to life.

However, we have not argued otherwise. Our key claim was:

(QD) The fact that an individual is a potential (descriptive) person is sufficient for it to possess a right to life.

This claim does connect a descriptive fact with a normative fact. But notice that the connection is not one of logical entailment. We are not claiming that the fact that an individual is a descriptive person logically entails that it is a normative person with the right to life. Our position is that certain descriptive facts (which are a matter of metaphysics) are what ground certain normative moral truths. So being a descriptive person grounds being a normative person and being a normative person is sufficient for having a right to life.[31] And this sort of claim is commonplace in discussions about persons. Recall Feinberg's explanation of the distinction between descriptive and normative persons. He says, "When we use the word 'person' in this wholly descriptive way . . . we are attributing characteristics that may be a ground for ascribing rights and duties."[32] So although we are making a robust philosophical claim here, we are not violating Hume's law and we are not suggesting that a descriptive claim logically entails a normative claim.

Another way this ontological objection could go would be to grant that, although we have not violated Hume's law and inferred an "ought" from an "is," our key claim is simply incorrect. It is not the case that "the fact that

---

31. We do not take a position on the precise nature of this "grounding" relationship other than that there are certain moral truths that are true in virtue of the fact that certain metaphysical facts are the case. For more on how this relation could be construed, see Väyrynen, "I—Grounding and Normative Explanation."

32. Feinberg, "Abortion," 186 (emphasis added).

an individual is a potential (descriptive) person is sufficient for it to possess a right to life." And there are two ways one might make such a case.

First, one could argue that it is a mistake to focus on "personhood" as being the relevant property that grants someone this special moral status and instead argue that it is our biological nature—the fact that we are organisms of the species homo sapiens—that is of greater moral relevance.[33] One reason someone might argue for this is because perhaps it might appear that certain humans are deserving of moral respect even if they fail to satisfy any particular conception of personhood (either due to lacking particular mental capacities or lacking the potential for such capacities). If that is correct, then the metaphysics of persons is an unhelpful aid in moral decision-making. However, even if this view is correct, it would not suggest that ethics is not grounded in metaphysics. It would simply refocus our moral attention on the metaphysics of human organisms instead of the metaphysics of (descriptive) persons. Some might think that talking about human organisms requires only work in biology and little (if any) robust metaphysical theorizing, but that underestimates the complexity of answering the questions "What is a human? When does a human life begin and end?" A plausible idea would be that the human organism begins at the moment of conception.[34] But others have argued that you—the human organism—begin to exist later than conception because you cannot be identical to your past single-celled zygote or even to your past two-celled blastocyst.[35] Yet others even argue that you begin to exist prior to conception because your organic life began as an egg cell or a sperm cell.[36] But however these questions get answered, the significance of metaphysics to ethics remains because the answers to these questions will directly impact issues in ethics and bioethics.

Second, one could go even further in rejecting our key claim by arguing that normative ethical truths are entirely independent from descriptive metaphysical truths. This would involve rejecting the idea that metaphysical truths somehow ground the moral or normative truths. On such a view, there might be facts about who counts as a descriptive person and there

---

33. For an analysis of these two approaches, see Kadlac, "Humanizing Personhood."
34. Lee, "Christian Philosopher's View."
35. Van Inwagen, *Material Beings*, 153. Although Van Inwagen argues that we cannot be identical to the first couple cells in the development of a human organism, he does not identify a point in development at which we are identical to that organism.
36. Sauchelli, "Animalism, Abortion, and Future."

might be facts about who has moral rights (or who counts as a human organism and who has what moral status), but such facts are unrelated to each other. So even if we were to sort out the descriptive metaphysical truths, that would not settle the normative ethical truths.

This kind of objection describes a logical possibility, but an implausible one. Although there is no logical contradiction in suggesting that a thing's moral status is unrelated to its metaphysical status, it runs counter to most approaches to theorizing about moral status. For example, if you ask a utilitarian why we have some particular ethical obligation, their answer will appeal to the amount of happiness or pain that would result from the action or how it would affect people's interests. John Stuart Mill goes as far as saying that every moral school of thought admits "that the influence of actions on happiness is a most material and even predominant consideration in many of the details of morals, however unwilling to acknowledge it as the fundamental principle of morality, and the source of moral obligation."[37] But the fact that certain beings are capable of having interests or experiencing pleasure or pain is a descriptive metaphysical issue, so utilitarianism grounds normative matters in descriptive matters about sentience. Or consider Kantian deontology. If you ask a Kantian why we have some particular ethical obligation, their answer will appeal to a robust notion of rational autonomy and whether one's actions are fully autonomous and whether they would interfere with someone else's autonomy.[38] Again, this approach takes descriptive metaphysical facts (whether an agent is interfering with anyone else's autonomy) to ground normative moral facts. So although these approaches disagree about which descriptive properties ground the moral properties, they agree that there must be some such descriptive properties to do that job.

There is one caveat to note here. In addition to grounding a thing's moral status in its intrinsic metaphysical properties, some theories will also ground a thing's moral status in its relational properties. That is, some will argue that x has some special moral status not because of any intrinsic feature of x, but because of x's relation to some y. For example, some have argued that some human fetuses have a certain moral status not because they are persons (potential or actual) but because they stand in special relationships to other persons. Eva Feder Kittay argues that simply being a person's child is sufficient to ground moral status even if the child does not

---

37. Mill, *Utilitarianism*, 1.4.
38. Wood, *Kant's Ethical Thought*, 156–59.

meet the criteria for personhood.³⁹ And Robert Nozick argues that being a member of a relevant species is sufficient to ground such moral status even if the individual in question has not sufficiently developed into a person.⁴⁰

However, even if these accounts are correct, they do not undermine the approach of grounding ethics in metaphysics. In fact, they reinforce it. First, they do not deny that a thing's intrinsic properties can ground that thing's moral status. They simply add that a thing's relational properties might also do such work. Second, a thing's possession of relational properties is still a descriptive and metaphysical issue. Whether x stands in some descriptive relation to y is what grounds x's normative moral status. And furthermore, relational approaches such as these still go on to appeal to y's intrinsic properties to explain why x's relationship to y is supposed to be sufficient for grounding its moral status. So even on relational approaches to moral status, descriptive metaphysical truths are used to ground normative ethical truths.

What all of these accounts have in common is that they all ground normative ethical truths in descriptive metaphysical truths. This approach makes sense because any time someone suggests that an individual has some special moral status, a reasonable question to ask is "Why does that thing in particular have such moral status?" It is logically possible that there is no answer to that question. Perhaps the fact that an individual has such a status is simply a brute fact—a fact that has no further explanation. But when theorizing about reality, it is best to have as few brute facts as possible because such inexplicable facts violate the highly plausible principle of sufficient reason (i.e., that for every fact there must be a sufficient reason that explains why it is the case).⁴¹ Instead, if something is a certain way, we should offer an explanation for why it is the case. So, when one posits that some things have moral status, it is reasonable to ask why those things and not others have that status. This question leads us to investigate which descriptive metaphysical truths are the best candidates for grounding normative moral truths.

At this point one might object by recalling an example from earlier—the debtor's paradox—and using it to support the idea that metaphysics is unrelated to ethics. Suppose your friend (call him "Roger") tries to avoid paying what he owes you by appealing to a metaphysical view about the

39. Kittay, "At the Margins."
40. Nozick, "Do Animals Have Rights?"
41. See Della Rocca, "PSR."

nature of (descriptive) persons. He says that persons are just collections of particles and, given the change in particles over time, the person now being called Roger is not identical to the Roger who borrowed the money. Call this the particle view of persons. So this person now called Roger does not owe you anything. Of course, such an excuse seems absurd. This Roger owes you the money, and you do not care about whether he is the same collection of atoms as the man who borrowed the money. If this is right, it could seem to support the idea that at least some normative matters about persons are independent from the metaphysics of persons. For whether this man called Roger is the same descriptive person as the man who borrowed the money (a metaphysical issue) turns out not to matter for whether this man called Roger owes you money (a normative issue). In other words, you might conclude that this Roger owes you the money regardless of whether he is the same descriptive person who borrowed the money.

Such an objection would be too hasty. We agree that it is absurd to think that Roger can get out of his commitment by appealing to the particle view of persons. But there is a much better explanation available than suggesting that metaphysics is unrelated to ethics. This Roger still owes you the money because, contra the particle view of persons, this Roger is the same descriptive person as the Roger that borrowed the money. And if a metaphysical theory of personhood says otherwise, then that theory must be wrong. In other words, we have some initial judgments on our hands:

- The normative claim: This Roger owes you the money.
- The metaphysical claim: This Roger is the same descriptive person as the Roger who borrowed the money.

These are our starting philosophical data. And the particle view of persons rejects the metaphysical judgment and says that this Roger is not the same descriptive person as the Roger who borrowed the money, which is a new theoretical philosophical datum. Taken together, the data are inconsistent. They cannot all be true, so we have a decision to make.

- Option 1:
    - Reject the idea that the normative claim depends on the metaphysics of descriptive persons.
    - Accept the particle view of descriptive persons.
    - Keep the normative claim.

- Reject the metaphysical claim.

- Option 2:
  - Keep the idea that the normative claim depends on the metaphysics of descriptive persons.
  - Reject the particle view of descriptive persons.
  - Keep the normative claim.
  - Keep the metaphysical claim.

To go with option 1 would be to accept two counterintuitive results—that whether this Roger owes you money does not depend on whether he is the same (descriptive) person as the man who borrowed the money, and that this Roger is not the same descriptive person as the man who borrowed the money. It is better to go with option 2, keep our intuitive judgments about personhood, and preserve the relation between metaphysics and ethics. The lesson of the debtor's paradox is not that normative matters are independent from metaphysical matters. Rather, the lesson is that when considering our philosophical data, we might find some conflicts and there are various ways to resolve them.

3.2 The Methodological Objection

The second objection is what we call the methodological objection. One might concede that metaphysical truths ground ethical truths in the way described above, yet still object that there is no significant relation between these disciplines in practice. These disciplines are epistemologically or methodologically autonomous. Knowing about one is not required, and does not help us, to know about the other. If that is correct, then this would show the practice of metaphysics is not necessary or helpful to the practice of ethics.

One reason to think that ethical theorizing need not rely on metaphysical theorizing is that we appear to be able to make rational moral judgments without needing to have a corresponding metaphysical theory to back them up. For example, one could argue that we should not theorize about "persons" and should instead make our best moral judgments. And it is possible that such judgments can be justified without having to base them on any particular metaphysical theory.[42]

42. We cannot explore all of the various ways in which normative judgments might

To further illustrate this idea of the autonomy of ethical theorizing, we can return to the discussion of the debtor's paradox. We argued that the debtor's paradox does not disprove the idea that ethics is grounded in metaphysics. In doing so, we used some philosophical data—both metaphysical and normative—as evidence of the falsity of a particular metaphysical view (the particle view of persons). If such a move is justified, then this reveals something important. It shows that there is an epistemological and methodological relation between metaphysics and ethics such that information about one domain can inform how we ought to think about the other domain. And this is precisely what we argued in the first part of this chapter when we argued that the metaphysics of personhood should inform our ethics.

However, further reflection also reveals another consequence of this case. It suggests that the epistemological and methodological relation between metaphysics and ethics is not unidirectional. Many might accept that metaphysics can, and should, inform ethics because ethics is grounded in metaphysics. But perhaps one can also use normative conclusions to inform one's metaphysics. In the discussion of the debtor's paradox, we used a normative judgment (e.g., "This Roger owes you the money") as evidence against the particle view of (descriptive) persons, which is a metaphysical theory.

One might further object that if the above is correct and ethical beliefs can inform metaphysical beliefs, then even if ethics is ontologically dependent on metaphysics, perhaps it need not be epistemologically or methodologically subordinate to it. If ethical judgments can be justified without specifically worked out metaphysics and they can be used to inform metaphysics, then perhaps to do ethics one need not do metaphysics at all. So those raising the methodological objection might reasonably say, "We do not need to theorize about metaphysics to do ethics. We can, and should, form justified beliefs about ethical issues without depending on theories in metaphysics."

We agree with part of this objection. As we discussed earlier, when asking why something or someone has a special moral status we typically look to identify which descriptive features would make it so. Metaphysics appears to be highly relevant to ethics in this way, so some might be inclined to suggest that metaphysics has an epistemological or methodological priority over ethics such that one's metaphysics can, and should, inform

---

be justified, but on some accounts particular moral judgments can be justified because they involve perceptions of moral features, while others suggest they can be justified on the basis of moral intuition. For more on this, see Audi, "Phenomenology of Moral Intuition."

one's ethics, but that it should never go in the other direction. But we think such a claim goes too far. It is true that one's metaphysics should inform one's ethics, but there is no reason, in principle, that one's ethics should not inform one's metaphysics. To see why, we need to take a look at philosophical methodology.

There is disagreement about what counts as good philosophical methodology and whether there is anything that can accurately be called the methodology of philosophy. However, one plausible view is that at least part of philosophical practice includes the aim of producing a coherent set of beliefs and avoiding contradictions. And one popular way to achieve this goal is by engaging in the method of reflective equilibrium.[43] Broadly speaking, this method involves three stages.[44] First, one notes their initial beliefs and considered judgments. Assuming that these have at least some kind of justification, they form the starting points for one's theorizing. We can call this one's initial philosophical data. Second, one reflects on the implications of these beliefs and attempts to develop more general principles based on them. We can call this one's theoretical data. And what one often finds after this step is that they run into some form of inconsistency; some theoretical data conflicts with the initial data. So that leads to the third step, which requires identifying these conflicts and resolving them by revising one or more of their judgments. This means that what was included in the initial philosophical data might ultimately be rejected or what initially appeared to be an implausible theoretical consequence of the initial data might be accepted in order to avoid the inconsistency. With this process one can work toward a more complete and coherent philosophical system.

The process of reflective equilibrium is typically applied to one particular domain at a time. We can implement it in ethics, metaphysics, epistemology, etc. To do so is to engage in a version of what is called narrow reflective equilibrium. But we can also use this process in philosophy as a whole and work to make one's moral and nonmoral beliefs more coherent. This broader approach is a version of wide reflective equilibrium.[45] Rather

43. This term was coined by Rawls, *Theory of Justice*, 18. He popularized the concept, but the idea did not originate with him.

44. Scanlon, "Rawls on Justification."

45. The terms "narrow reflective equilibrium" and "wide reflective equilibrium" have some variability. Sometimes "narrow" refers to using only one's own moral judgments and principles, whereas "wide" refers to also considering additional competing moral theories. Alternatively, as used here, "wide" can refer to using both moral and nonmoral data in the reflective process.

than limiting the process to some particular domain within philosophy, one can use it to help develop one's views across all branches of philosophy. And insofar as one domain might have implications for another, the process of wide reflective equilibrium seems appropriate.

We can now return to the methodological objection that we raised at the beginning of this section and offer a response. To suggest that ethics can, and should, remain methodologically and epistemologically isolated such that it should be done without interacting with metaphysics is to reject that one can, or should, engage in the process of reflective equilibrium across these two domains. It is to suggest that narrow reflective equilibrium is to be preferred over wide. But wide reflective equilibrium arguably provides stronger justification for one's beliefs because it involves reconciling them with a larger set of considerations—in this case ethical and metaphysical beliefs rather than ethical beliefs alone.[46] There is a cost, and no clear benefit, to neglecting this kind of cross-domain reflection. To engage in wide reflective equilibrium across these domains is to consider a source of data (metaphysics) that could have significant implications for ethics. Of course, after considering one's metaphysical beliefs, one could ultimately conclude that they are unhelpful in contributing to one's ethical beliefs. But to neglect to even consider what implications metaphysics might have for ethics is to ignore a source of information that could be relevant to ethical theory and practice. So although we do not think that ethics must be methodologically and epistemologically subordinate to metaphysics such that the latter can inform the former but not vice versa, we also do not think that ethics ought to be methodologically and epistemologically isolated from other areas of philosophy that could potentially help shape it.

4. CONCLUSION

It turns out that, despite conceptions of metaphysics in popular culture, metaphysics is not just about crystals and New Age practices. It is an area of study that spans a wide range of topics and involves considerations about the fundamental nature of reality. And some such parts of reality have practical implications for our everyday lives. Persons matter. And it matters how we treat them. But merely determining how persons ought to be treated leaves out the crucial issue of who rightfully counts as a person. So to settle ethical questions about how the individual is to be treated, it is

---

46. See Daniels, "Wide Reflective Equilibrium"; and Cath, "Reflective Equilibrium."

prudent to answer the metaphysical question of when an individual counts as a descriptive person.

We explored how different views about the metaphysics of persons will produce different answers to the question of whether an individual counts as a normative person with a right to life. At first glance, this discussion might seem abstract and disconnected from medical practice and bioethics. But it becomes deeply practical when considering potential issues one might face in the clinical context. Clinicians and medical care providers have to make ethical decisions about patient care. A patient's status as a person will at least partially determine which courses of action are ethically permissible and it extends beyond concerns for Frodo in the year 3005. Whether or not a patient in the hospital bed is a person affects which courses of actions are morally obligatory, permissible, or impermissible. Questions about personhood are directly relevant to issues surrounding end-of-life decision-making, reproductive ethics and abortion, severe cognitive impairment, comatose patients, organ donation, and more.

We have not argued that one must adopt any particular view in metaphysics of persons. Each view will have its strengths and weaknesses. The important point is the relation between metaphysics and ethics. Our discussion of personhood is just one example of metaphysics' significance to ethics and bioethics; it is by no means exhaustive. We discussed only the criteria for personhood, but there are additional issues in the metaphysics of personhood that impact ethics, such as determining what counts as "good" for a person. Two prominent bioethical principles are the principles of beneficence and non-maleficence, which say we are to do what is good for the patient and to do no harm. But what counts as "good" or "bad" for a person could depend on the nature of personhood. Furthermore, beyond the topic of personhood, issues in the metaphysics of free will intersect with issues on moral responsibility, which has significance for ethical questions about informed consent. The bottom line is this: knowing what things are impacts how we should treat them.

Given these ethical considerations, we should not take metaphysics for granted. It is true that there is much debate and disagreement in metaphysics, so settling these issues is no small task. Some might worry that we will never fully settle these questions. But to neglect them altogether is to naively proceed in ethics without considering issues that are directly relevant to the issues at hand. Minimally, we should seek to clarify what our metaphysical assumptions are when we engage in ethics and bioethics. We should reflect on what those assumptions mean for our moral decision-making. And we should then consider whether there are any good reasons for keeping or abandoning such assumptions. We might not arrive at complete answers. But we should try.

BIBLIOGRAPHY

Ashby, Muata. *The Kemetic Tree of Life: Ancient Egyptian Metaphysics and Cosmology for Higher Consciousness*. Miami: Sema Institute, 2008.
Audi, Robert. "The Phenomenology of Moral Intuition." *Ethical Theory and Moral Practice* 25 (2022) 53–69. https://doi.org/10.1007/s10677-021-10245-w.
Baier, Annette C. *A Progress of Sentiments: Reflections on Hume's "Treatise."* Cambridge, MA: Harvard University Press, 1991.
Benn, Stanley. "Abortion, Infanticide, and Respect for Persons." In *The Problem of Abortion*, edited by Joel Feinberg, 135–44. 2nd ed. Belmont, CA: Wadsworth, 1984.
Cath, Yuri. "Reflective Equilibrium." In *The Oxford Handbook of Philosophical Methodology*, edited by Cappelen Herman et al., 213–30. Oxford: Oxford University Press, 2016.
Daniels, Norman. "Wide Reflective Equilibrium and Theory Acceptance in Ethics." *Journal of Philosophy* 76 (1979) 256–82.
Della Rocca, Michael. "PSR." *Philosophers' Imprint* 10 (2010) 1–13.
DiSilvestro, Russell. *Human Capacities and Moral Status*. Philosophy and Medicine 108. Dordrecht: Springer, 2010.
———. "Reproductive Autonomy, the Non-Identity Problem, and the Non-Person Problem." *Bioethics* 23 (2009) 59–67.
Feinberg, Joel. "Abortion." In *Matters of Life and Death*, edited by Tom Regan, 183–217. Philadelphia: Temple University Press, 1980.
Seuss, Dr. [Theodor Seuss Geisel]. *Horton Hears a Who!* New York: Random House, 1954.
Hume, David. *A Treatise of Human Nature*. Edited by David Fate Norton and Mary J. Norton. 2 vols. Clarendon Edition of the Works of David Hume. Oxford: Clarendon, 2007.
Kadlac, Adam. "Humanizing Personhood." *Ethical Theory and Moral Practice* 13 (2010) 421–37.
Kittay, Eva Feder. "At the Margins of Moral Personhood." *Ethics* 116 (2005) 100–131.
Lee, Patrick. "A Christian Philosopher's View of Recent Directions in the Abortion Debate." *Christian Bioethics* 10 (2004) 7–32.
Lewis, C. S. *The Lion, the Witch, and the Wardrobe*. San Francisco: HarperCollins, 1950.
Lindsey-Billingsley, T. *Black Consciousness, Ancient Alien Gods, Metaphysics, Kemetic Spirituality & African Origins of Civilization*. Vol. 2 of *New Age Bible of Mother Africa*. N.p.: Create Space, 2018.
Locke, John. *An Essay Concerning Human Understanding*. Edited by Peter H. Nidditch. Clarendon Edition of the Works of John Locke. Oxford: Oxford University Press, 1975.
Mill, John Stuart. *"Utilitarianism" and "On Liberty": Including Mill's "Essay on Bentham" and Selections from the Writings of Jeremy Bentham and John Austin*. Edited by Mary Warnock. Oxford: Wiley-Blackwell, 2003.
Nozick, Robert. "Do Animals Have Rights?" In *Socratic Puzzles*, 305–310. Cambridge, MA: Harvard University Press, 1997.

Rawls, John. *A Theory of Justice*. Rev. ed. Cambridge, MA: Belknap, 1999.
Rea, Michael, ed. *Arguing about Metaphysics*. Arguing about Philosophy. New York: Routledge, 2009.
———, ed. *Material Constitution: A Reader*. Lanham, MD: Rowman & Littlefield, 1997.
———. *Metaphysics: The Basics*. Basics. New York: Routledge, 2014.
Sauchelli, Andrea. "Animalism, Abortion, and a Future Like Ours." *Journal of Ethics* 23 (2019) 317–32.
Scanlon, T. M. "Rawls on Justification." In *The Cambridge Companion to Rawls*, edited by Samuel Freeman, 139–67. Cambridge Companions to Philosophy. Cambridge: Cambridge University Press, 2003.
Sedley, David. "The Stoic Criterion of Identity." *Phronesis* 27 (1982) 255–75.
Singer, Peter. *Practical Ethics*. 2nd ed. Cambridge: Cambridge University Press, 1993.
Tolkien, J. R. R. *The Two Towers*. Vol. 2 of *The Lord of the Rings*. 50th anniv. ed. Boston: Houghton Mifflin, 2001.
Van Inwagen, Peter. "Introduction: What Is Metaphysics?" In *Metaphysics: The Big Questions*, edited by Peter van Inwagen and Dean W. Zimmerman, 1–13. Philosophy: The Big Questions. 2nd ed. Oxford: Wiley-Blackwell, 2008.
———. *Material Beings*. Ithaca, NY: Cornell University Press, 1990.
Väyrynen, Pekka. "I—Grounding and Normative Explanation." Supplement, *Aristotelian Society* 87 (2013) 155–78. https://doi.org/10.1111/J.1467-8349.2013.00224.x.
Warren, Mary Anne. "On the Moral and Legal Status of Abortion." *Monist* 57 (1973) 43–61.
Wiggins, David. *Identity and Spatio-Temporal Continuity*. Oxford: Blackwell, 1967.
———. *Sameness and Substance*. Cambridge, MA: Harvard University Press, 1980.
———. *Sameness and Substance Renewed*. Cambridge: Cambridge University Press, 2001.
Wood, Allen. *Kant's Ethical Thought*. Modern European Philosophy. Cambridge: Cambridge University Press, 1999.
Wreen, Michael. "The Possibility of Potentiality." In *Values and Moral Standing*, edited by Thomas Attig et al., 137–54. Bowling Green, OH: Bowling Green State University Press, 1986.

2

Modal Arguments for Generic Substance Dualism and Why the Soul Matters for Bioethics

J. P. Moreland

Philosophy is experiencing a resurgence of property and substance dualism.[1] According to property dualism, phenomenal consciousness is irreducibly/intrinsically mental. According to substance dualism, the soul (self, mind, ego) is not identical to anything physical but, rather, is an enduring spiritual substance that has/unifies consciousness, employs and is the referent of "I," exhibits a first-person point of view, and acts as an intentional agent. Currently, there are five major versions of substance dualism.[2] Rather than distinguishing them, I will discuss generic substance dualism (GSD), according to which the soul is a spiritual substance that is not identical to anything physical or to its body.

Several arguments have been advanced for substance dualism (SD), but I shall focus on one: a modal argument.[3] I present one form of the argument, clarify and defend its premises, and respond to objections. Initially, I

1. See Koons and Bealer, *Waning of Materialism*.
2. Loose et al., *Substance Dualism*.
3. See Moreland, *Soul*.

show why the soul is crucial for the sort of intrinsic, high value enjoyed by human persons and is relevant to bioethical reflection.

1. DOES PHYSICALITY PLAY AN IMPORTANT ROLE IN ACCOUNTING FOR THE HIGH INTRINSIC VALUE OF HUMAN PERSONS?

Richard Swinburne has reminded us that "it is also of great moral and practical importance to know what humans are. For surely the greater the difference between humans and machines, the more appropriate it is to treat them in very different ways from each other."[4]

In this section I advance two claims: (1) Human persons have high intrinsic value as expressed in the datum (see below). However, their physicality plays little or no role in grounding/explaining that value. Rather, it is the soul that does the heavy lifting. (2) Given this, I show why the human body is still a significantly valued entity.

By "physicality" I mean all of those constituents—e.g., properties, intrinsic relations, parts, events of a whole (or a collection of simples arranged whole-wise) that are and are only physical. A point of clarification is in order. We need to distinguish what I mean by an intrinsic relation versus an internal relation:

> Intrinsic relation: If a relation (R) is intrinsic to some whole (W), then R's relata and R itself are constituents of W and that reside within the being of W (example: a causal relation between one's brain and nervous system).
>
> Internal relation: R is an internal relation between a and b if (i) facts about R are grounded in facts about the natures of a and b, and (ii) necessarily, if R fails to obtain, a and b are altered (example: brighter than between yellow and purple).

If the R of aRb is internal to a (or both a and b), then for all x, if x does not stand in R to b, then $x \neq a$. An internal relation is grounded in the nature/essence of the relevant relata.

My characterization of "physicality" employs intrinsic and not internal relations. The point is that a strictly physical object (PO) is ontologically exhausted by physicality. According to standard physicalism (SP), we are

---

4. Swinburne, *Are We Bodies or Souls*, 3.

POs. Moreover, most philosophers hold that if some object (O) is a PO, then O is essentially a PO. Finally, let us assume that the human body is a PO.

Given these notions, let us turn to arguments for the irrelevance of the physical body and the importance of the soul (I, ego, etc.) for the sort of high, intrinsic value and special moral status enjoyed by human persons.[5]

1.1 Argument 1: A Modal and Grounding Argument

We start with the datum:

> Persons enjoy special intrinsic value and inherent moral status, having uniquely and extremely high worth. Persons as such are owed great respect. They matter.

For many thinkers, given the datum, it is also the case that persons as such are necessarily or essentially valuable. There is no possible world in which persons exist and the datum is false.

Prima facie, there is a conflict between a PO and the datum. POs do not seem to have the sort of value human persons do, and it is difficult to see how the constituents of physicality could fund the datum. It will not do to "solve" this problem along the lines of thinkers such as James Rachels and Erik Wielenberg.[6] In different ways, they appeal to emergent conscious states claiming that they have various degrees of value/disvalue; thus, human persons differ from other POs in virtue of having such states.

Unfortunately, this move is not helpful in solving the problem within our purview, viz., how can the high intrinsic value of human persons as such be reconciled with a PO. Surely, this question is different from one about the various degrees of value regarding different conscious states. For example, one is not less valuable if one wakes up in a bad mood and gains value as one gets happier during the day. Our conscious states wax and wane, but our intrinsic value remains constant. Clearly, such a move shifts one's ethical perspective from a sanctity of life to a quality of life approach and, moreover, it becomes difficult to justify the claim that all human persons have equal value as such since the value of conscious states involves degreed properties.[7]

---

5. I have adjusted a set of similar arguments in the excellent article by Bailey and Rasmussen, "How Valuable."

6. Rachels, *End of Life*; Craig and Wielenberg, *Debate on God*.

7. See Moreland, *Recalcitrant Imago Dei*, 144–45.

The argument employs a specific variation of ideal observer theory, according to which there is an ethics help desk staffed by moral experts with highly accurate moral intuitions and who deliver correct moral judgments when we turn to them for guidance. When asked, the desk affirms the datum. That said, here is the (generic) modal/grounding argument:

A_1: The datum is true irrespective of whether human persons possess physical bodies.

A_2: If A_1 is true, then our physicality is irrelevant to the truth of the datum.

Granting A_1 and A_2, we get:

A_3: Our physicality is irrelevant to the truth of the datum.

A_4: Since a human person's physical body is exhausted by physicality, then that physical body is irrelevant to the truth of the datum.

A_5: Either the soul or the physical body is what is relevant to the truth of the datum.

A_6: The soul is what is relevant to the truth of the datum.

A_1 is endorsed by the ethics help desk and may be taken to express a properly basic belief grounded in fundamental intuitions. Still, I mention two supporting considerations.

First, consider a possible world in which there is a disembodied intermediate state following death. In this state, persons are wholly immaterial, yet it would be wrong to treat them as mere things with little value, e.g., to insult, demean, agitate them. Clearly, the datum would apply to such persons even though they lacked physicality, including physical bodies. In fact, such persons would seem to have the same value as embodied persons in our world.[8] How could this be? The answer appears to be that our value is grounded in the soul, not in physicality.

Second, setting aside instrumental/functional and aesthetic value (see below), it is hard to see how paradigm-case POs have much intrinsic value. In a zombie world with no selves or conscious states, the humanlike zombies would lack intrinsic value, even though they have (were?) duplicate physical human bodies.

Regarding A_2, the consequent seems to follow from the antecedent. However, we will observe shortly that there are two different ways to interpret irrelevant, generating two different versions of the argument. So, our

---

8. I owe this point to Bailey and Rasmussen, "How Valuable," 339.

prima facie acceptance of A_2 may be exposed to defeaters when attention is given to interpreting irrelevant. Assuming the antecedent of A_4, together with A_3, we get the consequent of A_4. Finally, given the defeaters raised against identifying conscious states as and only as what have intrinsic value, and using "soul" in the generic dualist sense, A_5 appears to present an exhaustive dilemma, or, at least, it exhausts the live options for most thinkers.

We are left with the task of clarifying irrelevant/relevant in A_2–A_6. Irrelevant may be understood in either a modal or grounding way.

The Modal Version

A_{1M}: The datum is true irrespective of whether human persons possess physical bodies.

A_{2M}: If A_{1M} is true, then, possibly, human persons exist, satisfy the datum, and lack physicality (are immaterial).

Granting A_{1M} and A_{2M}, we get:

A_{3M}: Possibly, human persons exist, satisfy the datum, and lack physicality (are immaterial).

A_{4M}: Since a human person's physical body is exhausted by physicality, then, possibly, human persons exist, satisfy the datum, and lack physical bodies.

A_{5M}: Necessarily, either the human person's soul exists and satisfies the datum, or the physical body exists and satisfies the datum.

A_{6M}: The human soul exists and satisfies the datum.

Note carefully that the conclusion, A_{6M}, asserts a conjunction true at the actual world. And while it will require abandoning SP, a modified materialist position would reject the first conjunct of A_{6M}, and thus A_{6M} itself. Here's how. A materialist could propose contingent physicalism according to which a strictly physical object is not essentially physical and a strictly immaterial object is not essentially immaterial. Thus, while there is a possible world in which an object (O) is strictly physical, O could exist in another possible world and not be a strictly physical object. Thus, some material objects could have been immaterial, and the move from A_{3M} to A_{6M} is blocked.

The contingent physicalist could reject A_{5M} by pointing out that the dilemma is not exhaustive because of an ambiguity in "physical body." As stated, "physical body" actually means "physical body and not a person." But the contingent physicalist claims that there is a possible world in which the physical body exists and is a person, i.e., the person is identical to his body. One could argue further that in such a world, the body qua person does, in fact, satisfy the datum.[9] So, we must replace A_{5M} with A^*_{5M}:

A^*_{5M}: Necessarily, either the human person's soul exists and satisfies the datum; or the nonpersonal physical body exists and satisfies the datum; or the physical body exists, is identical to a person, and satisfies the datum.

I think few physicalists would abandon standard physicalism (SP) for contingent physicalism, and the modal version works against SP. Still, contingent physicalism has a way out and I will evaluate it later. Here, I note that granting a possible world (W) in which I am identical to my body, there remains the problem of why I would still satisfy the datum in W. To probe this problem further, let us turn to the grounding version of the argument.

The Grounding Version

A_{1G}: The datum is true irrespective of whether human persons possess physical bodies.

A_{2G}: If A_{1G} is true, then the truth of the datum is not grounded in our physicality.

Granting A_{1G} and A_{2G}, we get:

A_{3G}: The truth of the datum is not grounded in our physicality.

---

9. It has been suggested to me that contingent physicalism is a weak interlocutor, and a more subtle view with which I should interact is material constitutionalism proffered by Lynne Rudder Baker and others. For two reasons, I will not follow this suggestion. First, this view has increasingly fallen into disfavor among philosophers of mind and, consequently, it has fewer and fewer defenders due to the problems with the positions. For example, along with Baker, Kevin Corcoran was one of the early, main defenders of material constitution, but he has subsequently abandoned it in favor of some version of Russellian neutral monism. Second, I have subjected this view to rigorous critique elsewhere and will not repeat that critique here. See Moreland, *Recalcitrant Imago Dei*, 131–37.

A_{4G}: Since a human person's physical body is exhausted by physicality, then the truth of the datum is not grounded in a human person's physical body.

A_{5G}: Either the soul or the physical body, which one either has or to which one is identical, grounds the truth of the datum.

A_{6G}: The soul is what grounds the truth of the datum.

As Bailey and Rasmussen point out, the grounding argument is harder to reject than the modal version.[10] Specifically, A_{2G} is hard to reject. Why? Recall the disembodied, intermediate-state thought experiment above. It would be wrong to torture wholly nonphysical persons, and surely, such persons command the same respect as embodied persons. However, what if a physicalist responded by claiming that our physicality grounds the same value as our immateriality, so we have the same value whether disembodied or embodied. Unfortunately, this response is irrational since it implies a bizarre, utter coincidence: the physical and nonphysical ground the very same value for human persons. Bailey and Rasmussen note that without some deep explanation for this, such a coincidence defeats this response.

Clearly, SP is in trouble here. A modified physicalist could insist that our value is not grounded in our physicality in two ways: (1) the property of being valuable is exemplified by wholly physical persons in a basic, un-grounded way; (2) the property of being valuable is exemplified by wholly physical persons by being grounded in a more basic nonphysical property.

Beside the fact that either move seems to be inappropriately ad hoc, neither grounds our value in physicality. The SD proponent is cheered by this. Moreover, it is far from clear how an object could be wholly physical while exemplifying being valuable or a nonphysical property grounding being valuable. Taking a page from the history of philosophy, this last point has been thoroughly vetted in eighteenth-century Britain following John Locke's (infamous) claim that it was within the range of divine omnipotence to create thinking matter.[11] Thus, a material object could have irreducible properties of consciousness. For the next century, this claim was the focus of great debate, and a number of thinkers such as Gerdil and Stillingfleet correctly pointed out that if God were to do this, God would thereby change the substance. It would no longer be a material object since it would be characterized essentially as "thinking matter" by nonphysical properties. It

---

10. Moreland, *Recalcitrant Imago Dei*, 131–37.
11. Yolton, *Thinking Matter*.

may be some sort of psycho-material substance, but it would not be wholly physical. I believe the same point applies to the modified physicalist position under consideration. In my view, such a modified physicalism is not a modified physicalism; it is an abandonment of physicalism.

1.2 Argument 2: An Inductive Argument

I conclude this section with an inductive argument construed either as an inference to the best explanation (IBE) or in Bayesian terms. As an IBE, we begin with the datum as a fact that needs to be explained. Our pool of hypotheses is that we are/have souls or are POs. Now, it seems self-evident that if we are/have souls, then the datum is true whether we are disembodied or embodied. I have offered thought experiments above for this claim. Since this is an ethical argument attempting to explain certain value/moral facts, these thought experiments do not need to represent worlds that are possible.

This may sound strange but consider this. Suppose time travel to the past is impossible. We can still entertain a world in which someone goes back into the past and murders someone. The ethics help desk would judge such an act as deeply immoral since the time of occurrence is irrelevant.

Even if impossible, dualist thought experiments focus on fundamental, ubiquitous intuitions about the difficulty of any PO satisfying the datum. The simple fact is that this is a huge problem for SP. Modified physicalism does not ground our value in physicality, but in basic value properties or nonphysical properties that ground them. Thus, the soul view is the best explanation for the datum. In Bayesian terms, let D=the datum, S=the soul view, and SP=the wholly physical body view. It seems obvious that we have (D/S)>>(D/SP).

In conclusion, consider the following term of epistemic appraisal offered by Roderick Chisholm:

> Beyond reasonable doubt: A proposition p is beyond reasonable doubt for S if and only if S is more justified in believing p than withholding judgment on p.[12]

In my view, if p = "the datum and it is best explained by and grounded in the soul," then p is beyond reasonable doubt.

---

12. See Chisholm, *Theory of Knowledge*, 8–17.

2. DOES A HUMAN PERSON'S BODY HAVE VALUE?

But what of the body? Am I being Platonic and rejecting its worth? Not at all. I just don't think the body is of much value qua physical. The body has value for these reasons: (1) As a Thomist, I take the body to be an ensouled, extended, physical structure; thus, the body includes the soul to be a body, and is valuable accordingly. By contrast, a corpse has little intrinsic value. (2) It has secondary qualities that ground many of its aesthetic properties, and neither secondary qualities nor aesthetic properties are physical. (3) It exemplifies certain geometrical relations, e.g., shape and symmetry, but these are abstract, not physical. (4) It exemplifies a certain relational complexity of arrangement, but this complexity type is abstract, not physical. (5) It is owned by the person, it is the vehicle, perhaps by way of natural signs, in virtue of which the person is known, and it is intimately and causally related to the person. (6) Relatedly, the body is necessary for full human functioning and flourishing, e.g., expressions of sexual love. (7) It exists, and insofar as any existing thing has value, it does. (8) It is physical.

Factors (7) and (8) provide little value compared to the other factors. The intrinsic value/beauty of creation is due to factors like (2)–(4) above, not (8). This becomes clear as follows: if Berkeley's immaterialist ontology were true, little of value of the created world would be lost, metaphysically speaking. If I am correct about this, then while the body has incredible value, that is not largely due to its being physical.

We are now faced with the issue of whether or not there is a soul. With adjustments, each of the arguments presented above has been used on behalf of GSD. Rather than return to those arguments, I will present and defend a modal argument for SD.

3. A MODAL ARGUMENT FOR SD

3.1 The Modal Argument

Descartes was the first philosopher to advance modal arguments for substance dualism in *Meditations* 2 and 6, especially in 6. Since then, several different modal arguments have been formulated, but I shall focus on one specific form. I am not implying that other forms are not appropriate; it's just not my purpose to survey various versions, and instead, by presenting my own form of the argument, I can focus on what I take to be most important. Let SS be a wholly spiritual substance, e.g., a soul. Here is the argument:

1. The indiscernibility of identicals and $(x=y) \rightarrow \Box(x=y)$
2. POs are essentially and intrinsically physical, and SSs are essentially and intrinsically immaterial.
3. Possibly, I exist and no POs exist.
4. My physical body is a PO.
5. Therefore, possibly, I exist without my physical body existing.
6. Therefore, I am essentially and intrinsically not my body nor any PO.
7. I am essentially and intrinsically either a PO or SS.
8. Therefore, I am essentially and intrinsically a SS.

Certain clarifications are in order. In (1), x and y are Kripkean rigid designators or Swinburne's informative rigid designators. Thus, (1) expresses *de re* and not *de dicto* reference and modality. I will take up a defense of the essentialist part of (2) below, but here I want to clarify my use of "intrinsically." This is meant to capture the idea that what makes a PO physical are the physical natures of the constituents—e.g., properties, property instances, relations, relation instances, parts, stuff, or events—that "make up" a PO, that are inherent in its being. With proper substitution, the same goes for SS.

In (3), (4), and following, "I," "PO," and "my physical body" are *de re* rigid designators. I don't like using "my physical body," because "my" is an indexical possessive adjective, and I agree with those who take "I," "my" to be singular referring terms that refer to sui generis, irreducible, nonphysical (in these two cases, mental) entities.[13] Thus, designating something as "my body" is already to adopt a mental ontology as an "aspect" of the referent. But I set this issue aside, and for the sake of convenience and in conformity with standard statements of modal arguments for SD, I shall retain "my physical body."

Regarding (7), if we limit our domain of discourse to strictly physicalist views and various dualist views of the subject of consciousness, the I, and of the physical body, then (7) is an exhaustive dilemma. If we remove such a limitation, (7) still captures the live options for most who support or reject the modal argument(s), so I set aside other options, e.g., Berkeley's

---

13. See Madell, *Identity of the Self* and *Essence of the Self*.

idealism, for the sake of convenience. Let us grant (7) and my limited focus for the sake of argument.

I am assuming (1), (4), and (7). Premise (5) follows from (3) and (4); (6) follows from (2) and (5). Thus, (2) and (3) are the main premises subject to attack. In what follows, I defend (2) and (3) and respond to general defeaters of the modal argument.

3.2 Contingent Physicalism and Premise (2)

The vast majority of philosophers would embrace the notion that wholly physical and wholly mental particulars are essentially such. There are no possible worlds, W1 and W2, such that an object PO is wholly physical in W1 and wholly nonphysical in W2, and similarly with a wholly immaterial subject/self. But Trenton Merricks (and Dean Zimmerman) demurs, advocating contingent physicalism, which entails that an object could be wholly physical in the actual world but wholly immaterial in another world.[14]

Merricks begins with a consideration of this argument:

1. For all x and all y, if x is identical to y, then x is necessarily identical to y.
2. Possibly, I exist, and no physical thing exists.
3. I am identical with my body.

The dualism employs (1) and (2) to establish the negation of (3). Merricks seeks to block the inference from (2) to the negation of (3), and he claims that inference rests on (4):

4. M (my body) is essentially a physical thing.

Unfortunately, says Merricks, there is no argument for (4). Now consider (5):

5. Possibly, M (my body) exists, and no physical thing exists.
6. Therefore, it is not the case that I am essentially, wholly, and intrinsically my body or any PO.

Premise (5) entails the denial of (4), and deciding which to adopt depends on arguments/judgments re accepting (3) or (4). The contingent physicalist will prefer (3) and also accept (1) and (2). From the fact that

14. Merricks, "New Objection"; Zimmerman, "Two Cartesian Arguments."

there is a possible world in which I exist and no physical thing exists, it does not follow that in the actual world, I am not identical to my body.

But what if someone argues that (4) is intuitively evident and properly basic? Merricks responds that (4) rests on (7):

7. It is necessarily true that a body is a physical thing.

But (4) does not follow from (7) as can be seen in this counter example: It is necessarily true that the president of the United States is a member of the executive branch of the American government. But this does not entail that Bill Clinton is essentially a member of the executive branch.

Given that we have strong arguments/empirical evidence (e.g., split brain phenomena, mental/physical correlations) and modal intuitions (e.g., we have strong modal intuitions that mental/physical interaction is impossible) against (4) and for (3), and given that we have only weak intuitions for (3), the physicalist should adopt (4), even though the modal argument for SD may persuade those half-convinced of SD, or strengthen the faith of SDs. While this is a creative argument, I think it suffers from significant problems.

First, a dualist could hold that (4) is properly basic and grounded in very strong modal seemings. For two reasons, this need not be a mere assertion. For one thing, Husserl (see below) has provided a detailed account of how we procure the relevant intuitions that provide access-internalist grounds for (4). Even if Husserl is wrong, he shows that the proper-basicality claim need not be a mere assertion. Moreover, we will see below that dualist intuitions of disembodiment are historically and geographically ubiquitous, and they are naturally formed by little children with no exposure to dualist teaching. One could respond that this shows merely that the folk ontology of human beings includes the contingent fact that we are possibly, but not essentially, disembodiable. However, if that were the case, you would expect to find a fair number of children and adults sans prior physicalist indoctrination expressing physicalist understandings of the afterlife. But that is not the case, because people grasp the kind of thing they are—essentially immaterial.

Merricks counters that dualist commitment to (4) relies on (7):

7. It is necessarily true that a (wholly physical) body is a physical thing.

I disagree and embrace a Husserlian account of (4) relying on the relevant intuitions. But more importantly, in context, (7) is a *de dicto* claim with wide scope for the modal operator, and "a body" seems to be a non-rigid designator. If this is correct, then if there is a propositional ground for (4), it is not (7) but (7*):

7* My body is necessarily (more appropriately, essentially) a physical thing.

Here "my body" and "physical thing" are rigid designators; the premise involves *de re* necessity with the modal operator exhibiting narrow scope. So Merricks's employment of (7) is not relevant.

Second, in criticizing Van Inwagen's simulacrum hypothesis, Merricks says that even if there is a possible world in which Van Inwagen's view is true, nevertheless, it is the actual word that is of concern to us and his view is false in the actual world.[15] Analogously, he claims that (2) of his argument implies that there is a possible world in which I am a wholly immaterial object, but that world is not the actual one.

I offer two responses:

i. Modal intuitions, especially as understood by Husserl, are of kinds of objects—the kind "pure ego" and the sub-categorial kind "physical object" (including "wholly physical body"). Merricks could reject this as irrelevant, but he shoulders a burden of proof here since most philosophers and lay people find contingent physicalism to be unacceptable. He also needs to interact with modal epistemologies like Husserl's.

ii. I think Merricks's notion that a wholly physical body could exist in a possible world as a wholly immaterial entity is, in part, the result of taking possible-world talk as a useful semantics for modal operators/propositions and, in some way, ontologizing possible worlds. I can't argue the point here, but if something like Alexander Pruss's Aristotelean-Leibnizian view is correct, then it entails that modal truths are grounded by the causal/dispositional capacities of actual substances.[16] Assuming that this is correct, if an alleged "wholly physical body" in the actual world can exist wholly immaterially, then the former must have a wide range of immaterial capacities, and arguably, this would entail that it is not wholly physical in the actual world.

---

15. Merricks, "How to Live Forever"; "New Objection," 84.
16. Pruss, *Actuality, Possibility and Worlds*, pts. 5–6.

Third, it seems unintelligible how complex objects x and y could be identical (in this or across worlds) if they share no proper constituents. How could the angel Gabriel in one world be a frog's body in another when they share no proper constituents? To clarify, a complex object is one with two or more proper constituents. A proper constituent of some object x is an entity that would be included in an ontological assay/inventory of all and only those entities that are "within/enter into the being of" or that "make up" x. "Proper constituent" includes parts, properties/property instances, intrinsic relations/relation instances, structure/structure instances, and events. Finally, "being a proper constituent of" is primitive.

For Merricks, one's body in the actual world is a PO, and in another world an SS/IO. There is nothing shared between a PO and an SS/IO that could ground or account for their identity.

Look at it another way. If a PO is wholly physical in a contingent way, then physicality is accidental to one's body (PO). But if a proper constituent (or structural arrangement of such) is accidental to an entity (e), then (e) could exist without it. Drawing insights from other relevant cases, we conclude: The object has the accidental proper constituent, and thus, in another world where that proper constituent is lacking and the object exists, the object simply lacks the accidental proper constituent. Thus, the object is what has and is not identical to that constituent. The same would be true of a proper-constituent cluster. Thus, the object must be something "over and above" that cluster, and it has different clusters in different worlds. Thus, one's body has physicality and then immateriality and must be the same entity in each of the relevant possible worlds to make sense of what remains the same and has one and now the other proper-constituent clusters.

Merricks is not arguing that a wholly physical object could become a wholly immaterial object. Still, an analogy with Aristotelian accidental change is useful. Consider a dog changing from being black to grey. For this to be change and not successive replacement involving ceasing-to-be and coming-to-be, there must be some entity that is self-identical throughout the change and that had blackness and now has greyness. That entity is "over and above" the color properties.

How might a contingent physicalist respond? I think the best line would be to say that identity, including the identity of a complex object is brute and ungrounded, it is the object itself—a PO/IO—that is identical in the two worlds, and that's that.

Unfortunately, this claim comes very close to begging the question. I am disputing that a PO could be identical to an IO as Merricks depicts it, and this response says, in effect, that my arguments are ineffective because they are just identical and there's nothing more to be said. Surely, when it comes to complex objects as I have characterized them, we are owed at least some sort of account as to how such an identity could be brute. Not all brute primitives are created equal. I could see how a constituentless bare particular's self-identity could be brute, but complex objects are another matter altogether.

Further, I think the following claim is ambiguous: Identity is never grounded ("each thing is what it is and not something else" is about all one can say on the matter), including the identity of complexes, so the search for a ground is misguided. If this means that the identity relation is primitive and irreducible to some other relation, e.g., exact similarity or some persistence relation, then I agree. But I suspect that this isn't what is being affirmed. I suspect it means that there is no reductive analysis of cases of identity themselves, in these cases, identity is what it is and, consequently, uninformative.

A good place to begin evaluating this interpretation is the debate over diachronic personal identity between advocates of the simple and complex views.[17] One criticism of the simple view is that by taking personal identity to be primitive and brute, the simple view is uninformative and merely an assertion of diachronic identity.

This criticism is confused in that it conflates a reductive analysis of identity with an ontological assay of the entities that retain it. The simple view does entail that no reductive analysis of personal identity, e.g., in terms of sortal-dependent persistence conditions, is adequate. But it does not entail that identity is uninformative because in each case, an ontological assay may be given to the entity that retains identity to understand what must be the case for identity to obtain.

For example, a simple-view advocate could say that personal identity is identity of a specific type of soul, and moreover, the identity of that sort of thing requires identity of its constituents—the essence "human personhood," the nexus of exemplification, and a bare particular. Such an assay retains the basicality of identity itself but provides an ontological inventory of the relevant entity and what must stay the same for the entity to retain identity. Again, on a property exemplification view of event identity,

---

17. See Georg and Stefan, *Personal Identity*.

$(e_1=e_2) \rightarrow [(S_1=S_2)$ & $(P_1=P_2)$ & $(t_1=t_2)]$, where e_1, e_2 are events; S_1, S_2 are substances; P_1, P_2 are properties; and t_1, t_2 are times. Here, identity itself is primitive, but the natures of the entities (events) that are/are not identical are complex and in need of an ontological assay. I suggest this same response is sufficient to defeat this objection.

Finally, it may be objected that parthood is constituted by sameness of causal-functional role integration with respect to a whole or by being caught up into the same life. So, if the parts themselves are replaced by other types of parts that play the same role or are caught up into the same life, identity is retained.

In response, many philosophers, e.g., Jaegwon Kim, take functional roles as concepts, as ways of taking something, and not real entities that constitute the relevant objects. Sans some sort of Aristotelianism, I agree.

Second, this confuses an ontological account of what makes something a part with the nature of the part itself. The latter is essential for macro-identity. Thus, if all the parts of an object are replaced with different parts that play the same role, you have different objects that are functionally isomorphic, rather than the same object.

Third, it is far from clear that a functional role construed ontologically is a physical entity, and if not, then a PO is not wholly physical. Finally, being caught up in the same life faces this problem: If the activities of the parts of O_1 at t_1 are different from those of the parts of O_2 at t_2, how is it the same life? Since a life is an aggregate of living activities, it seems that if those activities change, so does the life. Thus, life is not stable enough to ground identity. And if all the physical parts are gradually replaced with immaterial parts and all parts exhibit life-constituting activities, then the life at t_1 will be a set of physical activities, the life at t_2 will be a set of mental activities, and the life at one time is just not identical to the life at another.[18]

I want to tweak this last point to support my second objection above. Suppose O_1 at t_1 = O_2 at t_2 because their parts' activities constitute the same life. Assuming O_1 is a physical object composed of and only of physical parts that exhibit physical activities, then O_2 seems to be a physical object. But suppose, instead, that O_2 at t_2 is composed of and only of purely immaterial animal spirits exhibiting immaterial activities. If we still assume that O_1 at t_1 is entirely physical and that the activities of the parts of O_1 and O_2 constitute the same life, then, based on our criterion of parthood, it would

---

18. I am indebted to Andrew Bailey and Joshua Rasmussen for their helpful input in this discussion of Merricks's view.

seem that O_2 is a physical object as well. But we have strong intuitions that resist this conclusion. O_2 is composed of and only of immaterial parts with no physical constituents. Given this, surely O_2 is an immaterial object and not identical to O_1. But, then, the nature of an object's constituents determine its ontological kind, and criteria for parthood simply tell us which parts are relevant in deciding the ontology of the whole.

To close out my response to Merricks, (1) I think that our modal intuitions for a real distinction between the self and body are much stronger than those against mental/physical interaction (note the ubiquitous dualist intuitions cited above and the ubiquitous intuitions that a wholly immaterial God could cause things to occur in a wholly physical world); (2) strict physicalism, mere property dualism, and substance dualism are empirically equivalent, and thus there is no empirical evidence that favors one of these three views (I invite the physicalist to present such empirical evidence that a substance dualism could not easily accommodate); and (3) I have tried to show that there are good arguments against contingent physicalism and that the arguments for it are weaker than Merricks supposes. Thus, I see no epistemic considerations that favor physicalism over substance dualism.

3.3 Clarification and Defense of Premise (3): Conceivability and Possibility

Historically, the main position on how we gain modal knowledge as expressed in (3) ("Possibly, I exist, and no POs exist") appeals to an epistemic or truth-tracking connection between something being conceivable (or rationally intuitive) and its being possible (necessary, etc.).[19] Unfortunately, there are at least fourteen different notions of "conceiving," many of which are widely disparate.[20] As a result, even though the notion of "rational intuition" also exhibits different interpretations, nevertheless, it is not as unwieldy as "conceiving" and further, with clarifications (see below), it is more appropriate for my own views in modal epistemology.

Before leaving the topic of conceiving, there are two important issues that are usually discussed in association with conceiving, so while I shall adjust them in appropriate ways to express my clarified notion of rational intuition, now is a good place to mention them. First, there is an important

---

19. Cf. Evnine, "Modal Epistemology," 665–70; Yablo, "Is Conceivability a Guide."

20. Gendler and Hawthorne, *Conceivability and Possibility*, 7–8; cf. Tidman, "Conceivability as a Test."

distinction between strong (positive) conceiving and weak (negative) conceiving. Limiting our understanding to possibility, if *s* strongly conceives some proposition (P) to be possibly true or some state of affairs (S) to be possible, then *s* "sees" that P is possibly true or S is possible. Strong conceiving confers positive epistemic status on P or S. If *s* weakly conceives P to be possibly true or S to be possible, then *s* fails to "see" that P is impossibly true or S is incompossible.[21] In my comments below, I will employ positive rational intuition and different specifications of it.

Second, another distinction is between *de re* and *de dicto* conceivings, the former being directed towards an entity, e.g., a state of affairs, and the latter towards a proposition.

3.4 Modal Epistemology, Rational Intuitions as Seemings, and Adequate Intuitive Presentation

In order to clarify my own concept of what confers positive epistemic status on modal claims whether they exhibit the status of being prima facie justified, secunda facie justified, or (usually) defeasible modal knowledge, it seems best to survey three representative samples of modal epistemology to give a proper context for my own views.[22] And such a survey can provide different approaches to countering modal skepticism, e.g., by giving different explanations for modal error.

Consider George Bealer's statement: "Intuition is the source of all a priori knowledge."[23] Setting aside purported a posterior modal knowledge, I take Bealer to be on the right track. Assuming this as a launching point, I first note Chisholm's comments about the concepts expressed in a class of important words used in a primitive phenomenological way: "seems," "appears," "looks."[24] Accordingly, I take phenomenological employments of "seemings" or "appearings" to express "intuitions." Expressed adverbially, a rational seeming is a way of being appeared to by a purported intentional object.

In my view, any account of modal knowledge (evidence, justified belief) must answer two questions:

21. Cleve, "Conceivability and Cartesian Argument."
22. Elsewhere, I have assessed Bonjour's modal epistemology. See Moreland, *Universals*, 123–26.
23. Bealer, "Modal Epistemology," esp. 73.
24. Chisholm, *Theory of Knowledge*, 26–34, 39–42.

1. What is the character of adequate intuitive acts, the intentional objects of such acts, and the tie that connects them in cases of modal knowledge?
2. How does one account for modal error?

As we will see, some reject (1) altogether and replace "intuitive acts" and "intentional objects" with causal or reliabilist considerations, while other retain (at least) some notion of intuition as a necessary but not sufficient condition for modal knowledge to be supplemented by access-externalist factors, e.g., modal reliabilism. With this in mind, let us examine three versions of modal knowledge.

Timothy O'Connor

According to O'Connor, modal beliefs are woven into our concept of the world.[25] From our theorizing, advancing scientific theories, our cognitive activities are replete with modal concepts. Thus, he adopts robust modal realism: the world contains primitive modal features.

These claims raise an epistemological problem, especially in light of modal error: How do we come to have modal knowledge? O'Connor's answer employs a version of truthmaker theory according to which for every truth—modal or otherwise—there is some entity that is its ground and whose obtaining metaphysically necessitates its truth.

Two initial observations are in order. First, it seems that O'Connor's sole focus in modal epistemology is the *de dicto* knowledge of a modal proposition's truth value (though he does believe in modal facts). He regularly talks about modal beliefs, concepts, or judgments, theoretical explanations that tacitly assume modalities that are not transparent to an idealized grasp of the relevant concepts. Here, it is concepts and not mind-independent modal entities that are known.

Second, O'Connor rejects the role of rational intuition in modal knowledge when understood as a form of seeming, directly perceiving and so forth. He explicitly equates intuition with belief.[26] He also rejects such seemings on empirical grounds, and he faults Bonjour's account of modal knowledge for employing rational "seeing" which, O'Connor says,

---

25. O'Connor, *Theism and Ultimate Explanation*, 1–62.
26. O'Connor, *Theism and Ultimate Explanation*, 149n11.

is not explicated beyond a mere disposition to believe.[27] Further, O'Connor faults earlier rationalist employment of intuition as a metaphor for "directly seeing the necessity" since it is too strong. Rather, once we embrace modal fallibilism, we should replace this metaphor with a strong disposition to believe certain propositions to be necessary, a disposition often fueled by a hidden, underlying commitment to the explanatory role of such necessities.

Turning to O'Connor's positive account of modal knowledge, four features are important for our purposes: the role of causality, reflective equilibrium and refinement, the tie between modal facts and modal knowledge, and sources of modal error.

First, O'Connor adopts a causal component for knowledge—including modal knowledge—as a necessary condition. Modal knowledge entails some sort of appropriate causal contact with modal facts.[28]

Second, in addition to a causal component, reflective equilibrium and refinement are necessary components of modal knowledge.[29] According to O'Connor, we begin our quest for developing a theory of modal knowledge by starting with the insight that modal beliefs play a unique, ineliminable role in commonsense and theoretical understanding of things. We begin with certain core "data" and through reflective equilibrium and refinement, we extend outward to a fuller theory of modal knowledge. For example, we have a strong propensity to accept certain obvious modal propositions, and we recognize that our explanatory schemes and theoretical rationality are built upon taking such basic modal notions as fundamentally legitimate. Moreover, we recognize that our perception of the actual is imbued with an implicit grasp and acceptance of the modal character of reality. As we build from this "ordinary folk" perspective, we develop theories of modal knowledge that extend the range of our modal beliefs and allow for correction, refinement and extension of our modal judgments.

Regarding the tie between modal facts and knowledge, O'Connor appropriates truthmaker theory:[30] Modal facts ground modal truths and by way of a causal chain, trigger a "strong propensity" to accept certain modal truths, a "disposition to strongly believe" them, particularly those involving necessity and impossibility. To give an account of why such dispositions are generally truth-tracking, we need to reflect on the causal origin of our

27. O'Connor, *Theism and Ultimate Explanation*, 9–10.
28. O'Connor, *Theism and Ultimate Explanation*, 8–10, 50–51, 58–59.
29 O'Connor, *Theism and Ultimate Explanation*, 41–43, 49.
30. O'Connor, *Theism and Ultimate Explanation*, 8, 10.

fundamental modal convictions and any account of this cannot be causally independent of the relevant truthmakers.[31] To fill out a sketch of more details, O'Connor presents a just-so story beginning:

> An evolutionary advantage accrued to cognizer types that readily ascent to the actual truth of core logical and mathematical principles and that systematize the world in terms of natural kinds; some such cognizers in our ancestral history were selected in part owing to this fact; and the truthmakers for these actual truths are none other than their modalized counterparts.[32]

Perhaps not exhaustive, but the following are the major sources of modal error for O'Connor:

- Deviant causal chains from modal fact/truth to modal propositional dispositions/attitudes
- Unreliably produced, non-truth-tracking modal dispositions
- Disagreement regarding the modal implications of non-modal facts (could the embodied person Socrates have been an alligator?)
- General theoretical disagreements where the role of imagination is far from clear (is time travel possible?)
- Extending modal cognitive processes to areas we cannot imagine in sufficient detail or which are such that they involve controversial philosophical possibility claims, e.g., remote and complicated unactualized possibilities

This precis does not do justice to the full extent of O'Connor's reflections, but this will do for my purposes. My goal in this section is to sketch out main and diverse versions of modal epistemology in order to show the resources available to one who embraces premise (3). Many accept O'Connor's approach and, accordingly, could use it with adjustments to defend (3). Still, for three reasons, I am unpersuaded by his view.

First, O'Connor mistakenly makes modal knowledge about *de dicto* modality with no room for *de re* modal knowledge as the epistemic grounds for the former. I recognize that O'Connor advances a version of epistemic access-externalism, so he may not be bothered by this criticism. But I think his doing so is uninformed. Surely, commonsense "folk epistemology" is

---

31. O'Connor, *Theism and Ultimate Explanation*, 58–59.
32. O'Connor, *Theism and Ultimate Explanation*, 59.

internalist in some way or another, and I think we should stick to that unless there are substantial defeaters that override its prima facie justification. Just as seeming to see red while looking at an apple provides good justification for believing the apple is red, so seeming to see modal entities does the same thing.

The only two defeaters I can find in O'Connor's writing are: (1) Philosophers who appeal to rational intuition fail to explain, e.g., how "seeing" redness and greenness allows us to "see" their mutual exclusivity. This is not explicated beyond claiming a mere disposition to believe the exclusion. (2) Those who appeal to rational intuition, at least historically, adopt infallibilism for modal knowledge and fail to account for (purported) modal error.

In response, (2) is simply not applicable in the current setting. Even Edmund Husserl acknowledged the defeasibility of modal awareness and propositional attitudes epistemically grounded in them, and he proffered a clear account of modal error. Regarding (1), Husserl provided the most detailed answer to this problem in the history of philosophy. We will examine his views below.

Second, due to his inadequate employment of irreducible intentionality, O'Connor turns to a causal account as an essential aspect of his overall view of modal knowledge. Unfortunately, (efficient) causality and appropriate causal chains are irrelevant to sensory (e.g., visual) and modal evidence, justified belief and knowledge.

The obtaining of such a causal relation/chain between an entity known and the knowing subject is not necessary for knowledge. Two considerations show this to be the case. (1) Consider a world in which relevant entities have causal powers and such chains obtain. Now suppose that God decides to shift this world to an occasionalist one every Sunday and is the sole direct cause of everything. If I was appeared to redly while looking at a red apple's surface (or used the concept of a dog to think about one) from Monday through Saturday, then if I had that same sensory state (or concept) on Sunday, I would still be seeing the apple's surface or thinking about the dog sans the relevant causal chain. If someone says that God would still be doing the relevant causal work, this won't do. What exactly does God cause in the subject such that it "hooks up" with the right object? If God were to cause a sensation of a grey elephant while looking at the red apple, the sensation simply would not be about the apple; it would be about the elephant.

(2) Another way to see the unnecessariness of a causal relation is to consider a case presented by Hillary Putnam.[33] In order to get rid of irreducible intentionality and replace it with wide mental contents and a causal chain analysis, he invites us to consider a being on some planet with no trees who suddenly gets a mental image of what we would describe as one of a tree. Putnam claims that the image is not a representation of a tree because mental states, e.g., images, are not intrinsically representational and there is no (appropriate) causal chain from a nonexistent object to the image.

In responding to Putnam's thought experiment, Geoffrey Madell grants the lack of intrinsic intentionality for the mental image, but goes on to give the reason why.[34] It is not due to the absence of a causal connection; rather, it is because no sense image is intrinsically referential. Images become representational when the subject stipulates or thinks of it as representing something, in this case, a tree.

In my view, this whole discussion is deeply confused. Because of a sensation's or concept's intrinsic character available to second-order introspection, it is of what it is of. It functions as a natural sign. You can't have a tree sensation without it being of a tree (even if no tree caused it.) Moreover, (at least clear) intentional mental states are necessarily of their intentional objects. In the alien's case, his image is of a tree, but unfortunately, since no trees exist, the image fails to "hit" a real target. Regarding Madell's response, he seems to liken visual images (I analyze them adverbially) to words, and this is wrong. The word-world connection is arbitrary and conventional. The visual sensation or conceptual relation to an intentional object in the world is necessary. As we will see in our examination of Husserl, (especially) certain kinds of sensations and propositional attitudes are intrinsically intentional and necessarily of their intentional objects, and this is why we know what we are thinking about or taking ourselves to see by a simple act of focused attention on the intentional state itself. This ability is hard to explain if a causal chain or stipulative analysis is embraced.

In addition, the obtaining of such a causal relation/chain between an entity known and the knowing subject is not sufficient for knowledge. Causal chains can always be deviant. This is why causal-connection advocates require that the chain is "appropriate." It is notoriously difficult to analyze this concept in a noncircular way. But waiving this problem, the dialectical

---

33. Putnam, *Reason, Truth and History*, ch. 1, esp. 4.
34. Madell, *Identity of the Self*, 17.

process of refining and giving content to "appropriate" casual chain inevitably involves appealing to the intrinsic character and intentionality of the relevant mental state to guide the deliberative process. An analysis of the notion of "appropriate" is advanced, and counterexamples offered. A new, patched-up analysis is offered and new counterexamples are provided, and so on until an allegedly acceptable final analysis is reached. What guides the process, providing the intuitive insight that a given analysis adequately solves the relevant counterexamples and providing the insight for generating new counterexamples? It is our (at least implicit) understanding of the intrinsic intentionality of the relevant mental state, of what it is supposed to be about. If I'm right about this, then the relevant intrinsic intentionality is irreducible/ineliminable, and it is conceptually and epistemically basic while the causal chain analysis is derivative.

Finally, advocates of "intuition as direct awareness" views face, but have met, the problem of modal fallibility. But the causal chain analyses face an associated difficulty lurking in the neighborhood: the problem of incorrigible or infallible modal judgments, along with the directness/immediacy of modal seemings. Granting widespread modal defeasibility, there still seem to be cases of modal infallibility, e.g., the transitivity of identity and certain other relations, the law of noncontradiction (with apologies to advocates of deviant logics). If causal chains are always subject to deviancy, how is one to account for these cases? And what are we to make of the apparent immediacy and directness of our intentional awarenesses? These are difficult questions, and causal chain advocates need to do a better job of answering them.

3.3 George Bealer[35]

As David Kasmier observes, because Bealer accepts the widely adopted JTB (plus Gettier modifications) analysis of knowledge, knowledge strictly entails "evidence," so a theory of evidence is all that is necessary for a theory of a priori knowledge, and a theory of the latter must answer two questions: (1) What are intuitions? (2) Why are they evidence?[36]

---

35. Key primary sources are Bealer, "Modal Epistemology"; "Philosophical Limits"; "Possibility of Philosophical Knowledge." Key secondary sources are Kasmier, "Husserl's Theory," 38–50, 96–103; Evnine, "Modal Epistemology"; Hopp, *Phenomenology*; Piazza, *A Priori Knowledge*, 137–81; Yablo, "Is Conceivability a Guide."

36. Kasmier, "Husserl's Theory," 38.

In answering these questions, *de re* modality seems not to play a role; rather, his theory is analyzed with respect to *de dicto* modal knowledge by focusing on analysis and knowledge of concepts and the truth of modal propositions. His is a theory of evidence as intuitions supplemented by modal reliabilism to explain why and under what conditions certain intuitions are defeasibly truth-tracking.

Intuitions are a basic source of evidence and, as such, are primitive and sui generis. Rational intuitions are seemings whose objects are modal concepts, modal propositions and their truth values, and seemings amount to intuitive understandings. Such intuitions do not involve some magical power or inner voice of some mysterious faculty. For example, upon reflection of a De Morgan's law, a modal seeming occurs, and upon further reflection, an alethic seeming obtains.

Why are intuitions evidential? According to Bealer, certain intuitions have an appropriately strong modal (i.e., necessitating) tie to modal truth elucidated by way of his version of modal reliabilism. And what is this version? To begin with, the appropriate tie requires properly understanding the concepts involved in the content of our modal intuitions. To possess a concept is to understand it to some degree or other. However, only a certain kind of concept possession—determinate concept possession—entails the needed tie. A subject possesses a concept determinately if:

1. The subject at least nominally possesses the concept, and this happens if the subject has a natural propositional attitude (e.g., a belief) towards the proposition that has that concept as a conceptual content.

2. The subject does not do this with misunderstanding or incomplete understanding or just by virtue of attributions practices or in any other such manner.[37]

Condition (2) is called robust or determinate concept possession. When this occurs, one's intuitions are truth tracking. Determinate understanding of this sort is that mode of understanding that constitutes the categorical base of the metaphysical possibility of truth-tracking intuitions.

Bealer acknowledges that historically speaking, rationalists accepted the following equivalence (E): For all propositions (P), necessarily, P is a priori if P is necessary. But since Kripke, scientific essentialist considerations have presented a challenge to E. Kripke famously showed the equivalence in E fails in both directions. Modal error occurs regarding necessary a

37. Bealer, "Modal Epistemology," 102.

posteriori truths (e.g., necessarily, water is H_2O) with respect to an illusion of possibility in cases where those in an epistemic duplicate community (e.g., twin earth) say something true (their aqueous stuff is *xyz*) but this doesn't imply that water itself is not H_2O. Similarly, modal error occurs regarding contingent a priori truths with respect to an illusion of necessity when one confuses a description (e.g., "stick S at time t_0") as a definite description versus as a reference fixer.

Bealer's way out of this problem is to say that E still holds for a certain class of propositions, viz., those that are semantically stable. According to Bealer, there are three relevant classes of concepts at play: (1) categorial concepts (identity, property, relation, stuff, compositional stuff, functional stuff); (2) content concepts (phenomenal concepts, concepts of psychological attitudes); (3) naturalistic concepts (natural kinds involved in scientific essentialism such as water=H_2O). The concepts in (1) and (2) are semantically stable, and those in (3) are not. A proposition is semantically stable iff its meaning remains invariant across epistemic duplicate communities.

Since the concepts employed in the traditional a priori disciplines (logic, mathematics, first philosophy) and those that express the relevant mental concepts are semantically stable, a posteriori necessities do not arise in these areas. Thus, Kripke's arguments apply to (3) and have no significance to (1) and (2). Below, I will briefly mention two current strategies for responding to Kripkean problems with E, but for now, I want to keep our focus on Bealer's modal epistemology.

In closing out my precis of Bealer's thought, I list his take on the major sources of modal errors along with a brief comment regarding his assessment of the modal argument for SD[38]:

- Confusing epistemic and metaphysical possibility
- In the context of scientific essentialism, Stephen Yablo's class *a* belief-based errors: mistaken a posteriori beliefs (e.g., that Hesperus≠Phosphorus)
- Stephen Yablo's class *b* beliefs: mistaken beliefs about the relationship between a posteriori beliefs and their relationship to modal truths (e.g., denying that if Hesperus=Phosphorus, Hesperus could not outlive Phosphorus)
- Those resulting from local categorial misunderstanding according to which categorial mastery of a concept is interrupted due to being

---

38. Due to space considerations, I omit Bealer's employment of a priori stability. See Bealer, "Modal Epistemology," 104–5.

locally disrupted. This occurs when one has the right primary categorial concept but does not know it applies to a local range of cases, perhaps due to having the wrong sub-categorial concept (e.g., having the categorial concept that water is macroscopic stuff but selecting the subcategory "functional stuff" when applying it to water in a local situation.)

- Those resulting from categorial misunderstanding (e.g., taking water to be a functional concept rather than a compositional-stuff concept)

Finally, for two reasons, Bealer rejects the modal argument for SD.[39] First, regarding intuitions that support the claim that one's disembodiment is possible, Bealer retorts that many fail to have such intuitions, and in fact, many report having the opposite intuitions, so these cancel out. Secondly, since "I" is a paradigm case of semantic instability, the question is raised as to which subcategory of thing is hit by "I." Granting that "a person" is the primary category, we just don't know if the correct subcategory is "essentially embodied person" or "disembodiable person."

Bealer has presented a careful, sophisticated account of modal evidence (justified belief, knowledge) and modal error. Given the current widespread acceptance of different versions of epistemic externalism, I think his views should be appealing to many philosophers, and surely, it shows that a plausible account of modal evidence et al. and error is available. Still, I think we can do better, and I have four problems with Bealer's account.

First, it is entirely *de dicto* in that the objects of modal knowledge are concepts, propositions, and truth values. This is especially odd, given the importance of rational intuitions as seemings. It is most natural to take such as direct awareness or apprehension of a relevant entity. Given this, I see no reason to limit those entities in the way he does; rather, it seems more fitting to hold that such seemings are also directed at relevant modal entities themselves (e.g., properties, relations) epistemically prior to *de dicto* seemings, such that *de re* seemings provide the epistemic grounds for *de dicto* seemings.

Bealer's omission of such *de re* seemings is responsible for his taking what I believe to be a wrong turn in analyzing why intuitions as seemings are evidence appropriately tied to truth. Given the importance of intuiting/"rational seeing" for Bealer, one would naturally expect an

---

39. Bealer, "Modal Epistemology," 114–16.

elucidation of the appropriate tie in terms of a careful analysis of the nature of seemings, truth, considering, reflecting, and propositions, and how they are made available to and are in consciousness, modal entities, and the like. One would also expect an account of how these are brought together in synchronic and diachronic mental acts so as to deliver modal knowledge. Instead, Bealer jumps to an externalist account in terms of his version of modal reliabilism. Given his starting point in seemings, it would have been simpler and more intuitive for Bealer to have continued along an access-internalist path, rather than changing horses midstream.

Second, the difficulties just surfaced actually make intuitive seemings superfluous to his overall account. To see this, consider functionalist accounts of mental types and tokens. Mental types are functional roles and mental tokens are realizers of those roles. Interestingly, the intrinsic nature of the realizer is irrelevant to making it a token of a particular type of mental event. Rather, it is the realizer playing the correct role in an input/output system whether causal or in a machine functionalist way. Thus, if the realizer is one with the intrinsic phenomenal texture of being hurtful, that is irrelevant to its being a pain. What makes it a pain is its playing the right role in the functional type being painful.

Applied to Bealer, he takes intuitions to be psychological conditions that serve as indicator evidence for various necessities. It is the reliable processes and correlations that make intuitions epistemically important. Thus, these processes/correlations need not be known or thought about for them to be relevant. All that must take place is that the appropriate reliable connections obtain between the processes that produce modal beliefs and their truth value. Thus, the intuition itself is no per se indicator at all. Intuitions are irrelevant as intuitions. Further, given the importance of determinate concept possession, especially in the sense that it entails understanding that concept in which proper categorial mastery is central, Bealer runs into a problem. Bealer's account depends on what it seeks to establish. Understanding the relevant concept and categorial mastery of it require a priori knowledge. That intuitions become evidence, therefore, depends on a priori knowledge and the former cannot constitute the latter.

Third, according to Bealer, intuitions are a basic source of evidence and, as such, are primitive and sui generis propositional attitude. He is quick to distance his view from those who hold that intuitions are a magical power or inner voice of a mysterious faculty. But these claims represent two significant confusions.

i. The idea of a faculty has a long and steady history and is still employed today. Many contemporary philosophers are irreducible realists regarding notions such as various kinds of powers, dispositions, potentialities, capacities, abilities, etc. Further, historically speaking, the sub-categorial classification of these notions was grounded in the kind of properties they actualized or activities they manifested.[40] Finally, a faculty is a natural grouping of relevantly resembling disposition. There is nothing particularly odd, spooky, or mysterious about the existence of faculties. Now a faculty of rational intuition (e.g., a natural grouping of dispositions for rational seeming/awareness) may be mysterious within, e.g., a naturalist ontology and anthropology, but Bealer's entire account is mysterious in this sense, as are the existence of modal knowledge and the powers required to have it.

ii. These claims (ironically) represent a category fallacy between a faculty containing dispositions for rational intuitive seemings and the actualized intuitive seemings themselves. No informed thinker would conflate and, therefore, identify intuitions and magical powers any more than they would do so regarding a disposition and its actualization.

Finally, while my account of modal knowledge is primarily directed at defending premise (3) of my modal argument for SD, nevertheless, I want to respond briefly to Bealer's rejection of that modal argument. Recall that Bealer rejects (3) on two grounds: (a) Many do not have the intuitions expressed in (3) or do have contrary intuitions; (b) "I" is semantically unstable, and this obfuscates the subcategory of entity it targets (disembodiable or essentially embodied person).

I will provide important defeaters for (a) later, so I set it aside for now. Regarding (b), there are several problems with it:

i. As Trenton Merricks points out, the indexical "I" could be removed in (3) and replaced with a premise with no indexicals, e.g., "Possibly, S exists, and no POs exist."[41] Acknowledging this point does not require abandoning the metaphysical significance of the irreducibility/uneliminability of "I."

ii. t may be the case that "I" has no meaning to begin with. It seems to be the paradigm case of a rigid designator that is purely and directly

---

40. Perler, *Faculties*, 11–12.
41. Merricks, "New Objection," 84n1.

referential.[42] Bealer could extend his view to include referentially stable and unstable terms, but to my knowledge, he has not done so; consequently, I do not know how he would respond to this objection.

iii. It may be that "I" has meaning, but in a relevant sense it is semantically stable. I will provide two ways of thinking about this, but before I do, recall that for Bealer, a sentence (proposition, concept) has semantic instability if the external environment contributes to its meaning. Scientific essentialist concepts are examples of semantic instability. But recall that phenomenal concepts are semantically stable, presumably, because their meanings are in some way fully fixed by something "internal" to the subject. This may mean "metaphysically intrinsic to" or, more likely, something to which the subject has private, direct access.

Given this, here is a plausible account of indexicality—we'll focus on "I"—that may be helpful. In a famous paper, David Kaplan analyzed indexicals such as "I" as follows.[43] Kaplan distinguished two levels of meaning of indexicals: content and character. Content is the contribution of an indexical term to what is said in a context. The content of "I" varies across contexts of utterance and may be understood as part of a singular proposition composed of the specific referent and the property attributed to it. Character is a rule for using indexical statements, and as such, it may be understood as a function that assigns to any appropriate context of utterance tokening an indexical proposition the content that would be expressed in that context. As such, it remains invariant across contexts. Thus, character would be semantically stable in Bealer's sense, and while content varies across different contexts, there is nothing in the external environment that contributes to its meaning, and thus it is disanalogous to scientific essentialist terms in that the latter but not the former exhibit what Bealer takes to be troublesome regarding the latter.

We have examined the accounts of modal knowledge proffered by O'Connor and Bealer. It is time to turn to the account I favor: Edmund Husserl's theory of modal knowledge.

---

42. See n12 above. [X-REF]
43. Kaplan, "On Logic of Demonstratives."

3.4 Edmund Husserl[44]

As David Kasmier observes, typical rationalist accounts of modal knowledge and a priori intuition suffer from a failure to provide an adequate phenomenology of rational intuition.[45] More generally, they lack an adequate ontology and phenomenology of modal knowledge by failing to answer two questions: (1) What synchronic and diachronic elements go into the makeup of a piece of immediate a priori modal knowledge? What is the essential character of various intuitive acts? (2) How are these elements appropriately connected (synchronically and diachronically) to achieve that result?

Husserl's account answers these questions, along with a careful description of the objects of modal knowledge (dependencies/independencies or compatibility/incompatibility relations binding objects and their "parts" into complex wholes whose type of unity is grounded in the essences of those objects and parts) and the tie between the relevant mental act and the modal object (an object, whether existent or nonexistent, is anything upon which an intentional act may be directed). For every existent object there corresponds the possibility of a set of mental acts and act qualities (the mode of attending to an object, roughly, the propositional attitude itself) through which the object in itself is fully present to consciousness and known.

Given this overview, I turn to a brief description of the epistemological side of modal knowledge followed by the ontological side. For Husserl, the epistemic task is to identify and describe those mental acts/act qualities through which one becomes fully presented with the modal entities deemed a priori. Four items are central to Husserl's epistemology of modal knowledge:

1. Knowledge and intentionality. For Husserl, *de re* knowledge obtains when a certain type of immediate intuition/presentation of (direct acquaintance with) the thing itself. Indirect *de re* knowledge involves inference(s) that trace back to immediate presentations. *De dicto* knowledge is the conscious possession of truth/adequation on an appropriate immediate or mediate basis in experience. Immediately based knowledge

---

44. It is hard to identify a particular location where Husserl treats rational a priori intuition and modal knowledge.

45. Kasmier, "Husserl's Theory," v. I have generally followed Kasmier's order of presentation in ch. 4 because of its clarity.

is the possession of truth in virtue of direct encounter with the facts/things themselves. Mediately based knowledge involves inferences from immediately based knowledge. In contemporary terms, Husserl would agree that *de dicto* knowledge is true warranted belief, but he would analyze "warranted" in this way: it is the possession of immediate or mediate evidence where evidence is provided by a certain kind of presentation in which the thing itself is directly given to consciousness. For Husserl, direct/immediate knowledge is defeasible.

Intentionality is a monadic property (not a relation) that is exemplified by most, if not all, mental states, and it consists in a primitive ofness, aboutness, directedness toward an object or possible object.

2. Fulfillment and fulfillment structures. For Husserl, knowledge involves the recognition of an identity between an object adequately intuited and the object as merely thought. The conscious awareness of this identity is called "fulfillment." Fulfillment is knowledge. And fulfillment is usually the final mental act of a diachronic series of relevantly ordered mental acts that lead a subject from an empty intention to an adequately filled intention in which the object known is directly, intuitively present as it really is. Such a direct awareness of the object provides *de re* knowledge of it and, on that basis, an awareness of the *de dicto* truth value (and, as we will see, modal status) of the corresponding proposition. Such a series is called a "fulfillment structure."

An example may help. Suppose my wife says there is a shirt in the closet ready for me to wear. Immediately, I form an empty intention, a vague, general concept of some shirt or other with very few details. But the empty intention has enough content to indicate a series of steps to take to verify or fulfill it. I know how to go to my closet instead of the garage and to look in the general area where my shirts and not my pants hang. So I embark on a trip to the closet. I look where the shirts are, and eventually, I see a specific short-sleeve blue shirt with a specific logo on the top left of the front side. I know that I see the shirt itself, and I have a fulfilled intention at which the shirt itself is directly present to me.[46] I have conceptually independent *de re* knowledge by acquaintance with the shirt, and on that basis, if I compare the shirt as merely thought of with the shirt itself, I can

---

46. For Husserl, a characteristic of material objects is that one can never have a full and complete awareness of it. There will always be an additional angle of awareness or unexamined aspect to it. By contrast, a mental content such as an image is fully, completely present to the proper mental acts.

become aware of the truth relation itself and form the relevant proposition expressing *de dicto* knowledge.

3. Eidetic and categorial intuition. Obviously, Husserl did not limit experience and fulfillment within the bounds of sensations. Specifically, he held to two other forms of fulfillment with fulfillment structures appropriate to the nature of the intentional object itself: direct awareness of universals and relations (eidetic intuition or *Wessenshau*) and categorial intuition. Each type of object has its own particular mode of being known, of finding fulfillment.

Elsewhere, I have given a rigorous analysis of eidetic intuition and cannot go into that here.[47] Briefly put, Husserl held to an Aristotelian constituent ontology according to which a universal is nonspatially in the concrete particular and, in a different way, is the property instance of that universal, constituting its essence. When one has a direct sensation of a property instance of red, one sees a particular. But by virtue of a sort of gestalt switch, one can attend to the universal itself that is in the instance. And similarly with relations. Categorial intuition is of the objects of formal ontology, e.g., ultimate and subcategories such as object, material object, part, essence, types of states of affairs.

4. Self-knowledge. For Husserl, the referent of "I" in premise (3) is the pure ego (aka transcendent ego), the irrefutable, secure starting point for First Philosophy. The pure ego is the subject of consciousness and the enduring continuant through a series of mental acts and consciousness-of states. It stands "beyond" the world as that to whom the world is given and is the subjective pole of the subject-object duality. Husserl holds that while the pure ego cannot be sensed (pace Hume), it can be apperceived, actively and directly attended to. On the basis of such intuitive apprehension (and factors to be addressed shortly), Husserl claims that the pure ego could survive the annihilation of the natural world, including the body. Thus, he would affirm (3).

In sum, an act of a priori, modal knowledge will involve the appropriate fulfillment structures and full, direct fulfillment in which the relevant entities constituting modal facts and the truth value of propositions about those modal facts are directly apprehended by way of eidetic or categorial intuition. But what, exactly, are these modal entities? To answer this, we need to look at that aspect of Husserl's ontology relevant to our question.

---

47. See Moreland, "Naturalism, Nominalism."

Husserl's ontology combines an Aristotelian constituent ontology according to which genuine universals—properties and relations (propositions are structural mental properties)—are immanent within and constitute the species/nature of their metaphysically complex instances (or concrete particulars) with a rich mereological ontology. This ontology provides a crucial backdrop for his modal epistemology, and accordingly, I will describe the former only as it is relevant to the latter.

As noted, Husserl was a realist regarding universals. Besides monadic properties, he held to the existence of what we would call external and internal relations. If the R of aRb is external to a (or a and b) then a can exist and retain identity if it fails to stand in R to b. Spatial relations are external. If the R of aRb is internal to a (or both), then for all x, if x does not stand in R to b, then $s \neq a$. An internal relation is grounded in the nature/essence of the relevant relatum or relata.

For Husserl, a part is any distinguishable particular "in" a whole. Husserlian mereology contains a crucial distinction between separable (pieces) and inseparable (moments) parts:

> p is a separable part of some whole W = def. p is a particular, p is a part of W, and p can exist if it is not a part of W (example: a table leg, an electron in an atom construed as a mereological aggregate).

> p is an inseparable part of some whole W = def. p is a particular, p is a part of W, and p cannot exist if it is not a part of W (example: surfaces, an instance of redness on an apple's surface).

A separable part is independent in the sense that it can exist if the rest of the whole of which it is a part is annihilated. Such parts are accidental to other such parts and their wholes in that they require an external relation to bond together into their wholes (e.g., mereological aggregates of separable parts). Such bonding does not follow from the parts' natures.

Inseparable parts (moments) are dependent entities. They are intrinsically partial in this sense: they require supplementation by something else to exist. That supplemental entity is called the moment's foundation. Foundation can be one-sided (e.g., an instance of redness cannot exist without foundation in an instance of extension but not conversely) or mutual (an instance of size cannot exist without an instance of shape and conversely.) For moments, no external relation is needed for their unification. Rather, their essences require them to be (modally or mutually) unified by way of internal relations into larger wholes.

It is the relations among the essences of various parts that determine the kind of unity various actual/possible wholes do or can have. Husserl's analysis of these wholes, along with the constitutive nature of the essences providing laws of combination among the instances of those essences that is the basis of modal relations.

Husserl distinguishes compatible and incompatible objects. Two objects are compatible if they can be joined together into a whole. And they are incompatible if they cannot be so joined. Compatibility/incompatibility is determined by the immanent essence of the relevant objects, that is, in virtue of what kind of object they are, and not by their individuality per se. Also relevant to compatibility/incompatibility is the form (essence, type of combinatorial structure) of the whole. If two objects can combine into the unity of a kind of whole, they can do so in part because of the form of unity of the whole. Thus, two objects can be compatible under one form of unity but not another. For example, no physical object can be red and green all over at the same time, but can be red and green when these moments are adjacent.

It should be clear that modal concepts are peppered throughout this account. If a set of parts are compatible, relative to a kind of whole, then that whole is metaphysically possible. If the set is incompatible, the whole is impossible. Thus, possibility and impossibility follows from the compatibility/incompatibility of the (usually complex) universals (essences/natures) immanent within the parts of and relative to the form of a kind of whole. *De dicto* modal judgments about possibility/impossibility will be epistemically grounded in eidetic/categorial intuition of the universals and the relevant relations constituting the natures of the parts and the form of the possible whole.

Further, modal knowledge involves the ontology of dependence and necessity. The universal essences and internal relations prescribe to their actual/possible instances their relative dependencies that serve as the ultimate ground of modality. For example, necessity and contingency are grounded in relations of dependence (one-way or mutual) and independence, respectively. This provides an analysis of the entities that constitute modal facts and for which eidetic intuition grounds modal knowledge. Modal intuitions begin with eidetic intuitions of universals, and they ground the further discovery of the dependency and compatibility relations that ground various modalities and are the objects of modal knowledge.

Since Husserl's views are not widely known, and given space considerations, I cannot provide an account of sources of modal error (it will involve problems with intuitive attentiveness, fulfillment structures that go off course, etc.) and answers to objections raised against his views.[48]

In this section, while Husserl's account of modal knowledge is close to my own, my purpose has been to provide a range of options regarding modal knowledge and error as part of the defense of (3). I now turn to a brief consideration of several objections against modal knowledge, premise (3), and/or the modal argument in general.

4. A POTPOURRI OF OBJECTIONS AGAINST MODAL ARGUMENTS FOR SD[49]

Objection 1: The modal argument is circular. Stewart Goetz has argued that the modal argument is viciously circular in this way: Knowledge of a premise like C_5 (I have the essential property of being such that I possibly survive disembodied [without my or any other physical body]) presupposes knowledge of C_4 (I am not identical with my [or any] physical body).[50] Knowledge of C_5 requires I already know C_4, which, in turn, is likely due to an awareness of a real distinction between me and my body due to an awareness of a difference in their essential properties (e.g., primarily being simple vs. being complex; but also being unextended vs. being extended, being constituted by psychological properties vs. being constituted by physical properties). If we reject this claim, then some sort of conceivability will be the only thing available to the modal dualist for C_5, and it will most likely be weak conceivability (failing to be aware of the necessary connection between me and my body), which is inadequate to support C_5 since an absence of awareness is not awareness of absence.

Reply 1: I am inclined to agree with Goetz that we have direct awareness of our own I and body (or other physical objects), and on that basis,

---

48. See Kasmier, "Husserl's Theory," chs. 7 and 8.

49. I am omitting a debate between William Hasker and Richard Swinburne about whether or not his unique version of the modal argument is a good one (Jaegwon Kim actually takes it to be an argument about persistence conditions). See Hasker, "Swinburne's Modal Argument"; Swinburne, "Modal Argument." I am also setting aside the view that one can accept all the premises of a modal argument and deny the conclusion advanced by advocates of material constitution physicalism. See Taliaferro, *Philosophy of Religion*, 126–27.

50. Goetz, "Modal Dualism."

we are aware of a real distinction between them. But Goetz's argument assumes direct awareness of the self (and its simplicity and unextendedness), and many philosophers reject such a thing. So, even if Goetz is correct, I see plenty of room for a modal argument for those who reject Goetz's approach.

Reply 2: Charles Taliaferro responds by claiming that we have strong conceivability plus the absence of epistemic negligence (roughly, inadvertently careless awareness or reflection with respect to the real distinction expressed in C_5) and this is adequate grounds for C_5.[51] Goetz responds that at best, Taliaferro's rejoinder supports property dualism because his strong conceivability targets the properties involved in our contingency. Moreover, Taliaferro never specifies what properties these are, and if they are psychological ones, property dualism is all Taliaferro can justify. The I and contingency are left out.

It may be that Taliaferro does not adequately specify the relevant properties. I don't have an opinion on that. But I think Husserl did. For Husserl, we have intuitive awareness of the I and an eidetic intuition of its essence (e.g., being simple with respect to separable parts; having mental properties or the capacities for them), and we have categorial intuitive awareness of the subcategory "material object"; and on that basis, we become aware of the independence and separability of the two. Husserl may be wrong, but this must be shown if his way out is to be rejected.

Objection 2: The modal argument merely establishes a duality of concepts and not objects. Jaegwon Kim is among a number of philosophers who have raised this objection.[52] The basic idea is that in certain intensional contexts, especially those involving *de dicto* beliefs, equals can be substituted for equals but the truth value is not preserved. Thus, the man who sped away is believed by the police to be a hit-and-run driver; the man who sped away is, in fact, my neighbor, but the police do not believe my neighbor is the alleged driver. Here we have two concepts that refer to the same object, not two different objects, even though it surely seems possible that there are truths about my neighbor that are not true of the man who sped away. And the same problem is exhibited by the modal argument.

Reply 1: My modal argument employs rigid designators in (3), (4), (5); they involve *de re* beliefs and are epistemically grounded in *de re* knowledge by acquaintance. Kim-style counterarguments exhibit *de dicto* beliefs

---

51. Taliaferro, "Modal Argument."
52. Kim, *Philosophy of Mind*, 35–36.

(and, often, nonrigid designators). So the counterargument is importantly dis-analogous to the relevant premises in the modal argument. To see this, substitute *de re* beliefs for the *de dicto* beliefs in his counterargument. We get the police to believe of that man there who sped away (namely, my neighbor) that he is the hit-and-run driver, but the police do not believe of the man who is, in fact, my neighbor that he is the hit-and-run driver. Here, the second belief is false because the police do, in fact, believe of my neighbor that he is the driver. They just don't believe that he is my neighbor.

Reply 2: It is clear that the problem surfaced in Kim-style arguments is based on a lack of knowledge of something relevant. And it's easy to see how one could have that lack of knowledge, e.g., that the police would have no idea that the speeding driver is my neighbor. But it isn't easy to see where the source of error is in the modal argument. If we do, in fact, have direct awareness of our I and find it to be essentially simple, non-extended, and constituted by mental properties, and if we have a pretty good third-person set of descriptions of physical objects, including one's body, where does the error come from? Husserl's account gives a detailed analysis of the sort of entities known relevant to the modal argument, and I see no non-question-begging identification of modal error involved in the argument.

Objection 3: Physicalist and dualism intuitions cancel out each other. Peter van Inwagen has argued that thought experiments with reverse modal or physicalist intuitions are easily constructed and cancel out dualist intuitions.[53] For example, Van Inwagen claims that "when I enter most deeply into that which I call myself, I seem to discover that I am a living animal. And, therefore, dualism seems to me to be an unnecessarily complicated theory about my nature."[54]

Reply 1: I doubt that such intuitions are actually possible, and if people have them, I would agree with Husserl that an inadequate concept of I and of a material body prevent fulfillment when the things themselves are given directly to intuitive awareness (which can occur with actual and merely possible entities). But setting that aside, even if such intuitions are possible, they are overwhelmed by dualist intuitions. Here's why. Almost everyone acknowledges that we all have, or at least start with, dualist intuitions. But this is not a throw-away line. It expresses overriding epistemic justification. Since Neanderthals, except for a few Western intellectuals, 99 percent of

---

53. Van Inwagen, "Modal Epistemology." For a response, see Taliaferro, "Sensibility and Possibilia."

54. Van Inwagen, "Dualism and Materialism," 476.

the human beings (even in nonreligious environments) have had dualist intuitions, though the precise form they take may vary. Further, there is a vast amount of psychological research demonstrating that little children don't have to be taught to be dualists. They find themselves to be dualists at a very early age.[55] If there is any place where the ontological/epistemological commitments of folk ontology carry overriding justification, surely it is here. People all over the world from a young age are simply aware that they are spiritual selves somehow "in" a body from which they will eventually be released. So, it is false that physicalist intuitions are sufficiently strong to cancel out dualist ones.

Reply 2: Even if we grant that physicalist/dualist intuitions cancel out, it is not clear what is supposed to follow. The growing literature in the epistemology of peer disagreement exemplifies disagreement about what the demands of rationality require when such disagreement occurs. Moreover, for those who adopt some version of the steadfast view, one may be justified or warranted in continuing to hold to one's view even when peer disagreement seems irresolvable.

Objection 4: Problems with dualist thought experiments. According to Van Inwagen, while we have modal knowledge in clear, everyday cases, we have no clear conception of how a thought experiment might work to provide credible views of what is possible, especially regarding more sophisticated philosophical claims. Moreover, presenting stories or detailed scenarios doesn't tell us how we know the state of affairs is possible. And such scenarios would have to be presented at such a high level of detail/comprehensiveness, they would surpass our capacities.[56]

Reply 1: Though defeasible, thought experiments are highly successful throughout philosophy for focusing our intuitive attention of specific items. I'm not claiming merely that because this is all we have, we just go with it. Rather, I am claiming that their use in focusing/clarifying modal seemings is demonstrably successful, and regarding the modal argument, since dualist intuitions conform to those of folk ontology, sans a question-begging

---

55. See Bering et al., "Development of 'Afterlife' Beliefs"; Bloom, *Descartes' Baby*; Bloom, "Religion Is Natural"; Rochat and Striano, "Social-Cognitive Development"; Kuhlmeier et al., "Do 5-Month-Old Infants See"; Wellman and Hickling, "The Minds 'I'; Spelke et al., "Infants' Knowledge"; Saxe et al., "Five-Month-Old Infants Know"; Bering, and Bjorklund, "Natural Emergence of Reasoning." I am indebted to Brandon Rickabaugh for these sources.

56. Van Inwagen, "Modal Epistemology," 70–71, 75–78.

commitment to physicalism, I see no reason to deny their use in the modal argument.

Reply 2: Van Inwagen accepts modal intuitions in clear, commonsense cases, but rejects them in more sophisticated philosophical cases. But dualist intuitions have been pervasive throughout the world for millennia, and very young children pervasively have them. All the modal argument does is to capture and focus these commonsense cases because a lot of philosophers don't like where they lead. So, the intuitions captured in the modal argument are clear and commonsensical.

Reply 3: You can know something, especially something basic and fundamental like dualist intuitions, without knowing how you know them. Moreover, the purpose of a thought experiment expressed as a scenario is to add a deeper, focused awareness to surface intuitions that we know such and such; it is not to show how we have such knowledge. That is the task of developing theories of modal knowledge.

Reply 4: It is not true that we don't have an account of how we have the modal knowledge relevant to the modal argument. I have presented three such accounts, and with slight adjustments, O'Connor's and Bealer's views can easily accommodate the intuitions relevant to the modal argument. And Husserl's view is a detailed, rigorous account of modal knowledge and how we have it, including such knowledge in the modal argument.

Reply 5: It is not true that adequate thought experiments require a level of detail that surpasses our cognitive capacities. There is a vast and sophisticated literature on near-death experiences. In them are literally thousands of highly detailed, comprehensive accounts of disembodied existence, far more so than successful thought experiments in other areas of philosophy. Upon examination, one becomes aware of their adequacy of detail/comprehensiveness, along with the intuitive insight that NDE accounts contain no incompossible states of affairs or other entities. They are metaphysically possible.

Objection 5: Kripke and the confusion between epistemic and metaphysical possibility. In most cases, a claim about the link between what seems possible and what is possible is defeasible. Accordingly, a widely employed criticism of the modal argument is that it establishes a mere epistemic, not a metaphysical, possibility in (3). This criticism was strengthened by and, currently, usually expressed in association with Kripke's arguments in support of a posteriori necessities.

Reply: It would take an entire paper to address this issue adequately, and due to space considerations, I can only gesture at two lines of response. First, Richard Swinburne has developed an account of informative rigid designators that, if successful, solves this problem by showing that the designators in the modal argument are informative ones, and thus, our modal knowledge of (3) is a priori.[57] David Chalmers (and Frank Jackson) have developed the widely known solution called two-dimensional semantics, which, if successful, show the relevant necessities, at least in Kripkean cases, are a priori.[58] Second, Kripke's argument about metaphysical/epistemic confusion rests on the relevant community failing to know something. But the accounts of modal knowledge presented above, especially Husserl's, show that the modal intuitions involved in the modal argument are grounded in positive intuitive awareness of the relevant entities and their metaphysical modality. Thus, Kripke's cases are dis-analogous to the modal argument.

CONCLUSION

I have sought to spell out a case for the relevance of SD for the high, intrinsic value enjoyed by human persons, and I have formulated and defended a modal argument for SD. I acknowledge that, granting the success of my modal argument, it doesn't follow that SD is true or the best philosophical anthropology to adopt. That judgment would need to be done in light of all of the relevant considerations, and the modal argument is just one of them. But it is an important one, and in any case, I trust my chapter will provide resources for further dialog.[59]

BIBLIOGRAPHY

Bailey, Andrew M., and Joshua Rasmussen. "How Valuable Could a Material Object Be?" *Journal of the American Philosophical Association* 2 (2016) 332–43.
Bealer, George. "Modal Epistemology and the Rationalist Renaissance." In *Conceivability and Possibility*, edited by Tamar Szabó Gendler and John Hawthorne, 71–125. Oxford: Clarendon, 2002.

---

57. Swinburne, *Mind, Brain, and Freewill*, 11–14, 23–24, 27–28, 36–38.
58. Chalmers, "Does Conceivability Entail Possibility?"
59. I am grateful to Mihretu Guta, Brandon Rickabaugh, and Eli Haitov for their helpful feedback on various parts of this chapter. For a comprehensive defense of GSD, see Rickabaugh and Moreland, *Substance of Consciousness*.

———. "On the Possibility of Philosophical Knowledge." In *Metaphysics*, edited by James E. Tomberlin, 1–34. Philosophical Perspectives 10. Cambridge, MA: Blackwell, 1996.

———. "Philosophical Limits of Scientific Essentialism." *Philosophical Perspectives* 1 (1987) 289–365.

Bering, Jesse M., and David F. Bjorklund. "The Natural Emergence of Reasoning about the Afterlife as a Developmental Regularity." *Developmental Psychology* 40 (2004) 217–33.

Bering, Jesse M., et al. "The Development of 'Afterlife' Beliefs in Religiously and Secularly Schooled Children." *British Journal of Developmental Psychology* 23 (2005) 587–607.

Bloom, Paul. *Descartes' Baby: How the Science of Child Development Explains What Makes Us Human*. New York: Basic, 2004.

———. "Religion Is Natural." *Developmental Science* 10 (2007) 147–51.

Chalmers, David J. "Does Conceivability Entail Possibility?" In *Conceivability and Possibility*, edited by Tamar Szabó Gendler and John Hawthorne, 145–200. Oxford: Oxford University Press, 2002.

Chisholm, Roderick M. *Theory of Knowledge*. 3rd ed. Englewood Cliffs, NJ: Prentice-Hall, 1989.

Cleve, James V. "Conceivability and the Cartesian Argument for Dualism." *Pacific Philosophical Quarterly* 64 (1983) 35–45.

Craig, William Lane, and Erik J. Wielenberg. *A Debate on God and Morality: What Is the Best Account of Objective Moral Values and Duties?* Edited by Adam Lloyd Johnson. New York: Routledge, 2020.

Evnine, Simon. "Modal Epistemology: Our Knowledge of Necessity and Possibility." *Philosophy Compass* 3 (2008) 664–84.

Georg, Gasser, and Matthias Stefan, eds. *Personal Identity: Complex or Simple?* Cambridge: Cambridge University Press, 2012.

Gendler, Tamar Szabó, and John Hawthorne, eds. *Conceivability and Possibility*. Oxford: Oxford University Press, 2002.

Goetz, Steward. "Modal Dualism: A Critique." In *Soul, Body, and Survival: Essays on the Metaphysics of Human Persons*, edited by Kevin Corcoran, 89–104. New York: Cornell University Press, 2001.

Hasker, William. *The Emergent Self*. Cornell Studies in the Philosophy of Religion. New York: Cornell University Press, 1999.

———. "Swinburne's Modal Argument for Dualism: Epistemically Circular." *Faith and Philosophy* 15 (1998) 366–70.

Hopp, Walter. *Phenomenology: A Contemporary Introduction*. Routledge Contemporary Introductions to Philosophy. New York: Routledge, 2020.

Kaplan, David. "On the Logic of Demonstratives." *Journal of Philosophical Logic* 8 (1970) 81–98.

Kasmier, David. "Husserl's Theory of a Priori Knowledge: A Response to the Failure of Contemporary Rationalism." PhD diss., University of Southern California, 2003.

Kim, Jaegwon. *Philosophy of Mind*. 2nd ed. Boulder, CO: Westview, 2006.

Koons, Robert C., and George Bealer, eds. *The Waning of Materialism*. Oxford: Oxford University Press, 2010.

Kuhlmeier, Valerie A., et al. "Do 5-Month-Old Infants See Humans as Material Objects?" *Cognition* 94 (2004) 95–103.

Loose, Jonathan J., et al., eds. *The Blackwell Companion to Substance Dualism*. Blackwell Companions to Philosophy. Oxford: Wiley-Blackwell, 2018.

Madell, Geoffrey. *The Essence of the Self: In Defense of the Simple View of Personal Identity.* Routledge Studies in Contemporary Philosophy. New York: Routledge, 2015.
———. *The Identity of the Self.* Edinburgh: Edinburgh University Press, 1981.
Merricks, Trenton. "How to Live Forever without Saving Your Soul." In *Soul, Body, and Survival: Essays on the Metaphysics of Human Persons*, edited by Kevin Corcoran, 183–200. New York: Cornell University Press, 2001.
———. "A New Objection to a Priori Arguments for Dualism." *American Philosophical Quarterly* 31 (1994) 81–85.
Moreland, J. P. "Naturalism, Nominalism, and Husserlian Moments." *Modern Schoolman* 79 (2002) 199–216.
———. *The Recalcitrant Imago Dei: Human Persons and the Failure of Naturalism.* Veritas. London: SCM, 2009.
———. *The Soul: How We Know It's Real and Why It Matters.* Chicago: Moody, 2014.
———. *Universals.* Central Problems of Philosophy 2. Montreal: McGill-Queen's University Press, 2001.
Moreland, J. P., and William Lane Craig. *Philosophical Foundations for a Christian Worldview.* 2nd ed. Downers Grove, IL: IVP Academic, 2017.
O'Connor, Timothy. *Theism and Ultimate Explanation.* Walden, MA: Wiley-Blackwell, 2012.
Perler, Dominik. *The Faculties: An Introduction.* Oxford Philosophical Concepts. Oxford: Oxford University Press, 2015.
Piazza, Tommaso. *A Priori Knowledge: Towards a Phenomenological Explanation.* Phenomenology & Mind 10. Frankfort: Ontos, 2007.
Pruss, Alexander R. *Actuality, Possibility and Worlds.* Continuum Studies in Philosophy of Religion. London: Bloomsbury, 2011.
Putnam, Hilary. *Reason, Truth and History.* Cambridge: Cambridge University Press, 1981.
Rachels, James. *The End of Life: Euthanasia and Morality.* Studies in Bioethics. New York: Oxford University Press, 1986.
Rickabaugh, Brandon, and J. P. Moreland. *The Substance of Consciousness: A Comprehensive Defense of Contemporary Substance Dualism.* Oxford: Wiley-Blackwell, 2023.
Rochat, P., and T. Striano. "Social-Cognitive Development in the First Year." In *Early Social Cognition: Understanding Others in the First Year of Life*, edited by Philippe Rochat, 3–34. Mahwah, NJ: Earlbaum, 1999.
Saxe, Rebecca, et al. "Five-Month-Old Infants Know Humans Are Solid, Like Inanimate Objects." *Cognition* 101 (2006) B1–B8.
Spelke, E. S., et al. "Infants' Knowledge of Object Motion and Human Action." In *Causal Cognition: A Multidisciplinary Debate*, edited by Dan Sperber et al., 44–78. Oxford: Oxford University Press, 1995.
Swinburne, Richard. *Are We Bodies or Souls?* Oxford: Oxford University Press, 2019.
———. *Mind, Brain, and Freewill.* Oxford: Oxford University Press, 2013.
———. "The Modal Argument Is Not Circular." *Faith and Philosophy* 15 (1998) 371–72.
Taliaferro, Charles. "A Modal Argument for Substance Dualism." *Southern Journal of Philosophy* 24 (1986) 95–108.
———. *Philosophy of Religion: A Beginner's Guide.* Beginner's Guides. Oxford: Oneworld, 2009.
———. "Sensibility and Possibilia: A Defense of Thought Experiments." *Philosophia Christi* 3 (2001) 403–20.

Tidman, Paul. "Conceivability as a Test for Possibility." *American Philosophical Quarterly* 31 (1994) 297–308.
Van Inwagen, Peter. "Dualism and Materialism: Athens and Jerusalem?" *Faith and Philosophy* 12 (1995) 475–88.
———. "Modal Epistemology." *Philosophical Studies* 92 (1998) 67–84.
Wellman, Henry, and A. K. Hickling. "The Minds 'I': Children's Conception of the Mind as an Active Agent." *Child Development* 65 (1994) 1564–80.
Yablo, Stephen. "Is Conceivability a Guide to Possibility?" *Philosophy and Phenomenological Research* 53 (1993) 1–42.
Yolton, John W. *Thinking Matter: Materialism in Eighteenth-Century Britain*. Minneapolis: University of Minnesota Press, 1983.
Zimmerman, Dean. "Two Cartesian Arguments for the Simplicity of the Soul." *American Philosophical Quarterly* 28 (1991) 217–26.

3

Aristotelian-Thomistic Framework for Detecting Covert Consciousness in Unresponsive Persons

Matthew Owen, Aryn D. Owen, Anthony G. Hudetz

INTRODUCTION

The standard methods medical practitioners use to discern a patient's level of conscious awareness rely on observable behaviors, such as a verbal response to a question or a behavioral reaction to an arousing stimulus. This methodology is pragmatically effective because it is reproducible and widely available. Unfortunately, however, it cannot detect consciousness in the absence of behavioral evidence. In other words, it cannot detect covert consciousness latently remaining in brain-injured patients who are unable to express their consciousness through a purposeful motor response. This is the medical motivation for many neuroscientists and neurologists trying to find a way to empirically discern the presence of consciousness based solely on neuronal activity that can be observed, for example, via neuroimaging.

For the care providers of an unresponsive brain-injured person who might be covertly conscious, the seemingly abstract topic of whether consciousness can be empirically discerned can be immensely practical.[1] First of all, it can be a way of ruling out the occurrence of death when technological intervention preserves vital bodily functions. Since consciousness is a capacity of a human person, the presence of consciousness indicates the presence of its bearer—the person who is conscious.[2] Empirical confirmation of consciousness would amount to empirical confirmation that the person is still present. Furthermore, the ability to detect the presence of a private conscious experience based on publicly observable neural processes in the brain would yield a more accurate diagnosis and prognosis. Such information can be invaluable when family members and medical doctors are making decisions about continuing care and specialized treatment, and insurance companies are making funding decisions. Hence, the topic of whether we can empirically detect consciousness using neuroimaging data in a behaviorally unresponsive patient is a pragmatic issue of bioethical importance.

Yet, it is also a theoretical topic tied to philosophy of mind. In their article "Measuring Consciousness in Severely Damaged Brains," Gosseries et al. point out that the accuracy of techniques employing neuroimaging to diagnose disorders of consciousness in unresponsive patients is "intrinsically linked to understanding the relationship between consciousness and the brain."[3] Their point can be easily grasped by considering the implications of the identity theory, a version of reductive physicalism. This theory says consciousness is correlated with specific neural mechanisms because it is ontologically identical to the neural mechanisms it corresponds to.[4] Given that, whenever the neural mechanisms are present, then consciousness is present, and one could know that consciousness is present by observing the neural mechanisms via neuroimaging. Hence the identity theory provides a philosophical foundation for empirically detecting consciousness. The same could be said of nonreductive views in the philosophy of mind that hold to the physicalist doctrine of supervenience. While there are various versions, this doctrine essentially says all mental properties are determined

1. See Young and Edlow, "Quest for Covert Consciousness."
2. See Guta, "Non-Causal Account," 132–33.
3. Gosseries et al., "Measuring Consciousness," 457; see also 466, 468. For similar claims, see Cecconi et al., "Islands of Awareness"; and Boly et al., "Consciousness in Humans," 2. For some theoretical background regarding why the relationship between consciousness and neural states matters for empirically diagnosing unresponsive patients, see M. Owen and Guta, "Physically Sufficient Neural Mechanisms."
4. Smart, "Sensations and Brain Processes."

by their physical substrate.⁵ Given supervenience, if you knew consciousness supervened on specific neural activity, you could know consciousness is present whenever the neural activity is present.

The scientific study of consciousness set its roots at the end of the twentieth century when physicalism was orthodoxy in the philosophy of mind.⁶ A key objective of the science of consciousness is to locate the neural correlates of consciousness that could be used to empirically detect consciousness. Within a materialist milieu that embraces a physicalist framework, this objective is theoretically reasonable, even if the practical details are daunting. However, since the early days of the neurobiological study of consciousness, physicalism has begun to falter.⁷ Although it remains the preeminent position, it is not unchallenged orthodoxy. The hard problem of consciousness and what is often called the exclusion problem regarding mental causation have presented physicalism with considerable challenges.⁸ Correspondingly, there has been a reconsideration of non-physicalist and dualist views.⁹ All this can prompt a worry that if physicalism fades so will the scientific study of consciousness along with the objective of empirically detecting consciousness, which could have clinical consequences.

The aim of this chapter is to counter this worry by demonstrating that physicalism is not the only view that provides a philosophical foundation for the science of consciousness and empirically detecting consciousness. It will be argued that the *mind-body powers model* of neural correlates of consciousness provides a metaphysical framework that yields the theoretical possibility of empirically detecting consciousness.¹⁰ Since the model is informed by an Aristotelian-Thomistic hylomorphic ontology rather than

---

5. Kim, *Philosophy of Mind*, 8–11.

6. Searle, *Rediscovery of the Mind*, xii. Crick and Koch, "Toward a Neurobiological Theory," jump-started the neurobiological study of consciousness with their seminal article and subsequent research (see Cavanna and Nani, "Francis Crick and Christof Koch").

7. See Göcke, *After Physicalism*; Koch, "Re-Enchanting the World," 519; Koons and Bealer, *Waning of Materialism*.

8. Kim, *Mind in a Physical World*, 30; *Physicalism*, 7–31, 70.

9. See Chalmers, *Conscious Mind*; Kim, *Physicalism*, 70; Lavazza and Robinson, *Contemporary Dualism*; Loose et al., *Substance Dualism*; O'Connor and Robb, *Philosophy of Mind*, 5.

10. For a full explication of the mind-body powers model, see M. Owen, *Measuring the Immeasurable Mind*, chs. 7–8.

a physicalist ontology, it provides a philosophical foundation for the science of consciousness and empirically detecting consciousness that is an alternative to physicalism. Our claim is not that the mind-body powers model provides the only alternative, but rather that it provides a sufficient framework for the possibility of empirically detecting and scientifically studying consciousness. Thus, if the philosophical foundation of physicalism continues to falter, that will be no reason for the research field to fret.

Bioethics is a subject that incorporates various disciplines. Therefore, readers of a bioethics volume will likely be specialists in different disciplines and will inevitably come to the topic of this chapter with different background knowledge.[11] In light of this, it is worth mentioning a way in which our thesis could be misunderstood. In discussions about the nature of consciousness or how it relates to the brain, philosophy of mind and neuroscience are sometimes seen as competitors. Someone who reads this chapter while assuming that philosophy and neuroscience are competitors might be primed to misinterpret our objective, thesis, and overall argument. They may read us as arguing for a philosophical method to empirically detect consciousness that is purportedly a replacement for a neuroscientific method.[12] This would be an unfortunate and complete misunderstanding of our objective to present a philosophical framework that yields the theoretical possibility of empirically detecting consciousness using a neuroscientific method.

In the neurological context of our topic, we see philosophy of mind and neuroscience as complementary. We are concerned with the question of how consciousness in an unresponsive patient could be detected on the basis of empirically observable neural activity in the patient's brain. This would require data about neural activity in the patient's brain, which may be gathered via neuroimaging. But if all you had was data about the neural activity in the patient's brain, it would not tell you whether the patient is conscious. In addition to possessing the data about the neural activity in the patient's brain, you would also need to have knowledge of what neural activity correlates with being conscious versus unconscious. This is where neurobiological theories about the neuronal correlate of consciousness become relevant, and where an accurate theory would be invaluable. Currently, there

---

11. M. Owen, *Measuring the Immeasurable Mind*, provides background information that space does not permit us to discuss here.

12. Such an objective is not even possible. We are indebted to an anonymous reviewer of this chapter for bringing to our attention the possible misunderstanding addressed here.

are different theories and hypotheses that predict different neural correlates of consciousness.[13] In the coming years, the neurobiological study of consciousness may reveal what neural activity correlates with being conscious versus unconscious. Yet, once it is confirmed what neural activity correlates with consciousness in a healthy patient capable of providing a behavioral response that is collaborative evidence of their consciousness, a diagnostic question concerning unresponsive brain-injured patients would remain.

The diagnostic question is: Could the presence of consciousness in an unresponsive patient be justifiably inferred based on the presence of neural activity that correlates with consciousness in a healthy human brain of a responsive subject? This is where philosophy of mind that addresses how consciousness relates to its neuronal correlates becomes relevant. As indicated above, the answer to the diagnostic question is affirmative if physicalism is correct that consciousness is ontologically identical to the neural correlate or supervenes upon it. That is to say that physicalism provides a philosophical framework that yields, or grounds, a theoretical possibility of empirically detecting consciousness in unresponsive patients using a neuroscientific method. Our goal is simply to show that there is another view in the philosophy of mind that does likewise. Put differently, our aim is to show that the mind-body powers model provides philosophical rationale for inferring that an unresponsive patient is conscious if neuroimaging data reveals the presence of neural activity that regularly correlates with consciousness in a healthy human brain. As the "if" in the previous sentence suggests, we are here talking about a theoretical possibility—because it is not yet conclusively known what neural activity correlates with being conscious versus unconscious.

An empirically verified theory or hypothesis about the neural correlate of being conscious is needed for the theoretical possibility we argue for to become a practical actuality in a clinical context. If it can be shown that this is theoretically possible given not only a physicalist but also a nonphysicalist understanding of consciousness and how it relates to the brain, the neurological research aimed at providing the physical and practical details is all the more warranted. It's often said that teamwork makes the dream work. In this neurological context, progress in discerning what is theoretically possible and then making it a clinical reality may well require

---

13. National Academies, *Human Neural Organoids*, 39; Sattin et al., "Theoretical Models of Consciousness"; Seth, "Models of Consciousness"; Seth and Bayne, "Theories of Consciousness."

collaborative teamwork between a diversity of specialists, including philosophers and neuroscientists. Abstract information from philosophy of mind about how consciousness relates to the brain will need to be combined with a neurobiological theory that accurately describes the neural correlate of being conscious.

Elsewhere, the integrated information theory's prediction about the neural correlate of being conscious has been used to illustrate how the mind-body powers model grounds the theoretical possibility of empirically detecting consciousness.[14] The theory's prediction was used as one plausible example of a hypothesis about the nature and location of the neural correlate that can be combined with the model. However, since there is no settled conclusion about which neurobiological theory of consciousness accurately identifies the neural mechanisms corresponding to being conscious, this work will employ another plausible neurobiological prediction provided by the temporal circuit hypothesis.[15] The hypothesis will be combined with the mind-body powers model to demonstrate that empirically detecting consciousness is metaphysically plausible wholly apart from a physicalist framework.[16] The following two sections set the stage by elucidating the epistemic challenge of diagnosing disorders of consciousness, as it involves discerning the presence of consciousness or lack thereof. The subsequent sections introduce the temporal circuit hypothesis and the mind-body powers model before they are combined to illustrate how the model yields the theoretical possibility of empirically detecting covert consciousness in unresponsive patients.

---

14. See M. Owen, *Measuring the Immeasurable Mind*, ch. 8.

15. For representative articles on TCH, see Huang et al., "Anterior Insula" and "Temporal Circuit."

16. The mind-body powers model is not a neurobiological theory of consciousness aimed at identifying and describing the neural mechanisms of consciousness. Rather, it is a model of how consciousness relates to the brain and its neural mechanisms. Therefore, it does not depend on any one neurobiological theory about the nature and location of the neural mechanisms of consciousness. It leaves open the possibility of any one of a variety of predictions about the neural mechanisms of consciousness made by various theories being verified as the correct hypothesis.

THE CHALLENGE OF DIAGNOSING DISORDERS OF CONSCIOUSNESS

To understand the epistemic conundrum of diagnosing disorders of consciousness (DOC), it will be helpful to begin with distinguishing three disorders. The first is coma, a pathological state in which the patient is unconscious and there is a continuous absence of eye-opening, while behaviors are limited to only reflexive movements.[17] The second relevant DOC is the vegetative state (VS), which is often abbreviated PVS for "persistent vegetative state" when the condition lasts longer than one month.[18] This state is also called unresponsive wakefulness syndrome (UWS).[19] This is a fitting term for this DOC since these patients can exhibit certain behaviors that might typically be associated with someone who is awake—such as spontaneous eye-opening or moaning—but their behaviors appear to be merely reflexive and unrelated to their surrounding environment. To a degree, the body appears to behaviorally function in subtle ways without the conscious mind.[20] The third relevant DOC is the minimally conscious state, abbreviated MCS. This state is often distinguished by the presence of inconsistent yet clear, recognizable behavioral signs of consciousness.[21]

For various reasons accurately diagnosing disorders of consciousness is crucial. To begin with, a patient's prognosis can depend on their diagnosis. For example, there is reason to believe a diagnosis of MCS corresponds with a better prognosis with a more favorable chance of functional recovery than a diagnosis of VS/UWS.[22] Secondly, a patient's diagnosis will inform plans regarding their treatment and overall care, which impacts their quality of life.[23] For example, if it is known that a patient has emerged from an unconscious state and is now minimally conscious, pain management becomes more important. Moreover, different medical departments implement different rehabilitation programs for patients based on the DOC

---

17. Schnakers et al., "Neuroimaging of Consciousness," 118.
18. Schnakers et al., "Neuroimaging of Consciousness," 118.
19. Laureys et al., "Unresponsive Wakefulness Syndrome."
20. Schnakers et al., "Neuroimaging of Consciousness," 118.
21. Schnakers et al., "Neuroimaging of Consciousness," 119. A distinction is also made between MCS- and MCS+ (Boly et al., "Consciousness in Humans," 3; Gosseries et al., "Measuring Consciousness," 458–59).
22. Giacino, "Vegetative and Minimally Conscious," 296; Giacino and Kalmar, Vegetative and Minimally Conscious."
23. See Giacino et al., "Disorders of Consciousness."

they are diagnosed with, so a patient's diagnosis often determines which department they are admitted to and the rehabilitation support they receive.[24] Insurance companies also have standards for medical expenses to be financially covered that are based on a patient's diagnosis.[25]

In addition to the clinical and financial reasons, there are also bioethical reasons why accurately diagnosing DOC patients is important.[26] Since whether a patient is conscious can correspond to their likelihood of clinical improvement,[27] it is important to know whether a patient is conscious when family members and healthcare providers are deciding whether to continue life support. Misdiagnosing a patient who is behaviorally unresponsive but nevertheless covertly conscious can lead to withdrawing life sustaining treatment prematurely.[28] The legality of withdrawing life support is also impacted by the patient's diagnosis. In several countries, withdrawing artificial hydration and nutrition is legal in VS/UWS cases but not in MCS cases.[29]

While accurately diagnosing DOC patients is important for the aforementioned reasons, it can be difficult to discern whether a patient is conscious and therefore what diagnosis is appropriate. A study done by Caroline Schnakers and colleagues is sobering—they found that 41 percent of forty-four patients in their study who were diagnosed as VS/UWS patients were in fact MCS.[30] More recently, an illuminating study led by Jiahui Pan used a novel machine-learning algorithm in the assessment of DOC patients.[31] In his scientific commentary on the study, Adrian Owen notes that 40 percent of patients in the study who were clinically diagnosed as VS/UWS were able to follow commands well enough to be reclassified as aware.[32] According to Joseph Giacino et al., "Reports consistently find that approximately 30–40% of people diagnosed with VS actually retain

24. Giacino et al., "Disorders of Consciousness," 103.

25. Giacino et al., "Disorders of Consciousness," 103.

26. See Fins, *Rights Come to Mind*; Fins et al., "Late Recovery"; Giacino et al., "Disorders of Consciousness," 108–9.

27. See A. Owen, "Improving Diagnosis and Prognosis," 1052.

28. Giacino et al., "Disorders of Consciousness," 103.

29. Schnakers et al., "Minimally Conscious State," 178; see also Manning, "Withdrawal of Life-Sustaining Treatment."

30. Schnakers et al., "Minimally Conscious State," 171; Schnakers et al., "Diagnostic Accuracy."

31. Pan et al., "Prognosis for Patients."

32. A. Owen, "Improving Diagnosis and Prognosis," 1052.

conscious awareness."[33] Marcello Massimini and Giulio Tononi offer an even starker estimate, writing: "Recent data show that nearly half of the patient[s] labelled as being in an unconscious VS/UWS are actually in a MCS... this low sensitivity in detecting conscious existence represents one of the most serious clinical and ethical issues of contemporary neurology."[34]

In the next section we will discuss methods for diagnosing DOC patients. This will elucidate why the diagnostic process is epistemically complex and how it could be aided by the ability to empirically discern consciousness without requiring any response from patients.

METHODS FOR DIAGNOSING DOC

As mentioned in the introduction, behaviors that indicate consciousness are commonly used to discern the degree to which patients are conscious. Medical practitioners regularly observe behavioral responses to stimuli to assess a patient's level of consciousness.[35] An articulate verbal response to a complex question can indicate a higher level of consciousness, while a stereotypical response to a sensory stimulus can indicate a lower level. Such behavioral correlates of consciousness can be very useful because this diagnostic method has few technological requirements. However, there are other prerequisites limiting the behavioral paradigm's scope of diagnostic effectiveness.[36]

One prerequisite is that patients must be conscious enough to perceive the stimuli and respond. But a patient could be conscious but nevertheless not conscious enough to perceive an external stimulus and respond in an appropriate manner. Moreover, specific sensory systems must be functioning well enough for a patient to sense the kinds of stimuli that medical practitioners decide to use. However, someone could remain conscious while a specific sensory system fails to function properly. When a person's vision is impaired, for example, it does not necessarily follow that they are unconscious simply because they cannot see. Likewise, a patient could be conscious while they are unable to hear due to a brain injury that damaged

---

33. Giacino et al., "Disorders of Consciousness," 103.

34. Massimini and Tononi, *Sizing Up Consciousness*, 33.

35. See Giacino et al., "JFK Coma Recovery Scale-Revised"; Teasdale and Jennett, "Assessment of Coma."

36. While we focus on three general limitations, Schnakers et al., "Minimally Conscious State," 171, provide a list of potential issues that could limit diagnostic accuracy.

their auditory cortex or the neural mechanisms that send signals to it. If a stimulus such as a loud noise is used to induce a response, the patient would remain behaviorally unresponsive to the stimulus not because she is unconscious but rather because she cannot sense that specific kind of stimulus.

An additional prerequisite is that a patient's motor systems must be sufficiently preserved to carry out behavioral responses necessitating motor movement. Yet again, a patient could lack motor movement while retaining consciousness. A patient with locked-in syndrome (LIS) might appear unconscious because they lack the necessary motor movement to respond to a command or sensory stimulus in a typical manner. However, this does not mean that they are unconscious, as we know from LIS patients who have minimal motor movements preserved that permit them to communicate via eye blinks.[37] Unique as it is, such communication makes it evident that the patient is conscious, even though they lack the motor movement required to give standard behavioral responses. Some patients can also hear the clinician's command to respond but lack the motivation or will to move.

Motor systems of normal healthy subjects are also suppressed during dreaming in rapid eye movement sleep—a state Sanders et al. define as disconnected consciousness.[38] Likewise, a goal of general anesthesia is to achieve unconsciousness or sensory-behavioral disconnection from the environment. However, clinical studies using the isolated forearm technique, in which muscle paralysis to one of the arms is prevented by a tourniquet, reveal that a small fraction (~5 percent) of anesthetized patients can still produce a purposeful behavioral response with their unparalyzed hand. With complete muscle paralysis, these patients would be unresponsive and considered unconscious, while in reality, they are conscious and connected to their environment.

Another diagnostic paradigm, which provides an alternative to relying on behavioral responses, employs neuronal responses from the patient to discern the presence of consciousness when patients lack motor movement. This paradigm was first used by a team of neuroscientists—led by Adrian Owen and Steven Laureys at the University of Cambridge and the University of Liege—who demonstrated that a brain-injured patient lacking motor movement yet retaining consciousness could provide a neuronal

---

37. Massimini and Tononi, *Sizing Up Consciousness*, 32.
38. Sanders et al., "Unresponsiveness ≠ Unconsciousness."

response to commands to do imaginative tasks.[39] Laying the groundwork for this neuronal response paradigm, Mélanie Boly and her colleagues did a study on healthy subjects and found that when they followed commands to carry out imaginative tasks there was specific neural activity corresponding to their specific mental activity.[40] When they were asked to imagine playing tennis there was corresponding neural activity in the supplementary motor area involved in planning movement. And when they were asked to imagine walking through their home different coalitions of neurons that correspond to processing spatial coordinates and memory of locations were activated in the posterior parietal cortex, the parahippocampal gyrus, and the lateral premotor cortex.[41] Having mapped the specific neural activity that corresponds to each mental activity, this information was then used to empirically identify the presence of consciousness when a severely brain injured patient lacked motor movement. As was done with healthy subjects, the researchers could give the commands and observe the corresponding neural activity one would expect if the patient imagined playing tennis and at another time imagined walking through their home in response to each command.[42]

When sufficient neuroimaging technology is available in medical settings, the neuronal response paradigm can be useful for detecting covert consciousness in some behaviorally unresponsive patients. Neuronal responses have also been used as a way for patients to provide basic yes/no answers to questions.[43] The neuronal response paradigm is truly remarkable, and yet, it still requires a type of active response from the patient—a neuronal response rather than a behavioral response.

There are multiple reasons why patients who are conscious might nevertheless be unable to provide even a neuronal response.[44] Many severely brain-injured patients are aphasic and therefore lack the facility to comprehend the language in a command such as "imagine playing tennis." Other patients may be unable to give a neuronal response because the area

39. A. Owen et al., "Detecting Awareness."

40. Boly et al., "When Thoughts Become Action."

41. Boly et al., "When Thoughts Become Action"; Massimini and Tononi, *Sizing Up Consciousness*, 37.

42. A. Owen et al., "Detecting Awareness." Cf. Pan et al., "Prognosis for Patients"; Naci et al., "Common Neural Code."

43. Monti et al., "Willful Modulation"; A. Owen, "Improving Diagnosis and Prognosis," 1051.

44. Boly et al., "Consciousness in Humans," 3.

of their brain that would be activated once they understood the command and tried to respond is damaged.[45] There can also be patients who are simply too depressed, unmotivated, or confused to respond to what seems to them like a meaningless game.[46] Furthermore, a patient must be able to sense the verbal command, whether it be a command to imagine playing tennis or to imagine navigating through their home. In the final analysis, the neuronal response paradigm not only requires patients to be able to sense commands but also to be conscious and cognizant enough to actively respond appropriately.[47] Using anesthesia as a pharmacological model for disorders of consciousness, Zirui Huang et al. tested the presence of tennis and navigation imagery to verbal command in healthy volunteers anesthetized with propofol titrated to the point of behavioral unresponsiveness.[48] Only one patient out of twenty-nine tested so far displayed convincing neuroimaging signs of mental imagery, suggesting that either covert consciousness during anesthesia is rare or the applied task-response approach for its detection is suboptimal.

For the aforementioned reasons, active paradigms necessitating either a behavioral or neuronal response from the patient are not sensitive enough to detect when a completely unresponsive person is covertly conscious.[49] Although an active response indicates consciousness, a lack of response is uninterpretable because the lack of a response does not necessarily indicate the absence of consciousness.[50] What we need is a passive, so-called "no-report," paradigm that allows us to detect consciousness without requiring the patient to give any response at all.[51] In other words, we need: (1) a publicly observable, empirically identifiable indicator of consciousness that is present whenever someone is conscious; and (2) warrant for inferring the presence of consciousness based on this empirically observable indicator, even when a patient is unable to give any willful response. The first desideratum is where research aimed at identifying the neural activity that corresponds to being conscious could become clinically invaluable. After

45. See Massimini and Tononi, *Sizing Up Consciousness*, 38–39.
46. See Massimini and Tononi, *Sizing Up Consciousness*, 38–39.
47. Giacino et al., "Disorders of Consciousness," 105.
48. Huang et al., "Brain Imaging."
49. See Boly et al., "Consciousness in Humans," 3; Giacino et al., "Disorders of Consciousness," 105; Gosseries et al., "Measuring Consciousness," 462.
50. Gosseries et al., "Measuring Consciousness," 462.
51. Gosseries et al., "Measuring Consciousness," 463.

outlining a theoretical perspective in this area of research in the following section, the mind-body powers model will be applied to meeting the second desideratum in the subsequent section.

THE NEURAL CORRELATE OF CONSCIOUSNESS

The search for the neural correlates of consciousness (NCC) is a research objective central to the neurobiological study of consciousness that has become prominent in the last four decades.[52] NCC can be understood as the minimal neuronal mechanisms physically sufficient for consciousness.[53] A distinction is often made between two main types of NCC—that is, content-specific NCC versus the full NCC.[54] Content-specific NCC are the neural mechanisms that correspond to conscious states with particular content, such as seeing a face or tasting a sweet strawberry. The full NCC corresponds to simply being conscious rather than unconscious, regardless of the content of one's conscious experience.

The full NCC is arguably most relevant to discerning the presence of consciousness in completely unresponsive patients. Yet, as previously mentioned, there's no consensus about which neurobiological theory accurately predicts its nature and location in the brain.[55] The two most well-known hypotheses are provided by the global neuronal workspace theory and the integrated information theory.[56] A more recent proposal gaining attention is the *temporal circuit hypothesis* (TCH).[57] This section will provide an overview of the TCH before it is combined with the mind-body powers model of NCC in the next section.

---

52. Koch, *Quest for Consciousness*; Metzinger, *Neural Correlates of Consciousness*; Storm et al., "Consciousness Regained."

53. Koch et al., "Neural Correlates of Consciousness," 307; M. Owen and Guta, "Physically Sufficient Neural Mechanisms."

54. Koch et al., "Neural Correlates of Consciousness," 308.

55. National Academies, *Human Neural Organoids*, 39; Sattin et al., "Theoretical Models of Consciousness"; Seth, "Models of Consciousness"; Seth and Bayne, "Theories of Consciousness."

56. See Mashour et al., "Conscious Processing"; Tononi et al., "Integrated Information Theory." For an overview and comparison of the integrated information theory, the global neuronal workspace theory, and the temporal circuit hypothesis, see M. Owen et al., "Theoretical Neurobiology of Consciousness."

57. Huang et al., "Anterior Insula"; Huang et al., "Temporal Circuit."

According to TCH, consciousness can be described as the awareness an individual has of something in one's environment. A human (or nonhuman) agent could have the ability to accurately represent its environment without such representations in themselves endowing the agent with awareness. Being conscious, or aware, also requires the agent perceiving itself in relation to the outside world. Given this, TCH suggests the crucial step for consciousness to be present is not just perception, but the percepts being our percepts, or more precisely the percepts of the individual who is perceiving something in her environment. On this framework, the self is crucial because it is the subject that is aware of the environment, and without a subject who is aware there is no awareness and therefore no consciousness.[58] In light of the nature of consciousness, TCH proposes that the neuronal substrate of consciousness is a temporal architecture of representational brain processes that change dynamically and probabilistically.[59] The presence of consciousness relies on a dynamic relation of two brain networks that relate to the self and the environment—the default mode network and the dorsal attention network—both of which consciousness depends upon.

TCH anchors the "self-environment" interaction in a reciprocal balance between two opposing cortical systems embedded in the spatiotemporal dynamics of neural activity. To grasp a real-life example, imagine driving to work along the same route you take every day. Your thoughts wander from one thing to the next. Suddenly, a car cuts you off, and wandering thoughts instantaneously vanish as all your attention focuses on maneuvering the steering wheel to avoid a collision. As we go about our waking lives, during which we are consciously aware, our stream of consciousness typically cycles through many such alternations between introspection and outward attention. This back-and-forth "dance" between inward-oriented and outward-oriented mental states happens naturally and automatically.

Evidence from noninvasive functional neuroimaging studies points to two distinct brain networks that mediate the stream of consciousness, an internally directed system and an externally directed system. The system that corresponds to internally oriented mental states is the default mode

---

58. Cf. Critchley et al., "Neural Systems"; Damasio, *Self Comes to Mind*; Faivre et al., "Visual Consciousness"; Guta, "Non-Causal Account"; Park and Tallon-Baudry, "Neural Subjective Frame."

59. Huang et al., "Anterior Insula"; Huang et al., "Temporal Circuit."

network (DMN).[60] The system that corresponds to externally oriented mental states is the dorsal attention network (DAN).[61] DMN corresponds to inward focus on ourselves and conceptually guided cognition, whereas DAN corresponds to our awareness of the environment around us. In the brain of a conscious individual, these two systems are in a dynamic balance, sliding back and forth, as both remain active to some degree as there is an ongoing switching between each network.

Recent research has revealed how cyclical patterns of brain activity, and how the push-pull relationship between DMN and DAN, may differ between conscious and unconscious individuals.[62] In the brain of a conscious individual the dynamic switching of networks including the DMN and DAN occurs along a set of structured transition trajectories conceived of as a "temporal circuit." The conscious brain passes through intermediate states between DMN and DAN rather than oscillating instantaneously between the two. By contrast, in the unconscious brain, there are fewer trajectories reaching the DMN and DAN. In subjects who were either under anesthesia or unconscious due to neuronal injury, both DMN and DAN are visited less often, so the number of times they are activated within the cycling patterns of networks is reduced. This suggests consciousness relies on a temporal circuit of dynamic brain activity representing balanced reciprocal accessibility of functional brain states. The absence of this "give-and-take" between the two systems is common to any form of diminished consciousness and its presence corresponds to full consciousness, including both the external and internal aspects corresponding to the two systems.

The dynamic network shifting between DMN and DAN is regulated by a critical brain structure, the anterior insula,[63] a key component of the brain's salience and ventral attention networks.[64] The anterior insula apparently identifies and prioritizes salient stimuli in the ongoing stream of sensory information and sends signals to systems responsible for the allocation of top-down attentional resources relevant to sensory representations.[65] The an-

60. Raichle, "Brain's Default Mode Network"; Raichle et al., "Default Mode of Brain Function."

61. Corbetta and Shulman, "Control"; Fornito et al., "Competitive and Cooperative Dynamics"; Vossel et al., "Dorsal and Ventral Attention."

62. Huang et al., "Temporal Circuit."

63. Huang et al., "Anterior Insula."

64. Fox et al., "Spontaneous Neuronal Activity"; Menon, "Large-Scale Brain Networks"; Seeley et al., "Dissociable Intrinsic Connectivity Networks."

65. Menon, "Large-Scale Brain Networks"; Michel, "Anterior Insular Cortex"; Uddin, "Salience Processing."

terior insula is composed of distinct clusters of large spindle-shaped pyramidal neurons in layer 5, called von Economo neurons,[66] which establish a fast long-distance relay of information throughout the cortex.[67] These neurons play a role in spatial-awareness as well as self-awareness; and, historically, their abnormality was associated with psychiatric disorders.[68] Interestingly, they have been found only in species able to pass the standard mirror test for self-recognition, such as macaque monkeys and elephants.[69] Moreover, the dysfunction of the anterior insula during anesthesia, when patients are unconscious, disables the cyclic DMN-DAN network transitions.[70]

In sum, TCH proposes that consciousness is enabled by a temporal architecture involving a back-and-forth dance of mental states about the inner self and outer world mediated by attentional switching. This is principally supported by the observed spatiotemporal dynamics of brain activity that displays a shifting balance between DMN and DAN, governed by the anterior insula. This neuronal activity is hypothesized to be the full NCC that corresponds to being conscious versus unconscious. Although there is no consensus conclusion about which theoretical prediction regarding the nature and brain location of the full NCC is correct, TCH provides an example hypothesis with considerable empirical support. We will rely on it in the subsequent section, and assume its validity, to illustrate how the mind-body powers model of NCC provides a philosophical foundation for empirically detecting covert consciousness in unresponsive patients.

THE MIND-BODY POWERS MODEL OF NCC

A passive paradigm for empirically identifying consciousness in unresponsive patients will not only require knowledge of the neural activity that corresponds to being conscious. It will also require knowledge of how consciousness relates to the full NCC, and more precisely, whether it relates

---

66. Allman et al., "Von Economo Neurons."
67. Craig, "How Do You Feel."
68. Economo, *Encephalitis Lethargica*.
69. Critchley and Seth, "Studies of Macaque Insula"; Evrard et al., "Von Economo Neurons."
70. Huang et al., "Anterior Insula."

in such a way that justifies inferring the presence of consciousness based on the presence of the NCC alone, in the absence of any response.[71]

The way physicalism depicts consciousness relating to the brain warrants inferring the presence of consciousness based solely on the presence of the neural correlate. But given contemporary challenges to physicalism,[72] it would be advantageous for the neurology of consciousness if it had an alternative philosophical foundation. The purpose of this section is to present such an alternative by outlining how the mind-body powers model of NCC warrants inferring the presence of consciousness based on the presence of the full NCC alone. The model, which is informed by Aquinas's hylomorphic human ontology and Aristotle's understanding of causal powers, was originally developed to provide a metaphysical explanation of NCC. Prior works discuss the details of the model and the philosophical ideas of Aristotle and Aquinas that inform it.[73] Here, we merely outline the model's metaphysical underpinnings before briefly summarizing the model itself and how it applies to empirically detecting consciousness when combined with a plausible neurobiological theory identifying the full NCC, such as TCH.

Hylomorphism and Causal Powers

The mind-body powers model is undergirded by a view of human nature called "neo-Thomistic hylomorphism" inspired by Thomas Aquinas, who often followed Aristotle's philosophy. As will become clear, this view is noticeably distinct from physicalism. The term hylomorphism is a compound Greek word, with *hyle* meaning "matter," while *morphe* means "form." As these words together constitute the word "hylomorphism," a real form and matter together constitute a real hylomorphic object. According to hylomorphism, there are accidental forms that modify already existing entities, such as the blue color of a door. Yet, there are also substantial forms that ground

---

71. M. Owen, *Measuring the Immeasurable Mind*, 1–5, 169–87; see also M. Owen and Guta, "Physically Sufficient Neural Mechanisms."

72. For a list of works presenting such challenges, see M. Owen, *Measuring the Immeasurable Mind*, 6–10.

73. See M. Owen, "Aristotelian Causation" and *Measuring the Immeasurable Mind*. The model also benefitted from the works of contemporary philosophers (see M. Owen, *Measuring the Immeasurable Mind*, 140–41), such as Haldane, "Return to Form"; Moreland, "Nancey Murphy's Christian Physicalism"; Moreland, "Defense of Thomistic-like Dualism"; Oderberg, "Hylemorphic Dualism."

the existence of a material substance, such as a dog or a human person. A material substance consists of matter that is unified by a substantial form.

To grasp a key role of a substantial form on this ontological framework, suppose Plato gives Socrates a hardy hug. Though we may not know why they are hugging (perhaps it is to reconcile after a philosophical debate became a bitter dispute), we surely know that there are two bodies present. But why isn't there only one physical body present when the matter of each body is connected as they are in direct contact? Why are there still two bodies, not one, given the physical connection? After all, if their bodies consisted merely of two sets of fundamental physical constituents (e.g., atoms) being in physical proximity, then when the two sets become physically connected by direct contact, it seems that they would be combined into one single set that is larger than the prior individual sets. Yet, this doubtfully happens. It is doubtful, in other words, that Plato's body and Socrates's body become a single larger body as they hug. Their bodies remain distinct bodies, despite their direct physical, spatial connection.

Hylomorphism provides an explanation for why Plato's body and Socrates's body are distinct bodies at all times and even when the two bodies are in direct contact as they hug. That is, the two bodies are comprised of not only their physical constituents, but also what unifies the physical constituents of each body into a single unified organism. That which unifies the physical matter of each body is the substantial form of each body, which Aristotle and Aquinas thought was the soul of each person.[74] There are two distinct bodies present, not one, because each body has its own distinct substantial form that unifies it. The substantial form unifying the physical parts of Plato's body is Plato's soul; the substantial form unifying the physical parts of Socrates's body is Socrates's soul.

On this hylomorphic human ontology, a human person is not a bundle or set of physical parts that we call a body, but rather a material substance consisting of matter unified by a substantial form that is a human soul. While that is noticeably different from a physicalist view of human nature, Aristotle and Aquinas would certainly have agreed with an intuition that seemingly supports physicalism. That is the intuition that our bodies are essential to our human nature and what it means to be human. They thought a human person is a material substance in the sense that each human is an internally unified being consisting of a soul that is by nature the substantial form of a physical body.

---

74. See Aquinas *ST* 1a 76.1c; 76.3c; 76.8c; Aristotle *DA* 2.1–2.

The rationale Aquinas gave for why the human soul is naturally the substantial form of a physical body appeals to the soul's powers, or capacities.[75] On his view, the soul is no powerless abstract object tantamount to a "free-floating-shape."[76] Rather, the soul is a powerful entity and due to human nature it relies on the body to manifest its powers.[77] As a Dominican friar, Aquinas conscientiously placed his philosophical positions within a theological context. Like God and angels, the nature of human persons is rational, but it is also sensory, like animals, according to Aquinas.[78] Given that, and that he followed Aristotle's thought that the body is required for the soul to sense, Aquinas considered the body necessary for human persons to operate consistently with their nature and therefore essential to human nature.[79]

The body, Aquinas thought, has the variety of organs it has so the soul can manifest its various powers/capacities.[80] The human soul, with its variety of capacities, "requires various dispositions in the parts of the body to which it is united."[81] Different capacities of the soul rely on different organs that have different structures sufficient to manifest different powers.[82] As this is true of all capacities and their corresponding organs, it likewise applies to the brain and corresponding mental capacities. Hence it is not surprising that Aquinas floats the following empirically verifiable/falsifiable prediction:

> If anyone wants to examine also the particular organs of the human body, he will discover that they are organized so that a human being might sense most effectively. Consequently, because a well ordered brain is necessary for the effective condition of the internal

---

75. In this context, several terms—powers, capacities, dispositions, operations—are synonymous.

76. Pasnau, "Philosophy of Mind," 353.

77. See *ST* 1a 76.5c.

78. See Aquinas, *Creation*, §§46, 57; *ST* 1a 89.1c; 75.7 ad 3.

79. See Aquinas, *Creation*, §57; *ST* 1a 84.4c; 89.1c; 75.4c; 75.7 ad 3. On how this is compatible with statements Aquinas makes about rationality being an independent operation not needing the body and the Christian doctrine of the intermediate state Aquinas held, see M. Owen, "Aristotelian Causation," sect. 3. Cohoe, "Separability of Nous," is a worthwhile read on the related topic of the separability and possible persistence of *psuchē* and *nous* in Aristotle's philosophy.

80. *ST* 1a 78.3c; 78.4c.

81. *ST* 1a 76.5 ad 3.

82. *QDA* 8c ad 14–16.

sense powers, for example, the imagination, the memory and the cogitative power, a human being was made in such a way that in proportion to his size he has a brain that is larger than that of any other animal.[83]

The concept of interdependent powers between the soul and bodily organs evident in Aquinas's understanding of human nature has roots in the Aristotelian philosophical tradition he is part of. There are interdependent powers all throughout the natural world, according to an Aristotelian ontology of causal powers.

Aristotle thought that the causal powers (or capacities) possessed by natural entities throughout the world are the source of change.[84] On this view, powers are not mere projections of ours about reality, but are rather objective features of the world that cannot be reduced to non-powers.[85] Fundamentally, there are two kinds of powers in this Aristotelian landscape. Active powers are capacities to bring about change whereas passive powers are capacities to undergo change; and "Aristotle defines an active power as one that exercises its powerfulness on a corresponding passive one."[86] The upshot is an interdependence of active and passive powers.

The cold, crisp water in Colchuck Lake in the Cascade Mountains has the passive power to be heated by the noonday sun. Likewise, the sun has the active power to heat the water. It is important to recognize, however, that both the active power of the sun and the passive power of the water must be co-manifested in order for either one to be manifested. In this way, the manifestations of powers depend on the manifestations of their "mutual partner-powers."[87] And, as Anna Marmodoro clarifies, "Because of their mutual dependence for activation, partner-powers realize their natures in activities that are co-determined, co-varying, and co-extensive in time."[88] It will become apparent, in due course, that this aspect of the Aristotelian metaphysics of causation informing the mind-body powers model is vital to discerning covert consciousness.

---

83. QDA 8c.

84. See *Meta* 5.12.

85. Cf. Hume, *Enquiry Concerning Human Understanding*, 55; Mayr, *Understanding Human Agency*, 166.

86. Marmodoro, *Aristotle On Perceiving Objects*, 13.

87. Marmodoro, *Aristotle On Perceiving Objects*, 32.

88. Marmodoro, *Aristotle On Perceiving Objects*, 32.

Mind-Body Powers, Consciousness, and Neural Mechanisms

Aquinas thought about how the soul depends on the body to exercise its powers in light of the scientific understanding during his lifetime in the thirteenth century. Hence, he thought about it at the level of organs, not the cellular level, which was unobservable during his lifetime, that predated the first use of the term "neuron" and Santiago Ramón y Cajal's neuron doctrine by six centuries.[89] The mind-body powers model of NCC applies Aquinas's thought to the cellular level and beyond, in light of what we now know from neurobiology. According to the model, human persons have both mental powers of the mind and bodily powers of biological structures in the body that are interdependent partner-powers. These interdependent mental and bodily powers are called mind-body powers.

We could give countless examples of mind-body powers, and the complexities could easily become confusing. Yet, a couple examples can sufficiently convey the gist of mind-body powers. The power to feel what it's like to taste Swiss chocolate is a mental power to be in that particular state of phenomenal consciousness. Though this capacity is a mental power, it relies on the co-manifestation of the powers of biological parts in the body that are suitably structured, from the macro-level of the tongue to the micro level of neurons in the gustatory cortex, to manifest such bodily powers. The power to experience what it's like to see the Matterhorn's north face is also a mental power, but not the same mental power as the capacity to feel what it's like to taste Swiss chocolate. Accordingly, this mental power co-manifests with a different set of bodily powers manifested by biological body parts which are sufficiently structured—from the organic level of the eyes to brain structures such as the optic chiasm, to neurons in the visual cortex. Since the bodily powers that correspond to each distinct mental power are likewise distinct, they are manifested by distinct biological parts with particular structures sufficient to manifest the particular bodily powers.

As Aquinas recognized that different organs correspond to particular mental powers, the mind-body powers model focuses on the fact that different structures in the brain even at the neuronal and subcellular levels correspond to particular mental powers. This is because the mental powers rely on the manifestation of bodily powers in biological parts that are suitably structured at multiple levels. Due to technological advances since

---

89. Cf. Finger, *Minds behind the Brain*, ch. 13.

Aquinas's day, we have learned much about the human body well beyond the level of organs. The model applies Aquinas's line of thought not only to macro but also micro levels, inferring that biological mechanisms with sufficient physical properties are needed at each level to manifest bodily powers that are interdependent partner-powers of mental powers.

The basic idea is that mind-body powers rely on certain types of physical properties at every level of bodily composition, and the correspondence between conscious states and neuronal states are grounded in the metaphysics of mind-body powers. Each conscious state and its corresponding neural activity correlate with consistent regularity because they manifest a mental power and bodily power(s) that are interdependent partner-powers which naturally co-manifest, as co-constituents of a mind-body power. And since the mental and bodily powers naturally co-manifest as co-constituents of a mind-body power, the manifestation of one can indicate the manifestation of the other. Therefore, once a researcher knows what the NCC of a particular conscious state is then they can reasonably infer the presence of the conscious state based on the presence of its empirically observable NCC. For example, once a neuroscientist knows what neural activity corresponds to seeing Bill Clinton's face, the neuroscientist can know when the conscious state of seeing Clinton's face is present by observing the neural correlate via neuroimaging.[90]

It is important to keep in mind that the purpose of the mind-body powers model of NCC is not to tell us what neural properties and processes correlate with particular conscious states. In other words, it does not tell us what and where specific NCC are. This is the task of neuroscience research aimed at identifying what specific neuronal structures, states, and processes are physically sufficient to support particular conscious states. What the model does, however, is provide a metaphysical explanation of the correspondence between conscious states and their neural correlates.

In addition to providing a metaphysical explanation of NCC, the model has several additional strengths worth briefly mentioning (even though we cannot defend them here). For one, the model is consistent with the irreducibility of consciousness—it does not explain the correspondence between consciousness and NCC by identifying the former with the latter. This abolishes the burden of finding a way to counterintuitively explain how consciousness can be identical to physical brain processes in the face of

---

90. See Koch, *Consciousness*, 65–66.

powerful arguments to the contrary.[91] At the same time, the model is consistent with the intuition that our bodies are essential to human nature. Moreover, the human ontology informing the model fits well with philosophical data relevant to consciousness studies, such as the unity of consciousness, the simplicity of the self, and the persistence of human persons through time and bodily change.[92] This is ultimately because a human person is (according to the neo-Thomistic hylomorphism informing the model) identical to a metaphysically simple soul that is the bearer of consciousness, rather than the physical constituents of the body it en-forms.[93] While these strengths are worth briefly noting, we must focus here on a strength of the model that can have practical implications in clinical neurology.

Detecting Covert Consciousness

Having introduced the metaphysical underpinnings of the mind-body powers model, we can now address how it provides a metaphysical foundation for the possibility of empirically discerning covert consciousness in unresponsive patients. To illustrate how this is the case, we will combine the model with TCH, a plausible hypothesis about the nature and location of the full NCC. Recall that TCH predicts consciousness involves a back-and-forth dance of mental states about the inner self and outer world mediated by attentional switching supported by spatiotemporal dynamics of brain activity displaying a shifting balance between DMN and DAN. And this shifting balance is governed by the anterior insula. This neuronal activity is predicted to be the full NCC that corresponds to being conscious versus unconscious. TCH's theoretical framework easily maps onto the metaphysical picture presented by the mind-body powers model of NCC. The substantial form of the body would be the internal self TCH refers to, which has the power to be conscious, which TCH characterizes as the self being aware of something in its environment. The shifting balance between DMN and DAN governed by the anterior insula is the neuronal activity

91. For examples of pertinent arguments, see Chalmers, *Conscious Mind*; Mørch, "Phenomenal Knowledge *Why*"; Robinson, *From the Knowledge Argument*.

92. For helpful discussions of the unity consciousness, see Hasker, "Persons and the Unity"; of the simplicity of the self, see Lowe, "Identity, Composition, and Simplicity"; Barnett, "You Are Simple"; of the persistence of an individual through time and bodily change, see Brown, *Aquinas and the Ship*, ch. 5.

93. For a more detailed description of neo-Thomistic hylomorphism that makes this apparent, see M. Owen, *Measuring the Immeasurable Mind*, chs. 5–7.

manifesting bodily powers, which are the partner-powers of the self's mental power to be aware.

Aquinas thought our rational cognition relies on sense images.[94] If that is the case, there's no substitute for a diagram that provides a visual representation of abstract ideas. Diagram 1 illustrates the metaphysical interdependence between the mental power to be aware and its mutual partner bodily powers, which co-manifest via the conscious state of being aware and the full NCC, respectively. The bottom row represents these interdependent partner-powers. The top represents their mutual manifestation, as the mental power is manifested through the conscious state of being aware and the bodily powers are manifested by the corresponding shifting balance between DMN and DAN, which TCH predicts is the neural correlate of being conscious (i.e., the full NCC). The double arrow on the top represents the resulting natural correlation between the neural mechanisms and the conscious state that's rooted in the metaphysical interdependence between the partner-powers, represented by the bottom double arrow.

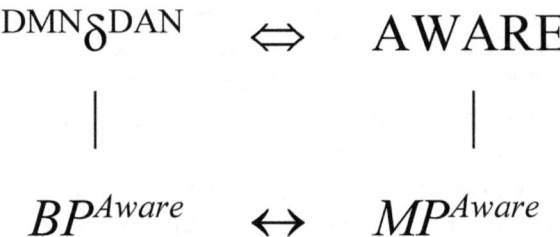

Figure 1—Mind-Body Powers and the Full NCC: The mental power to be conscious (MP^{Aware}) is manifested via the mental state of being aware (AWARE) with partner bodily power (BP^{Aware}), which is manifested via the full neural correlate ($^{DMN\delta DAN}$).
The double arrow on the bottom represents the metaphysical interdependence between the mental and bodily powers. The double arrow on the top represents the resulting natural correlation between the conscious state and corresponding neuronal mechanisms. The vertical lines represent that the bodily and mental powers are manifested via the corresponding neural activity and conscious state, respectively. Whenever MP^{Aware} manifests via AWARE, then BP^{Aware} co-manifests via $^{DMN\delta DAN}$. Likewise, whenever BP^{Aware} manifests via $^{DMN\delta DAN}$, then MP^{Aware} co-manifests via AWARE. Therefore, $^{DMN\delta DAN}$ is indicative of AWARE.

---

94. *ST* 1a 89.1c.

The metaphysical interdependence of the powers entailing their co-manifestation grounds the correspondence between the conscious state and the NCC studied by neurobiologists. The mental and bodily powers the mental state and neural activity manifest are interdependent partner-powers that constitute the mind-body power to be conscious. Given that they are interdependent partner-powers that together constitute the mind-body power to be conscious, the mental and bodily powers naturally co-manifest with each other. Consequently, if the mental power manifests, then the bodily power manifests; and if the bodily power manifests, then the mental power manifests, which is vitally important to detecting covert consciousness. Assuming TCH's prediction about the full NCC is accurate, a shifting balance between DMN and DAN would strongly indicate the presence of consciousness. Because that would be the manifestation of a bodily power that naturally co-manifests with the mental power to be aware, as they are interdependent partner-powers that mutually manifest.

Thus, when TCH's prediction about the full NCC is coupled with the mind-body powers model, a philosophical foundation emerges for empirically discerning the presence of consciousness apart from any intentional response from the patient. The neuronal activity that's the full NCC would be the manifestation of a bodily power that naturally co-manifests with its mutual mental power to be conscious. So, if the model accurately describes the relationship between consciousness and its neural mechanisms, and if TCH accurately describes the full NCC, then medical practitioners are well justified to infer that an unresponsive person is conscious based on the neural activity TCH predicts is the full NCC. In other words, the model provides a metaphysical basis that epistemically justifies inferring the presence of consciousness based on the presence of the full NCC.

In sum, the mind-body powers model of NCC provides philosophical justification for inferring that an unresponsive patient is conscious based on neural activity alone that can be publicly observed via neuroimaging. However, the practical utility of this inferential method rooted in the model will require empirical confirmation of the neural correlate of being conscious.[95] This is why the neurobiological study of consciousness, and research aimed at confirming or falsifying plausible theories such as TCH, is of great importance to clinical neurology.

---

95. It will also require the development of the technological tools (i.e., neuroimaging) to identify it in clinical contexts, ideally at the bedside of patients.

PART I | ONTOLOGY AND PERSONHOOD

CONCLUSION AND CAVEATS CONCERNING DEATH

We have focused here on the possibility of empirically discerning covert consciousness in unresponsive patients. Our aim has been to demonstrate that it is metaphysically possible given the philosophical framework provided by the mind-body powers model combined with a plausible prediction about the full NCC. A related topic is how the presence or absence of consciousness is related to death and to epistemically determining when it has occurred. This topic is not only important but also quite complicated in our modern world with technology capable of sustaining vital functions (e.g., oxygenation and cardiovascular circulation).[96] We want to conclude with several relevant caveats and points of clarification about how detecting consciousness relates to death and discerning when it has taken place.

We have argued that based on the presence of specific neural activity, it is possible, in theory, to know whether a person is conscious. If there is neural activity indicating that an unresponsive person is conscious, then the person is alive, not dead. Therefore, demonstrating that consciousness is present is one way to show that the person is alive. It does not follow, however, that if consciousness is absent then the person is dead. Consciousness is not the boundary between life and death. All of us have lost consciousness numerous times—every night when we go to sleep, or when under anesthesia, or perhaps in a car accident, etc.—and yet, we're still alive. Thus, while the presence of consciousness entails life, a loss of consciousness does not entail death. One cannot infer that someone has died solely on the basis that consciousness is absent. That could be a fatal fallacy if the choice was made to discontinue life sustaining measures based on such a conclusion unjustifiably arrived at.

We should also note an important distinction between being conscious and being capable of being conscious. When a person is asleep, the individual may not be conscious, but that does not entail that the person is not capable of being conscious. The distinction between being conscious and the capacity to be conscious is important because a person might be unconscious yet still capable of being conscious. Once again, we can make a positive inference—from the fact that someone is conscious, we can know they are still capable of being conscious. However, we cannot infer that if one is not conscious,

96. See Laureys, "Death, Unconsciousness and Brain"; Nair-Collins and Miller, "Do the 'Brain Dead'"; Verheijde et al., "Neuroscience and Brain Death"; Shewmon, "Recovery from 'Brain Death'"; Eberl, *Thomistic Principles and Bioethics*, ch. 3; Bernat, "Defense of Whole-Brain Concept"; and Esmaeilzadeh et al., "One Life Ends."

then they are necessarily incapable of being conscious. From the Thomistic perspective informing the mind-body powers model, the neural activity that is the full NCC can indicate the manifestation of the capacity (or power) to be conscious, but the absence of the activity does not entail the absence of the capacity. For a capacity, or power, can be present but unmanifested. As Jason Eberl points out, "While Aquinas notes that one can determine the presence of a certain capacity based upon observation of its corresponding activity, it does not follow that failure to observe an activity entails the lack of its corresponding capacity."[97]

Finally, even if the capacity for consciousness itself (not just its manifestation) is lost, there is more to consider from an Aristotelian-Thomistic perspective. Because, according to this view, the human soul is a substantial form that is not only rational and sensitive but also nutritive.[98] And the manifestation of any of the soul's capacities—rational, sensitive, or nutritive—could indicate its presence and therefore that the person is alive. Accordingly, even when a person does not have access to their cognitive faculties and will not reawake mentally, if their body is still a living organism then the soul would seem to be present, manifesting its nutritive capacity, according to an Aristotelian-Thomistic human ontology. When exactly the body ceases to be a unified living biological organism can be difficult to discern, but until it ceases to be such, there is reason to think death has not occurred.[99]

With the aforementioned caveats and qualifications made, we can conclude with some positive points. The philosophical foundation for the neurobiology of consciousness is broader than physicalism, and the mind-body powers model informed by Aristotelian-Thomistic metaphysics also entails that empirically detecting consciousness is theoretically possible. If neurobiologists can identify the full NCC, then inferring the presence of consciousness based on the presence of the neural correlate will be well justified in clinical neurology even in the absence of any response to stimuli. This is true given either a physicalist philosophical framework or the Aristotelian-Thomistic alternative presented here.

---

97. Eberl, *Thomistic Principles and Bioethics*, 48, referring to Aquinas, *Treatise on Human Nature*, 1a.87.1.

98. Cf. Eberl, *Thomistic Principles and Bioethics*, ch. 3; Norkowski, "Brain Based Criteria"; Shewmon, "Recovery from 'Brain Death'"; Moreland and Wallace, "Aquinas versus Locke."

99. See Eberl, *Thomistic Principles and Bioethics*, ch. 3; *Nature of Human Persons*, ch. 6.

PART I | ONTOLOGY AND PERSONHOOD

BIBLIOGRAPHY

Allman, John M., et al. "The Von Economo Neurons in the Frontoinsular and Anterior Cingulate Cortex." *Ann N Y Acad Sci* 1225 (2011) 59–71. doi: 10.1111/j.1749-6632.2011.06011.x.

Aquinas, Thomas. *Creation*. Translated by James F. Anderson. Summa Contra Gentiles 2. Notre Dame, IN: University of Notre Dame Press, 1956.

———. *Questions on the Soul*. Translated by James H. Robb. Milwaukee: Marquette University Press, 1984.

———. *Summa Theologica*. Translated by Fathers of the English Dominican Province. New York: Benziger, 1947.

———. *The Treatise on Human Nature: Summa Theologiae 1a 75–89*. Translated by Robert Pasnau. Hackett Aquinas Project. Indianapolis: Hackett, 2002.

Aristotle. *Metaphysics*. In *The Complete Works of Aristotle: The Revised Oxford Translation*, edited by Jonathan Barnes, translated by W. D. Ross, 2:1552–728. Princeton, NJ: Princeton University Press, 1984.

———. *On the Soul*. In *The Complete Works of Aristotle: The Revised Oxford Translation*, edited by Jonathan Barnes, translated by J. A. Smith, 1:641–92. Princeton, NJ: Princeton University Press, 1984.

Barnett, David. "You Are Simple." In *The Waning of Materialism*, edited by Robert C. Koons and George Bealer, 161–74. New York: Oxford University Press, 2010.

Bernat, James L. "A Defense of the Whole-Brain Concept of Death." *Hastings Center Report* 28 (1998)14–23. https://doi.org/10.2307/3527567.

Boly, M., et al. "When Thoughts Become Action: An fMRI Paradigm to Study Volitional Brain Activity in Non-communicative Brain Injured Patients." *NeuroImage* 36 (2007) 979–92. https://doi.org/10.1016/j.neuroimage.2007.02.047.

Boly, Melanie, et al. "Consciousness in Humans and Non-human Animals: Recent Advances and Future Directions." *Frontiers in Psychology* 4 (2013) https://doi.org/10.3389/fpsyg.2013.00625.

Brown, Christopher. *Aquinas and the Ship of Theseus: Solving Puzzles about Material Objects*. Continuum Studies in Philosophy 10. New York: Continuum, 2005.

Cavanna, Andrea Eugenio, and Andrea Nani. "Francis Crick and Christof Koch." In *Consciousness: Theories in Neuroscience and Philosophy of Mind*, edited by Andrea Eugenio Cavanna and Andrea Nani, 99–103. Berlin: Springer, 2014.

Cecconi, Benedetta, et al. "Islands of Awareness or Cortical Complexity?" *Trends in Neurosciences* 43 (2020) 545–46. https://doi.org/10.1016/j.tins.2020.05.007.

Chalmers, David. J. *The Conscious Mind: In Search of a Fundamental Theory*. Philosophy of Mind. New York: Oxford University Press, 1996.

Cohoe, Caleb M. "The Separability of Nous." In *Aristotle's "On the Soul": A Critical Guide*, edited by Caleb M. Cohoe, 229–46. Cambridge Critical Guides. Cambridge: Cambridge University Press, 2022.

Corbetta, Maurizio, and Gordon L. Shulman. "Control of Goal-Directed and Stimulus-Driven Attention in the Brain." *Nature Reviews Neuroscience* 3 (2002) 201–15. https://doi.org/10.1038/nrn755.

Craig, A. D. "How Do You Feel—Now? The Anterior Insula and Human Awareness." *Nature Reviews Neuroscience* 10 (2009) 59–70. https://doi.org/10.1038/nrn2555.

Crick, Francis, and Christof Koch. "Toward a Neurobiological Theory of Consciousness." *Seminars in the Neurosciences* 2 (1990) 263–75.

Critchley, Hugo, and Anil Seth. "Will Studies of Macaque Insula Reveal the Neural Mechanisms of Self-Awareness?" *Neuron* 74 (2012) 423–26. https://doi.org/10.1016/j.neuron.2012.04.012.

Critchley, Hugo D., et al. "Neural Systems Supporting Interoceptive Awareness." *Nature Neuroscience* 7 (2004) 189–95. https://doi.org/10.1038/nn1176.

Damasio, Antonio. *Self Comes to Mind: Constructing the Conscious Brain*. New York: Pantheon, 2010.

Eberl, Jason T. *The Nature of Human Persons: Metaphysics and Bioethics*. Notre Dame Studies in Medical Ethics and Bioethics. Notre Dame, IN: University of Notre Dame Press, 2020.

———. *Thomistic Principles and Bioethics*. Routledge Annals of Bioethics. New York: Routledge, 2006.

Economo, Constantin. *Die Encephalitis Lethargica*. Vienna: Deuticke, 1918.

Esmaeilzadeh, Majid, et al. "One Life Ends, Another Begins: Management of a Brain-Dead Pregnant Mother—A Systematic Review." *BMC Medicine* 8 (2010). https://doi.org/10.1186/1741-7015-8-74.

Evrard, Henry C., et al. "Von Economo Neurons in the Anterior Insula of the Macaque Monkey." *Neuron* 74 (2012) 482–89. https://doi.org/10.1016/j.neuron.2012.03.003.

Faivre, N., et al. "Visual Consciousness and Bodily Self-Consciousness." *Current Opinion in Neurology* 28 (2015) 23–28. doi: 10.1097/WCO.0000000000000160.

Finger, S. *Minds behind the Brain: A History of the Pioneers and Their Discoveries*. New York: Oxford University Press, 2000.

Fins, Joseph J. *Rights Come to Mind: Brain Injury, Ethics, and the Struggle for Consciousness*. New York: Cambridge University Press, 2015.

Fins, Joseph J., et al. "Late Recovery from the Minimally Conscious State: Ethical and Policy Implications." *Neurology* 68 (2007) 304–7. doi: 10.1212/01.wnl.0000252376.43779.96.

Fornito, A., et al. "Competitive and Cooperative Dynamics of Large-Scale Brain Functional Networks Supporting Recollection." *Proceedings of the National Academy of Sciences* 109 (2012) 12788–93. https://doi.org/10.1073/pnas.1204185109.

Fox, Michael D., et al. "Spontaneous Neuronal Activity Distinguishes Human Dorsal and Ventral Attention Systems." *Proceedings of the National Academy of Sciences* 103 (2006) 10046–51. https://doi.org/10.1073/pnas.0604187103.

Giacino, Joseph T. "The Vegetative and Minimally Conscious States: Consensus-Based Criteria for Establishing Diagnosis and Prognosis." *NeuroRehabilitation* 19 (2004) 293–98.

Giacino, Joseph T., and Kathleen Kalmar. "The Vegetative and Minimally Conscious States: A Comparison of Clinical Features and Functional Outcome." *Journal of Head Trauma Rehabilitation* 12 (1997) 36–51.

Giacino, Joseph T., et al. "Disorders of Consciousness after Acquired Brain Injury: the State of the Science." *Nature Reviews Neurology* (2014) 99–114. doi: 10.1038/nrneurol.2013.279.

———. "The JFK Coma Recovery Scale-Revised: Measurement Characteristics and Diagnostic Utility." *Archives of Physical Medicine and Rehabilitation* 85 (2004) 2020–29. https://doi.org/10.1016/j.apmr.2004.02.033

Göcke, Benedikt Paul, ed. *After Physicalism*. Notre Dame, IN: University of Notre Dame Press, 2012.

Gosseries, Olivia, et al. "Measuring Consciousness in Severely Damaged Brains." *Annual Review of Neuroscience* (2014) 457–78. doi: 10.1146/annurev-neuro-062012-170339.

Guta, Mihretu P. "The Non-Causal Account of the Spontaneous Emergence of Phenomenal Consciousness." In *Consciousness and the Ontology of Properties*, edited by Mihretu P. Guta, 126–51. New York: Routledge, 2019.

Haldane, John. "A Return to Form in the Philosophy of Mind." *Ratio* 11 (2010) 253–77.

Hasker, William. "Persons and the Unity of Consciousness." In *The Waning of Materialism*, edited by Robert C. Koons and George Bealer, 175–90. New York: Oxford University Press, 2010.

Huang, Zirui, et al. "Anterior Insula Regulates Brain Network Transitions That Gate Conscious Access." *Cell Reports* 35 (2021). https://doi.org/10.1016/j.celrep.2021.109081.

———. "Brain Imaging Reveals Covert Consciousness during Behavioral Unresponsiveness Induced by Propofol." *Scientific Reports* 8 (2018). https://doi.org/10.1038/s41598-018-31436-z.

———. "Temporal Circuit of Macroscale Dynamic Brain Activity Supports Human Consciousness." *Science Advances* 6 (2020). DOI: 10.1126/sciadv.aaz0o.

Hume, David. *An Enquiry Concerning Human Understanding*. Edited by Peter Millican. Oxford World's Classics. New York: Oxford University Press, 2007.

Kim, Jaegwon. *Mind in a Physical World: An Essay on the Mind-Body Problem and Mental Causation*. Representation and Mind. Cambridge, MA: MIT Press, 2000.

———. *Philosophy of Mind*. 3rd ed. Boulder, CO: Westview, 2011.

———. *Physicalism, or Something Near Enough*. Princeton, NJ: Princeton University Press, 2005.

Koch, Christof. *Consciousness: Confessions of a Romantic Reductionist*. Cambridge, MA: MIT Press, 2012.

———. "Re-Enchanting the World." *American Journal of Psychology* 133 (2020) 519–22. https://doi.org/10.5406/amerjpsyc.133.4.0519.

———. *The Quest for Consciousness: A Neurobiological Approach*. Englewood, CO: Roberts, 2004.

Koch, Christof, et al. "Neural Correlates of Consciousness: Progress and Problems." *Nature Reviews Neuroscience* 17 (2016) 307–21.

Koons, Robert C., and George Bealer, eds. *The Waning of Materialism*. New York: Oxford University Press, 2010.

Laureys, Steven. "Death, Unconsciousness and the Brain." *Nature Reviews Neuroscience* 6 (2005) 899–909. https://doi.org/10.1038/nrn1789.

Laureys, Steven, et al. "Unresponsive Wakefulness Syndrome: A New Name for the Vegetative State or Apallic Syndrome." *BMC Medicine* (2010) 8. https://doi.org/10.1186/1741-7015-8-68.

Lavazza, Andrea, and Howard Robinson, eds. *Contemporary Dualism: A Defense*. Routledge Studies in Contemporary Philosophy. New York: Routledge, 2014.

Loose, Jonathan J., et al., eds. *The Blackwell Companion to Substance Dualism*. Blackwell Companions to Philosophy. Oxford: Wiley-Blackwell, 2018.

Lowe, E. J. "Identity, Composition, and the Simplicity of the Self." In *Soul, Body, and Survival: Essays on the Metaphysics of Human Persons*, edited by Kevin Corcoran, 139–58. New York: Cornell University Press, 2001.

Manning, Joanna. "Withdrawal of Life-Sustaining Treatment from a Patient in a Minimally Conscious State." *Journal of Law & Medicine* 19 (2012) 430–35.

Marmodoro, Anna. *Aristotle on Perceiving Objects*. New York: Oxford University Press, 2014.

Mashour, George A., et al. "Conscious Processing and the Global Neuronal Workspace Hypothesis." *Neuron* 105 (2010) 776–98. https://doi.org/10.1016/j.neuron.2020.01.026

Massimini, Marcello, and Giulio Tononi. *Sizing Up Consciousness: Towards an Objective Measure of the Capacity for Experience*. New York: Oxford University Press, 2018.

Mayr, Erasmus. *Understanding Human Agency*. New York: Oxford University Press, 2011.

Menon, Vinod. "Large-Scale Brain Networks and Psychopathology: A Unifying Triple Network Model." *Trends Cogn Sci* 15 (2011) 483–506. doi:10.1016/j.tics.2011.08.003.

Metzinger, Thomas, ed. *Neural Correlates of Consciousness: Empirical and Conceptual Questions*. Cambridge, MA: MIT Press, 2000.

Michel, Matthias. "A Role for the Anterior Insular Cortex in the Global Neuronal Workspace Model of Consciousness." *Conscious Cogn* 49 (2017) 333–46. doi: 10.1016/j.concog.2017.02.004.

Monti, Martin M., et al. "Willful Modulation of Brain Activity in Disorders of Consciousness." *New England Journal of Medicine* 362 (2010) 579–89. doi: 10.1056/NEJMoa0905370.

Mørch, Hedda Hassel. "Phenomenal Knowledge *Why*: The Explanatory Knowledge Argument against Physicalism." In *The Knowledge Argument*, edited by Sam Coleman, 223–53. Classic Philosophical Arguments. Cambridge University Press, 2019.

Moreland, J. P. "A Critique of and Alternative to Nancey Murphy's Christian Physicalism." *European Journal for Philosophy of Religion* 8 (2016) 107–28.

———. "In Defense of a Thomistic-like Dualism." In *The Blackwell Companion to Substance Dualism*, edited by Jonathan J. Loose et al., 102–22. Blackwell Companions to Philosophy. Oxford: Wiley-Blackwell, 2018.

Moreland, J. P., and Sam Wallace. "Aquinas versus Locke and Descartes on the Human Person and End-of-Life Ethics." *International Philosophical Quarterly* 35 (1995) 319–30. doi: 10.5840/ipq199535327.

Naci, Lorina, et al. "A Common Neural Code for Similar Conscious Experiences in Different Individuals." *Proceedings of the National Academy of Sciences of the USA* 111 (39) 14277–82. https://doi.org/10.1073/pnas.1407007111

Nair-Collins, Michael, and Franklin G. Miller. "Do the 'Brain Dead' Merely Appear to Be Alive?" *Journal of Medical Ethics* 43 (2017) 747753. doi: 10.1136/medethics-2016-103867.

National Academies of Sciences, Engineering, and Medicine. *The Emerging Field of Human Neural Organoids, Transplants, and Chimeras: Science, Ethics, and Governance*. Washington, DC: National Academies Press, 2021. https://doi.org/10.17226/26078.

Norkowski, Jacek Maria. "Brain Based Criteria for Death in the Light of the Aristotelian-Scholastic Anthropology." *Scientia et Fides* 6 (2018) 153–88. http://dx.doi.org/10.12775/SetF.2018.002.

O'Connor, Timothy and David Robb, eds. *Philosophy of Mind: Contemporary Readings*. Routledge Contemporary Readings in Philosophy. New York: Routledge, 2003.

Oderberg, David S. "Hylemorphic Dualism." In *Personal Identity*, edited by Ellen Frankel Paul et al., 70–99. Social Philosophy and Policy 22. New York: Cambridge University Press, 2005.

Owen, Adrian M. "Improving Diagnosis and Prognosis in Disorders of Consciousness." *BRAIN* 143 (2020) 1046–56.

Owen, Adrian M., et al. "Detecting Awareness in the Vegetative State." *Science* 313 (2006) 1402. doi: 10.1126/science.1130197.

Owen, Matthew. "Aristotelian Causation and Neural Correlates of Consciousness." *Topoi* 39 (2020) 1113–24. https://doi.org/10.1007/s11245-018-9606-9.

———. *Measuring the Immeasurable Mind: Where Contemporary Neuroscience Meets the Aristotelian Tradition*. Lanham, MD: Lexington, 2021.

Owen, Matthew, and Mihretu P. Guta. "Physically Sufficient Neural Mechanisms of Consciousness." *Frontiers in Systems Neuroscience* 13 (2019) 1–14. https://doi.org/10.3389/fnsys.2019.00024.

Owen, Matthew, et al. "Theoretical Neurobiology of Consciousness Applied to Human Cerebral Organoids." *Cambridge Quarterly of Health Care Ethics* (2023) 1–21. https://doi.org/10.1017/S0963180123000543.

Pan, Jiahui, et al. "Prognosis for Patients with Cognitive Motor Dissociation Identified by Brain-Computer Interface Brain." *BRAIN* 143 (2020) 1177–89. https://doi.org/10.1093/brain/awaa026.

Park, Hyeong-Dong, and Catherine Tallon-Baudry. "The Neural Subjective Frame: From Bodily Signals to Perceptual Consciousness." *Philos Trans R Soc Lond B Biol Sci* 369 (2014) 20130208. doi: 10.1098/rstb.2013.0208.

Pasnau, Robert. "Philosophy of Mind and Human Nature." In *The Oxford Handbook of Aquinas*, edited by Brian Davies and Eleonore Stump, 348–68. Oxford Handbooks. New York: Oxford University Press, 2012.

———. *Thomas Aquinas on Human Nature: A Philosophical Study of "Summa Theologiae" 1a 75–89*. Cambridge: Cambridge University Press, 2002.

Raichle, Marcus E. "The Brain's Default Mode Network." *Annu Rev Neurosci* 38 (2015) 433–47. doi: 10.1146/annurev-neuro-071013-014030.

Raichle, Marcus E., et al. "A Default Mode of Brain Function." *Proceedings of the National Academy of Sciences* 98 (2001) 676–82. doi: 10.1073/pnas.98.2.676.

Robinson, Howard. *From the Knowledge Argument to Mental Substance: Resurrecting the Mind*. New York: Cambridge University Press, 2016.

Sanders, Robert D., et al. "Unresponsiveness ≠ Unconsciousness." *Anesthesiology* 116 (2012) 946–59. doi: 10.1097/ALN.0b013e318249d0a7.

Sattin, Davide, et al. "Theoretical Models of Consciousness: A Scoping Review." *Brain Sciences* 11 (2021) 535.

Schnakers, Caroline, et al. "Diagnostic Accuracy of the Vegetative and Minimally Conscious State: Clinical Consensus versus Standardized Neurobehavioral Assessment." *BMC Neurology* 9 (2009). https://doi.org/10.1186/1471-2377-9-35.

———. "Minimally Conscious State." In *The Neurology of Consciousness: Cognitive Neuroscience and Neuropathology*, edited by Steven Laureys et al., 167–81. 2nd ed. San Diego, CA: Elsevier, 2016.

———. "Neuroimaging of Consciousness in the Vegetative and Minimally Conscious State." In *Neuroimaging of Consciousness*, edited by Andrea Eugenio Cavanna et al., 117–32. Heidelberg: Springer, 2013.

Searle, John. R. *The Rediscovery of the Mind*. Representation and Mind. Cambridge, MA: MIT Press, 1992.

Seeley, William W., et al. "Dissociable Intrinsic Connectivity Networks for Salience Processing and Executive Control." *Journal of Neuroscience* 27 (2007) 2349–56. https://doi.org/10.1523/JNEUROSCI.5587-06.2007.

Seth, Anil. "Models of Consciousness." *Scholarpedia* 2 (2017) 1328. doi:10.4249/scholarpedia.1328.

Seth, Anil K., and Tim Bayne. "Theories of Consciousness." *Nature Reviews Neuroscience* (2022). doi: 10.1038/s41583-022-00587-4.

Shewmon, D. Alan. "Recovery from 'Brain Death': A Neurologist's Apologia." *Linacre Quarterly* 64 (1997) 31–96.

Smart, J. J. C. "Sensations and Brain Processes." *Philosophical Review* 68 (1959) 141–56.

Storm, Johann F., et al. "Consciousness Regained: Disentangling Mechanisms, Brain Systems, and Behavioral Responses." *Journal of Neuroscience* 37 (2017) 10882–93. https://doi.org/10.1523/JNEUROSCI.1838-17.2017.

Teasdale, G., and B. Jennett. "Assessment of Coma and Impaired Consciousness." *Lancet* 304 (1974) 81–84. doi: 10.1016/s0140-6736(74)91639-0.

Tononi, Giulio., et al. "Integrated Information Theory: From Consciousness to Its Physical Substrate." *Nature Reviews Neuroscience* 17 (2016) 450–61.

Uddin, Lucina Q. "Salience Processing and Insular Cortical Function and Dysfunction." *Nature Reviews Neuroscience* 16 (2015) 55–61. doi: 10.1038/nrn3857.

Verheijde, Joseph L., et al. "Neuroscience and Brain Death Controversies: The Elephant in the Room." *Journal of Religion and Health* 57 (2018) 1745–63. https://doi.org/10.1007/s10943-018-0654-7.

Vossel, Simone, et al. "Dorsal and Ventral Attention Systems: Distinct Neural Circuits but Collaborative Roles." *Neuroscientist* 20 (2014) 150–59. doi: 10.1177/1073858413494269.

Young, Michael J., and Brian L. Edlow. "The Quest for Covert Consciousness: Bringing Neuroethics to the Bedside." *Neurology* 96 (2021) 893–96. doi: 10.1212/WNL.0000000000011734.

4

Consciousness and the Self without Reductionism
Touching Churchland's Nerve

Eric LaRock and Mostyn Jones

What am I? What is consciousness? Securing adequate answers would be tantamount to a discovery of the "holy grail" of neuroscience and philosophy. Some neuroscientists and philosophers believe that neurobiological facts alone are relevant to answering the forgoing questions. A leading example is Patricia Churchland, who has argued in her recent book, *Touching a Nerve: The Self as Brain*, that naturalism provides a better account of the self and consciousness than dualism. Churchland defines naturalism in terms of "the brain alone" (or only brain stuff) and dualism in terms of "soul stuff and brain stuff." To clarify, we use the terms "soul," "self," "person," and "subject" interchangeably. What all these terms indicate in our view is the bearer of rights, duties, free will, and mental properties in general, both conscious and unconscious.[1]

Churchland is an eloquent leader for the views that comprehending minds require comprehending brains and that minds will ultimately be reduced to neuroscientific terms with no need for dualism. But we embrace dualism (and the relevant empirical data) and try to turn the tables on

---

1. This isn't meant as a hard and fast point—for example, apes arguably have self-awareness but aren't persons.

Churchland's naturalism by showing that certain kinds of dualism explain minds better than neuroscience can. What's most novel below is that while most critiques of reductionism have confronted its metaphysical problems, we focus more on its serious empirical problems in accounting for the self, its unified experience, its powers of agency, and its various impairments involving amnesia, blindsight, split brains, and paralysis. In what follows, we take a brief tour and analysis of Churchland's naturalism and conclude that it doesn't threaten the existence of soul stuff. Our arguments challenge a great many reductive theories of mind today.

I. CHURCHLAND'S BRAIN-ALONE HYPOTHESIS

Churchland maintains that all mental phenomena, including consciousness and the self, point to and can be explained in terms of the brain alone: "There is just the brain—there is no separate thing, me, existing apart from my brain."[2] From the moral sphere to the sparks of scientific creativity, all mental phenomena boil down to our brain's capacities: "Our moral nature is what it is because our brains are as they are; so too, for our capacities to learn, reason, invent, and do science."[3] Churchland is not making the noncontroversial claim that our moral nature and mental capacities, in general, merely correlate with our brains. For any proponent of a non-materialist position—from Cartesian substance dualism (where souls and bodies are two radically different substances that can exist apart) to non-reductive physicalism—could make that claim. Rather she's asserting that our moral nature and mental capacities in general can be explained by "the brain alone."[4] Churchland originally tended to deny the existence of conscious mental life, but in her more recent book we focus mainly on here she accepts its existence and tries to reduce it to brain activities (see the discussion of the hard problem below).

To bolster the preceding claim, her "brain-alone" hypothesis argues that the phenomena of neural dependence have greater consilience under this hypothesis than (Cartesian) substance dualism. Simply stated, her objection to dualism is that the mind depends on the brain, so they can't be radically different entities. We will now cover examples of the self's dependence on brain activities in cases of the self's awareness of its own body, its

2. Churchland, *Touching a Nerve*, 34.
3. Churchland, "Moral Decision-Making," 3.
4. Churchland, "Moral Decision-Making," 5; see also Churchland, *Touching a Nerve*, 50.

impairments, its decision-making, its agency, its own unity, and the unity of its experiences.

To start with, Churchland's account of neural dependency stresses how the brain supports the self's awareness of its own body. She argues that the brain's circuitry "supports a neural model of the inner world."[5] Presumably, this inner neural model maps, or spatially represents, our bodies' skin, muscles, stomach, arms, head, etc. This neural model, for example, enables us to know the spatial positions of our arms and legs while biking down a challenging mountain trail or playing the drums in the dark. When this neural model breaks down, so does our capacity to represent the spatial positions of our bodily parts, also known as proprioception.

There are other data that one might enlist to show how highly dependent the mental is on the physical not only for sensory stimuli and behavior but for our conscious lives as well. This is evident in the self's impairment due to neural damage. For example, a fall accident involving a head injury can lead to significant memory problems and personality changes. And damage to the right parietal cortex can lead to visual neglect (or a lack of awareness of the stimulus contents associated with the left half of one's visual field) and to somatoparaphrenia (which can involve a lack of awareness of the limbs on the left side of one's body). Further, severing the corpus callosum can lead to a split-mind effect (under carefully controlled empirical constraints). Regarding the latter, Churchland maintains that split-brain results "were powerful support for the hypothesis that mental states are in fact states of the physical brain itself, not states of a nonphysical soul."[6] Churchland articulates her view of neural dependence deftly in the following pithy passage:

> The more we know about neurology and about neuropharmacology, the more evident it is that the functions in question [reasoning, judgments, consciousness, etc.] are not remotely as independent as the classical [dualist] hypothesis asserts. On the materialist hypothesis, the observed interdependence is precisely what would be expected, but it is distinctly embarrassing to the dualist hypothesis.[7]

Churchland also argues that the self's powers of agency depend on brain states. She argues that the brain is a "causal machine" (presumably

---

5. Churchland, *Touching a Nerve*, 38 (emphasis original).
6. Churchland, *Touching a Nerve*, 50.
7. Churchland, *Neurophilosophy*, 319.

within the logic of a linear, deterministic framework).[8] The brain has different states at different times. A brain state at any given time is caused by antecedent conditions. Antecedent conditions include, among other events, the effects of external stimuli (e.g., encoding the prototypes of exploitation and altruism in early childhood development) and internal hormonal changes (e.g., feeling down or feeling uplifted). These sorts of antecedent conditions are both necessary and sufficient for the generation of any brain state: "If the antecedent conditions had been different, the result would have been different; if the antecedent conditions remained the same, the same result would obtain."[9] She motivates this claim by deploying the logic of transitivity: "If choices are brain events, and if brain events have causal antecedents, then choices have causal antecedents."[10] Churchland surmises that if the brain as a causal machine hypothesis were true, then the brain could be regarded as the sole cause of human choice and action. Hence, there would be no need to appeal to nonphysical substances or properties to explain human choice and action: "The most plausible hypothesis on the table is that the brain, and the brain alone, makes choices and decides upon actions."[11] An illustration about character development might be useful here. If brains cause actions, and actions cause characters, then brains cause characters. Inspired by the Scottish philosopher David Hume, Churchland maintains that if a choice could be made without reference to one's brain (and thus without reference to the causal basis of one's character), "the choice would be so bizarre, so 'out of the blue' as to raise the question of whether it was a real choice at all."[12] In further attacking this dualist account of choices, Churchland asks "How can energy be transferred from a completely nonphysical thing to a physical thing? Where does the soul get its oomph to have such an effect?"[13] This is one reason that she assimilates consciousness and its causal role to neural activities.

Further elaborating on this dependence of the mental upon the neural, Churchland turns to how the self's own unity depends on neural

8. Churchland, "Moral Decision-Making"; Churchland, *Touching a Nerve*. This view contrasts with the logic of nonlinear dynamical systems, in which the mind is thought to act back upon the brain through recurrent interactions, also known as downward causation by mind on brain.

9. Churchland, "Moral Decision-Making," 5.

10. Churchland, "Moral Decision-Making," 6.

11. Churchland, "Moral Decision-Making," 5.

12. Churchland, "Moral Decision-Making," 7; see also Churchland, *Touching a Nerve*, 12.

13. Churchland, *Touching a Nerve*, 51.

events. She alleges that human choice and action can be accounted for without a commander-in-chief but by mere reference to the dynamics of billions of neurons performing functions together. Self-control on her account depends solely upon the synapses between a subset of neurons in "the prefrontal cortex and subcortical structures, mainly the basal ganglia and nucleus accumbens."[14] From these data, she then draws the inference that there is currently no known single area of the brain (or unique module) where the will resides and carries out its functions. An analogy might be useful. Just as there is no known convergence zone for the integration of sensory information, so too there is no known single place in the brain where the self wills, conducts, or fulfills its commands.

Turning to the dependence of the self's unified experiences on neural events, Churchland further suggests that current neurobiology is converging upon several properties central to consciousness: (1) local and global connections are required for the integration of information; (2) posterior events in the frontal areas are required for consciousness; (3) the central thalamus is required for enabling specific contents of consciousness; and (4) the common underlying mechanism of the aforementioned (1–3) neurobiological properties is the synchronous activations of widely distributed neurons: "The linkages, it is thought, may consist in synchrony in the activities of populations of neurons."[15] This approach has several strengths.

In these ways, Churchland argues that the self depends on neural events for its awareness of its own body, its various impairments, its decision-making and agency, its own unity, and the unity of its experiences. So, there is no need for nonneural dualist causes which radically differ from neural causes. These cases of neural dependence are better explained by her brain-alone hypothesis than by dualism.

Finally, Churchland adds that her brain-only view allows for free will. Here, she embraces soft determinism's claim that free will is self-determined instead of being externally determined or not determined at all. This is the ordinary sense of free will.[16]

Having taken a brief tour of Churchland's naturalism (or brain-alone hypothesis), we shall now argue that dualism can not only counter—but also turn the tables on—her anti-dualist arguments concerning neural dependence, especially in regard to the self's various impairments, unified

---

14. Churchland, *Touching a Nerve*, 176.
15. Churchland, *Touching a Nerve*, 147.
16. Churchland, *Touching a Nerve*, 178.

experiences, and powers of agency. But we'll start with the hard problem facing her reductionism, which will figure in some of our other comments below.

II. ANALYSIS OF CHURCHLAND'S BRAIN-ALONE HYPOTHESIS

Reply to Churchland's Treatment of the Hard Problem

Most of Churchland's writings address the so-called "easy problem" of consciousness concerning how brains integrate information and perform other activities associated with consciousness. Our paper is concerned mostly with the easy problems that she addresses.

But Churchland also addresses the hard problem of why these neural activities are accompanied by an experienced inner life.[17] Here, Churchland originally supported eliminative materialism, which predicts that naive folk psychology's acceptance of consciousness will ultimately be replaced by a mature neuroscience that makes no use of consciousness.[18] This argument has fared poorly because of Descartes's well-known point that if we know anything exists, it's our own consciousness. More recently, Churchland adopts the weaker contention that consciousness exists, but is reducible to neural events: "there is just the brain—there is no separate thing, me, existing apart from my brain,"[19] so "probably the soul and brain are one and the same."[20] This implies ontological reductionism.

But such reductionist views face several well-known problems that will just be summarized here:

1. Putnam's multiple realization argument is that pain probably doesn't have the same neurochemical correlate in all species across evolutionary history.[21] Yet pain always has a functional correlate that involves detecting and reacting to tissue damage. So, pain is a mental function realizable in multiple hardwares but irreducible to any particular hardware.

---

17. Chalmers, *Conscious Mind*, xi–xii.
18. Churchland, *Neurophilosophy*, 395.
19. Churchland, *Touching a Nerve*, 34.
20. Churchland, *Touching a Nerve*, 60.
21. Putnam, "Nature of Mental States."

2. Conceivability arguments basically say that it's always conceivable that a zombie world can exist where qualia don't accompany physical events. So it's metaphysically possible that God could have created a zombie world if he wished (or so it's argued). This shows that purely physical accounts can't distinguish between zombie worlds and our world where qualia exist. So, physicalism is false, for counter to its claims, physical accounts are incomplete.

3. Knowledge arguments basically say that if a scientist learns all about the science of color vision yet only experiences color later, then at that time the scientist gets new knowledge that's beyond physical science, that is, not physical.

4. Levine feels that conceivability and knowledge arguments undercut physicalism just epistemologically, not metaphysically.[22] They thus leave an explanatory or intelligibility gap between physical events and qualia. This gap doesn't exist between identities, such as water is H_2O. For the latter offers a deeper explanation of water and its behavior, such as its ability to dissolve salts. By contrast, identifying qualia with brain events doesn't offer any explanation—it leaves their relation unexplained. This strong explanatory argument harks back to Leibniz's argument that if we could enter into our bodies like we enter a windmill, we'd see just figures and motions—not anything by which to explain a perception.[23] The two differ too much here to be the same.

The last argument is perhaps the strongest, for reasons Levine gives above.[24] But the best reply to it is that our present inability to explain how reductions work doesn't imply that they are impossible to ever explain.[25] Nonetheless, it's safe to say that until reductionists show how to bridge the explanatory gap between consciousness and brains, any claims of their identity will continue to face an intelligibility problem. We'll suggest a dualism below that avoids both physicalism's problem with reductions and dualism's problem with causality.

But, as just noted, the main focus of this paper isn't on Churchland's hard problem, but on her easy problems concerning what neural activities are associated with consciousness. We'll turn to these problems now.

22. E.g., Levine, "On Leaving Out."
23. Leibniz, "Monadology."
24. Also see Jones, "Growing Evidence."
25. Churchland, *Touching a Nerve*, 56–60.

Reply to Churchland's Neural Dependence Objection

Let's now take a closer examination of Churchland's brain-alone hypothesis and why it doesn't threaten the existence of soul stuff. Simply stated, Churchland's objection to dualism here is that the mind depends on the brain, so they can't be radically different entities.

Nonetheless, here, Churchland overlooks the fact here that many dualisms are compatible with this neural dependence of minds on brains. Most contemporary non-Cartesian dualists hold to a naturalistic approach (without reductionism), which could be called naturalistic dualism.[26] Naturalistic dualism treats the brain as the natural seat of the soul, so the soul depends on the brain. For the naturalistic dualist, the term "soul" might refer only to (a) irreducible mental properties that are causally dependent on neural properties (e.g., weakly emergent mental properties); or to (b) an irreducible mental substance (in possession of irreducible mental properties) that strongly emerges from, and possesses causal power to act back upon, its neural properties (i.e., a species of strong emergent dualism).[27]

For option (a), John Searle's biological naturalism will suffice for illustrative purposes, wherein specialized neural properties are thought to causally realize mental properties, such as thirst sensations (like certain molecular structures realize solidity). Those properties are reducible causally but not with respect to certain conscious phenomena, such as subjectivity, unity, and qualia.[28] The trouble here is that an explanatory gap remains. How can something entirely physical produce something nonphysical? William Hasker articulates option (b) as follows: "The human mind [or soul] is produced by the human brain and is not a separate element 'added to' the brain from the outside."[29] Option (b) insists that the human brain is the "natural seat" of the human soul: without the human brain, there could be no human soul that undergoes phenomenal and non-phenomenal (information processing) events. Moreover, because the human brain is the "natural seat" of the human soul, the human soul derives certain properties

---

26. This phrase was introduced by Chalmers, "Problem of Consciousness," to name his preferred brand of dualism. I use it here because it clearly applies (in different senses) to other contemporary brands of dualism.

27. Option (a) traces all the way back to Aristotle (see LaRock, "Is Consciousness"), while option (b) is advocated by several contemporary philosophers (see Hasker, *Emergent Self*; Lowe, *Personal Agency*; LaRock, "From Biological Naturalism").

28. E.g., Searle, *Rediscovery of Mind*.

29. Hasker, *Emergent Self*, 189.

from the human brain, such as being located in space and being functionally related to the natural world. Further, option (b) is at least open to the idea that mind could be fundamental in some sense, and thus a question about how irreducible mental entities are produced is not as mysterious as standard versions of property dualism. Hence, options (a) and (b) actually entail the neural dependence of our conscious lives on the physical.[30] This shows that non-Cartesian brands of dualism (in which souls are irreducible to brains but don't exist apart from brains) are not vulnerable to Churchland's neural dependence objection.

Perhaps what Churchland has in mind when she uses the phrase "nonphysical soul" is a popular ("folk-psychological") theistic approach to soul. However, not every theistic approach is equivalent, and some formulations entail soul-brain dependence in a very detailed way. For example, consider option (c): God simply wires the human soul (an irreducible entity that has subjective and nonsubjective properties) to the human brain, so to speak; a consequence of that wiring process is that the human soul is dependent on the human brain in a very detailed way in this life. Like (b), this is strong emergence, inexplicable by physical science. Now, option (c) might be an actual nonstarter for those who reject theism, including some dualists committed to option (a). Granted. Our point here is modest. We only mean to suggest that option (c) illustrates how some theistically minded dualists have postulated neural dependence as a core theoretical entity. And this observation aligns with a core theoretical entity of Churchland's hypothesis, namely, neural dependence.

Another non-Cartesian dualist option with a rather different view of neural dependence is (d): the mind is seated in the brain's electromagnetic (EM) field.[31] This is our own dualist field theory (DFT). It avoids reducing minds to neuroscience's observable electrical activity by treating minds as the underlying reality of this electrical activity beyond neuroscience's descriptions of it. We access our mental activity directly while accessing neural

---

30. Moreover, option (b) possesses the explanatory power needed to address Jaegwon Kim's famous pairing relations objection to Cartesian dualism. Also, entity dualism entails property dualism, but the reverse does not follow. It's also important to note that some non-Cartesian dualists, like Alvin Plantinga and J. P. Moreland, do think souls can exist apart from bodies.

31. Jones and LaRock, "From Murphy's Christian Physicalism." Field theories of mind have been held by renowned thinkers like Kohler, Libet, Eccles, and Popper (see Jones, "Electromagnetic-Field Theories of Mind," for references). They draw on considerable experimental evidence, withstand past criticisms, and help avoid neuroscience's issues in explaining the mind's consciousness, unity, and causality.

matter quite indirectly through instruments, reflected light, etc. Since we therefore cannot know what brain matter is really like beyond perceptions of it, for all we do know, this underlying reality could be conscious.[32]

If all matter-energy is treated as consciousness, this yields a nonreductive monist field theory—while treating just EM activity as conscious yields DFT where EM fields are conscious and everything else is nonconscious. The brain's sensory-processing circuitry helps generate a conscious EM field with visual images and emotions, for example. Cognitive and limbic processing yields a conscious, intelligent field—a mind. This conscious EM field is a simple, unified substance, unlike the separate neurons that generate it. For the waves comprising it reach across space as a continuous whole.

These conscious fields exert EM forces which interact with the neurons that generate them. This yields mind-brain interactions.[33] Here, the conscious activity has its own subjective, qualitative dynamics apart from the blind mechanics of physical science. This is evident when we weigh moral choices or even choose which foods taste best. In DFT, consciousness and its causality are thus necessarily irreducible to the physical science.[34]

DFT's account of neural dependence both resembles and differs from other dualisms. First, in DFT, minds depend on brains in that the brain generates the conscious EM field and helps shape its conscious content (e.g., visual images). But unlike in (a), minds act back on brains—and with dynamics irreducible to neural dynamics.[35] Second, DFT also rejects (a) and (c)'s claim that consciousness emerges from brain activity that is nonconscious. Instead, the mind's overall consciousness arises when the neural EM field joins the small-scale consciousness in the myriad neuroelectrical activities of separate cells into a simple, unified whole reaching across overall circuitries.[36] So, while there's no single place in brains where informa-

---

32. Cf. Strawson, "Realistic Monism."

33. See Jones and LaRock, "From Murphy's Christian Physicalism," for experimental evidence for this account of mental unity and causality.

34. This DFT is a modified form of Lowe's non-Cartesian substance dualism (NCSD) (Jones and LaRock, "From Murphy's Christian Physicalism"). DFT addresses two issues Lowe wasn't clear about. First, Lowe treated subjects as unified, simple substances but wasn't clear on how subjects come to be this way. Second, Lowe insisted that subjects lack forces and energy, but wasn't clear on how the conscious purposes of subjects affect bodily behavior without any forces or energy transfers. Treating subjects as the underlying reality of unified, simple neural EM energy fields thus helps clarify Lowe's NCSD.

35. LaRock and Jones, "How Subjects Can Emerge"; Jones and LaRock, "From Murphy's Christian Physicalism."

36. In DFT, consciousness doesn't mysteriously pop into existence from what lacks

tion processing converges,[37] there is a single field that unifies consciousness together. To summarize, DFT avoids some other dualisms' claims that consciousness emerges from nonconscious brains and has no causal dynamics apart from brains. DFT is emergent here in that consciousness and its dynamics aren't explicable by natural science, as we'll see.

DFT's interpretation of neural dependence differs not only from that of the other dualisms above (as just explained), but also from that of Churchland. While minds do depend on brains in DFT, they do so in ontologically and causally irreducible ways. To start with, brains alone don't account for behavior in DFT. As already noted, mental causality brings subjective, qualitative dynamics to behavior. In contrast, Churchland's reductionism doesn't explain how neuronal circuits alone can have subjective, qualitative dynamics (e.g., choosing which food tastes best or which face looks prettier). Also, DFT rejects her claim that brains alone exist. This reductive (or eliminative) claim leaves her unable to explain the conscious percepts, thoughts, and feelings we obviously possess. As already noted, DFT also explains how minds get their unity, while Churchland offers no explanations here. All this arguably turns the tables on her claim that experimental evidence about brains has greater consilience under her brain-alone hypothesis than under dualism.

In sum, all forms of naturalistic dualism hold that the human soul is highly dependent on the human brain in very detailed ways. Unlike some others, option (d) adds that consciousness doesn't emerge from brains that lack consciousness—and that the soul has its own causal dynamics irreducible to the brain's dynamics. A broader theoretical implication of all the naturalistic dualisms above is that we would expect to discover highly detailed physical correlates upon which our phenomenal and non-phenomenal lives depend. Not surprisingly, some dualists these days are, in fact, interested in discovering those highly detailed physical correlates for the sake of developing a testable theory.[38] Thus, whatever Churchland might mean by a "nonphysical soul," one thing is clear about the issue of neural

---

consciousness, as in some other dualisms. Instead, consciousness is the underlying reality of fundamental electromagnetic energy fields (beyond what we observe of them via electrodes and other instruments). Yet only in brains is consciousness organized to form images, thoughts, and overall minds.

37. Zeki, "Disunity of Consciousness."

38. For example, see LaRock, "Disambiguation, Binding"; LaRock, "From Biological Naturalism"; LaRock and Jones, "How Subjects Can Emerge"; LaRock et al., "Strong Emergence Hypothesis"; Jones and LaRock, "From Murphy's Christian Physicalism."

dependence: over the past 2400 years, very few, if any, noteworthy dualists have denied that the "soul" causally depends in a very detailed way on the physical. This dualism is, of course, compatible with souls having their own causal dynamics and interacting with brains.[39]

Neural Dependence: Hard vs. Easy Cases

Churchland might push back on grounds that, so far, our response to the neural dependence objection to dualism has not addressed any of the hard cases, such as those involving impairments to the self, such as amnesia and blindsight. One might claim that these cases reveal key properties of consciousness that are dependent upon and probably explainable in terms of our neural hardware without remainder. We think these key properties of consciousness boil down to easy problems of consciousness (which are really just problems about physical structures and functions associated with consciousness). Philosophers point out here that the former concerns hard problems (about experience) but the latter concerns easy problems (about functions and their related structures). For example, amnesia concerns problems about information encoding, storage, and access, but not the harder problem of subjective experience. When a computer begins to lose its capacity to encode, store, and access information, we do not thereby conclude that it has begun to lose its subjective experience. It never had subjective experience. So why would we ever conclude that persons are subjects of experience on the basis of encoding, storing, and accessing information? Perhaps we would not, unless we've already conflated the hard problem with one or more of the easy problems of consciousness. Also, none of the specific data surrounding amnesia cases entail the absence of a subjective point of view. It's just that one's experience of being a subject is truncated in time because the physical structures responsible for encoding, storing, and accessing information have undergone damage. One could still know what it is like to be a subject of experience, if only over brief periods of time.[40]

In the case of blindsight, one could draw a distinction between information processing versus phenomenal experience.[41] Information processing refers to a system's capacity to encode and react to information in the

---

39. LaRock, "Aristotle and Agent-Directed Neuroplasticity"; LaRock and Jones, "How Subjects Can Emerge"; Jones and LaRock, "From Murphy's Christian Physicalism."
40. LaRock and Collins, "Saving Our Souls."
41. See Flanagan, *Consciousness Rediscovered*; Holt, *Blindsight and Nature of Consciousness*.

natural world. Information processing, however, does not require phenomenal experience. Something as simple as a motion detector on a security system engages in information processing. Our brains, too, have evolved several specialized subsystems that engage in information processing of the stimuli they distinguish, including the capacity to encode motion (e.g., in visual area 5 [V5]). Yet a subject cannot be phenomenally aware of motion (or of other stimuli) without information processing. The relation is asymmetric: phenomenal experience requires information processing, but the reverse does not hold.[42] This suggests that while blindsight patients are still engaged in information processing of certain stimuli; they're just not phenomenally aware of the stimuli they process and differentiate.[43]

While blindsight suggests that brains can fully explain some cognitive responses, there is currently no evidence that brains alone can explain higher cognition, including creative imagination.

In any case, the data surrounding neural dependence map elegantly onto dualist options (b), (c), and (d) above: human subjects undergo both phenomenal and non-phenomenal events; thus, some of what we do (as embodied subjects) is likely influenced by and dependent on the non-phenomenal (information processing) events that we undergo via our brains. Contrary to Churchland's inference above, the data surrounding neural dependence do not have greater consilience under the brain-alone hypothesis.

Reply to Churchland's Split-Brain Objection

Churchland could push back in another way. She could suggest that split-brain phenomena run counter to a subject (or self or soul) that's irreducible to the brain. If the brain can split, but the soul cannot, then don't split brains challenge the existence of soul stuff? In fact, Churchland maintains that split-brain results "were powerful support for the hypothesis that mental states are in fact states of the physical brain itself, not states of a nonphysical soul."[44] However, our DFT in fact doesn't assume the soul is indivisible, for severing connections between the hemispheres blocks the flow of electrical currents and their highly localized fields between hemispheres. This can

---

42. Holt, *Blindsight and Nature of Consciousness*; see also Chalmers, "Problem of Consciousness"; LaRock, "Aristotle and Agent-Directed Neuroplasticity"; LaRock and Collins, "Saving Our Souls."

43. See also Persuh et al., "Working Memory and Consciousness."

44. Churchland, *Touching a Nerve*, 50.

yield two separate subjects in DFT—which aligns with behavioral evidence (such as the battling of opposing hands) in these patients. So split brains don't undermine DFT but help illuminate its explanatory power as well. (The preceding suggestion does not settle the matter, for there are competing explanations on this issue, such as the possibility that what breaks down is access consciousness rather than subject or phenomenal consciousness.)

Reply to Churchland's Purported Common Link

Further, recall Churchland's claim that the common link to, or neural correlate of, consciousness is the synchronous activations of widely distributed neurons: "The linkages, it is thought, may consist in synchrony in the activities of populations of neurons."[45] However, extensive data show that neuronal synchronization is present (and actually strengthens) in the relevant striate and extra-striate regions of the primary sensory networks when an animal is rendered unconscious by means of anesthesia.[46] Furthermore, posterior-to-anterior processing of the primary sensory networks is actually preserved during anesthetic-induced unconsciousness in humans[47] and nonhuman animals.[48] Not only do these data punch squarely against Churchland's purported common link, but they also challenge recent related hypotheses grounded in the claim that neuronal synchrony plus amplification (via attention and/or some other mechanism) could count as the distinctive correlate of consciousness. For example, recent advocates of this claim include Carruthers, Dehaene, Levy, and Prinz.[49] By implication, this widely purported common link (neuronal synchrony) cannot be the unique (or distinctive) correlate of consciousness.[50]

While several more objections to her view of common links exist,[51] we'll focus on a foundational one that directly challenges the connectionist

---

45. Churchland, *Touching a Nerve*, 147.

46. Bola et al., "Loss of Consciousness"; Hudetz, "Suppressing Consciousness"; Hudetz, "Feedback Suppression"; Imas et al. 2005; Mashour, "Cognitive Unbinding"; Mashour, "Consciousness, Anesthesia."

47. Ku et al., "Preferential Inhibition"; Mashour, "Cognitive Unbinding"; Mashour, "Consciousness, Anesthesia."

48. Imas et al., "Volatile Anesthetics Disrupt."

49. Carruthers, *Centered Mind*; Dehaene, *Consciousness and the Brain*; Levy, *Consciousness and Moral Responsibility*; Prinz, *Conscious Brain*.

50. LaRock, "Hard Problems."

51. See LaRock, "Why Neural Synchrony Fails"; LaRock, "Disambiguation, Binding";

assumption of her hypothesis. Churchland's common link to consciousness assumes that spatial connections (synapses) and temporal connections (synchronous activations) exist between all relevant neuronal subassemblies. However, current data suggest otherwise: the properties of an object are not only distributed in space, owing to a lack of direct anatomical links between processing sites,[52] but they are "distributed in time" as well, owing to a lack of temporal connections between processing sites.[53] For example, while a subject is exposed to an object, Zeki and colleagues have systematically observed a temporal gap as great as eighty milliseconds between visual processing subsystems V4 and V5. In effect, the current evidence reveals an asynchronous relation between geographically separate processing sites—an observable datum that cuts directly against Churchland's (and many other scholars') purported common link to, or neural correlate of, consciousness.[54]

Here, again, DFT may turn the tables on Churchland's claim that experimental evidence has greater consilience under her brain-alone hypothesis than under dualism. For DFT explains how perceptions and other kinds of conscious activities are unified, while (as just explained) her synchronic approach doesn't. In DFT, the brain's single, continuous EM field in diffuse currents can unify numerous dispersed circuits to produce a single unified consciousness, even where these circuits don't synapse with each other. The neural EM field is thus a better candidate for the neural correlate of consciousness (i.e., unified consciousness) than her candidate of neural

---

LaRock, "Philosophical Implications"; LaRock and Jones, "How Subjects Can Emerge"; Jones and LaRock, "From Murphy's Christian Physicalism."

52. While there are no direct anatomical links between brain areas, this claim cannot be generalized. Certain regions of the brain are anatomically linked whereas others are not as connectionism assumes; as explained below, there are often diffuse ion currents (with their strong internal fields) among these circuitries (in, for example, cortical modules), as our field approach assumes.

53. Zeki, "Disunity of Consciousness," 215; Zeki, "Massively Asynchronous, Parallel Brain"; LaRock, "Disambiguation, Binding"; LaRock, "Philosophical Implications"; LaRock et al., "Strong Emergence Hypothesis."

54. It might be argued that while no single frequency of synchronized activity links geographically separate processing sites, various frequencies couple together to do so, as when theta (or alpha and beta) frequencies help control gamma frequency activities in memory, attention, and working memory (Buszáki, *Rhythms of the Brain*). But such "cross-frequency coupling" just serves to reinforce the neural EM fields that do the actual binding (Jones, "Growing Evidence"). Indeed, it's hard to see how synchronic or coherent EM frequencies alone could ever unify consciousness. One of several reasons is that, given the sheer numbers of brains on earth, it's highly likely their EM frequencies will often cohere—yet there's no evidence that they actually share any unified consciousness.

synchrony. Experimental evidence for this conclusion comes from Koch et al.[55] They argue that locally activated EEGs track conscious perceptions across brains better than other events such as synchrony. This EEG evidence correlates unified perceptions with local neuroelectrical fields.

Reply to Churchland's Naturalist Account of Agency

As we observed earlier, Churchland also maintains that if a choice could be made without reference to one's brain (and thus without reference to the causal basis of one's character), "the choice would be so bizarre, so 'out of the blue' as to raise the question of whether it was a real choice at all."[56] In transitive form, for example, if brains cause actions, and actions cause characters, then brains cause characters. We think her linear, deterministic approach to agency raises deeper puzzles in clinical neuropsychiatry about a subject's (or self's) capacity to rewire its brain (or to engage in subject-directed neuroplasticity), say, in the case of stroke, OCD, or certain other pathologies. We do not think the brain-alone hypothesis can adequately accommodate such feats, though the brain is most certainly involved in them. According to our (strong) emergent subject hypothesis (ESH), when a brain's EM field is activated, an ontologically irreducible (and simple) subject emerges and possesses causal power (in its own right) to influence the structures and functions of its brain.

It's important to note that our rejection above of weakly emergent consciousness doesn't conflict with our acceptance of a strongly emergent subject. The former tries to explain the rise of the conscious subject and its causality in terms of physical science (as in the first kind of naturalistic dualism discussed earlier). The latter doesn't try to explain the conscious subject and its causality in terms of physical science. Instead, this subject intelligibly arises with its own dynamics from simpler forms of consciousness in neural activities engaged in perception, emotion, memory, etc.[57] ESH is a species of non-Cartesian substance dualism. Is there empirical evidence to support ESH with respect to mental causation, thereby challenging Churchland's claim that exceptions to the brain-alone hypothesis are bizarre? There is growing evidence along these lines from recent neuroplasticity studies.

55. Koch et al., "Neural Correlates of Consciousness."
56. Churchland, "Moral Decision-Making," 7; see also Churchland, *Touching a Nerve*, 12.
57. LaRock and Jones, "How Subjects Can Emerge"; Jones and LaRock, "From Murphy's Christian Physicalism"; LaRock, "Philosophical Implications"; LaRock, "From Biological Naturalism"; LaRock et al., "Strong Emergence Hypothesis."

Consider the key role that modified constraint-induced movement therapy (CIMT) can play in the aftermath of severe cerebral strokes. This species of therapy involves constraining the intact arm so that the patient has to use the paretic arm. When this occurs, a self is carrying out an operation that requires considerable mental effort.[58] Abundant evidence suggests that patients who engage in such cognitive (or subject-directed) behavioral therapy are actually stronger after the stroke event.[59] For example, severe cardiac strokes can cause significant neurological damage in a part of one of the motor cortices. If severe damage occurs in the right motor cortex, immobility on the left side of the body usually follows. But immobility of this sort is not necessarily permanent. Some stroke patients can, through sustained conscious effort, rewire adjacent neural areas in the same motor cortex, enabling them to execute (overt) actions prior to the stroke event, say, moving one's left arm. In most stroke cases, the conscious subject usually causes adjacent neural wiring in the motor cortex impacted by the stroke. However, there are rare cases of stroke patients with severe right motor cortical damage who have been known to recruit and rewire neural areas in their left motor cortex. When this unusual form of neuroplasticity occurs, the left motor cortex is used not only for right-sided movements but for left-sided movements as well.

The initial stages of this unusual form of subject-directed neuroplasticity can create a strange phenomenal experience for the subject. For example, a patient described the phenomenology of the initial stages of the rewiring process as involving a strange battle between her left and right thumbs. While trying to exercise her left thumb, the patient would experience her right thumb moving along with her left thumb in an almost mirrorlike fashion. She experienced her consciously directed left thumb movements in tandem with her nonconsciously directed right thumb movements. That strange experience occurred because, in the early stages of the subject-directed neural rewiring process, her conscious effort to bring about left thumb movements had recruited some neurons in the left motor cortex that were normally used to carry out right thumb movements. Through sustained conscious effort, she eventually carved out new neural pathways in her left motor cortex for left-sided movements that did not involve right-sided interference. Through sheer will power this patient totally defied her doctors' prognosis; she was told that she would never be able to move her left side, owing to the magnitude of

58. LaRock et al., "Strong Emergence Hypothesis."
59. Yadav et al., "Efficacy of Modified Constraint."

neurological damage in her right motor cortex. These empirical data underscore the power of subject-directed neuroplasticity and thus how "plastic or adaptable" the brain can be in relation to the conscious voluntary power of a subject.[60] This subject-directed plasticity counters Churchland's brain-alone hypothesis. Our view here is a sensible account of this phenomenon, rather than being bizarre, as she claims.

More recently, LaRock et al. advocate a strong emergence hypothesis and argue on logical and empirical grounds that when a subject (or self) is engaged in CIMT, and other tasks that require considerable mental effort, the subject is causing its brain to change (i.e., subject-directed neuroplasticity).[61] Subject-directed neuroplasticity has also been deployed to effectively treat obsessive-compulsive disorders, addiction disorders, attention disorders, and to preempt the onset of full-blown seizures.[62]

The philosophical upshot is that we possess causal power to reorganize our neural wetware. Having this causal power not only increases the survival value of subjects in possession of it, but the associated empirical evidence above runs directly counter to Churchland's deterministic, brain-alone hypothesis. By implication, our emergent subject hypothesis provides a better fit of this data than materialism in general and Churchland's brain-alone hypothesis in particular. We conclude that dualism is not floundering but quite feasible compared to Churchland's naturalism today. The evidence of subject-directed neuroplasticity works hand in hand with DFT and ESH to counter Churchland's brain-alone hypothesis and its implication that mental causation is merely neural causation.

DFT can go further and turn the tables here on Churchland's brain-alone hypothesis in two ways. First, her anti-dualist, brain-alone hypothesis relies partly on the argument that souls lack causal powers (which she calls "oompf") to affect brains.[63] Yet DFT counters this argument by showing how souls can be the underlying nature of the neural EM field which has considerable causal powers in brains. Second, her hypothesis fails to establish that only brains exist—after all, we exist. As argued above, we know our own consciousness exists, and it's not clear how consciousness and its

---

60. Schwartz and Gladding, *You Are Not Your Brain*, 37–38; LaRock, "From Biological Naturalism."

61. LaRock et al., "Strong Emergence Hypothesis."

62. LaRock et a., "Strong Emergence Hypothesis"; LaRock, "From Biological Naturalism"; LaRock, "Aristotle and Agent-Directed Neuroplasticity."

63. Churchland, *Touching a Nerve*, 51.

causality can be nothing but brain activity as her hypothesis claims. In contrast, DFT readily explains consciousness and its causality.

Implications for Free Will and Ethics

Churchland's naturalism (only brain stuff) raises issues surrounding the free will of selves (which is another example of the self's powers of agency). Our field theories may be able to avoid such issues. We begin with a brief description of three standard theories of free will. In hard determinism, our choices are determined, so we can't choose otherwise than we actually did, as free will requires. In indeterminism (or libertarianism), our choices aren't determined (at least not by physical causes), so we have free will. We're free to act as we choose (which involves liberty), and we do so without determinism (which requires indeterminism). In soft determinism, our choices are both determined and free, for freedom is self-determinism (autonomy). Only in this view are free will and determinism compatible.

Churchland sees indeterminism's claim that free will requires indeterminism as being irrelevant to practical life. She embraces soft determinism's claim that free will is self-determined instead of being externally determined or not determined at all. This is the ordinary sense of free will, which is used in law courts and addresses different sorts of diminished self-control.[64]

But this free will may be illusory, given her naturalist view that selves (or minds) are just brains. This naturalist view arguably leaves us as mere puppets of the neurobiological forces controlling brains. We don't control these or any other laws of nature, so we don't really control ourselves—we're just puppets of our neurons, mistakenly thinking we're free. Further, if we're determined by neurobiological forces, then arguably we aren't free to do otherwise than we do—we're locked into what we do and can't be held responsible for doing otherwise. Unfortunately, Churchland doesn't reply to these standard anti-free will arguments.

Our DFT can also adopt soft determinism, yet in ways that may be able to avoid the preceding issues. To start with, we base autonomy on top-down causation involving emergent causality based around qualia that transcends physical science. We thus avoid Churchland's causal reductionism, which arguably renders us into puppets of neurobiological forces. Furthermore, following Kane's ideas on free will,[65] we combine elements of soft determinism

---

64. Churchland, *Touching a Nerve*, 178.
65. Kane, *Significance of Free Will*.

and indeterminism, (which involves altering standard soft determinism). We allow for indeterminism in top-down causation at quantum levels, which avoids deterministic claims that we couldn't have acted otherwise.[66] Note that this indeterminism doesn't make our choices erratic, it just helps randomly create options for our more deliberate levels of thinking to draw upon. In these ways, we arguably avoid Churchland's standard free will problems.

Moreover, in our DFT, emotions and other qualia play a vital role in soft determinism's core idea of autonomy. But Churchland fails to account for qualia in terms of neural information processing. She thus fails to account for the crucial role of emotions in free will. What is this role of emotions? To start with, our choices involve weighing our inner feelings in ways that transcend the principles of neural networks. We construct our own autonomous goals in the form of ideals and values imbued with strong feelings. Through these feelings, the will draws its controlling power from the primal emotional powers it controls, much like power steering.[67] These passionate principles bring their own unfolding logics to our creative imaginations, a logic of ideas. New ideologies, art forms, etc. arise with lives of their own. They harness the external forces that partly create them, transforming them into new directions. This is the vital role of our qualia's inner life in free will. Here, our wills are autonomous, not puppets of neurobiological forces. Without our qualia, we'd be vegetative and robotic, devoid of feelings and purposes. This is, in effect, what we become under Churchland's brain-alone hypothesis.

The analyses above have ethical implications. To start with, we have argued that Churchland's reductionism fails to account for the mind's qualia and free will. Her naturalism (in which selves are brains) is thus an impoverished account of human life. We also argued that DFT is, by contrast, causally and ontologically nonreductive. Its naturalism (in which minds merely depend on brains) can thus readily account for the mind's qualia and free will.

By implication, there are arguably two ways in which DFT's naturalism can account for the value of human life.

First, by doing justice to qualia, DFT arguably does justice to the value of human life from the hedonistic perspective. Here only feelings such as pleasure and happiness are of moral value. This applies to all sentient life.

---

66. See Jones and LaRock, "From Murphy's Christian Physicalism," on all this.
67. Lorenz, *On Aggression* and *Behind the Mirror*.

In contrast, a purely robotic universe would be devoid of qualia and would thus lack any value.

Second, by doing justice to human free will, DFT arguably does justice to the value of human life from the perspective of various metaethical theories of value. For example, one familiar perspective here is that humans are free, responsible beings who can plan their lives—so they should be left alone to do just that. This arguably gives them more value than robots who do not evaluate ultimate values, nor plan their lives accordingly, but instead derive their ultimate purposes from human's qualia and plans.

III. CONCLUSION

Churchland's thesis is that the self (which typically involves free will and consciousness) is nothing but the brain. She argues here that neuroscience can explain the self better than dualism. For, counter to dualism, the self is dependent upon neural activities—as shown by its various impairments, its unified experiences, and its powers of agency.

We have tried to turn the tables on Churchland with three arguments: (1) She fails to explain the self due to the easy problems and by extension the hard problem as well. (2) Our new non-Cartesian substance dualism explains all the dependencies she points to. (3) Our dualism avoids her problematic reductionist accounts of qualia and free will—and traditional dualism's problematic account of mental causality. We conclude that this dualism may avoid traditional physicalism's problems and traditional dualism's problems. These arguments have ethical implications. They imply that dualism can account for two sources of moral value in human life—our qualia and free will—that reductionism fails to account for.

BIBLIOGRAPHY

Bola, Michal, et al. "Loss of Consciousness Is Related to Hyper-Correlated Gamma-Band Activity in Anesthetized Macaques and Sleeping Humans." *NeuroImage* 167 (2018) 130–42.

Buszáki, György. *Rhythms of the Brain*. Oxford: Oxford University Press, 2006.

Carruthers, Peter. *The Centered Mind: What the Science of Working Memory Shows Us about the Nature of Human Thought*. Oxford: Oxford University Press, 2015.

Chalmers, David J. *The Conscious Mind: In Search of a Fundamental Theory*. Philosophy of Mind. Oxford: Oxford University Press, 1996.

———. "Facing Up to the Problem of Consciousness." *Journal of Consciousness Studies* 2 (1995) 200–219.

Churchland, Patricia S. "Moral Decision-Making and the Brain." In *Neuroethics: Defining the Issues in Theory, Practice and Policy*, edited by Judy Illes, 3–16. Oxford: Oxford University Press, 2006.

———. *Neurophilosophy: Toward a Unified Science of the Mind-Brain*. Cambridge, MA: MIT Press, 1996.

———. *Touching a Nerve: The Self as Brain*. Illustrated ed. New York: Norton, 2013.

Dehaene, Stanislas. *Consciousness and the Brain: Deciphering How the Brain Codes Our Thoughts*. New York: Penguin, 2014.

Flanagan, Owen. *Consciousness Rediscovered*. Cambridge, MA: MIT Press, 1992.

Hasker, William. *The Emergent Self*. Cornell Studies in the Philosophy of Religion. New York: Cornell University Press, 1999.

Holt, Jason. *Blindsight and the Nature of Consciousness*. New York: Broadview, 2003.

Hudetz, Anthony G. "Feedback Suppression in Anesthesia: Is It Reversible?" *Consciousness and Cognition* 18 (2009) 1079–81.

———. "Suppressing Consciousness: Mechanisms of General Anesthesia." *Seminars in Anesthesia* 25 (2006) 196–204.

Imas, Olga A., et al. "Volatile Anesthetics Disrupt Frontal-Posterior Recurrent Information Transfer at Gamma Frequencies in Rat." *Neuroscience Letters* 387 (2005) 145–50.

Jackson, Frank. "What Mary Didn't Know." *Journal of Philosophy* 83 (1986) 291–95.

Jones, Mostyn W. "Avoiding Perennial Mind-Body Problems." *Journal of Consciousness Studies* 23 (2016) 111–33.

———. "Electromagnetic-Field Theories of Mind." *Journal of Consciousness Studies* 20 (2013) 124–49.

———. "Growing Evidence That Perceptual Qualia Are Neuroelectrical Not Computational." *Journal of Consciousness Studies* 26 (2019) 89–116.

Jones, Mostyn, and Eric LaRock. "From Murphy's Christian Physicalism to Lowe's Dualism." *TheoLogica* 5 (2021). https://doi.org/10.14428/thl.v5i2.56273.

Kane, Robert. *The Significance of Free Will*. Oxford: Oxford University Press, 1996.

Koch, Christof, et al. "Neural Correlates of Consciousness: Progress and Problems." *Nature Reviews Neuroscience* 17 (2016) 307–21.

Ku, Seung-Woo, et al. "Preferential Inhibition of Frontal-to-Parietal Feedback Connectivity Is a Neurophysiologic Correlate of General Anesthesia in Surgical Patients." *PLoS ONE* 6 (2011) e25155.

LaRock, Eric. "Aristotle and Agent-Directed Neuroplasticity." *International Philosophical Quarterly* 53 (2013) 385–408.

———. "Disambiguation, Binding, and the Unity of Visual Consciousness." *International Society for Theoretical Psychology* 17 (2007) 747–77.

———. "From Biological Naturalism to Emergent Subject Dualism." *Philosophia Christi* 15 (2013) 97–118.

———. "Hard Problems of Unified Experience from the Perspective of Neuroscience." In *Consciousness and the Ontology of Properties*, edited by Mihretu P. Guta, 223–40. New York: Routledge, 2019.

———. "Is Consciousness Really a Brain Process?" *International Philosophical Quarterly* 48 (2008) 201–29.

———. "The Philosophical Implications of Awareness during General Anesthesia." In *Consciousness, Awareness, and Anesthesia*, edited by George A. Mashour, 233–51. Cambridge: Cambridge University Press, 2010.

———. "Why Neural Synchrony Fails to Explain the Unity of Consciousness." *Behavior and Philosophy* 34 (2006) 39–58.

LaRock, Eric, and Robin Collins. "Saving Our Souls from Materialism." In *Neuroscience and the Soul: The Human Person in Philosophy, Science, and Theology*, edited by Thomas M. Crisp et al., 137–46. Grand Rapids: Eerdmans, 2016.

LaRock, Eric, and Mostyn Jones. "How Subjects Can Emerge from Neurons." *Process Studies* 48 (2019) 40–58.

LaRock, Eric, et al. "A Strong Emergence Hypothesis of Conscious Integration and Neural Rewiring." *International Philosophical Quarterly* 60 (2020) 97–115.

Leibniz, Gottfried. "Monadology." In *Philosophical Writings*, edited by G. H. R. Parkinson, translated by Mary Morris, 179–94. Everyman's University Library. London: Dent and Sons, 1973.

Levine, Joseph. "On Leaving Out What It's Like." In *Consciousness: Psychological and Philosophical Essays*, edited by Martin Davies and Glyn W. Humphreys, 543–57. Readings in Mind & Language. Oxford: Blackwell, 1993.

Levy, Neil. *Consciousness and Moral Responsibility*. Oxford: Oxford University Press, 2014.

Lowe, E. J. *Personal Agency: The Metaphysics of Mind and Action*. Oxford: Oxford University Press, 2008.

Lorenz, Konrad. *Behind the Mirror*. London: Methuen, 1977.

———. *On Aggression*. New York: Harcourt Brace and World, 1966.

Mashour, George A. "Cognitive Unbinding: A Neuroscientific Paradigm of General Anesthesia and Related States of Unconsciousness." *Neuroscience and Behavioral Reviews* 37 (2013a) 2751–59.

———. "Consciousness, Anesthesia, and Neural Synchrony." *Anesthesiology* 119 (2013b) 7–9.

Mashour, George A., and Eric LaRock. "Inverse Zombies, Anesthesia Awareness, and the Hard Problem of Unconsciousness." *Consciousness and Cognition* 17 (2008) 1163–68.

Persuh, Marjan, et al. "Working Memory and Consciousness: The Current State of Play." *Frontiers in Human Neuroscience* 12 (2018). https://doi.org/10.3389/fnhum.2018.00078.

Prinz, Jesse. *The Conscious Brain: How Attention Engenders Experience*. Philosophy of Mind. Oxford: Oxford University Press, 2012.

Putnam, Hillary. "The Nature of Mental States." In *Art, Mind, and Religion*, edited by W. H. Capitan and D. D. Merrill. Pittsburgh: University of Pittsburgh Press, 1967.

Schwartz, Jeffrey M., and Rebecca Gladding. *You Are Not Your Brain: The 4-Step Solution for Changing Bad Habits, Ending Unhealthy Thinking, and Taking Control of Your Life*. New York: Penguin, 2011.

Searle, John R. *The Rediscovery of the Mind*. Representation and Mind. Cambridge, MA: MIT Press, 1992.

Strawson, Galen. "Realistic Monism: Why Physicalism Entails Panpsychism." *Journal of Consciousness Studies* 13 (2006) 3–31.

Yadav, Raj K., et al. "Efficacy of Modified Constraint Induced Movement Therapy in the Treatment of Hemiparetic Upper Limb in Stroke Patients: A Randomized Controlled Trial." *Journal of Clinical Diagnostic Research* 11 (2016) YC01–YC05. doi: 10.7860/JCDR/2016/23468.8899.

Zeki, Semir. "The Disunity of Consciousness." *Trends in Cognitive Sciences* 7 (2003) 214–18.

———. "A Massively Asynchronous, Parallel Brain." *Philosophical Transactions of the Royal Society B* 370 (2015) 1–14. https://doi.org/10.1098/rstb.2014.0174.

5

Does Personhood Come in Degrees?

Mihretu P. Guta

INTRODUCTION

What is a person? Let's call this the personhood question (P-question, hereafter). We run into the P-question both in philosophical as well as nonphilosophical circles.[1] The issues that come up in philosophical circle regarding the P-question are both multifaceted and known for stirring up spirited debate compared to the ones in nonphilosophical circles.[2] In this regard, the philosophical discussions set the tone for other disciplines as they make their own attempts in their own ways to work through the P-question. As a matter of fact, the present volume reinforces my point in the sense of demonstrating why it is accurate to think that bioethical issues are not immune to philosophical assumptions. It is in this spirit that I set out to advance my discussion.

The controversies associated with the P-question begin with the ambiguity that underlies the term "person." That is, the term "person" is used to refer to different things. For example, we can answer the P-question in

---

1. Examples of the nonmainstream philosophical circles where issues related to personhood are discussed include applied ethics, of which bioethics takes a center stage; cognitive psychology; cognitive neuroscience; and the social sciences (e.g., anthropology).

2. For present purposes, I am interested only in philosophical questions.

relation to nonhuman entities that are taken to be persons—God, demons, and angles (as widely held in Christianity). We can also answer the P-question in relation to human beings like you and me because we, too, are persons. Similarly, one could answer the P-question in relation to higher-level animals such as apes and dolphins because they are said to qualify as persons. In the face of ever-growing technological advances, discussions are already underway to answer the P-question in relation to artefacts such as robots and digital computers, corporations as well as extra-terrestrial beings (if there are any such things).[3] Whenever philosophers talk about something being a person, they often have in mind certain sorts of psychological properties such as self-consciousness and others like it to distinguish a person from a nonperson. However, as we shall see, such personhood establishing criteria are highly disputed.

Assuming that the term "person" has a wide range of applications, two conditions must be satisfied for the supposed application in question to work: (1) the various entities that are said to be persons must share some features in common and (2) the entities in question must be suitable to make up a natural set. As I understand it, a set is said to be natural just in case members of the set in question share some features in common. Here an example would be a set of red objects: {red apple, red T-shirt, red car, red flag . . .}[4]

By contrast, a set is said to be contrived just in case members of a set in question share no features in common. An example of such a set would be an amalgamation of haphazardly put together objects: {a car, President Joe Biden, Mars, a rock, an apple, the 2022 World Cup . . .}

It could be said that the P-question can be answered in light of both (1) and (2). But unfortunately, there does not seem to be a promising way to secure an answer for the P-question. I say this because, as they stand, (1)

---

3. An external reviewer wondered that the ambiguity attributed to the term "person" could be understood as analogical predication as discussed in Aristotle and Aquinas. In that case, we can ask whether the term "person" is ambiguous, or is it analogical with some core meaning that applies in various cases. My own take is that the term "person" can be understood as ambiguous as well as analogical when we evaluate it in different contexts. Due to space limitations, I won't belabor this point. For an excellent discussion on analogical predication, see Bonevac, "Two Theories." On personhood-related matters, see further Guta, "Two Natures"; Van Inwagen and Zimmerman, *Persons*, chs. 12–15; Olson, "Metaphysics of Transhumanism," ch. 12; Miller, *Critiquing Transhumanism*; Puccetti, *Persons*; DeGrazia, "On Question of Personhood," ch. 3; Teichman, "Definition of Person."

4. Notice that the objects of this set need not be the same kind or similar to each other in every way insofar as they share similarity in at least one respect. In this example, the objects share the property of being red in common.

and (2) raise incredibly complex metaphysical/ontological issues that pose potentially insurmountable difficulties to tackle. For example, (1) implies that the different entities described as persons can be shown to have some common feature(s). However, here one faces an uphill battle. To see the problem here, one only needs to make note of how metaphysically the sense in which say, God is said to be a person is radically different from the sense in which a computer or corporations are said to be persons. Similarly, the sense in which humans are said to be persons is radically different from the sense in which say, dolphins are said to be persons.

If one were to work out the details of what it would take to satisfy condition (1), then one would have to take up the task of establishing the ontology of a being like God and demonstrate how it is similar and dissimilar to that of the ontology of artifacts like computers as well as the ontology of social/conventional beings such as corporations and vice versa.[5] Likewise, one would have to show how the ontology of human beings is similar and dissimilar to that of the ontology of dolphins and vice versa. The fruit of such labor at the end must translate into how the term "person" applies to all the parties involved on somewhat equal ground. It is only after one is able to work out the details required of (1) that one would hope for a promising prospect to satisfying (2). In fact (2) comes with its own set of challenges, one of which concerns determining if the set consisting of all the different entities in question should be understood as a natural set or a contrived set. But determining this matter is entirely contingent on one's success in satisfying condition (1).[6] So, I conclude that, as things stand, no

---

5. For details on social ontology, see Epstein, "Social Ontology"; and on the ontology of artifacts, see Thomasson, *Ordinary Objects*.

6. Here it could be asked: Why can't we understand (1) and (2) in the words of Ludwig Wittgenstein as family resemblances? In a nutshell, this is the idea that different things despite their differences can come together under one umbrella descriptor term, implying that the entities in question share certain similarities. Wittgenstein's own widely discussed term "games" is a good case in point. There are different games, each with its own rules, but we group them all under one umbrella term, "games." Likewise, we call the different entities in question under the umbrella term "persons." Wittgenstein claims, "Consider for example the proceedings that we call 'games.' I mean board-games, card-games, ball-games, Olympic games, and so on. What is common to them all?—Don't say: 'There must be something common, or they would not be called "games"'—but look and see whether there is anything common to all.—For if you look at them you will not see something that is common to all, but similarities, relationships, and a whole series of them at that" (Wittgenstein, *Philosophical Investigations*, 31?, §66). Wittgensteinian "game" example may be said to be relevant to make sense of a functionalist conception of personhood. But I will argue that such conception of personhood is highly problematic.

univocal answer can be established for the P-question when different entities are involved in the sense discussed above.

In the rest of this chapter, my focus will be solely on the question of human personhood. More precisely: What is a human person? Let's call this the HP-question. Unlike the P-question, which as we saw is wide in scope, the HP-question is narrow in scope focusing on one kind of entity, that is, us, human beings. So, in this chapter, I use the term "person" exclusively in relation to human beings. I also use the term "personhood" to refer to qualities or properties that are responsible for being a person. Taken this way, the notion of a person and the notion of personhood are inter-definable in the sense that what a person is cannot be divorced from the property of being a person and vice versa. Although these two notions are inter-definable, in my view, there is a real (not just a mere conceptual) ontological categorial distinction that holds between them. Here I am echoing a long-standing Aristotelian tradition which draws an ontological distinction between substance and property.[7] I will argue that a human person belongs to a category of substance whereas personhood belongs to a category of property. As I understand it, a substance is a property bearer, and a property is the way a substance is.[8] In light of this, my own conception of human personhood is very much echoes that of Boethius's who describes a person as, "naturae rationabilis indiuidua substantia" or an individual nature of a rational substance.[9]

However, the sort of characterization of human personhood briefly sketched out above is deeply unpopular in some philosophical circles. For example, some contemporary analytic philosophers claim that personhood must be attributed only to those human beings who can meet certain criteria required for it. In saying this, these philosophers are strongly implying that human personhood is something that comes in degrees. That is, if this

---

So, I fail to see its relevance to motivate its application to (1) and (2).

7. In this regard, for an excellent overview and discussion on Aristotle's metaphysics, see Loux and Crisp, *Metaphysics*.

8. For details on such characterization of substance, properties, and other related matters, see Lowe, *Four-Category Ontology*, chs. 1–7; Lowe, *Possibility of Metaphysics*, chs. 5–10; Heil, *Universe*, chs. 1–5; Galluzzo and Loux, *Problem of Universals*.

9. See Boethuis, "Contra Eutychen et Nestorium," 3. I take Boethuis's conception of personhood as having its roots in the Aristotelian tradition. Aristotle's views on the nature of substance (*ousia*) and rationality (*nous*) in the *Categories* and *De Anima* may have influenced Boethuis's own thinking, which is evident in his characterization of the notion of a person.

is true, then we should embrace the idea that there is (can be) such a thing as: (a) more, or (b) less, or (c) no personhood at all. Here both the inclusive and the exclusive senses of the disjunctive operator "or" are at work. In this case, (a) and (b) taken together imply the inclusive use of a disjunctive operator "or." By contrast, in (c), the exclusive sense of "or" is implied. In this chapter, I will argue that there are excellent reasons to reject a conception of human personhood taken along the lines of (a), (b), and (c). In this case, I will examine the views of Michael Tooley, Daniel Dennett, and Peter Singer, each of whose views on human personhood strongly entails (a), (b), and (c). For these philosophers, human personhood understood along (a), (b), and (c) constitutes the best answer to the HP-question.

Alternatively, I will defend a non-degreed conception of human personhood as the best answer to the HP-question. I will develop my arguments and discussion against the backdrop of the metaphysics of powers ontology as advocated by contemporary philosophers: C. B. Martin, John Heil, and others. In this chapter, I will take some small steps in an attempt to shed some light on this important issue of human personhood. In the relevant philosophical literature, discussions on human personhood are not connected, at least in any direct manner, to the contemporary discussion on the metaphysics of dispositions or powers ontology. My essay in this chapter will remedy that missing connection without getting into the mainstream controversies on the metaphysics of dispositions.[10] The chapter is structured as follows: In section 1, I will briefly present Locke's characterizations of a person. In section 2, I will introduce and examine Tooley-Dennett-Singer's conditions on human personhood. In section 3, I will discuss the metaphysics of powers ontology. In section 4, I will respond to Tooley-Dennett-Singer's conditions on human personhood within the framework of the powers ontology. In section 5, I will conclude that the powers ontology gives us excellent reasons to reject an implausible notion of a degreed human personhood.

---

10. For details on contemporary controversies on powers or dispositions, see, e.g., N. Williams, *Powers Metaphysic*; Koons and Pickavance, *Atlas of Reality*, chs. 4–6; Groff and Greco, *Powers and Capacities*; Bird et al., *Properties, Powers and Structures*; Ellis, *Philosophy of Nature*, esp. chs. 3–5; Lowe, *Four-Category Ontology*, ch. 8; Heil, "Dispositions"; Cross, "Dispositions"; Molnar, "Are Dispositions Reducible?"; Mumford, *Dispositions*; Crane, *Dispositions*.

PART I | ONTOLOGY AND PERSONHOOD

1. JOHN LOCKE'S CONCEPTION OF HUMAN PERSONHOOD AND CONTEMPORARY CONTROVERSIES

1.1 Locke's Two Notions of a Person

In his seminal book, *An Essay Concerning Human Understanding*, Locke introduced two notions of a person.[11] According to the first notion, a person is said to be a thinking intelligent being, with capacities such as reason, reflection, self-concept, and an ability to track one's own identity over time. I describe this notion of a person as ontological. According to the second notion, a person is said to be a forensic term, appropriating actions, and their merit.[12] I describe this notion of a person as forensic or moral. Taken together, I describe these two notions of a person as *onto-forensic/moral notions of personhood*. Locke's onto-forensic/moral notions of personhood are intimately related in that the moral notion of a person is rooted in the ontological notion of a person. That is, in Locke's view, only intelligent agents or persons are capable of obeying a law, happiness and misery.[13] By "intelligent person," Locke has in mind the kinds of features such as reason, reflection, and the ability for self-concept. What comes out of Locke's characterization or, as some call it, "definition" of a person, is that besides their biological nature, which is grounded in their physical body, persons are also psychological beings.[14] As we shall see, it is the psychologi-

---

11. Locke discusses this issue in the second edition.

12. Locke, *Essay Concerning Human Understanding*, 346. The reasons that led Locke to this conclusion primarily have to do with three theological convictions he had, namely, personal immortality, resurrection, and the last judgment day. Locke thought that God, on the last day, could justly punish or reward his people provided only that the receivers of his punishment or reward were capable of assuming accountability for their actions (Locke, *Essay Concerning Human Understanding*, 2.27.26 [346–47]; see also King, *Life and Letters*, 316–23; Forstrom, *John Locke*, ch. 1).

Recently Galen Strawson argued that Locke's theological convictions are entirely peripheral to his central theory of the forensic/moral notion of a person (see G. Strawson, *Locke on Personal Identity*, xii–xiii). But Strawson is wrong. Locke's discussion of the forensic notion of a person does not even get off the ground unless the theological convictions that prompted Locke to suggest it in the first place are considered. But this is a discussion for another time, and I shall say no more here.

13. Locke, *Essay Concerning Human Understanding*, 346.

14. For an excellent discussion of Locke's views of a person as well as its appropriation to personal identity at a time (synchronic) and over time (diachronic) and the difficulties raised against it, see Lowe, *Routledge Guidebook*, 100–112.

cal properties or capacities aspect of Locke's onto-forensic/moral notions of personhood, that sets the tone for contemporary discussions besetting the HP-question. Directly or indirectly most contemporary discussions on human personhood draw their inspiration from Locke.

1.2 Lockean Framework

Lockean conception of a person has provided a framework within which contemporary philosophical discussions on human personhood are developed. We can see this, most noticeably, in discussions that take place over the metaphysics of personal identity as well as various issues that come up in bioethics. For example, in metaphysics, philosophers debate about whether the notion of a person is coextensive with the notion of human being/living organism. In this regard, the two dominant views are animalism and neo-Lockeanism. As Eric Olson points out, the primary focus of animalism is to answer the question: What are we? But the primary focus of Lockeanism is to answer the question: What does it take for us to persist through time? Animalism states that we are human organisms, not human persons. Olson claims that although animalism does not answer the persistence question albeit it implies that a human animal's persistence over time consists in brute physical continuity. In contrast, Lockeanism states that a person's persistence overtime consists in some sort of psychological continuity.[15]

Contemporary philosophers also debate about whether the notion of a person is primitive.[16] If it is, then it is said that everything else is analyzed in terms of the notion of a person, but the converse does not hold. Here the well-known Peter Strawson's P-predicate (e.g., size) and M-Predicate (e.g., feeling sad) are good cases in point. These are two classes of predicates ascribed to persons.[17] Other philosophers reject the primitive notion of a person.[18] Moreover, philosophers debate about whether or not a person

---

15. Olson, "What Does It Mean," 85. The controversies over these issues are complex and rich involving other views besides the two mentioned here. For further details, see also Noonan, "Plenitude, Pluralism"; Georg and Stefan, *Personal Identity*; Noonan, *Personal Identity*; Olson, *What Are We?*; Olson, *Human Animal*; and Parfit, *Reasons and Persons*.

16. P. Strawson, *Individuals*, ch.3.

17. See also B. Williams, *Problems of the Self*, ch. 7; Lowe, "Probable Simplicity"; Lowe, *Subjects of Experience*; Lowe, *Personal Agency*, pt. 1.

18. See, e.g., Shoemaker, "Against Simplicity."

is a sortal concept.[19] It was Locke who first coined the term "sortal."[20] By *sortal concepts*, following David Wiggins, I mean those concepts "that present tensedly apply to an individual X at every moment throughout X's existence."[21] More specifically, Wiggins draws a distinction between phased sortal and substance sortal. An example of a *phased sortal* would be the titles such as "president," "child," etc., whose application to a human entity is time bound. An example of a *substance sortal* would be the term "human being," which is used to designate a particular human entity for as long as that entity continues in existence. As we shall see, the phased sortal notion is similar to what is known as a functional concept of a person, which focuses on the role-playing notion of a person. My own sympathy strongly lies with those who take the term "person" as a substance sortal notion.

Similarly, when it comes to bioethics, there are well-known debates about issues such as the morality of abortion, euthanasia, and physician-assisted suicide where the point of contention mainly revolves around issues directly related to human personhood. This is in the sense that one's view on human personhood paves the way for approving or disapproving such practices within the larger context of metaphysical, moral/ethical and legal considerations.[22] Once again, the Lockean conception of human personhood, which is rooted in psychological properties/capacities, plays a great role in providing a background against which these debates evolve. Other bioethical issues that deal with healthcare, the ethical treatment of animals, capital punishment, environmental ethics, equality, racism, sexual morality, the ethics of immigration, economic justice, personal liberty, torture, and the like all, in one way or another, bring human personhood into consideration.[23]

So, both in metaphysics and in bioethics, the most pressing issue concerns spelling out what constitutes the right conception of a person and, if there is one, how to figure that out. In the next section, we will see how Tooley, Dennett, and Singer attempt to answer the HP-question. Unlike Dennett, both Tooley and Singer attempt to answer the HP-question within the context of the current debates on the moral status of abortion. But for present

---

19. Kanzian, "Is 'Person' Sortal Term?"
20. See Locke, *Essay Concerning Human Understanding*, 3.3.15 (417).
21. Wiggins, *Sameness and Substance*, 30; also see Lowe, *More Kinds of Being*, chs. 2–3.
22. See Vaughn, *Doing Ethics*, chs. 9–10; Oderberg, *Abortion in Applied Ethics*, 174–84; Moreland and Rae, *Body & Soul*.
23. See Vaughn, *Doing Ethics*, chs. 11–21.

purposes, I won't focus on the mainstream debates on abortion. My focus will be on the way these philosophers attempt to answer the HP-question.

2. TOOLEY-DENNETT-SINGER'S CONDITIONS ON PERSONHOOD

2.1 The HP-Question Clarified and Answered

Central to Tooley-Dennett-Singer's notion of personhood is what I shall call the Lockean person-making or person-constituting properties/capacities. First, in his influential article "Abortion and Infanticide," Tooley remarks:

> What properties must something have in order to be a person? ... If it possesses the concept of a self as a continuing subject of experiences and other mental states, and believes that it is itself such a continuing entity ... which I will call the self-consciousness requirement.[24]

Second, Singer remarks:

> [The term] person is often used as if it meant the same as "human being." Yet the terms are not equivalent; there could be a person who is not a member of our species. There could also be members of our species who are not persons. The word "person" has its origin in the Latin term for a mask worn by an actor in classical drama. By putting on masks the actors signified that they were acting a role. Subsequently "person" came to mean one who plays a role in life, one who is an agent. I propose to use "person" in the sense of a rational and self-conscious being, to capture those elements of the popular sense of "human being" that are not covered by members of the species Homo Sapiens.[25]

Third, Dennett remarks:

> The first theme is that persons are rational beings. ... The second theme is that persons are beings to which states of consciousness are attributed, or to which psychological or mental or intentional predicates, are ascribed. ... The third theme is that whether something counts as a person depends in some way on an attitude taken toward it, a stance adopted with respect to it. ... The fourth theme is that the object toward which this personal stance is taken must

---

24. Tooley, "Abortion and Infanticide," 64; see also Tooley, "Abortion."
25. Singer, *Practical Ethics*, 87.

be capable of reciprocating in some way.... The fifth theme is that persons must be capable of verbal communication.... The sixth theme is that persons are distinguishable from other entities by being conscious in some special way.... This is identified as self-consciousness.[26]

Tooley, Singer, and Dennett all agree in characterizing a person as a psychological being with capacities such as rationality, self-consciousness, self-concept, and so on. As pointed out earlier, these are the sorts of capacities that Locke explicitly mentions in his characterization of the notion of a person. Furthermore, Tooley, Singer, and Dennett also agree in restricting the class of personhood to those who meet the sorts of conditions listed in their characterization of the notion of a person. In doing so, they tell us who is (should be) excluded from the class of persons.

In this regard, Dennett's list of the excluded group includes:[27]

(D-i) Infant human beings

(D-ii) Mentally defective human beings

(D-iii) Human beings [who are] declared insane by licensed psychiatrists

Singer's list of the excluded group includes:[28]

(S-i) Nonhuman animals

(S-ii) Newborn infants

(S-iii) Some intellectually disabled humans

Tooley's list of the excluded group includes:[29]

(T-i) Fetus

(T-ii) Newborn babies

---

26. Dennett, "Conditions of Personhood," 177–78.

27. Dennett, "Conditions of Personhood," 175. In describing the list, for Dennett we use the first letter of his name as (D-i); for Singer, (S-i); for Tooley, (T-i); and so on.

28. Singer, *Practical Ethics*, 101.

29. Tooley, "Abortion and Infanticide," 60–62.

2.1 Square of Personhood Opposition

To see the internal logical structure of Tooley-Singer-Dennett's answer to the HP-question, it would be very helpful to deploy some machinery from logic. For our purpose, classical logic and first-order predicate logic would do. Let's begin first with classical logic. Here categorical propositions take center stage. But what is a proposition? In this context, a proposition is something that is said to relate two classes denoted by a subject term (S) and a predicate term (P). Understood this way, a proposition denies or affirms that one class, say, S, is included in some other class, say, P, either in whole or in part. In doing so, classical logic identifies four kinds of categorical propositions, which are represented by four special letters, namely, A, E, I, and O.

A represents universal affirmative propositions, E represents universal negative propositions, I represents particular affirmative propositions, and O represents particular negative propositions. The standard form of these propositions or statements is stated as follows:

1. A—All S are P.
2. E—No S are P.
3. I—Some S are P.
4. O—Some S are not P.

We can use the foregoing four kinds of propositions as tools to establish the HP-question into a statement. The conversion takes the following form:

1. All humans are persons.
2. No humans are persons.
3. Some humans are persons.
4. Some humans are not persons.

Using Hs to represent humans and Ps to represent persons, we can formalize the propositions in (1)–(4) as follows:

1. All Hs are Ps.
2. No Hs are Ps.
3. Some Hs are Ps.
4. Some Hs are not Ps.

PART I | ONTOLOGY AND PERSONHOOD

Logical Relations

Notice that (1) is a universal affirmative proposition of an A type, (2) is a universal negative proposition of an E type, (3) is a particular affirmative proposition of an I type, and (4) is a particular negative proposition of an O type. These four statements are logically related. This can be shown by using Aristotle's square of opposition which I labelled it here as the square of personhood opposition.

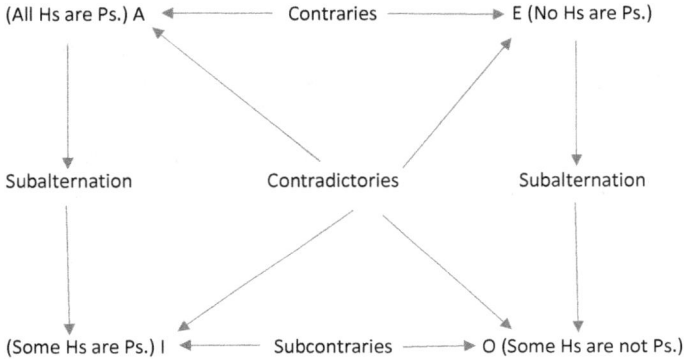

Figure 2—Square of Personhood Opposition

In the above square of personhood opposition, (1) "All Hs are Ps" and (2) "No Hs are Ps" are contraries, or they cannot both be true. That is, if the proposition "All humans are persons" is true, then its opposite proposition, "No humans are persons," must be ruled out and vice versa. However, both of these statements can be false. (3) "Some Hs are Ps" and (4) "Some Hs are not Ps" are subcontraries. These propositions cannot both be false. But they may both be true. In the case of subalternation, a universal affirmative proposition A implies its corresponding particular affirmative proposition I. That is, the proposition "All humans are persons" implies its corresponding proposition, "Some humans are persons." But the converse does not hold. Similarly, a universal negative proposition E implies its corresponding particular negative proposition O. That is, the proposition "No humans are persons" implies its corresponding proposition, "Some humans are not persons." But the converse does not hold.

Finally, a universal affirmative proposition A and a particular negative proposition O are contradictories. That is, the proposition "All humans are persons" and the proposition "Some humans are not persons" are contradictories. Similarly, a universal negative proposition E and a particular affirmative proposition I are contradictories. That is, the proposition "No humans are persons" and the proposition "Some humans are persons" are contradictories. In a nutshell, any given two propositions are said to be contradictory if one is the negation of the other. Contradictories cannot both be true. They cannot also both be false either.

Notice that here our goal is to show the internal structure of the HP-question that Tooley-Dennett-Singer tackled. To this effect, we have already taken the crucial step of stating the four categorical propositions as explained above. The question remains: Which one of the categorical statements should be adopted to establish the conversion of the HP-question into a statement? We can answer this question based on determining the scope of the HP-question. In this case, the scope in question extends to all humans. In light of this, of the four categorical propositions, (1) captures the statement form of the HP-question that we need for present discussion. As we recall, (1) is a universal affirmative proposition that takes the form "All Hs are Ps" (i.e., all humans are persons). Although our main focus is on (1), the other remaining propositions, namely, (2), (3), and (4), also play their own distinctive roles in our analysis of the HP-question. But our main focus remains on (1).

Competing Interpretations

There are two competing interpretations of (1) that must be noted. These are the Aristotelian and the Boolean interpretations. The interpretations in question revolve around the idea of existential import. As Copi, Cohen, and McMahon state, "A proposition is said to have existential import if it typically is uttered to assert the existence of objects of some kind."[30] Details aside, for Aristotle, all the four kinds of categorical propositions briefly discussed above do have existential import. As we recall, a universal affirmative proposition A implies a particular affirmative proposition I. Similarly, a universal negative proposition E implies a particular negative proposition O. Aristotle fully embraced and endorsed such inferences. For Aristotle, all these four kinds of propositions have existential import.

However, George Boole partly agreed and partly disagreed with Aristotle. Like Aristotle, Boole also endorsed that particular propositions I and O do have existential import. However, unlike Aristotle, Boole rejected that

30. Copi et al., *Introduction to Logic*, 190.

such particular propositions can be inferred from their corresponding A and E propositions. That is, for Boole, we cannot infer the truth of "Some humans are persons" from its corresponding proposition, "All humans are persons." Similarly, we cannot infer the truth of "Some humans are not persons" from its corresponding proposition, "No humans are persons." In commenting on Boole's rejection of the inference in question, Copi et al. remark that if the I and O propositions have existential import, then they validly follow from their corresponding A and E propositions. This means that A and E propositions must also have existential import. But this is said to create a serious problem, say, in forcing us to reason mistakenly that some class has members when in fact it does not.[31]

Thus, Boole argued that the best way to handle the A and the E propositions is to interpret them conditionally. For example, "All humans are persons" becomes "If there are such things as humans, they are persons." Similarly, "No humans are persons" becomes "If there are such things as humans, they are not persons." Notice that understood conditionally, the A and the E propositions do not have existential import at all. Conditionally stated, such universal propositions neither categorically assert nor deny the existence of anything. For Boole, this is one of the key advantages of the modification he made in Aristotle's classical logic. In light of this, Aristotle's interpretation of the A and the E propositions can be said to be strong whereas the Boolean interpretation of the propositions in question can be said to be weaker. Making note of the difference between these interpretations is important for our analysis of the HP-question as we examine the three views of Tooley, Singer, and Dennett.

Limitations

Having analyzed and converted the HP-question into a statement form (i.e., "All humans are persons") we can now construct an example of a formal deductive argument as follows:

>All humans are persons.
>Angie is a human.
>Therefore, Angie is a person.

The above argument is valid. However, there is one problem with it. That is, by using the resources of classical logic alone, we cannot show

---

31. For details, see Copi et al., *Introduction to Logic*, chs. 5–7.

adequately the inner logical structure of (1). For example, if we symbolize the foregoing argument, it takes the following form:

A
A
Therefore, P

But as it stands, the symbolized argument here does not seem to be valid. This is because the argument form does not allow us to capture the inner structure of the premises of the argument. To show the inner logical structure, we need a more advanced logical machinery or technique. In this case, a quantification theory is preferable to undertake the task at hand.

2.2 Predicate Logic

Quantification allows us to interpret noncompound premises (we saw above) as compound statements without a loss of meaning. Predicate logic enables us to show the inner structure of propositions that deal with the relations between subjects and predicates. In this case, we rely on quantifiers, namely, "all," "no," and "some." These quantifiers range over a certain domain. For general propositions, we use what is known as the universal quantifier. This is symbolized as (x) or $(\forall x)$. It is read as: "Given any x" or "for all x." For particular propositions, we use what is known as the existential quantifier. This is symbolized as: $(\exists x)$. We read this symbol as: "There is at least one x such that . . ." We also use the horseshoe symbol ($\supset$) or an arrow sign ($\rightarrow$). This is read as: "if—then." We use a dot symbol, ($\bullet$) to indicate a conjunction, "and." We use the tilde symbol ($\sim$) to indicate a negation, "not."

By deploying these technical tools of the predicate logic, we can symbolize the four kinds of, A, E, I, and O propositions as follows:

1. All humans are persons: (x) $(Hx \supset Px)$. This is read as: Given any x, if x is a human, then x is a person.
2. No humans are persons: (x) $(Hx \supset \sim Px)$. This is read as: Given any x, if x is a human, then x is not a person.
3. Some humans are persons: $(\exists x)$ $(Hx \bullet Px)$. This is read as: There is at least one x such that x is a human and x is a person.
4. Some humans are not persons: $(\exists x)$ $(Hx \bullet \sim Px)$. This is read as: There is at least one x such that x is a human and x is not a person.

Quantificationally, when (1) is symbolized as $(x)\ (Hx \supset Px)$, it is easy to see its inner logical structure. In this case, the quantifier (x) governs the entire statement function stated inside parentheses, namely, $(Hx \supset Px)$. That means that the variables that occur in the statement function $Hx \supset Px$ are bound variables, since they fall within the scope of the quantifier (x). The substitution instance of the statement function $Hx \supset Px$ can take truth evaluable form. For instance, if we put an input value for the variable x, say, Angie (a), we get a substitution instance of the conditional statement: $Ha \supset Pa$. We read this conditional statement as: if Angie is a human, then Angie is a person. Put this way, such a conditional statement can be evaluated for its truth value. But any adequate assessment of the truth value of the substitution instance of (1) as shown above must consider an interrelated but one distinct aspect of the HP-question, which concerns determining the scope of the quantifier in (1). Here, the focus should be on whether the universe of discourse associated with the universal quantifier (x) is restricted. If it is restricted, then what determines the domain of the quantifier?

In light of the above quantified analysis of the HP-question, we can clearly see that for Tooley-Dennett-Singer, the terms "human being" and "person" come apart and thus cannot be used interchangeably. This is because, as they see it, these terms belong to members that belong to two distinct classes.[32] But we have a coined phrase, "human person." That means that for Tooley-Dennett-Singer, the universe of discourse associated with the universal quantifier (x) is restricted. To see this, recall from §2.1 Tooley's excluded group, (T-i) and (T-ii); Singer's excluded group, (S-i), (S-ii), and (S-iii); and Dennett's excluded group, (D-i), (D-ii), and (D-iii). In light of this, Tooley-Dennett-Singer determine the domain of the quantifier by restricting it from quantifying over excluded groups. That is, its application is restricted to a domain to which only humans who also instantiate Lockean psychological properties/capacities belong. Of the four quantificationally formulated statement functions, the one that Tooley-Dennett-Singer would rightly reject is (2), which takes the form: $(x)\ (Hx \supset \sim Px)$. So, by restricting the domain of (1), Tooley-Dennett-Singer are fully embracing (3) and (4).

The question remains: Who is then privileged to be included in the class of persons laid out by Tooley-Dennett-Singer? Unlike what they did with the excluded group, Tooley-Dennett-Singer do not give us any

---

32. See, e.g., Tooley, "Abortion and Infanticide," 60–62; Singer, *Practical Ethics*, 86–87; Dennett, "Conditions of Personhood," 175–76.

explicit list of the privileged group. Of course, were they to give us such a list, their list would probably suffer from the problem of vagueness, since the Lockean person-making properties come in degrees.[33] Yet regardless of such difficulties, Tooley-Dennett-Singer still require the Lockean person-making properties as a basis in their attempt to establish the class of persons that does not have as its members anyone from the excluded group mentioned above. In saying this, I also have in mind a functional notion of a person. For example, Sprague claims that the term "person" is not a name that stands for a distinctive kind of thing, as "frog" or "diamond" may do. Rather as Sprague claims, we use the term "person" as a sort of title that we bestow on something if that thing satisfies certain appropriate criteria, as "doctor" or "policeman" may do.[34]

As we shall see in §2.3 and more closely in §§3 and 4, using the Lockean person-making properties to draw a demarcation between who qualifies as a person and who does not eventually results in a deeply implausible notion of human personhood.

2.3. ARE THERE FUZZY BOUNDARIES OF PERSONHOOD?

A divorce introduced by Tooley-Dennett-Singer between "human being" and "human person" forces us to wonder if personhood comes in degrees. Recall that earlier, I claimed that a degreed notion of personhood presents us with three and only three options, namely, (a) more, or (b) less, or (c) no personhood at all. If we follow Tooley-Dennett-Singer in answering the HP-question, then what we get is nothing other than the options presented in (a), (b), and (c). Suppose we follow these philosophers' lead and just settle for the options given to us in (a), (b), and (c). In such cases, what would human personhood amount to? In the case of (c) it is straightforward. That is, if the sorts of Lockean person-making properties are not manifested, then no person exists after all. But let's suppose that there are person-making properties. In that case, what exactly is the number of properties that one would need as a threshold to satisfy the conditions set by Tooley-Dennett-Singer? Probably asking such a question is unfair to these philosophers because no one can be in a position to set the threshold or

---

33. Cf. B. Williams, *Ethics and the Limits*, 114; see also Snowdon, "Persons and Personal Identity," 36.

34. Sprague, *Metaphysical Thinking*, 61.

establish the number of capacities one needs to have to be considered as a full-fledged human person. But if this is not possible, at least there is one thing we can do. That is, we can just work with what we have, that is, with the sorts of Lockean person-constituting properties that Tooley-Dennett-Singer suggested.

At this point, we run into a big problem. Consider, for example, John satisfies only some, but not all, of Dennett's conditions for personhood. Furthermore, suppose Parfit satisfies all of Dennett's conditions. So, the question now is, how should we go about determining the extent to which John is a person relative to Parfit and vice versa? The answer for this question oscillates between (a) and (b). Notice that Dennett's own conditions are underdetermined, which raises its own serious problems, among other things, arbitrary selection bias. Let's put aside this worry for now and stick to our question. The only way one can answer the question at hand is by embracing what I call fuzzy or vague boundary. Such vagueness may be true of other things, say deciding the initial point of the origin of a certain mountain range. But can we make sense of such vagueness as it pertains to human personhood? To see the absurdity of a degreed notion of personhood, we need to turn to the best logical system, which is fuzzy logic.

In his *Deduction: Introductory Symbolic Logic*, Daniel Bonevac remarks that fuzzy logic attempts to represent the possibility of continuous change. It does this by allowing sentences to have as truth values any real numbers between 0 and 1. If a sentence is definitely false, then the numerical value 0 is assigned. If a sentence is definitely true, then the numerical value 1 is assigned. However, sentences are said to have any numerical value in between, thereby implying truth values having degrees of truths. That is, as Bonevac further points out, a sentence with a value 1 is said to be completely true whereas one with a value of 0.5 is half-true.[35]

Let's suppose that Parfit fully satisfied Dennett's conditions and is given the value 1 whereas John is given 0.5. Furthermore, suppose that Mark satisfies even fewer psychological capacities than John. In that case, let's assign 0.2 to Mark. Given fuzzy logic, we can keep on assigning 0.1, 0.3, and any combination of decimal points. Trying to map human personhood along assigning such numerical values makes no sense at all. To do so only shows a confusion of first-order magnitude. How else should we go about making sense of the three options stated in (a), (b), and (c) then?

---

35. For details, see Bonevac, *Deduction*, 332–43; also see Mukaidono, *Fuzzy Logic for Beginners*.

The answer to this question is not clear because there is no such thing as a person attaining more, or less, or no personhood in the way implied by Tooley-Dennett-Singer's conditions of personhood. Such a flawed way of thinking was crystal clear to Aristotle, who argues that a substance does not come in degrees. As Aristotle remarks:

> Substance, it seems, does not admit of a more and a less. I do not mean that one substance is not more a substance than another (we have said that it is), but that any given substance is not called more, or less, that which it is. For example, if this substance is a man, it will not be more a man or less a man either than itself or than another man. For one man is not more a man than another, as one pale thing is more pale than another and one beautiful thing more beautiful than another.[36]

Aristotle continues,

> Again, a thing is called more, or less, such-and-such than itself; for example, the body that is pale is called more pale now than before, and the one that is hot is called more, or less, hot. Substance, however, is not spoken of thus. For a man is not called more a man now than before, nor is anything else that is a substance. Thus substance does not admit of a more and a less.[37]

If we were to seriously take the view that personhood comes in degrees, it could be only because we entertain a widely popular, but a wholly unsatisfactory, conception of the manifestation of dispositions or capacities. But if we get our thinking on this issue back on the right track, then there seems to be no good reason to embrace a degreed notion of personhood. I now turn to that discussion.

3. OBJECTS, DISPOSITIONS, AND THEIR MANIFESTATIONS

Suppose that a certain object O exists. What can we know about O? Depending on how it is specified, we may know a good deal about O. For example: (i) We may know what dispositions O possesses (here, following Heil, I understand dispositions as powers);[38] (ii) we may know under what

---

36. Aristotle, *Categories*, 3b32.
37. Aristotle, *Categories*, 3b32.
38. Heil, *Universe*, 120–30; cf. Mumford, "Causal Powers and Capacities," 269–70.

PART I | ONTOLOGY AND PERSONHOOD

circumstances those dispositions could be manifested; (iii) we may know what sorts of circumstances may hinder the manifestation of those dispositions, and so on. If we grant this, then at least initially, following Martin, we can make some assumptions. As Martin remarks:

> A particular disposition exists or it does not. You could say of any unmanifesting disposition that it straight-out exists, even if it is not, at that time or at any other time, manifesting any manifestation. It is the unmanifested manifestation, not the disposition itself, that is the would-be-if or would-have-been-if anything is. There can be a disposition A for the manifestation of acquiring a further disposition B and, of course, disposition B need not itself have any manifestation, but disposition B can still be unfulfilled terminus of that for which A has a specific directedness.[39]

In this passage, Martin has made two critical points with respect to the nature of dispositions. First, the absence of the manifestation of certain dispositions does not in any way show that they do not exist. Second, if for whatever reason(s) dispositions are not manifested, then they can be taken as unmanifested manifestations. Consider a china cup. It has certain dispositions, for example, the disposition to shatter if struck. Here the verb "struck" stands for what is taken to be a stimulus condition, and "shatter" stands for what is understood to be a manifestation.

So, the question remains: Will it be the case that, every time a stimulus condition is met, that we should necessarily expect to see a manifestation of a certain disposition? More specifically, should we expect to see a china cup shatter when struck? Of course, under normal circumstances, the answer to such questions will be yes. However, consider again a slightly modified scenario whereby a china cup is placed inside a sturdy box, such that when struck, the sturdy box completely absorbs the forceful impact—blocking it from reaching the china cup. In this case, the china cup remains un-shattered. Such is an example that seems to capture Martin's phrase "unmanifested manifestation." But is there any other way by which we can take the unmanifested manifestations themselves to be the actual manifestations of a different kind? Following Heil,[40] I would say yes. For example, Heil remarks:

> A ball's sphericity endows it with a power to roll. But it is also in virtue of being spherical that the ball has the power to make

39. Martin, "Dispositions and Conditionals," 1–2.
40. Heil, *Universe*, 120–30.

a concave, circular impression in a cushion, the power to reflect light so as to look spherical, the power to feel spherical to the touch. Talk of single- and multi-track dispositions or powers is confused from the outset. Powers quite generally are multi-track, if this means that they would manifest themselves differently with different reciprocal partners.[41]

Here Heil is echoing Martin's two points that concern the nature of dispositions. Martin is an ardent defender of multi-track dispositions. Originally, the term "multi-track" was coined by Ryle.[42] These are dispositions that are believed to have more than one kind of stimulus condition or manifestation, or both.[43] Taken this way, powers or dispositions have many reciprocal partners. That means that negative interfering factors such as absences, preventers, antidotes, blockers, inhibitors, etc., will no longer be taken as stopping a certain power from being manifested. This is because such things themselves are dispositions manifesting themselves with various reciprocal partners.[44] Again, as Heil remarks:

> What of scurvy and the lack of vitamin C? A living body's healthy condition is a mutual manifestation of myriad finely tuned reciprocal disposition partners. When one of these is missing, you have a different sort of manifestation, just as you have a different sort of manifestation when you remove one of the cards from a pair of propped-up playing cards. . . . An absence is not an entity, not something with properties providing it with distinctive powers. But certain kinds of manifestation require appropriately propertied something as reciprocal partners. When these are missing, the result is a different kind of manifestation.[45]

The gist of Heil's point here is that, once we take a multi-track powers model, the manifestation of dispositions is not a one-way street, whereby one thing causes another in a linear fashion. On the contrary, the manifestation of powers is the result of causings, i.e., mutual manifestings of various reciprocal partners.[46] Such considerations help us to have a good grip on Martin's earlier remarks. That is to say that, rather than talking

---

41. Heil, *Universe*, 21.
42. Ryle, *Concept of Mind*, 114.
43. Bird, *Nature's Metaphysics*, 21.
44. Heil, *Universe*, 126–30.
45. Heil, *Universe*, 127.
46. Heil, *Universe*, 120; see also Guta, "Two Natures."

about unmanifested manifestation, now we can talk about manifestations *tout court*. The manifestation of powers is multifaceted in that the apparent absence of the manifestation of certain powers does not show that no manifestation is taking place. Rather, it only means that a different kind of manifestation is happening. So, where does all this leave us? I will use the hitherto discussion on powers to respond to Tooley-Dennett-Singer's conditions on personhood.

4. RESPONSES

In this case, the issue can be examined from two standpoints, namely, the functionalist approach and the ontological approach. The functionalist approach shares a lot in common with a "functionalist" conception of mind in philosophy of mind. Setting aside the details for now, a functionalist view of the mind describes mental states within the framework of the input and the output causal role that they are said to play. On this view, as Jaegwon Kim remarks, "A mental kind [e.g., pain] is a functional kind, or a causal-functional kind, since the 'function' involved is to fill a certain causal role."[47]

Suppose, for example, yesterday in Belgium a Brazilian football star, Neymar, broke one of his knees while playing. In this case, the functionalists analyze Neymar's pain in terms of the bodily input (e.g., damaged tissues), which they say is responsible for causing the pain. Such pain in turn is responsible for causing Neymar's wincing, groaning, and engaging in avoidance behavior, each of which is said to be a pain output. In short, in the functionalist view, the concept of a pain consists in the input-output causal function and nothing beyond. Notice that taken this way, functionalism does not concern itself with the nature of pain at all. That is, pains do not have their own intrinsic nature.

But someone who does not embrace a functionalist theory of mind rejects the analysis of the concept of pain in terms of an input-output causal mechanism. For one thing, a pain experience does not seem to be something that is entirely capturable via an input-output causal mechanism. This can be seen by attending to one's own pain experience(s). In this regard, one of the clearest features of the sensation of pain has to do with one's awareness of the hurtfulness or painfulness of pain. What this in turn implies, among other things, is that one's knowledge of the painfulness of pain is first personal in nature. But what does the painfulness of pain reveal

---

47. Kim, *Philosophy of Mind*, 119.

about what pain is? One answer that the anti-functionalist could give for this question can be summed up along the following lines. In talking about the painfulness of pain, at the least, one is implying how one came to know about the property of pain, that it is painful/hurtful. In other words, painfulness is what defines what pain is. That is to say that the property of being painful is intrinsic to the pain itself. In short, the intrinsic nature of pain consists in its painfulness.

One's knowledge of the intrinsic nature of pain is rooted in one's own first-person knowledge, which is private, inner, and immediate to its subject. The implication here is that given their experiential aspect(s), any attempt one makes to fully functionalize mental states will be doomed to fail. This is because what it is like to have a certain pain sensation (subjective experience in general) is not something that can be known primarily via a third-person analysis. Each one of the above remarks could be objected to. Unfortunately, this is not the place to take up such discussions. I have argued such matters extensively elsewhere.[48] For now, it is not hard to see why functionalism leaves out the intrinsic/experiential aspect(s) of mental states, of which a pain state is just one example. However, by being indifferent with respect to the intrinsic nature of mental states, functionalism proves to be a deeply unsatisfactory view.

How, then, does the foregone brief discussion on the functionalist theory of mind provide us with a framework within which some of the implications of Tooley-Dennett-Singer's conception of personhood can be spelled out? To answer this question, we need to remind ourselves that in Tooley-Dennett-Singer's view, x is said to be a person if and only if x exercises/manifests capacities that are taken to be person constituting (see again §2). If, for any reason, x fails to manifest person-constituting capacities, then x will cease to be a person. Taken this way, the application of the term "person" is directly related to its function. In this case, the term "person" functions like a sort of title that is conferred upon a certain entity when such an entity manifests person-constituting capacities. Such reasoning follows a similar strategy adopted by defenders of a functionalist theory of mind, as discussed earlier.

The conception of personhood advanced by Tooley-Dennett-Singer can be spelled out via the language of *role-playing*. This can be put as follows:

> (i) X is a person if and only if x manages to play certain agreed-upon roles by exercising the relevant person-constituting capacities.

---

48. See, e.g., Guta, "Consciousness, First-Person Perspective."

This notion of a person directly coincides with the etymological meaning of the term "person," which derives from the Latin *persona*: a mask worn by an actor who plays some kind of role or character. The same meaning applies to its closest Greek cognate *prosopon*. This notion was originated in the Roman law, where persons are perceived to be bearers of legal rights. The notion of the person also became associated with moral value through the influence of Christian tradition.[49]

Notice that here, the role in question has to do with manifesting/exercising person-constituting capacities as opposed to figuring out the ontological status of personhood. That is, as it is true in the case of functionalism (concerning mental states), the focus of the functional approach in relation to personhood has to do with fulfilling certain functional roles. In light of this, the extension of (i) is open ended, allowing both nonhuman artefacts and biological organisms—for example, robots, corporations, computers, dolphins, chimpanzees, and the like—to fall under the sortal term "person." In this case, we can talk about "robotic persons," "artificial persons" (e.g., computers), "biological human persons," nonhuman biological entities (e.g., dolphins, chimpanzees), or social persons (e.g., corporations) and suchlike.

However, the underlying assumption behind Tooley-Dennett-Singer's conception of personhood is straightforwardly ontological in nature. The assumption I have in mind can be described as follows:

(ii) X is a person if and only if x manifests certain properties that are believed to constitute personhood.

So, my own focus will be on (ii). Notice that in (ii), unlike (i), the notion of role-playing is not implicated. In this case, (ii) marks the transition from ontologically noncommittal talk of role-playing to that of ontologically committal. Moreover, the inadequacies inherent in the functional approach will be obvious, once Tooley-Dennett-Singer's conception of personhood is examined from the standpoint of an ontological approach. What is to follow will draw upon the discussion on the metaphysics of dispositions sketched out in §3.

Going back to the multi-track powers model discussed in §3, which takes the manifestation of dispositions as multidirectional, we can ask the following question. That is: What is the merit of the class distinction Tooley-Dennett-Singer introduced between "human being" and "human

---

49. For details, see Mauss, "Category of Human Mind"; Peacocke and Gillett, *Persons and Personality*.

person"? Tooley-Dennett-Singer think that fetuses, newly born babies, and mentally disabled humans are not human persons. This is because, as they see it, humans with various sorts of mental disability have stopped manifesting powers essential for personhood. On the other hand, fetuses and newly born babies have not yet begun to manifest powers essential for personhood. In light of such reasoning, Tooley-Dennett-Singer freely assume that the class of "human beings" is different from that of the class of "human persons." However, it remains far from clear how Tooley-Dennett-Singer's class distinction can be plausibly maintained, if examined from the standpoint of the multi-track dispositions' model.

Whether it is in the case of fetus or mentally disabled people, the manifestation of powers is always taking place. In the case of a developing fetus or newly born baby, we can understand personhood in light of the concept of potentiality, which is often contrasted with actuality. Although I do not speak French, I have a second-order capacity to acquire the first-order capacity to speak French. Notice that here both the first-order and the second-order capacities are equal capacities. Simply because I do not speak French now, it does not follow that the second-order capacity I have to learn French is not an actual capacity.[50] So, the notion of potentiality I suggested above should not be understood as docile, since it is an instance of the manifestation of power.[51]

In light of such similar considerations, Oderberg remarks, "Conception does not bring into existence potential human beings, but an actual human being with a potential to develop, given the right external factors, into a mature human being [human person]."[52] Similarly, Puccetti remarks, "A human infant, for example, is not expected to make moral judgments: but since he can enter the human conceptual scheme, he is a developing person and is expected to have a moral character of his own someday."[53] Both Oderberg's and Puccetti's remarks echo the central assumption that underlies the multi-track powers ontology.

Moreover, in the case of anencephalic infants (i.e., without brains), we can see powers being manifested, albeit in a very different way than we normally expect. Ditto with mentally disabled people. For example, if a person

---

50. Cf. Frankfurt, "Freedom of the Will."

51. Cf. Aristotle, *Metaphysics Theta*.

52. Oderberg, *Abortion in Applied Ethics*, 21; see also Oderberg, "Metaphysical Status," 263–67.

53. Puccetti, *Persons*, 9; see also B. Williams, *Ethics and the Limits*, 114.

becomes totally amnesiac, adopting Tooley-Dennett-Singer's conception of personhood forces us to conclude that the amnesiac is no longer a person. However, if we adopt the multi-track powers model, the right thing to say would be that an amnesiac is still a person like the rest of us—despite suffering from a neurodegenerative disease.

The only difference between a normal person and that of an amnesiac person lies in the latter no longer being able to utilize his/her cognitive abilities. This happens due to an entirely different kind of manifestation that led to the apparent loss of the amnesiac person's cognitive abilities. The same is true of comatose patients and other cases of severely disabled people. So, despite the current orthodoxy that attempts to divide humans into entirely conventionally created classes, the powers ontology briefly discussed above shows why there is no justification for such a move. In light of such considerations, the class distinction suggested by Tooley-Dennett-Singer should be rejected. In rejecting the class distinction, however, one need not thereby also deny the distinction that obtains between a person and the animal body that embodies it. I have argued for this elsewhere.[54]

To all of these, Tooley-Dennett-Singer might respond in three ways. First, they might reject the multi-track dispositions model altogether. In that case, it is hard to see what compelling reasons there could be for rejecting it. Moreover, in rejecting the multi-track dispositions model, Tooley-Dennett-Singer owe us a better model. Again, it is hard to see what that might be.

Second, they might insist that the class distinction between "human being" and "human person" is not something they originated. Rather, it is the standard view that is accepted by an overwhelming majority of contemporary philosophers. The standard view invoked here primarily takes a person as a functional concept in a sense described at the beginning of this section. But in light of what I have argued so far, the functional concept of a person seems to be deeply unsatisfactory. So, the ground for maintaining the class distinction as suggested by Tooley-Dennett-Singer turns out to be less than adequate, to say the least.

Third, and more importantly, they might say, "All right, we will concede your powers ontology to you, human beings (which include fetuses, the mentally disabled, etc.) can be said to have the powers of 'self-consciousness,' 'rationality,' etc.; but now we will just specify that only

---

54. See, e.g., Guta, "Frank Jackson's Location Problem." See also Lowe, *Personal Agency*, part 1.

certain manifestations of those powers are morally relevant. Now we can make meaningful moral distinctions between 'mere humans' and 'human persons'; we just have to do it in terms of the particular manifestation of certain powers."[55]

For at least two reasons, I remain unpersuaded by this objection: (a) The immediate problem with this objection has to do with the very idea of specifying the manifestation of only certain dispositional properties as criteria on the basis of which one determines between "mere humans" and "human persons." Such a proposal seems to be entirely ad hoc. For example, what principled reason is there for one to choose certain manifestations of dispositions as "human person constituting" and certain others as not "human person constituting"? To properly answer this question, one has to show why a moral relevance has to be contingent on the manifestations of certain dispositions, which is not an easy thing to do without begging a question. (b) Appealing to moral considerations to establish the status of someone's personhood gives rise to a Euthyphro sort of dilemma: Is x a person because x satisfies certain conditions of morality, or does x satisfy certain conditions of morality because x is a person? In response to the first horn of the above dilemma, one could appeal to a Lockean solution.

As I pointed out in §1, Locke operates with two notions of the term "person," namely, ontological and forensic/moral. In the case of the latter, Locke claims that only a person is fit for moral accountability, or reward, or punishment, or legal right. In this case, the Lockean assumption is that only persons are the proper objects who can satisfy conditions that morality demands. But if the powers ontology sketched out so far is on the right track, which I believe it is, then the Lockean solution turns out to be less than helpful. But this is by no means to imply that satisfying moral conditions is irrelevant. The point here is that satisfying moral conditions, if understood along the lines of Tooley-Dennett-Singer's conception of personhood, turns out to be deeply mistaken. This leaves us with the second horn of the dilemma. Again, if the basic thesis of the powers ontology defended so far is adopted, then the proper way to think about the moral notion of personhood is precisely in the sense stated in the second horn of the dilemma. While Tooley-Dennett-Singer's conception of personhood supports what

---

55. This objection was pointed out to me by Benjamin Yelle, who commented on my paper at the International Conference on Persons at Boston University (Aug. 2015), for which I am very grateful.

is stated in the first horn of the dilemma, the position taken in this paper categorically rejects it.

So, what should we say about (ii) above? Recall that (ii) states that: x is a person if x manifests certain properties that are believed to constitute personhood. As it stands, (ii) is too restrictive in that it allows something to be included in the category of persons provided only that certain properties are exercised. In light of the powers ontology adopted here, (ii) also suffers from an implausible assumption that the idea of unexercised powers implies their absence altogether. As we saw, many realists about powers are perfectly happy with the idea of a power existing unexercised. But here there is a more pressing ontological issue. That is, how does an object acquire the powers it possesses? No doubt this question receives different answers in different contexts. But in relation to human persons, we can give a broadly Aristotelian answer for it. In this case, the key assumption that a defender of powers ontology brings to the table is this. That is, human persons have both natural as well as acquired/learned dispositions.

As I understand it, a disposition is said to be natural, just in case an object possesses it in virtue of being the kind of entity that it is. On the other hand, a disposition is said to be learned just in case an object acquires it through learning. There are two qualifications to keep in mind here, however. First, to have acquired dispositions, sometimes natural powers may be prerequisites. Second, to have acquired dispositions, natural powers may not be prerequisites. For example, we may teach a dog a certain skill, say of, riding on the scooter, which is a learned disposition. But no matter how hard we try, we cannot teach a dog to speak a natural language, since the dog lacks the natural disposition for it.

But in the case of Lockean person-making properties, all humans have the natural dispositions for self-consciousness, self-concept, and so on, in virtue of being the kinds of entities that they are. So, whether or not these dispositions are manifested in normal ways, no human being is more privileged in having them than the other. Therefore, there is no good reason to bifurcate human beings into two distinct classes, namely: "mere human beings," on the one hand, and "human persons" on the other. If I am right about this matter, then it follows that all humans have equal, i.e., unconditional, ontological status. In light of such considerations, (ii) above collapses. This is my answer for the HP-question.

5. CONCLUSION

I conclude then that a broadly Martin-Heil-type powers ontology that shows how the powers that objects have can exist even when they are not manifested (due to various reasons) is far superior to the kind of conventionalist and seemingly an ad hoc approach adopted by Tooley-Dennett-Singer in explicating the question of what constitutes human personhood.

A lot could have been said in defense of this conclusion. However, for now, space limitations will not allow us to go any further. That said, having cleared one key conceptual confusion out of the way with respect to how the notion of a person needs to be understood, the most demanding aspect of the ontology of a person has to do with giving an account of the emergence of a person—a bearer of consciousness. This is a homework assignment for another time.[56]

BIBLIOGRAPHY

Ackrill, John L., ed. *A New Aristotle Reader*. Princeton, NJ: Princeton University Press, 1978.

Aristotle. *De Anima (On the Soul)*. Translated by Hugh Lawson-Tancred. Penguin Classics. London: Penguin, 1986.

———. *"Categories" and "De Interpretatione."* Edited and translated by J. L. Ackrill. Oxford: Clarendon, 1963.

Bird, Alexander. *Nature's Metaphysics: Laws and Properties*. Oxford: Oxford University Press, 2007.

Bird, Alexander, et al., eds. *Properties, Powers and Structures: Issues in the Metaphysics of Realism*. Routledge Studies in Metaphysics. New York: Routledge, 2013.

Bonevac, Daniel. *Deduction: Introductory Symbolic Logic*. 2nd ed. Oxford: Wiley-Blackwell, 2003.

———. "Two Theories of Analogical Predication." Philosophical Space, Dec. 24, 2010. http://philosophical.space/papers/AnalogicalPredication.pdf.

Boethius. "Anicii Manlii Severini Boethii: Contra Eutychen et Nestorium." Documenta Catholica Omnia, n.d. http://web.documentacatholicaomnia.eu/03d/0480-0524,_Boethius,_Contra_Eutychen_et_Nestorium,_LT.pdf.

---

56. *Acknowledgments: I wrote this chapter based on my previously published paper "Looking into Objects." Originally, I presented the paper at the International Conference on Persons at Boston University (Aug. 6, 2015). My thinking on powers ontology was greatly shaped during my time as a research fellow at Durham University in the UK, where I had the privilege of discussing it with excellent philosophers: John Heil, Alex Carruth, Sophie Gibb, the late professor E. J. Lowe, and many others in the Philosophy Department. I greatly benefited from each of them. My thanks go to the three blind reviewers of this essay whose comments resulted in significant improvement.

Choi, Sungho, and Michael Fara. "Dispositions." *Stanford Encyclopedia of Philosophy*, July 26, 2006; revised June 22, 2018. Edited by Edward N. Zalta. https://plato.stanford.edu/entries/dispositions/.
Copi, Irving M., et al. *Introduction to Logic*. 14th ed. New York: Routledge, 2011.
Crane, Tim, et al. *Dispositions: A Debate*. International Library of Philosophy. New York: Routledge, 1996.
Cross, Troy. "Dispositions." *Synthese* 144 (2005) 321–41.
DeGrazia, David. "On the Question of Personhood beyond Homo Sapiens." In *In Defense of Animals: The Second Wave*, edited by Peter Singer, 40–53. Oxford: Blackwell, 2006.
Dennett, Daniel. "Conditions of Personhood." In *The Identities of Persons*, edited by Amélie Oksenberg Rorty, 175–96. Topics in Philosophy 3. Berkeley: University of California Press, 1976.
Ellis, Brian. *The Philosophy of Nature: A Guide to the New Essentialism*. Montreal: McGill-Queen's University Press, 2002.
Epstein, Brian. "Social Ontology." *Stanford Encyclopedia of Philosophy*, Mar. 21, 2018. Edited by Edward N. Zalta. https://plato.stanford.edu/archives/win2021/entries/social-ontology/.
Forstrom, K. Joanna S. *John Locke and Personal Identity: Immortality and Bodily Resurrection in Seventeenth-Century Philosophy*. Continuum Studies in British Philosophy 103. London: Continuum, 2010.
Frankfurt, Harry. G. "Freedom of the Will and the Concept of Person." *Journal of Philosophy* 68 (1971) 5–20.
Galluzzo, Gabriele, and Michael J. Loux, eds. *The Problem of Universals in Contemporary Philosophy*. Cambridge: Cambridge University Press, 2015.
Georg, Gasser, and Matthias Stefan, eds. *Personal Identity: Complex or Simple?* Cambridge: Cambridge University Press, 2012.
Groff, Ruth, and John Greco. *Powers and Capacities in Philosophy: The New Aristotelianism*. New York: Routledge, 2013.
Guta, Mihretu P. "Consciousness, First-Person Perspective and Neuroimaging." *Journal of Consciousness Studies* 11–12 (2015) 218–45.
———. "Frank Jackson's Location Problem and Argument from the Self." *Philosophi Christi Journal* 13 (2011) 35–58.
———. "John Locke's Contemporaries' Reaction against the Theory of Substratum." In *Metaphysics or Modernity: Contributions to the Bamberg Summer School 2012*, edited by Simon Baumgartner et al., 9–28. Schriften aus der Fakultät Geistes- und Kulturwissenschaften der Otto-Friedrich-Universität Bamberg 15. Bamberg, Germ.: Bamberg University Press, 2013. https://philarchive.org/archive/RANSIA.
———. "Looking into Objects, Dispositions and the Lockean Person-Making Properties." *Appraisal* 11 (2016) 4–11.
———. "The Two Natures of the Incarnate Christ and the Bearer Question." *TheoLogica* 3 (2019) 113–43.
Heil, John. "Dispositions." *Synthese* 144 (2005) 343–56.
———. *The Universe as We Find It*. Oxford: Oxford University Press, 2012.
Kanzian, Christian. "Is 'Person' a Sortal Term?" In *Personal Identity: Complex or Simple?*, edited by Georg Gasser and Matthias Stefan, 192–205. Cambridge: Cambridge University Press, 2012.
Kim, Jaegwon. *Philosophy of Mind*. 2nd ed. Boulder, CO: Westview, 2006.
King, Lord. *Life and Letters of John Locke*. London: John and Son, 1829.

Koons, Robert C., and Timothy Pickavance. *The Atlas of Reality: A Comprehensive Guide to Metaphysics*. Oxford: Wiley-Blackwell, 2017.
Locke, John. *An Essay Concerning Human Understanding*. Edited by P. H. Nidditch. Clarendon Edition of the Works of John Locke. Oxford: Clarendon, 1975.
Loux, Michael J., and Thomas M. Crisp. *Metaphysics: A Contemporary Introduction*. 4th ed. Routledge Contemporary Introductions to Philosophy. New York: Routledge, 2017.
Lowe, E. J. *The Four-Category Ontology: A Metaphysical Foundation for Natural Science*. Oxford: Clarendon, 2006.
———. *More Kinds of Being: A Study of Individuation, Identity, and the Logic of Sortal Terms*. Oxford: Wiley-Blackwell, 2009.
———. *Personal Agency: The Metaphysics of Mind and Action*. Oxford: Oxford University Press, 2008.
———. *The Possibility of Metaphysics: Substance, Identity, and Time*. Oxford: Clarendon, 1998.
———. "The Probable Simplicity of Personal Identity." In *Personal Identity: Complex or Simple?*, edited by Georg Gasser and Matthias Stefan, 137–55. Cambridge: Cambridge University Press, 2012.
———. *The Routledge Guidebook to Locke's Essay Concerning Human Understanding*. Routledge Guides to the Great Books. London: Routledge, 2013.
———. *Subjects of Experience*. Cambridge Studies in Philosophy. Cambridge: Cambridge University Press, 1996.
Martin, C. B. "Dispositions and Conditionals." *Philosophical Quarterly* 44 (1994) 1–8.
Mauss, Marcel. "A Category of the Human Mind: The Notion of Person; the Notion of Self." In *The Category of the Person: Anthropology, Philosophy, History*, edited by Michael Carrithers et al., translated by W. D. Halls, 1–25. Cambridge: Cambridge University Press, 1985.
Miller, Julie. *Critiquing Transhumanism: The Human Cost of Pursuing Techno-Utopia*. Phoenix: Public Philosophy, 2022.
Molnar, George. "Are Dispositions Reducible?" *Philosophical Quarterly* 49 (1999) 1–17.
Moreland, J. P., and Scott B. Rae. *Body & Soul: Human Nature & the Crisis in Ethics*. Downers Grove, IL: IVP Academic, 2000.
Mukaidono, Masao. *Fuzzy Logic for Beginners*. London: World Scientific, 2001.
Mumford, Stephen. "Causal Powers and Capacities." In *The Oxford Handbook of Causation*, edited by Beebee Helen et al., 265–78. Oxford Handbooks. Oxford: Oxford University Press, 2009.
———. *Dispositions*. Oxford: Oxford University Press, 1998.
Noonan, Harold. *Personal Identity*. 2nd ed. London: Routledge, 2003.
———. "Plenitude, Pluralism, and Neo-Lockean Persons." In *Selfhood, Autism and Thought Insertion*, edited by Mihretu P. Guta and Sophie Gibb, 108–31. Journal of Consciousness Studies. Exeter, UK: Imprint Academic, 2021.
Oderberg, David S. *Abortion in Applied Ethics: A Non-Consequentialist Approach*. Oxford: Blackwell, 2000.
———. "The Metaphysical Status of the Embryo: Some Arguments Revisited." *Journal of Applied Philosophy* 25 (2008) 263–76.
Olson, Eric T. *The Human Animal: Personal Identity without Psychology*. Philosophy of Mind Series. Oxford: Oxford University Press, 1997.

———. "The Metaphysics of Transhumanism." In *Human: A History*, edited by Karolina Hübner, 381–404. Oxford University Press, 2022.

———. *What Are We? A Study of Personal Ontology*. Philosophy of Mind. Oxford: Oxford University Press, 2007.

———. "What Does It Mean to Say That We Are Animals?" In *Selfhood, Autism and Thought Insertion*, edited by Mihretu P. Guta and Sophie Gibb, 84–107. Journal of Consciousness Studies. Exeter, UK: Imprint Academic, 2021.

Parfit, Derek. *Reasons and Persons*. Oxford: Clarendon Press, 1984.

Peacocke, Arthur R., and Grant R. Gillett, eds. *Persons and Personality: A Contemporary Inquiry*. Oxford: Blackwell, 1987.

Puccetti, Roland. *Persons: A Study of Possible Moral Agents in the Universe*. London: Macmillan, 1968.

Ryle, Gilbert. *The Concept of Mind*. Harmondsworth, UK: Penguin, 1963.

Shoemaker, Sydney. "Against Simplicity." In *Personal Identity: Complex or Simple?*, edited by Georg Gasser and Matthias Stefan, 123–36. Cambridge: Cambridge University Press, 2012.

Singer, Peter. *In Defense of Animals*. Oxford: Blackwell, 2006.

———. *Practical Ethics*. 2nd ed. Cambridge: Cambridge University Press, 1993.

Snowdon, Paul F. "Persons and Personal Identity." In *Essays for David Wiggins: Identity, Truth and Value*, edited by Sabina Lovibond and S. G. Williams, 33–48. Aristotelian Society Series. Oxford: Blackwell, 1996.

Sprague, Elmer W. *Metaphysical Thinking*. New York: Oxford University Press, 1978.

Steven, Luper, ed. *The Cambridge Companion to Life and Death*. Cambridge Companions to Philosophy. Cambridge: Cambridge University Press, 2014.

Strawson, Galen. *Locke on Personal Identity: Consciousness and Concernment*. Princeton Monographs in Philosophy. Princeton, NJ: Princeton University Press, 2011.

Strawson, Peter F. *Individuals: An Essay in Descriptive Metaphysics*. London: Methuen, 1959.

Teichman, Jenny. "The Definition of Person." *Philosophy* 60 (1985) 175–85.

Thomasson, Amie L. *Ordinary Objects*. Oxford: Oxford University Press, 2007.

Tooley, Michael. "Abortion." In *The Cambridge Companion to Life and Death*, edited by Luper Steven, 243–63. Cambridge Companions to Philosophy. Cambridge: Cambridge University Press, 2014.

———. "Abortion and Infanticide." In *Applied Ethics*, edited by Peter Singer, 57–85. Oxford Readings in Philosophy. Oxford: Oxford University Press, 1986.

Van Inwagen, Peter, and Dean Zimmerman, eds. *Persons: Human and Divine*. Oxford: Oxford University Press, 2007.

Vaughn, Lewis. *Doing Ethics: Moral Reasoning, Theory, and Contemporary Issues*. 6th ed. New York: Norton, 2022.

Wiggins, David. *Sameness and Substance Renewed*. Cambridge: Cambridge University Press, 2001.

Williams, Bernard. *Ethics and the Limits of Philosophy*. Cambridge, MA: Harvard University Press, 1985.

———. *Problems of the Self*. Cambridge: Cambridge University Press, 1973.

Williams, Neil E. *The Powers Metaphysic*. Oxford: Oxford University Press, 2019.

Wittgenstein, Ludwig. *Philosophical Investigations*. Translated by G. E. Anscombe. Oxford: Blackwell, 1958.

6

Ethics and the Generous Ontology

Eric T. Olson

THE GENEROUS ONTOLOGY

Metaphysics can impinge on ethics. Consider what it would mean for ethics if solipsism or theism were true. Claims about the metaphysics of human beings are especially pertinent: it would certainly make a difference to the morality of killing if (as Plato thought) we are indestructible and death only releases us from our corporeal prison.

I want to consider the ethical implications of a more widely held view, which we might call the *generous ontology*. In its strongest form it makes two claims. First, for every period in a person's life, there is a being just like that person except that it exists only during that period. For example, there is a thing that came into existence at midnight last night, slept in my bed until waking just when I did, ate my breakfast, and is now writing these words. He will continue to go where I go and do as I do until, at the stroke of midnight tonight, he will cease to exist—though because *I* shall go on living, his passing will be unnoticeable. Another thing, also coinciding with me now and writing these words, came into being at the beginning of this month and will perish at the end of it. A third thing exists during even-numbered days by the calendar but not during odd-numbered days. And there are many more beings that are sitting here writing whose careers are even more arbitrary and gerrymandered than these. The same goes for every human person.

Call such beings *subpeople*. Note that the generous ontology assigns subpeople the same metaphysical status as we have. They are no mere set-theoretic constructions or parts of a person's life or history. Rather, a subperson is supposed to stand to a segment of a person's life as the person stands to her entire life. It is a flesh-and-blood being just like a person, only briefer.

The second claim is that for any nonoverlapping periods during the lives of several people, there is a being just like those people are then, except that it exists at no other times. One such being coincides with me from my beginning till now and with Barack Obama from now until his demise: a thing that is just like me up to now and just like Obama afterwards, whose location and character change instantaneously in mid-career. Another coincides with Socrates throughout the whole of his life, with me during the whole of mine, and with the first Norwegian born in the twenty-fifth century. Call such beings *crosspeople*.

I would guess that at least half of all contemporary metaphysicians accept some species of generous ontology.[1] On the strong form I have been describing, every segment of a person's life is the life of a subperson, and every combination of segments of the lives of several people is the life of a crossperson. There are weaker versions that restrict the population of such beings. Perhaps only some segments of a person's life are the lives of subpeople—those that are in some way natural or unified. There may be a subperson coinciding with me throughout a given contiguous period during which I am conscious, and only then, but no subperson coinciding with me throughout a given calendar day and only then.

There are also different accounts of the metaphysical basis of the generous ontology—of why all these beings exist. The best understood is that a subperson is a temporal part of a person, standing to the person as the first lap of a race stands to the race as a whole. This makes the generous ontology a corollary of the ontology of temporal parts or "four-dimensionalism," according to which every matter-filled space-time region exactly contains a material thing. But "constitution" views of Baker's sort have similar

---

1. Those advocating a strong version include Quine, Lewis, Armstrong, and Sider. For what it's worth, I don't accept any version.

implications.² For reasons that need not detain us, four-dimensionalists almost invariably accept the strongest form of the generous ontology, whereas most constitutionalists prefer weaker versions. Because it is simplest and easiest to think about, I will discuss the strongest form. But some of my remarks will apply to weaker forms as well.

SUBPEOPLE, CROSSPEOPLE, AND PEOPLE

Generous ontologists agree that subpeople and crosspeople are not themselves people. Why not? What do they think it is to be a person? Philosophers ordinarily say that to be a person is to have certain mental properties, such as rationality and self-consciousness: everyone knows Locke's definition of "person" as "a thinking intelligent being, that has reason and reflection, and can consider it self as it self, the same thinking thing in different times and places."³ Most friends of the generous ontology deny that having such properties suffices for personhood: sub- and crosspeople have them, yet are not people. The being coinciding with me from midnight last night till midnight tonight—my "today part"—is, we have been supposing, psychologically indistinguishable from me as I am today, and so are all the other sub- and crosspeople now coinciding with me. Yet none of them are people. There is only one person here: me.⁴ So what do I have that the others lack? The most common view is that a person is a maximal aggregate of psychologically interconnected person-stages.⁵ A person-stage is a more-or-less momentary being with the right sorts of mental properties—roughly those that figure in traditional accounts of personhood such as Locke's. Two person-stages are psychologically connected when one "inherits" its psychological properties from the other via some appropriate causal connection. An aggregate of psychologically interconnected person-stages is a being composed of person-stages, each of which is psychologically connected with every other, and it is "maximal" when it is not a part of any other such aggregate. There are disputes over what counts

---

2. Baker, *Persons and Bodies*.

3. Locke, *Essay Concerning Human Understanding*, 335.

4. Insofar as I begin or end gradually, the generous ontology is likely to supply many beings, with precise temporal boundaries, that are ideal candidates for personhood, and thus for being me. But their differences may be slight enough for ethicists to ignore.

5. Lewis, "Survival and Identity."

as a person-stage, the nature of the psychological connections among the stages, and other details, but we can ignore them.

What makes this the right account of personhood, if indeed it is right? Why are maximal aggregates of psychologically interconnected person-stages people, and the countless other rational, self-conscious beings whose existence the generous ontology entails not people? The usual answer is linguistic convention. People are those beings in the extension of the word "person" and the referents of our personal pronouns and proper names, such as "I" or "Socrates." The question of what makes something a person is therefore equivalent to the question of what sort of things we use these expressions to denote. And it is up to us as a linguistic community to decide which of the eligible candidates—the ones with the right mental properties—those are. Had our habits of speech and thought differed only slightly, beings that are in fact subpeople would have been called people, and the beings who are in fact people would have been called nonpeople.

WHY ACCEPT THE GENEROUS ONTOLOGY?

Many arguments are offered for the generous ontology, most of them technical and not easily summarized.[6] But here is a more familiar consideration: the generous ontology goes with a "relaxed" attitude towards identity over time. Some of us worry about whether the conditions governing things' persistence are what we naïvely think they are. Others think these worries are misplaced. The no-worriers are usually presupposing some sort of generous ontology.

Think of your favorite puzzle about identity over time: I have some or all of my brain replaced with something new, undergo Star Trek teleportation, fall into a persistent vegetative state, or what have you. Do I survive? Is the being emerging from the adventure me or someone else? The worriers take this question to have an answer and worry that we might get it wrong. The no-worriers say there is nothing to get wrong; it is an empty question. Debates about whether I survive are merely arguments about words. The thought is not that I and the resulting being are neither definitely one nor definitely two—a case of vague identity. That would merely add a third possible answer without altering the appearance that only one of them can be true. The worry that we might get it wrong would remain. The no-worriers

6. Sider, *Four-Dimensionalism*.

think we can say what we like—identical, nonidentical, or indeterminate—with no danger of error.

But if it is right to say that I survive, how could it also be right to say that I do not survive? There must be ambiguity at work. The two (or three) sides in the debate might mean something different by "survive." But to say that I survive is just to say that something existing after the procedure is numerically identical with me, and most no-worriers agree that there is only one relation of numerical identity. The ambiguity is more likely to lie in the term "I" (or "Olson"): those who say that I survive are referring to one thing by that word, and those who say I do not survive are referring to another. There are (at least) two different candidates for the term's reference: one that survives and one that does not. Each side in the debate is saying something true about its own man. More generally, almost any view about identity over time will be true of some beings or other. So there is no chance of mistake and nothing to worry about. This presupposes the generous ontology.

THE INTERESTS OF SUBPEOPLE

The generous ontology has implications for ethics only if subpeople or crosspeople have moral status: if they act and are responsible for their actions, are harmed and benefited, have interests, and so on. Otherwise we can treat them as we do sticks and stones.

As I stated it, the ontology says that sub- and crosspeople are exactly like us apart from their temporal boundaries, implying that they think and act just as we do.[7] And any being psychologically and behaviorally indistinguishable at some time from a being with moral status ought to have moral status then too. My today part may not have precisely the same moral status as I have: he may not be responsible for what I did yesterday. But I can see no grounds for denying him moral status altogether.

If sub- and crosspeople have interests, what are they? Suppose that it is in the interests of a *person* to acquire as much benefit and as little harm or detriment as possible. (Set aside worries about what counts as a benefit or harm, how to weigh one against another, or whether benefits and harms far in the future count for less than imminent ones.) If it is also in the interests of sub- and crosspeople to maximize *their* benefit and minimize their

---

7. A few generous ontologists (e.g., Shoemaker, "Self, Body, and Coincidence") argue that such beings would have no mental properties; but this is a minority view.

harm, then their interests differ from ours. It is in my interests to buy milk tonight in order to have something for breakfast tomorrow. If I do not, I shall go hungry in the morning, which would be far worse for me than the tedium of visiting the supermarket. But my today part will get no such compensating benefit. It seems to be in his interest to seize the day—to eat, drink, and be merry, sparing no expense, mortgaging the house if need be. The doleful effect of all this on me tomorrow is of no concern to him, unless he wants to do me a favor and promote my interests over his own.

In fact, almost anything I could do that would be in my interest would go against the interests of countless subpeople. Any effort I could make—even opening the bottle or raising the glass to my lips—will be an effort on the part of subpeople who will pass away before they can benefit.

WHY SUBPEOPLE ACT SELFLESSLY

One might wonder why these beings act with such spectacular irrationality. My today part, if he exists, acts consistently in my interests and against his own. He acts in his interests only when they coincide with mine. He has no more intention of seeking short-term pleasure and ignoring tomorrow than I do. Or consider the crossperson coinciding with me until midnight and with Barack Obama thereafter. Though it would be in his interests to sign over all my money to Obama before the banks close, the thought never even occurs to him. He thinks only of me.

The reason is that these beings don't know who they are. My today part is not aware that he has only hours to live or that he came into being just this morning. Nor is the crossperson jumping from me to Obama tonight aware that he will do so. That is because their current beliefs are *my* beliefs—we share the same brain, after all—and I believe no such thing. If my today part is asked whether he will exist tomorrow, he will give the same answer as I would: of course, barring some sudden disaster.

What *do* these beings believe, then? The usual answer is that they have no beliefs about themselves at all, or at least none about themselves as such: no first-person or *de se* beliefs.[8] When they think or say "I," they do not refer to themselves but to me, the person. So when my today part says, "I'll finish this paper tomorrow," he does not express the false belief that he himself will finish tomorrow but the true belief that I will. Why do their first-person pronouns, and the first-person thoughts those words express,

---

8. Noonan, "Animalism versus Lockeanism."

refer to me and not to them? Why can't they refer to themselves in the first person? Well, that is simply how we, and they, think and speak. We all use the personal pronouns and related expressions to refer to maximal aggregates of psychologically interconnected person-stages, or some such. Sub- and crosspeople are linguistic helots, deprived by conventions of reference of the ability to speak and think about themselves as such. (A strange view, perhaps, but the sort of thing generous ontologists have to accept.) So the sub- and crosspeople coinciding with me consistently act for my benefit and ignore their own because their first-person thoughts are always about me and never about themselves.

Someone might argue that their inability to think about themselves as themselves means that they don't count as people in the Lockean sense. When *I* wonder, "Shall I be alive in 2050?" I am engaging in self-awareness, but when my today part has that thought, he is not; he is not thinking about himself as himself, but rather, if I may so speak, about *me* as himself. Even so, this is unlikely to affect his moral status. The sort of self-awareness that sub- and crosspeople lack is an extrinsic property. It is a property that a genuine person just like my today part, only created out of nothing and then annihilated, would have. It would be extraordinary if this difference had any moral significance: it would give linguistic convention the power to bestow or withhold moral status. Remember, which beings one's personal pronouns and first-person thoughts refer to is a matter of convention. Conventions of reference might change so that someone's first-person thought and talk no longer refers to herself—the being it in fact refers to—but to a subperson. The difference could be so subtle that no one would notice. Moral status could hardly be such a delicate condition as that.

CLASHING INTERESTS

If this is the right account of the interests of sub- and crosspeople, then our interests constantly clash with theirs. Almost anything I could do in my own interests would go against the interests of vast numbers of sub- and crosspeople.

This may not by itself imply that one has any obligations to these beings, as one does to other people. How could I fail to have obligations to my sub- and crosspeople? Not because they are mere parts of me—that would not apply to crosspeople—but perhaps because they coincide with me. Their consciousness is my consciousness. I have obligations to others only when their conscious states are independent of mine (or of any person's). But this would imply that my subpeople have no obligations to me either. My today part could indulge himself today with a clear conscience. At any rate, the fact that his celebrations might ruin me would give him no reason to restrain himself. That hardly seems fair.

It looks as if I ought to take the interests of sub- and crosspeople into account in my moral thinking, just as they must consider my interests in theirs. But how? In many cases the way to promote their interests is simply to promote my own. Whatever benefits or harms me at a given time will benefit or harm the subpeople coinciding with me then. The better off I am, the better off they will be. But not always. It could be in my interests to learn a difficult language or undergo a series of painful medical procedures. The long-term benefits may be enormous and success likely. But those of my subpeople who have the misfortune to exist only during the period of hardship would bear the burdens without any compensating benefit. I should be making their entire lives a misery in order to benefit myself. Granted, this also benefits the subpeople coinciding with me during the period when the benefits accrue. But no matter how many benefit, it seems unjust to those who suffer with no chance of any reward for themselves.

This may be no problem for maximizing utilitarians. If our sole duty is to maximize happiness, perhaps we ought to do the best by the stages and never mind about how the good is distributed. (Maximizing utilitarianism is the analog in the moral sphere of the relaxed attitude towards identity over time.) But if morality demands some measure of equality or minimizing of harm to the worst-off, we cannot have this simple solution.

Of course, the subpeople sacrifice their interests willingly: if I decide to suffer now for the sake of some future benefit, all the beings now coinciding with me do too, even those who will not themselves benefit. And it is not normally unjust for a being willingly to make the remainder of his existence miserable in order to benefit others after his demise; in fact, it is admirable. But not in this case, for the subpeople are unaware of their sacrifice. They are motivated by beliefs that they would express by saying such things as "Learning Russian will make me miserable for two years, but I shall have a brilliant career in the Foreign Office afterwards." Yet many of them have no chance of existing in two years' time. It is not that their beliefs about their future are false. Because those beliefs are about me and not them, they may be true: their sacrifice may well give *me* a brilliant career. But they have no beliefs about themselves. (They may believe that a person of a certain description will suffer and then benefit and that certain subpeople will suffer without benefiting. But they have no beliefs about which of these beings they themselves are.) So their actions are not based on informed choices. If they *did* know that they were not going to enjoy the fruits of their sacrifice, they would be no more likely to do it than anyone else would. Causing a being to devote the remainder of his existence to the benefit of others when he is entirely ignorant of its effects on him is unjust.

This seems to imply that anyone who suffers for the sake of a later benefit coincides with sub- and crosspeople whose decision is not based on informed consent: beings who are entirely ignorant of its likely consequences for themselves. More strongly, it suggests that we have a moral obligation to avoid periods of intense misery, no matter what rewards it may bring. Polar expeditions and divorce would be morally dubious at best. For the sake of my subpeople, it seems that I ought to live a life that is fairly pleasant at all times and forego benefits that I can achieve only at the cost of great sacrifice. Suffering for the sake of a future benefit would make beings like me suffer throughout their lives for my benefit. Moral duty would compel us to be comfortable and unambitious.

THE PARFITIAN PROPOSAL

I have been assuming up to now that the interests of sub- and crosspeople differ from our own. But it could be that their interests are always the same as ours. The interests of a subperson might be to maximize benefits and minimize harms not to herself but to the person she coincides with. That way, all the beings now coinciding with me would now have the same interests. If it is in my interests to suffer today to gain a benefit tomorrow, it would be equally in the interests of my today part to suffer, even though he will never benefit. It would be in his interests because it benefits *me*. Or think of the crossperson coinciding with me until midnight tonight and with Obama thereafter. It would not now be in his interests to transfer the contents of my bank account to Obama's tonight, even though that would benefit him considerably. He has no interest in benefiting himself, unless it also benefits me. (Tomorrow, of course, it will be in his interests to benefit Obama.) The interests of sub- and crosspeople are parasitic on our own: they are moral helots as well as linguistic ones. In that case, I do not violate their interests by suffering now in order to benefit later, and there is no moral duty to avoid temporary discomfort. The generous ontology might not require us to change our behavior at all.

How could it be in the interests of a rational being to sacrifice for the sake of benefits that only others will enjoy, or fail to be in his interests to benefit himself? This would be an application of the idea, familiar from Parfit and others, that numerical identity over time lacks the practical importance it is traditionally ascribed, and that what does matter practically is some other relation (R) that normally coincides with identity—some sort of psychological continuity, perhaps.[9] If each of a person's cerebral hemispheres were transplanted into a different head, so that both resulting people were psychologically continuous with her, their welfare might bear on her current interests in the same way that her own future welfare does in normal circumstances. (They might both be responsible for her actions too.) Yet it may be that neither offshoot would *be* her because if either were, both would be, and that is impossible because they are two and she is one. So it might be in her interests to sacrifice now to benefit them later, even though she herself will not benefit. In that case we should have what matters practically in identity without identity itself.

Just so, it might be in the interests of my today part to sacrifice now for my benefit tomorrow: my welfare tomorrow might matter to him today in the same way that it matters to me today. It might likewise be in the current interests of any crossperson coinciding with me now and with someone else tomorrow to benefit me tomorrow. And if we can have what matters without identity, it might also be possible to have identity without what matters. In that case, it might not be in that crossperson's interests now to benefit himself tomorrow: it may be no more in his prudential interest to promote his own welfare tomorrow than it is for you to promote mine. Whereas Parfit thought that what matters comes apart from identity only in unusual cases, it might happen constantly—whenever any sub- or crossperson ceases to coincide with one of us.

Parfitians are not forced to accept this: the general claim that what matters can obtain without identity (or vice versa) does not imply that this is the case with sub- or crosspeople. Because it is an application of that general claim, however, I will call it the Parfitian proposal.

---

9. Parfit, *Reasons and Persons*, 215.

COULD I BE A MORAL HELOT?

The proposal has important implications. For one thing, the standard four-dimensionalist version of the generous ontology implies that a person can survive the double transplant: both offshoots would be that person, insofar as they share their temporal parts located before the operation, and talk of "that person" then refers ambiguously to each. This leads Lewis and others to argue that identity really has got the practical importance traditionally ascribed to it.[10] If they have to adopt the *Parfitian proposal* in order to deal with sub- and crosspeople, this is mistaken.

Here is a more disquieting thought. The proposal is that the interests of a sub- or crossperson at a given time are the interests at that time of the person it coincides with then. So although all rational, self-conscious beings may have interests, *people* have a special moral status: they are the primary bearers of interests. The interests of other beings derive from those of people. It is tempting to say that to be a primary bearer of interests is what it is to be a person. We might call this status *moral personhood*.

I described the Parfitian proposal by saying that we are moral people, because I took it that we ourselves are the primary interest bearers. *My* interests, surely, could not be merely derivative. It could not be in my interests to benefit some other being that I now coincide with rather than myself. I am no moral helot. This comfortable assumption would be warranted if I were the only candidate for being the primary bearer of my interests—the only rational moral agent thinking these thoughts and writing these words. But the generous ontology says that I am only one of a vast number of such beings, nearly all of whom are moral helots. How do I know I am not one of them?

I can know, of course, that I am the being I refer to when I say "I": one of the beings we call "people" in ordinary English. I know that linguistic fact by virtue of being a competent speaker. And that is what it is to be a person according to advocates of the generous ontology. We might call this status *linguistic personhood*. I know that I am a linguistic person. And because sub- and crosspeople, by definition, are not linguistic people, I know that I am not one of them. But this would enable me to know that I am a moral person only if moral personhood and linguistic personhood are coextensive—if all and only moral people are linguistic people. And that is indeed what the Parfitian proposal says. But what reason is there to believe

10. Lewis, "Survival and Identity."

that this is the case? To put the point another way, a moral person, on the Parfitian proposal, is by definition a maximal aggregate of R-interrelated person-stages, where R is the relation that matters practically. At any rate, that seems to be the obvious way of developing the proposal.[11] And we might call the relation that binds together the stages of a linguistic person R*, so that a linguistic person is by definition a maximal aggregate of R*-interrelated person-stages. Moral and linguistic personhood are coextensive only if R and R* are coextensive. But what grounds have we to suppose that they are?

Moral personhood and linguistic personhood appear to be independent properties. The reason why we, as a linguistic community, came to use the personal referring expressions to denote beings unified by R*, rather than beings unified by some other relation, lies in the vagaries of human linguistic behavior. These vagaries do not even guarantee that all speakers use those expressions to refer to the same sorts of beings: Chinese linguistic people might be maximal aggregates of stages interrelated in some slightly different way from those of British linguistic people. If all human beings used personal referring expressions to denote the same beings, it would seem to be only an unlikely coincidence. And it would be all the more unlikely if those beings were also the moral people.

MORAL AND LINGUISTIC PERSONHOOD

Or maybe moral personhood and linguistic personhood are not independent after all. Perhaps the conventions of reference track moral status, so that personal pronouns, and the thoughts we use them to express, always refer to moral people. The difficulty for this proposal is that we do not know (on the Parfitian proposal) which beings the moral people are. We know that a moral person is a maximal aggregate of R-interrelated person stages, where R is the "mattering" relation, but philosophers debate about what relation that is. Even if everyone agrees that R is some kind of psychological continuity, there are many such kinds, each of which would determine a different class of beings. And if we cannot agree about which, of the many candidates, are the moral people, how can our linguistic conventions pick them out?

11. I am assuming for the sake of argument that there is only one "mattering" relation, and thus (on the Parfitian proposal) only one species of moral person. Otherwise the connection between moral and linguistic personhood would be even looser.

Perhaps we use the personal pronouns to refer to moral people without knowing which beings they are, just as we can use the word "water" to refer to a chemical substance without knowing what substance it is. The word "I" might mean something like "the being with nonderivative interests, whatever it may be, that is speaking or thinking this," just as "water" means something like "the chemical substance, whatever it may be, that fills rivers and lakes." This proposal would enable us to know that we are moral people.

That would infect the semantics of personal reference with moral content. To call something a person, or to refer to it as "I" or as "Socrates," would be to make a value judgment. These would be at least implicitly moral terms, just as "water" is (on this account of its meaning) implicitly a scientific term—vindicating Locke's claim that "person" is "a forensic term,"[12] though not in the way he intended.

It would also mean that in an important sense we do not know which beings we are. I could know that I am a maximal aggregate of R-interrelated person stages, but insofar as I do not know exactly what relation R is, I do not know which being that aggregate is. Likewise, we do not know what our identity over time consists in. We may know that it consists in R, but we do not know under what conditions R holds. That would make it a mistake to be relaxed about personal identity. If we ask what it takes for a person to persist through time, or whether someone would still exist after a certain event, there would be a unique right answer in terms of R. Any other judgment would be false. Our judgments about our identity over time would be only as reliable as our judgments about what relation it is that matters in identity. These judgments could be badly mistaken, just as moral judgments can be. That would undermine one of the main reasons for accepting the generous ontology in the first place.

What if conventions of personal reference are independent of the way nonderivative interests are distributed among moral agents? What if, in other words, linguistic and moral personhood are independent? Then something could be a linguistic person without being a moral person. And it is hard to see how we could be certain that we linguistic people are moral people. If anything, it would be highly unlikely for the conventions governing the reference of the word "I" and related terms to pick out the one moral person from among the multitude of beings writing this paper. It is far more probable that I am one of those whose interests are merely derivative: my interests are those of some other being that I coincide with. We

12. Locke, *Essay Concerning Human Understanding*, 346.

ourselves are moral helots. Though we fancy ourselves at the center of the moral universe, these are almost certainly delusions of grandeur, and our true place is on the periphery. And the beings who really are at the center are unaware of their exalted status. An accident of linguistic convention has made them blind to it: not being linguistic people, they have no thoughts at all about themselves as such. That would be a deeply absurd situation.

HOW ONTOLOGY IMPINGES ON ETHICS

The generous ontology appears, at least, to have troubling ethical consequences. Let me make one final remark. The Parfitian proposal is that the primary interest bearers—moral people—are maximal aggregates of R-interrelated person-stages. All other beings with moral status derive their interests from them. Assuming that R is a kind of psychological continuity, it follows that only a being that is always psychologically continuous in that way with itself as it is at every other time when it exists can have nonderivative interests. It would be important for ethics if this were true.

It is unlikely to be true, however, without the generous ontology. Suppose there are no sub- or crosspeople. In that case the only rational beings walking the earth are likely to be human organisms. (They might be immaterial substances or Humean bundles of impressions instead, but that is less likely.) If so, there are no maximal aggregates of R-interrelated person-stages. Not only are there no person-stages, but there are no beings R-related to themselves at every time when they exist as they are at every other time when they exist. Every human organism starts out as an embryo, and nothing is ever psychologically continuous in any way with itself as it was as an embryo. To put it the other way round, those who think there are beings who are R-related to themselves at all times will almost invariably accept some form of generous ontology. And if there are no such beings, it can hardly be the case that a thing must be always R-related to itself in order to have nonderivative interests; otherwise it would follow that no beings have nonderivative interests, and hence that no beings have interests at all.

So what it takes for a being to have full moral status may depend on the truth of the generous ontology: if it is true, a being might have to be always R-related to itself in order to have it; if not, the conditions for full moral status may have to be less stringent. Here, again, metaphysics impinges on ethics.[13]

13. Acknowledgments: I thank David Shoemaker, Fiona Woollard, an anonymous

BIBLIOGRAPHY

Baker, Lynne Rudder. *Persons and Bodies: A Constitution View*. Cambridge Studies in Philosophy. Cambridge: Cambridge University Press, 2000.

Lewis, David. "Survival and Identity." In *The Identities of Persons*, edited by Amélie Oksenberg Rorty, 17–40. Topics in Philosophy 3. Berkeley: University of California Press, 1976.

Locke, John. *An Essay Concerning Human Understanding*. Edited by P. H. Nidditch. Clarendon Edition of the Works of John Locke. Oxford: Clarendon, 1976.

Noonan, Harold. "Animalism versus Lockeanism: A Current Controversy." *Philosophical Quarterly* 48 (1998) 302–18.

Parfit, Derek. *Reasons and Persons*. Oxford: Clarendon Press, 1984.

Shoemaker, Sidney. "Self, Body, and Coincidence." Supplement, *Proceedings of the Aristotelian Society* 73 (1999) 287–306.

Sider, Theodore. *Four-Dimensionalism: An Ontology of Persistence and Time*. Oxford: Clarendon Press, 2001.

---

referee, and especially David Hershenov for their help. This essay was first published in 2010.

PART II

Bioethics and Personhood

7

Taking Persons Seriously
Applications to Bioethics

Scott B. Rae

Who and what constitutes a human person is central to many of the most controversial bioethical issues—in fact, what makes the issues so controversial is the contested views of the person. From the status of fetuses in abortion to embryos in reproductive technology to the elderly/terminally ill at the end of life, metaphysical views of the person are at the heart of these issues. Yet in my experience in bioethics over the past twenty-five years I have noticed a bracketing out of metaphysics in many discussions. In my view, this comes, in part, from the bedside, practical context for much of contemporary bioethics, in which the dignity of the patient can be reasonably assumed. In addition, this comes from the public policy emphasis in bioethics, which required bridge building among diverse ideological constituencies. It is often among these constituencies that metaphysical considerations are the principal things that divide the groups, thus they are often bracketed out in order to achieve a rough, though limited, consensus. Among theists who are eager to enter the bioethical discussion, this bracketing is often considered part of the price of admission to get into the conversation.

In the mainstream bioethics community, metaphysical considerations are often assumed without being explicitly articulated. Various forms of naturalism and physicalism are the default metaphysical positions that are assumed and must be adopted if one is to be a credible participant. Even something such as Peter Singer's preference utilitarianism makes no explicit metaphysical commitments, but underlying the system is the assumption of naturalism.[1] Even in some religious bioethics circles, particularly Christian ones, I've observed this bracketing out of metaphysics. For example, substance dualists, in one form or another, such as the contributors to this volume, who hold that human beings are a unity of material body and immaterial soul, at times attempt to find common ground with Christian physicalists, who hold to a form of physicalism that they maintain is consistent with their understanding of the Bible's view of human persons.[2]

In this chapter, I will attempt to build on the metaphysical work in part 1 and begin the application of the metaphysics of human persons to the various issues in bioethics. The central theme of this volume is that metaphysics matters to ethics, both to metaethics and applied ethics, particularly in the field of bioethics and, more specifically, to bioethical issues at the bedside and the clinic.[3] This is not to say that every health care professional needs to be conversant with the metaphysics of human persons at the depth presented so far. But views of persons are often assumed uncritically by both professionals at the bedside and practicing bioethicists. Our emphasis here is to insist on as much metaphysical rigor as possible given its importance to the ethical deliberations that take place in health care practice and public policy as well as the academic discussions in bioethics.

The metaphysical foundations for a substance dualist view of a person have been ably laid out and defended in part 1 of this volume. Timothy Houk and Russell DiSilvestro maintain that persons matter. They argue that it matters how we treat them. Yet, for Houk and DiSilvestro, merely determining how persons ought to be treated leaves out the question of who rightfully counts as a person. That means that in order to settle the ethical questions regarding how the individual is to be treated, it is advisable first to answer the metaphysical question of when an individual counts as a descriptive person. They cite the "debtor's paradox" to illustrate the importance of persons maintaining personal identity through time and change.

---

1. See, e.g., Singer, *Practical Ethics* and *Writings on Ethical Life*.

2. For examples of Christian physicalism, see Brown et al., *Whatever Happened to Soul*; Murphy and Brown, *Did My Neurons*.

3. The metaethical implications of our view of persons are beyond the scope of this volume and have been well considered elsewhere.

In addition, they defend the notion that different metaphysical views of persons result in different views of our moral obligations to such persons. They helpfully distinguish between normative and descriptive senses of persons, and critique the notion of the "potential person," contrasting with the concept of the "person with potential," which they argue is a more coherent concept. They illustrate this with the temporarily brain-damaged teenager who has lost the crucial functions necessary for personhood laid out by Mary Ann Warren, but is still clearly a person.

J. P. Moreland defends substance dualism and the existence of the soul as the immaterial essence of a human person. The soul is key to personhood and the body has value precisely because it is ensouled. According to substance dualism, the soul (self, mind, ego) is said to be not identical to anything physical. Instead, the soul is an enduring spiritual substance that has/unifies consciousness it employs and is said to be the referent of "I." It is said to exhibit a first-person point of view, as well as acting as an intentional agent. This is what gives persons both significant and intrinsic value, regardless of their ability to perform various functions.

Mihretu Guta examines certain influential contemporary philosophical analyses of the notion of a person and shows why they are misguided. Inspired largely by the Lockean conception of a person, some contemporary analytic philosophers claim that personhood must be attributed only to those human beings who can meet certain criteria required for it. Here the views of Tooley, Dennett, and Singer are discussed against the backdrop of the metaphysics of powers ontology as advocated by contemporary philosophers: C. B. Martin, John Heil, and others.

Eric LaRock, Mostyn Jones, Matthew Owen, Aryn D. Owen, and Anthony G. Hudetz address one of the most challenging issues for any metaphysical view of persons—that of consciousness. La Rock and Jones specifically address Patricia Churchland's metaphysical physicalism with her insistence that the self is entirely constituted by the brain and that the neurosciences are the best guide for understanding the self. They defend a non-Cartesian substance dualism that avoids her reductionism and, at the same time, avoids the well-known causal objections raised against free will. They turn the tables on Churchland and touch a nerve themselves by showing a view of dualism that accounts for consciousness and the mind better than the neuroscience on which Churchland relies.

Owen, Owen, and Hudetz address a more specific issue with consciousness—that of covert consciousness in unresponsive patients at the bedside. They maintain that their mind-body powers model of consciousness could empirically account for consciousness in patients that are otherwise unresponsive. They distinguish between consciousness and the ability to express that consciousness, insisting that the latter does not rule out the possibility of the former. They maintain that the mind-body powers model they propose gives philosophical reasons for inferring that an unresponsive patient is conscious. This is the case if neuroimaging data reveal the presence of neural activity that is said to correlate with consciousness in a normally functioning human brain.

Eric Olson discusses the way in which metaphysics impinges on ethics. In this regard, Olson examines a temporal parts ontology/generous ontology and its implications for issues related to personal identity. He explores, among other things, whether short-lived entities or, as he calls them, "subpeople," have moral status. Olson further explores whether their interests clashes with ours. He also explores if the interests of sub- and crosspeople (combinations of several people) differ from our own. He also discusses the Parfitian proposal that postulates that the primary interest bearers or moral people are said to be maximal aggregates of R-interrelated person-stages.

But for Olson, without generous ontology, there would be no sub- or crosspeople. In that case, for Olson, every human organism starts out as an embryo with no need for psychological continuity as a condition for issues related to personal identity, and persistence.

As Olson sees it, a being's having full moral status seems to be contingent on the truth of the generous ontology. If this turns out to be true, then a being in question might have to be always R-related to itself in order to have it. But if this is not the case, then the conditions for full moral status can be said to be less demanding. For Olson, all of this shows the impact of metaphysics upon ethics.

The arena of bioethics is often the place where one's views of person are revealed, even if one's metaphysical commitments are not explicit. For example, in much of the discussion of fetuses and embryos in the wider bioethics community, often the framework of metaphysical naturalism is simply assumed. The notion that fetuses and embryos could be persons, or could be constituted metaphysically any differently than on the basis of naturalism, is often simply ruled out of court. Similarly, at the end of life, the elderly or terminally ill are often the subject of a distinction between a person and a human being—as James Rachels laid out the distinction between biological and biographical life.[4] To make that distinction requires the assumption of naturalism, but on the basis of a different metaphysic—that of substance dualism, the distinction between a human being and a person, or between biological and biographical life, makes little sense. For if there is a continuity of personal identity, which is difficult to maintain under naturalism, which is somehow grounded in something that transcends time and change, such as an immaterial soul, then to be a human being is by definition to be a human person as well.

ABORTION AND INFANTICIDE

At the beginning of life, personhood comes into play in a variety of issues, first and foremost that of abortion. Of course, the moral status of fetuses and embryos is central to this discussion. In the conflict between a woman's right over her own body and the right to life of the fetus, the moral status of the fetus is determinative of the weighting of those competing interests. According to many opponents of abortion, it is the only issue that matters, and once that is settled, in their view, the debate is over. The weighting of the right to life more heavily than the woman's right is obvious and self-evident. For abortion proponents, the status of the fetus, generally regarded as something less than the status recognized by abortion opponents, allows for weighting the woman's rights more heavily than those of the fetus.

The 2022 Dobbs decision that overturned Roe v. Wade did not make any determination about the moral status of the unborn, leaving this issue to be decided by the states. In overturning Roe, the court called into question the now-outdated three-trimester framework in which the right of the fetus to life was situated. States are now free to set the threshold for fetal protection at a variety of points along the continuum from conception to birth. Mississippi, for example, in the Dobbs case, set the decisive point at fifteen weeks, admittedly a somewhat arbitrary point in the gestational age of the fetus. Other states, such as Texas, have set a fetal heartbeat threshold, which prohibits abortion at a much earlier stage of gestation.

It should be noted that no "decisive moment" between conception and birth makes any necessary metaphysical difference in what kind of a thing the fetus precisely is. For example, perhaps the most common point along the gestation continuum, and the one recognized by Roe, is viability, the ability of the fetus to survive outside the mother's womb. Viability at the

---

4. Rachels, *End of Life*. See the discussion of Rachels later in this chapter.

time of Roe was roughly at the end of the second trimester, making the trimester framework the court adopted more understandable. What makes that framework out of date today is that viability has been pushed back much earlier in the second trimester to between twenty-two and twenty-six weeks, varying because every fetus and pregnancy is different. In addition, in virtually every case of delivery at this stage, the notion of viability (the ability to survive outside the womb) is somewhat misleading. This is because in order to survive for weeks after delivery, the newborn child has simply exchanged a natural life-support system in the mother for an entirely artificial life-support system in the NICU (neo-natal intensive care unit). Many of them stay there for weeks, if not months, and ongoing complications from such an early delivery are not uncommon. What viability actually measures is the state and progress of neonatal medical technology, which renders viability quite different in less advantaged communities as opposed to tertiary care, high-risk pregnancy centers. The state of neonatal medical technology makes no necessary commentary on the metaphysical status of the fetus and is, ultimately, an arbitrary threshold for determining personhood and the attendant rights of the fetus.

The same holds true for other so-called decisive moments. Implantation simply marks a change of location for the fetus, which makes no metaphysical difference. Fetal heartbeat awareness, parallel to the medieval notion of quickening, are both epistemological markers that depend on the mother's cognizance of the fetus, and as any first-year philosophy student knows, one cannot confuse epistemology with ontology. The appearance of brain activity is similar to these markers, but with a more compelling parallel to the definition of death. The difference, of course, is that at the end of life, the loss of all brain activity is permanent and irreversible, whereas, at the beginning of life, it is only temporary and developmentally appropriate for the stage of maturity at which the fetus is. In addition, the temporary lack of brain function is an unactualized capacity, which is possessed by the fetus from the point at which conception is complete. Birth, parallel to implantation, marks merely a change in location and only a slight change in the degree of dependence of the newborn baby on the mother.

Some abortion proponents have recognized that there is nothing metaphysically significant about birth, even though the law in most parts of the world still recognizes birth as the point at which personhood undeniably begins. Early proponents of infanticide, such as Peter Singer and Michael Tooley, made the case that even for a time after birth, the newborn still did not necessarily possess an inalienable right to life.[5] More recent proponents have moved the defense of infanticide into more of the mainstream discussion of abortion, now calling infanticide the "after-birth abortion."[6] These proponents make clear that birth has no metaphysical significance, and the door to infanticide was opened wider than Singer and Tooley originally had in mind, as their focus was on the severely disabled child. Of course, infanticide has been practiced for some time, without regard to personhood considerations, namely, in parts of the world where parents have strong preferences for one sex over the other. What's different about the work of the Singer, Tooley, and the more recent philosophers is the academic justification for infanticide that centers around the notion of the personhood of the newborn as well as the fetus.

The shortcomings of these various "decisive moments" and the movement toward justifying infanticide led to some different ways of determining the personhood of the fetus/newborn. Rather than a point along the conception-birth continuum, the fetus/newborn was required to demonstrate a handful of functions that were deemed critical to someone being designated a person. DiSilvestro and Houk recognize the work of earlier philosophers such as Mary Ann Warren and Joseph Fletcher in identifying some of these necessary functions.[7] In addition, philosopher Bonnie Steinbock has focused on one of these functions—that of sentience as the critical determinant of personhood and attendant rights.[8]

DiSilvestro and Houk recognize the flaws in these various functional views of persons with their illustration of the teenager in a coma. Any functional view of the fetus/embryo, whether that of Steinbock, Warren, Fletcher, or numerous others who have put such a view forth, must account for the temporary losses of these functions during times of reversible coma, or even general anesthesia, in human beings who are uncontestably full human persons. Guta's essay also shows why the contemporary powers ontology provides us with a powerful explanatory advantage to show why personhood is retained at all times no matter what happens to the manifestation of cognitive capacities. The counterargument that these states are only temporary misses the point, since that appeal assumes that during

---

5. See, e.g., Singer and Kuhse, *Should the Baby Live?*

6. See, e.g., the lead article in an entire symposium on this subject, Giubilini and Minerva, "After-Birth Abortion."

7. Warren, *Moral Status*; Fletcher, "Indicators of Humanhood."

8. Steinbock, *Life before Birth*.

those temporary states, something else besides those functions actually grounds their remaining persons. We would suggest that that something else is something intrinsic to the person that is not dependent on any ability to perform specific functions, for which the substance dualist view of a person accounts quite well. Persons function in certain predicable ways because they are things of a certain type, not the reverse. That is, the ability to perform those supposedly necessary functions are not determinative of personhood. Rather those functions, for example, in the fetus, are the capacities that have been latent but are now being actualized, as part of the appropriate stages of maturity. This is why substance dualists do not speak of the embryo becoming a fetus, or developing into a fetus, newborn, etc. Rather, embryos mature into fetuses, who then mature into newborns, etc.

This continuity is the reason why embryos are seen as having the same moral and ontological status as fetuses and newborns. Whether they are inside or outside the womb is simply a difference in location, with no ontological significance. This is true even though the lab environment cannot, at this point, sustain the embryo and its maturity for all of the time needed for embryos to mature into newborns. But the suitability of the lab environment does not make an ontological difference either. For example, if astronauts were stranded on the moon without the necessary equipment to survive there, and the moon was thus an unsuitable environment for persons to flourish, these marooned astronauts would still unquestionably be full persons. We recognize that it is counterintuitive for many to consider embryos as having the status of full persons. Some want to consider embryos as nothing more than a clump of cells, or a "bag of marbles." But from the time conception is complete, the human embryo is fully human, having come from human parents and possessing a full complement of DNA, and has all the capacities it will ever have and need in order to mature into a full-grown adult. The fact that these capacities are latent in the process of fetal maturity does not mean that they are not possessed. They are not yet actualized as part of the normal process of maturing. Embryos do not become something ontologically different than what they are—they mature into what they already are.

Some will concede that the embryo/fetus is a person and still advocate for full abortion rights for the pregnant woman. For example, in the classic example of world-famous violinist with a kidney disease, someone is kidnapped and strapped to a bed to be a substitute kidney for the person for nine months. Judith Jarvis Thomson concludes that surely the kidnapped person, here analogous to the pregnant woman, is not obligated to provide the life-support system.[9] It is not entirely clear whether Thomson is conceding the personhood of the fetus for the sake of argument or whether she actually holds that position. She seems to indicate that at some point during pregnancy, unidentified, the fetus can be rightly seen as a person with the right to life, but that right is outweighed by the right of the mother over her own body.

A similar concession is made by Naomi Wolf in a well-publicized article that served as an admonition to her pro-choice colleagues to concede that the unborn are persons.[10] This concession was based on what medical technology such as ultrasound was making available to pregnant women, at earlier stages of their pregnancies. In her view it was becoming less and less plausible to conclude that the fetus was nothing more than impersonal tissue or something analogous to bodily organs. Like Thomson, she argues that the woman's right to choose what happens to her own body should be weighted more heavily than the right to life of her full-person fetus. Different from Thomson, Wolf sees the tragedy of a woman being in the position of having to make that choice to end her pregnancy as situated in the Jewish tradition of redemption.

One more recent assignment of personhood to fetuses assumes a different metaphysical framework—not of naturalism, but of postmodernism, in which there is no metanarrative framework in which to situate the human person.[11] In this framework, the assignment of personhood to fetuses is conferred by the mother. Being a person is seen as a social construct, not anything fundamentally ontological. Philosopher Hilde Lindemann refers to this process as the pregnant woman "calling the fetus into personhood." She describes personhood as a social practice—what the pregnant woman does is "call the fetus into personhood, by making physical arrangements for it, creating social space for it within her family and the wider community,

---

9. Thomson, "Defense of Abortion." For critique of Thomson, see Beckwith, *Defending Life*, 172–201.

10. Wolf, "Our Bodies, Our Souls." For a more recent work combining the concession of personhood with vigorous advocacy for abortion rights, see Boonin, *Beyond Roe*. For critique of both Wolf and Boonin, see Kaczor, *Ethics of Abortion*.

11. One of the common critiques of postmodernism is that the postmodern framework is itself a metanarrative, and the postmodern insistence that it is not is something akin to the emperor having no clothes. The metaphysical assumptions of postmodernism, such as the denial of objective truth and its knowability, are beyond the scope of this chapter.

and in an imaginative projection, conceiving of it as if it were already the born child she hopes it will become . . . she takes an attitude toward them of the kind reserved for persons.[12]

To be sure, there are numerous social practices that are characteristic of families welcoming children into the world that begin well before the child is born. But the notion of a pregnant woman "calling her fetus into personhood" bypasses any metaphysical considerations and leaves the notion of personhood as ultimately dependent on whether or not he or she is wanted by the mother. Of course, the mother could choose not to call the fetus into personhood by ending the pregnancy But wantedness is a commentary on the subjective mental state of the mother, not on the ontological status of the fetus. Whether or not the fetus is called into personhood has little connection to what kind of a thing it inherently is. The phrase "calling into personhood" is actually more a recognition of personhood as opposed to a determination of it, thereby confusing what is recognized about the fetus, which is different than what is actually is—again, a confusion of epistemology and ontology. In addition, it seems possible that the process of calling the fetus into personhood would not be complete until after the child is born, especially if the mother is ambivalent about keeping the pregnancy. If so, then the postmodern framework for personhood in this case could be logically extended to include infanticide.

EMBRYO RESEARCH AND REPRODUCTIVE TECHNOLOGIES

The moral status of embryos carries its own set of ethical issues that are dependent on the metaphysical view outlined and defended in the first part of this volume. Though somewhat counterintuitive, the notion of embryos being persons is ably defended by Houk and DiSilvestro, and Moreland's argument can be extended to include embryos. If, as he has argued, the soul is the essence of the human person, and the body has value precisely because it is ensouled, Moreland maintains that the soul is the engine that drives all of the bodily maturity of the person. Thus, the notion of "soulless person" would be an oxymoron for the substance dualist. For the body without the soul would constitute a corpse, and the only moral obligations in such a case would be those in keeping with the general respect for the

---

12. Lindemann, "Miscarriage and the Stories." See also Lindemann, "But I Could Never."

dead. Thus, it would follow that embryos would have souls from conception forward, or else they would be nonliving clumps of cells. But embryology is clear that from conception, the embryo is a human being—if it were not so, I suspect scientists would not be nearly as interested in embryonic stem cells as they are. And the substance dualist view we've defended in the first section makes it clear that there is a continuity of personal identity from conception forward, and, from that point, the embryo has all the capacities it will need to actualize in order to mature into a fully grown adult. It is a complete human person from the time that conception is complete.

This has ethical implications for both embryonic stem cell research and reproductive technologies. As long as the process of harvesting stem cells from human embryos involves the destruction of the embryo, which, at present, it does in the ongoing practice, that is morally problematic. One reason that this issue has receded from public attention is that the vast majority of clinical applications for stem cells, now numbering in the hundreds, are coming from stem cells harvested from non-embryonic sources. These are commonly referred to as "adult stem cells," and they come from several different sources, including bone marrow and umbilical-cord blood. There have been very few workable clinical applications from embryonic stem cells to date, despite the billions of dollars invested by governments and private entities. For example, the state of California has invested over $3 billion over the past two decades, with very little to show for it in terms of usable treatments for suffering patients. In part, the reason for this is an issue that has to do with donor-recipient compatibility. Adult stem cells are normally taken from the patient himself or herself, thus guaranteeing histocompatibility, and for this reason, parents of newborns are now routinely encouraged to freeze the umbilical cord blood of their child, in the event that it is needed for a future stem cell treatment. Whether these successes will eventually render the need for embryonic stem cells unnecessary remains to be seen, and it may be that at some point in the future, embryonic stem cells can be harvested without destroying the embryo in the process. Until that day, with embryos being full persons but at a very stage of maturity, harvesting their stem cells will be problematic, since as a general rule, inflicting harm (especially mortal harm) on one person in order to benefit another remains difficult to justify.

A more complex moral issue around the moral status of embryos involves several different reproductive technologies, especially the standard of practice with in vitro fertilization (IVF). In IVF, the goal is to give the infertile couple the best chance at achieving at least one live birth. To do this, the woman is given fertility hormones to enable her to release as many eggs as possible in her current cycle. Sperm is obtained from the man and is placed in a petri dish with the eggs—then they wait to see how many eggs are successfully fertilized. Normally the woman produces more eggs than can be used at that time, and often, more embryos are fertilized than can be safely implanted. This leaves the likelihood that, after the first group of two to three embryos is implanted, the couple will have embryos left over (which are frozen for future use). This is especially the case if the couple succeeds in having a live birth on the first attempt. If they have multiple children from that attempt, it is not uncommon for their childbearing days to be over, yet with multiple embryos (their children) remaining in storage. At this point, the couple has several different options. They can implant the remaining embryos themselves, perhaps in stages (the ideal), assuming the woman is still capable of carrying pregnancies to term. Or they can allow another couple to implant them, essentially giving up their embryonic children for adoption.[13] These would both be morally acceptable options that protect the life of the embryo. Other options that are less difficult for the couple, but morally problematic, include discarding the embryos, donating them to research (which normally results in their destruction), or continuing to keep the embryos in storage (which is not a decision at all). Whether embryos can be frozen at all is a moral issue as well, since doing something similar with fetuses or newborns, even for their own good, would be unthinkable for many people. The number of couples who elect to keep their embryos in storage is significant, and perhaps telling, about the ambivalence of couples toward destroying or donating their embryos. This may be particularly the case if couples have had children through IVF, since it is not hard to imagine that they recognize the continuity between the embryos in the lab and the child/children they are holding in their arms.

Reproductive technologies, including IVF, also involve moral issues with fetuses, issues that could arise after embryos are implanted. With IVF those are somewhat easier to control, since the couple and their infertility physician can elect to implant only the number of embryos that the woman can safely carry, or even the number of children that the couple ideally would prefer to raise. Of course, there are no guarantees that every embryo

13. For example, see the Snowflake Program at Nightlight Christian Adoptions—the first and largest embryo adoption program in the US (https://nightlight.org/snowflakes-embryo-adoption-donation/).

implanted will result in a live birth, and this is the reason why normally more than one embryo is implanted. In some cases, the age of the woman will be a factor in implanting more embryos than would be attempted if the woman were younger. If multiple embryos are successfully implanted, the couple will have the option of selective termination of some of the pregnancies, if the number of fetuses endangers the life or health of the woman, or even if the number of pregnancies exceeds the number of children the couple wants to raise. Not only are these dilemmas avoidable, but they are also morally problematic. It is irresponsible to implant more embryos than the woman can safely carry. It is equally irresponsible for the couple to go through IVF, have several successful pregnancies, and then decide that they are now pregnant with more children than they care to raise. Selective termination is virtually always morally problematic, except in those rare cases when it is necessary to save the mother's life. But that situation is the one that is entirely avoidable, simply by limiting the number of embryos implanted to the number that the woman can carry safely.

One other scenario with reproductive technologies can result in the need for selective termination of fetuses, and this one is more difficult to control. In some cases of intra-uterine insemination, the physician will give the woman some of the multiple ovulation hormones that are used in IVF, often at a lesser strength, but still enabling the woman to release multiple, but ultimately an unknown, number of eggs in one cycle. She is then inseminated with the sperm of her husband or a donor, and then, all involved wait and see how many pregnancies result. For example, if the woman releases six eggs and is then inseminated, it is possible that she could become pregnant with more fetuses than she can safely carry, and doing so may threaten her life. At that point, selective termination is usually strongly encouraged and may be necessary to save her life. This is a much more risky application of reproductive technology that raises the prospect of selective termination, and the physician will always advise the woman that this is a possibility that must be considered.

BIOTECHNOLOGY, GENETIC TESTING, AND GENE EDITING

In the field of genetics and biotechnology, the moral status of human persons, namely, fetuses and embryos, comes into focus. Take the area of prenatal genetic testing, for example. Many genetic abnormalities are detectable by ultrasound alone, and if preliminary ultrasound exams reveal something for further testing, normally amniocentesis is recommended. This has a minor level of risk to the fetus, and ultrasound is virtually risk free. The issue with this testing is not with the tests themselves, but with the decisions the pregnant woman/couple will make with the information they receive from these tests. If they get bad news back from prenatal testing, they can elect to end the pregnancy, which is what most couples elect to do. Or they can carry the child to term and elect to raise a child with genetic challenges. The couple needs to be aware that the genetic testing they undergo will give them a diagnosis, but for many genetic diseases, the severity of the disease the child will experience exists on a broad continuum. For example, the experience of Down syndrome can range from mild to severe, and where the child's experience will fall on that continuum is not always clear from the results of the genetic testing. In addition, in a substance dualist view of persons, disability does not disqualify someone from inclusion in the community of human persons. Often this is done out of understandable compassion for the child (and likely for the parents as well). However, one can make an argument that the assumption underlying this compassion for the child is actually somewhat presumptuous. The assumption in view is that disability and unhappiness necessarily go together. But such an assumption is often false, as kids and adults with challenges often find their lives fulfilling and bring great joy to their family. I suspect that if you took a poll of genetically challenged kids and asked them if they thought they would have been better off never having been born, they would think that quite an odd question. If, in fact, fetuses are persons, then aborting fetuses for genetic anomalies is morally equivalent to eliminating newborns or toddlers for the same anomalies.

For couples with a history of genetic disease, there is another method of prenatal testing that does not involve abortion of fetuses. Preimplantation genetic diagnosis (PGD) takes very early-stage embryos created by IVF, removes a cell (somewhat analogous to a biopsy), and then examines the cell for genetic abnormalities or for the specific abnormality for which the couple is at risk. Embryos that are free of the genetic problem are available for implantation and those that are not are then discarded. On the surface, this seems like a responsible way to address the prospect of someone passing on a genetic disease. However, it involves discarding genetically anomalous embryos, which is morally equivalent to aborting genetically anomalous fetuses, which is equivalent to killing newborns or toddlers for the same genetic anomaly.

Some even utilize genetic testing not to select out various of what they consider clearly harmful traits, but to select in for some of those same traits. For example, deaf couples have used testing to give them the best chance at giving birth to a non-hearing child.[14] There is considerable controversy about this application of genetic testing, since the deaf community does not consider deafness a disability. Critics see the parents deliberately limiting the potential of their child. What is interesting about this discussion is listening to critics of this matter justify their criticism in a secular culture that is overwhelmingly autonomy based. With personal/parental autonomy the overriding moral value, the resources available for putting moral limits on applications of genetic testing like this are thin, at best.

Gene editing presents its own set of both challenges and opportunities. In this volume, Luman Wing lays out the technology, opportunity, and ethical challenges involved with this exciting new discovery. He explains that some applications are called somatic cell alterations, and some are germline alterations. The difference is that somatic cell changes cannot be passed on to succeeding generations, whereas it is possible for germline alterations to be inherited. Given all that we still don't know much about the human genome and the potential unintended side effects of any particular genetic modification, there is still a moratorium on germline alterations in most of the West. What is problematic about gene editing has do with the embryos that are destroyed in the process of perfecting this technology, as well as the prospect of parents reproducing designer children according to their own specifications. Emily Stevens's chapter ably demonstrates that this technology is not neutral, either in its ideology or its various applications, particularly as it concerns the human person and who qualifies to be included in the community of persons. Similarly, Matthew Eppinette's chapter deals with important questions about human persons in the posthumanist vision for humanity, as the goal of this vision is for biotechnology to enable human beings to control their evolution and eventually transcend the limits of being human. Given the substance dualist view of a human person defended in the first half of this volume, and given that the material and immaterial aspects of a person dynamically interact, it is difficult to see

---

14. See the case of Sharon Duchesneau and Candy McCullough, a British lesbian couple, who used a deaf sperm donor to give them the best chance at having a deaf child. This is documented and the ethics are discussed in Glover, *Choosing Children*.

how any technological intervention on the body can impact the immaterial essence of a person such that they would no longer be considered persons or have transcended the designation of persons.[15]

Gene editing also raises the question of how it will be applied—will it be used for treating disease, or will it also be used for enhancing otherwise normal traits? This is the long-time distinction between treatment and enhancement in the bioethics literature, and the question of how gene editing fits with the goals of medicine is again at the forefront of the discussion.[16] There is little controversy about enhancement technologies such as gene editing when used for treating disease (with the germline therapy caveat mentioned above), since that is consistent with the goals of medicine. The debate deals with using technology to enhance otherwise normal traits, creating human beings who are "better than well."[17] Human beings have, for some time, utilized many technologies, some simple and some complicated, to better themselves and to improve on otherwise normal traits. For example, exercise improves muscle and cardiovascular function. Vaccinations enhance otherwise normal immune systems. Orthodontics sometimes treats disorders of the mouth and jaw, but more commonly is for cosmetic reasons for which few people have objections. Some medications have dual uses, in part to treat disease and in part to provide enhancement of related traits. For example, beta-blockers used to treat social anxiety disorders are also used by concert musicians and even by some surgeons to steady their nerves and hands. It is well known that ADHD medications such as Ritalin and Adderall are used by college students (with no diagnosable ADHD) during final exams to give them an added bit of focus and concentration. Though the treatment-enhancement distinction is often clear, there are some where the distinction is fuzzy. Take male pattern baldness, for example. Is hair loss a disease to be corrected, or is it for cosmetic purposes only? It is hard to say that treatment for baldness would be morally problematic even if it's unclear if such treatments would fit within the goals of medicine.

These enhancement therapies raise ethical issues concerning the just distribution of health care resources. Critics have argued that simply allowing the market to distribute these resources according to price will

---

15. For further reading on this subject, see Smith, "Privilege of Being Human."
16. See, e.g., Parens, *Enhancing Human Traits*; Parens and Johnston, *Human Flourishing*.
17. I've taken this term from Elliott, *Better Than Well*.

exacerbate the already yawning gap between the medical haves and have-nots.[18] Some have even suggested that enhancement therapies should be distributed in such a way as to level the playing field for the disadvantaged and reduce social inequalities, thus making them available in ways quite different than market based means.[19] Given our autonomy-based culture, it is difficult to see how meaningful limits can be put on the application of these technologies, especially for parents who feel the pressure to give their children all the advantages that they can.

HUMAN PERSONS AT THE END OF LIFE: REMOVING TREATMENTS AND PHYSICIAN-ASSISTED SUICIDE/EUTHANASIA

At the end of life, who counts as a person comes into focus as well as at the beginning of life. The debate over end-of-life treatments, particularly for those with terminal illnesses or in severely neurologically compromised states such as the persistent vegetative state (PVS), is ongoing, as are the morality and legality of physician-assisted suicide (PAS, more often referred to as physician aid in dying) and euthanasia. PAS and euthanasia are not the same procedures, since the former is actually administered by the patient and the latter is administered by the physician. For the seriously ill patient, it is often counterintuitive to many to see them as full persons. But to apply the substance dualist view of a person that frames this volume, one's ability to function, or lack of it, does not determine one's designation as a person. If what makes someone a person is essential and not functional, then the loss of capacities at the end of life, even if permanent, should not be considered differently than the temporary latency of capacities at the beginning of life, when it comes to the value and dignity of the patient. Erik Clary's chapter outlines the patient in the PVS, showing precisely what the PVS is, and defending the personhood and dignity of the PVS patient. He also argues for the position these patients can have treatments removed if their wishes are clear to that effect, but they cannot be considered disposable nonpersons with a "duty to die."

However, it does not follow from that that physicians and families are obligated to treat every condition at the end of life. One's view of the sacredness of human life from conception to death does not necessarily

18. See, e.g., Stock, *Redesigning Humans*.
19. Ray, "Not Just 'Study Drugs.'"

obligate medicine to keep everyone alive at all times and at all costs. There are clearly times in which further treatments are doing nothing more than delaying an inevitable dying process where death is imminent. In those cases, in which the prognosis is very poor and further treatments are either futile (that is, they won't arrest the downward spiral toward death), or they are more burdensome than beneficial, it is morally acceptable for the patient and/or family (if the patient can no longer make decisions) to say "enough" to medicine and allow death to take its natural course, without any further interventions from medicine except for pain management. Further, it is unethical for families to authorize treatments that increase the net pain and suffering for their loved one, that is, treatments in which the burden clearly outweighs the benefit. In addition, it is unethical for families to authorize treatments for their benefit, not the patient's, as often happens when families are not emotionally prepared to say goodbye to the patient.

In many cases, the personhood of the patient is not an issue in the decision to remove or withhold treatments. Their dignity is considered and the justification for ending treatments is not generally because the family/physicians no longer consider them persons with dignity. In fact, the palliative care industry, about which Michael Bacon so movingly writes in his chapter, presumes the dignity of seriously ill patients and requires adequate pain management in order to avoid an assault on their dignity. The seriously neurologically compromised patient, or the PVS patient, is sometimes the exception to this, as families will insist that their loved one "is no longer there." What they mean by that is they are unresponsive, incapable of doing anything that would seem to give their life value or to make any contribution to those around them. Sometimes, they will insist that "they are just a body." Some will insist that they have actually died, and the PVS patient is often used as an example of the need to alter the definition of death to include higher-brain death (as opposed to whole-brain death).[20] This is where the chapter by Owen, Owen, and Hudetz is so helpful in proposing that a seriously compromised person may have more conscious awareness than previously thought, and that the degree of conscious awareness can actually be empirically measured.

When it comes to PAS/euthanasia, that is an entirely different scenario since the cause of death for the patient is not the underlying disease or condition, but the intentional action of the patient/physician in administering

---

20. For an example of someone who maintains that the PVS patient has essentially died—and no longer has the image of God—see Wennberg, *Terminal Choices*.

the lethal dose of medication. Some of the justifications for PAS/euthanasia include mercy toward suffering patients and the autonomy of persons to decide their fate on their own, without restrictions from government. Both these justifications for PAS/euthanasia presume that the seriously ill patient contemplating either of these is a full person, with dignity and autonomy to be protected. If they are not full persons, then it's not clear why either of those justifications matter. In fact, it's not clear why even their consent matters if they are no longer persons. The same would hold true for the PVS patient. If they are just bodies, or they are no longer living persons in any meaningful sense, then their prior consent to have feeding tubes removed or ventilator support removed would be unnecessary and irrelevant.

Some have suggested that at the end of life (and applicable to the beginning of life as well) that medicine should distinguish between a human being and a human person. One way that this has been done is by making a distinction between biological life and biographical life.[21] It could also be expressed as the difference between being alive and having a life. One's biographical life consists of those aspects that give life meaning. This notion presumes that the person has the requisite functions necessary for having a life, as opposed to simply maintaining bodily existence. It defaults to much of the same functional views of a person that we critiqued in part 1 of this volume and in the earlier discussion of the beginning of life issues. Opponents of PAS/euthanasia argue that if "having a life" is what gives life its value and gives someone their dignity, then when biographical life is lost, what prevents us from taking away all other rights, consistent with our general respect for the dead? Could we simply bury the person, treating him or her like a corpse that still has vital functions? Could we take his or her organs with consent of family? Could we conduct experiments on him or her, as we would on a corpse? In fact, if the patient is no longer a person, it would seem that the distinction between PAS and euthanasia would be irrelevant. There would be no need to consider it necessary or important for the patient to self-administer the needed lethal medication. Further, one can ask why consent for euthanasia would need to be obtained at all, since only persons with rights need give consent for medical procedures.

---

21. See, e.g., the classic exposition of this view in Rachels, *End of Life*. See also Singer, *Rethinking Life and Death*.

CONCLUSION

To be consistent with the substance dualist view of persons presented throughout this volume and applied in this second section of this volume, we would maintain that persons are something you are, not something you do. In order to prevent getting the metaphysical cart before the horse, a person functions because they are a being of a certain type, as opposed to the notion that their functions determine what type of being they are. The application of this view of human persons is particularly relevant to the field of bioethics, not just theoretically, but at the bedside with patients, physicians, and families. In this arena, metaphysics puts on shoe leather and traffics in the real-life applications to decisions of life and death.

BIBLIOGRAPHY

Beckwith, Francis J. *Defending Life: A Moral and Legal Case against Abortion Choice.* London: Cambridge University Press, 2007.

Boonin, David. *Beyond Roe: Why Abortion Should Be Legal—Even if the Fetus is a Person.* New York: Oxford University Press, 2019.

Brown, Warren S., et al., eds. *Whatever Happened to the Soul? Scientific and Theological Portraits of Human Nature.* Theology and the Sciences. Minneapolis: Fortress, 1998.

Elliott, Carl. *Better Than Well: American Medicine Meets the American Dream.* New York: Norton, 2004.

Fletcher, Joseph. "Indicators of Humanhood: A Tentative Profile of Man." *Hastings Center Report* 2 (1972) 1–4.

Giubilini, Alberto, and Francesca Minerva. "After-Birth Abortion: Why Should the Baby Live?" *Journal of Medical Ethics* 39 (2012) 261–63.

Glover, Jonathan. *Choosing Children: Genes, Disability and Design.* New York: Oxford University Press, 2008.

Kaczor, Christopher. *The Ethics of Abortion: Women's Rights, Human Life and the Question of Justice.* 3rd ed. New York: Routledge, 2022.

Kilner, John F., ed. *Why People Matter: A Christian Engagement with Rival Views of Human Significance.* Grand Rapids: Baker Academic, 2017.

Lindemann, Hilde, ". . . But I Could Never Have One: The Abortion Intuition and Moral Luck." *Hypatia* 24 (2009) 41–55, 45.

———. "Miscarriage and the Stories We Live By." *Journal of Social Philosophy* 46 (2015) 80–90, 84.

Murphy, Nancey, and Warren S. Brown. *Did My Neurons Make Me Do It?: Philosophical and Neurobiological Perspectives on Moral Responsibility and Free Will.* New York: Clarendon, 2007.

Parens, Erik, ed. *Enhancing Human Traits: Ethical and Social Implications.* Hastings Center Studies in Ethics. Washington, DC: Georgetown University Press, 2000.

Parens, Erik, and Josephine Johnston, eds. *Human Flourishing in an Age of Gene Editing.* New York: Oxford University Press, 2019.

Rachels, James. *The End of Life: Euthanasia and Morality*. New York: Oxford University Press, 1986.
Ray, Keisha Shantel. "Not Just 'Study Drugs' for the Rich: Stimulants as Moral Tools for Creating Opportunities for Socially Disadvantaged Students." *American Journal of Bioethics* 6 (2016) 29–38.
Singer, Peter. *Practical Ethics*. 3rd ed. New York: Cambridge University Press, 2011.
———. *Rethinking Life and Death: The Collapse of Our Traditional Ethics*. New York: St. Martin's, 1994.
———. *Writings on an Ethical Life*. New York: Ecco, 2000.
Singer, Peter, and Helga Kuhse. *Should the Baby Live? The Problem of Handicapped Infants*. New York: Oxford University Press, 1986.
Smith, Patrick T. "The Privilege of Being Human: Transhumanism and Human Significance." In *Why People Matter: A Christian Engagement with Rival Views of Human Significance*, edited by John F. Kilner, 109–32. Grand Rapids: Baker Academic, 2017.
Steinbock, Bonnie. *Life before Birth: On the Moral and Legal Status of Embryos and Fetuses*. 2nd ed. New York: Oxford University Press, 2011.
Stock, Gregory. *Redesigning Humans: Choosing Our Genes, Changing Our Future*. New York: Mariners, 2003.
Thomson, Judith J. "A Defense of Abortion." *Philosophy and Public Affairs* 1 (1971) 1–8.
Warren, Mary Anne. *Moral Status: Obligations to Persons and Other Living Things*. Issues in Biomedical Ethics. New York: Oxford University Press, 1997.
Wennberg, Robert N. *Terminal Choices: Euthanasia, Suicide, and the Right to Die*. Grand Rapids: Eerdmans, 1989.
Wolf, Naomi. "Our Bodies, Our Souls: Rethinking Pro-Choice Rhetoric." *New Republic* 16 (1995) 26–35.

8

The Permanent (?) Vegetative (?) State

Erik M. Clary

In this essay we shall consider one of the more challenging issues in medical ethics, which still perplexes nearly fifty years after it first grabbed the national spotlight and which forces every student of introductory bioethics and medical law to learn the names of Quinlan, Cruzan, and Schiavo—specifically, it is the question of ceasing indefinite life support for patients who, in their recovery from coma following severe brain injury, stall in a highly debilitated condition that neurospecialists Bryan Jennett and Fred Plum labelled five decades ago as the persistent vegetative state (PVS).[1] By Jennett and Plum's seminal description, affected individuals are insensate and uninterruptedly unconscious on account of a cerebrum that has ceased to function. With brainstem preserved, however, they are also wakeful, generally capable of breathing without ventilatory assistance, and visibly responsive to a variety of stimuli, and such phenomena can lead kin and caregivers ministering at the bedside to conclude a measure of awareness contra the clinical assessment. Looking to clear up confusion and anticipating a public debate over "the wisdom of continuing supportive measures," Jennett and Plum chose a descriptor ("vegetative") they believed would effectively communicate to a wide audience the notion of "mindless" existence (surely

---

1. Jennett and Plum, "Persistent Vegetative State."

anticipating—and correctly so—that medical laypersons would conjure the depiction of vegetable[2]) and, more importantly, that would help convey their deep reservations over the indefinite provision of artificial nutrition and hydration (ANH) and other life-sustaining interventions.

Despite some early protestations of violative terminology,[3] over time, the language and concept of vegetative existence became deeply embedded in the medical literature and received much amplification as the effort to stake out moral and legal space for ceasing life support broadened. Such was the clear aim, for example, when, as the U. S. Supreme Court took up the ANH-PVS issue in early 1990 with the case of Cruzan v. Missouri Department of Health, the highly influential American Medical Association declared patients bearing the PVS diagnosis to be "residual collection[s] of systemic body organs."[4] Influential physicians buttressed the depiction, including internist Lawrence Schneiderman of the University of California, San Diego, School of Medicine, who proposed incorporating the vegetative state into the very definition of medical futility. Reiterating Jennett and Plum's chief conclusion with no holds barred, Schneiderman insisted that patients have no right to be sustained in the condition and that physicians should do nothing to facilitate it.[5]

---

2. See, e.g., Forte, "Getting Rid of Vegetables."

3. Theological ethicist Paul Ramsey, a stalwart defender of human dignity and seminal figure in the development of bioethics as an academic discipline, saw great reason for concern as he wrote nearly fifty years ago, "One can pause at this point and ask whether any living human being ought to be described as a 'vegetable' or reduced to metabolism" (Ramsey, *Ethics at the Edges*, 276). Ramsey clearly understood the rationale behind Jennett and Plum's descriptor, noting, "Use of variants of the word vegetable ... helps rhetorically to sustain an emphasis on quality-of-life decisions." If surrogate decision-makers can be convinced to view their charge as the functional equivalent of a vegetable, it is not a hard sell to procure a decision to cease life support (Ramsey, *Ethics at the Edges*, 294n25).

4. Council on Scientific Affairs and Council on Ethical and Judicial Affairs, "Persistent Vegetative State," 426; Cruzan v. Director, Missouri Department of Health, 497 U. S. 261. In a five to four ruling, the court held back from proclaiming a constitutional right to die, but it nonetheless found that a decision to forgo indefinite ANH could find anchor in a "liberty interest" secured under the due process clause of the Fourteenth Amendment. Provided Missouri's evidentiary standard for an advance medical directive could be met, the court presumed Ms. Cruzan's reported prior request to forego life-sustaining interventions if rendered a "vegetable" would carry the day over the state's effort to prohibit it in the interest of preserving human life.

5. Schneiderman et al., "Medical Futility." Schneiderman maintained the approach in his subsequently released book on medical futility now in its second edition. See Schneiderman and Jecker, *Wrong Medicine*.

Piling on, ethicists drawing from the well of personhood theory dug by Joe Fletcher worked the vegetative thesis to the conclusion that affected patients are dead—not figuratively dead, but actually dead.[6] According to Fletcher, writing in the early 1970s, a functioning cerebral cortex is "the human sine qua non . . . the key to the definition of a human being," and so he concluded that patients permanently robbed of cognitive capacity by disease or injury have ceased to be human even as they may breathe spontaneously and manifest other bodily functions.[7] With some terminological refinement, this proposition of bodily existence sans humanhood came to be expressed in the novel categories of (human) "nonperson" and "personal death" (as distinct from "biological death"). Although generally advanced with philosophical rationale à la Fletcher, some scholars addressing the ANH-PVS issue have offered overtly theological accounts. These include evangelical ethicist Robert V. Rakestraw. In a 1992 article published in the *Journal of the Evangelical Theological Society*, Rakestraw countered fellow Evangelicals' denunciation of ANH withdrawal in the case of PVS, arguing that patients in view are "theologically dead" on account of a nonfunctioning cerebral cortex that renders them incapable of imaging God. Since one cannot kill what is already dead, Rakestraw drew the simple conclusion, "If we can determine that the PVS individual is dead, then we need not hesitate to withdraw food and water."[8]

Clearly, in processing the tragic condition of people declared permanently vegetative, kin, caregiver, and commentator all discern severe disability and a level of function incapable of supporting even the barest conception of desirable living. The existential question of "Who would want to live like this?" is quite natural, and for many, it drives the analysis and decision-making. Periodic surveys consistently reveal a very strong

---

6. See, e.g., Buchanan, "Limits of Proxy Decision-Making," 164; Wennberg, *Terminal Choices*, 159; Davis, "Case of 'Mr. Stevens'"; Veatch, "Impending Collapse." As for proper disposition of the "remains," as of yet no one advocating this "higher-brain" concept of death has called for burying still-breathing bodies. Some, however, dwell considerably on the perceived prospects for vital organ sourcing and replacing live animals in invasive medical research. See, e.g., Fritz, "Can 'Best Interests'"; Ravelingien et al., "Proceeding with Clinical Trials"; Draper, "Research and Patients."

7. Fletcher, "Indicators of Humanhood"; Fletcher, "Four Indicators of Humanhood"; Fletcher, *Morals and Medicine*. The minimum level of cerebral (cognitive) function required for retaining (or attaining) the status of person generally goes unstated though Fletcher himself is on record as requiring a minimum Binet IQ score of twenty. See Bard and Fletcher, "Right to Die."

8. Rakestraw, "Persistent Vegetative State," 394.

preference among the general public for ceasing life support in the case of PVS,[9] and the language and concepts of vegetable, organ reservoir, death, nonperson, vacated body, etc, all grease the skids for advancing the inclination. Yet, useful as they may be to some in processing the ANH-PVS question, these depictions are highly problematic. Not only do they dehumanize highly vulnerable individuals, but also they project a very dubious anthropology in personhood theory and predicate an unwarranted empirical narrative in pushing a higher-brain definition of death. Because truth matters in ethics—and not just in the practical conclusions reached but also in the underlying warrant—the attempt to resolve the ANH-PVS question by declaring that the patients in view are dead must be addressed.

One may find in the literature substantive and compelling philosophical and theological critiques of personhood theory quite pertinent to end-of-life medical ethics stretching back to the ground-breaking analysis on death determination in the modern medical age by Fletcher's contemporary and frequent nemesis in debate, Paul Ramsey, in his classic work *The Patient as Person*.[10] We shall not rehash those critiques, but, instead, will add another prong to the argument. Routinely, ethicists wielding the personhood distinction in the PVS context assume that we are dealing en masse with individuals who are uninterruptedly unconscious and will remain so however long ANH might be employed to sustain them. Yet, this narrative of "permanent unconsciousness" proves unsustainable when considered in light of medical research published in the fifty years since Jennett and Plum penned their report. After demonstrating such, we shall conclude with an analysis of the ANH-PVS question developed sans the faulty assumption.

---

9. Lindgren, "Death by Default"; Moore, "Three in Four Americans."

10. Ramsey, *Patient as Person*, 59–112. Ramsey tackles the issue of "brain death" and finds the higher-brain (cerebral) criterion out of touch with the Scriptures that "know no life that is not embodied life" (Ramsey, *Patient as Person*, 60). It is simply unacceptable, he contends, "to resolve the problem of 'vegetable' cases by pronouncing them dead upon some humanistic definition of life" because "patients who still breathe and/or circulate themselves are *not* dead. These cases are rather to be addressed by an ethics of the proper care of the still living, the dying, the not yet dying" (Ramsey, *Patient as Person*, 97–98 [emphasis original]). For more recent critiques with greater philosophical bent, see Moreland and Rae, *Body & Soul*, 318–19, 378–79n46; Rae, "Views of Human Nature," 250–51; Meilaender, "Confused, Voiceless, Perverse"; Cooper, *Body, Soul, Life Everlasting*; Hoekema, *Created in God's Image*.

PART II | BIOETHICS AND PERSONHOOD

THE "SYNDROME IN SEARCH OF A NAME"

By Jennett and Plum's description, PVS is principally marked by the combination of (1) prolonged, uninterrupted lack of awareness; and (2) alternating periods of wakefulness and sleep.[11] The condition is relatively uncommon, affecting approximately thirty-three thousand individuals in the United States at any given time.[12] Most often, it develops subsequent to acute and severe brain injury (e.g., head trauma, cerebrovascular accident, anesthetic accident) that manifests first in coma, a sleeplike state characterized by complete unresponsiveness.[13] Prior to the advent of intensive life-support technologies beginning with the Drinker respirator (iron lung) in the 1920s, such injuries were uniformly fatal, but in the modern medical age, survival and recovery are distinct possibilities.[14] In the process of recovery, transition from coma to a vegetative state may occur in days or weeks as lower-brain (brainstem) swelling resolves and function returns.[15] Jennett and Plum did not specify how long a patient must be in the vegetative state before the condition could rightly be considered "persistent," but subsequent researchers have recommended a few weeks of observation prior to making that determination.[16]

By medical definition, both comatose and "vegetative" patients are unconscious. Clinically, it is the wakeful state that distinguishes the PVS

11. Jennett and Plum, "Persistent Vegetative State," 734. Following Jennett and Plum, a 1994 report—a joint collaboration between the Academy of Neurology, the American Neurological Association, the Association of Neurological Surgeons, the Academy of Pediatrics and the Child Neurology Society—defined the vegetative state as "a condition of complete unawareness of the self and the environment accompanied by sleep-wake cycles with either complete or partial preservation of hypothalamic and brain stem autonomic functions." See Multi-Society Task Force on PVS, "Persistent Vegetative State [pt. 1]."

12. This estimate of 33,000 PVS patients is based on an approximate population of 330 million and a mid-range estimate of 100 PVS patients per 1 million population, drawn from Jennett's review of the literature. See Jennett, *Vegetative State*, 36.

13. Jennett, *Vegetative State*, 42–48. Less commonly, PVS may be associated with congenital malformations (e.g., anencephaly) or degenerative conditions that include Alzheimer's disease.

14. Drinker and Shaw, "Apparatus for Prolonged Administration."

15. With acute injuries, the chief issue is oxygen deprivation or "hypoxia" in the brain. The higher brain (cerebrum) is much more sensitive to hypoxia than the lower brain (brain stem), and as a consequence, there may some patients in which the latter but not the former returns to functioning—this, neurologists believe, is precisely the case in PVS.

16. Multi-Society Task Force on PVS, "Persistent Vegetative State [pt. 1]," 1501.

condition.[17] This "wakefulness without awareness," as Jennett and Plum called it, may manifest in a number of ways, including eyes opening and even fixating on an object for a brief period of time, bolting upright in bed, chewing, swallowing, blinking, and vocalizing (grunting and, in some cases, shouting).[18] Transition to and from the wakeful state is generally cyclic, but wakefulness can, they also noted, be induced by vigorous stimulation of the sleeping patient.

To the ordinary observer, patients declared vegetative may, in manifesting wakefulness and various bodily movements, appear to be alert—i.e., conscious and aware. That interpretation, according to Jennett and Plum, fails to distinguish between functions that are purely reflexive and those that require some measure of cognition. All of the activities with PVS that might be construed as giving evidence of awareness, the theory goes, are roughly of the same order as the instantaneous withdrawal of one's hand when touching a hot stove or the quick jerk of the lower leg elicited by the physician's rubber hammer applied to the front of the knee—they are reflexes mediated by nerves running to and from the target muscle(s) that connect in the lower segments of the central nervous system (CNS).[19] Yet, whereas a person with no neurologic abnormality touching the hot stove would, concurrent with the reflexive action, also consciously perceive the noxious stimulus (i.e., experience pain)—and this by means of nerve pathways that run from the lower CNS (spinal cord) to the higher brain—patients deemed vegetative

---

17. Recognizing that the term "unconscious" was generally understood as to "imply a sleeplike insensibility," Jennett and Plum opted to avoid the term and instead described the vegetative patient's mental status as lacking "awareness." Jennett later explained, "Both patients in coma and those in a vegetative stage are unconscious but this term fails to distinguish between the two because it does not acknowledge that arousal and awareness can be independently affected." On the heels of Jennett and Plum, the MSTF sought to clarify the terminology, stating, "Consciousness has two dimensions: wakefulness and awareness.... Patients in a coma are unconscious because they lack both wakefulness and awareness. Patients in a vegetative state are unconscious because, although they are wakeful, they lack awareness" (Multi-Society Task Force on PVS, "Persistent Vegetative State [pt. 1]," 1501). See also Jennett, *Vegetative State*, 2; Jennett and Plum, "Persistent Vegetative State," 734.

18. Jennett and Plum, "Persistent Vegetative State," 734–35.

19. For some reflexes, the central nervous connections are located in the spinal cord (e.g., limb withdrawal, knee jerk, hand grasp), and for others, in the brain stem or "medulla oblongata" (e.g., eye movements, blinking of the eyelids, dilation of the pupils in response to light, swallowing, coughing, and various "autonomic" functions that include control of breathing and circulation).

purportedly feel nothing. They are, neurologists declare, "insentient" on account of a "cerebral cortex [that] is out of action."[20]

The Diagnostic Challenge

At the level of neuroanatomical description, it is the cerebral cortex (the neocortex) that matters most to clinicians relating PVS pathology to patient dysfunction, for it is in this part of the brain that the capacity for consciousness is believed to reside.[21] When this outermost layer of the cerebrum is rendered inoperative by trauma or disease, behaviors and activities normally taken as evidence of consciousness cease. From the failure of the patient to demonstrate outward signs of consciousness, the inference is then made that the individual is, in fact, "noncognitive, nonsentient, and incapable of conscious experience."[22]

Neurologists may, and often do, supplement their clinical observations of patient behavior with studies that image the brain or indirectly measure its function.[23] Although these tests typically demonstrate evidence of brain injury or dysfunction in patients declared vegetative, they fail to consistently distinguish PVS from other conditions of severe neurological impairment in which consciousness still manifests.[24] And so, fifty years after Jennett and Plum's original description of the condition, the vegetative state remains a "clinical" diagnosis—that is, one made chiefly on the basis of a physical (behavioral) examination of the patient.

As presented by Jennett and Plum, the persistent vegetative state is conceptually simple, yet significant challenges attend clinical application

---

20. Jennett and Plum, "Persistent Vegetative State," 734.

21. Medical descriptions and discussions of PVS generally reduce the mind (consciousness) en toto to an outworking of material processes (i.e., a functioning cerebral cortex). Such a notion presents significant challenges to the traditional (dualistic) conception of human nature that posits material (body) and immaterial (soul/spirit) components to the human constitution. Though clearly important, space constraints preclude a discussion of this question.

22. Multi-Society Task Force on PVS, "Persistent Vegetative State [pt. 1]," 1501.

23. These studies include computed tomography (CT), magnetic resonance imaging (MRI), brain wave analysis (electroencephalography or EEG), cerebral blood flow (CBF) measurements, and positron emission tomography (PET).

24. Concerning the diagnostic unreliability of brain imaging and function studies, Jennett cites numerous reports, including one involving PET scans that reported "virtually normal metabolism in most of the cortex in one patient . . . who had been vegetative for 6 years" (Jennett, *Vegetative State*, 25–28).

largely because there is no way to prove definitively that an unresponsive patient is, in fact, unaware or unconscious because there are no means for directly measuring mental states. "We can," the Multi-Society Task Force on PVS (MSTF) acknowledged in 1994, "only *infer* the presence or absence of conscious experience in another person."[25] Thus, neurologists admit to at least a "theoretical possibility," as Jennet wrote in 2002, "that a patient who is believed to be vegetative might retain some awareness without behavioural evidence."[26] In other words, no canon of neurological science is necessarily violated in assuming that a wakeful but unresponsive patient may be conscious.

With no objective means for identifying an unconscious state, there exists the real possibility for misdiagnosis of the vegetative state—i.e., failing to identify evidence of cognitive function when present and thus errantly concluding the patient to be vegetative (unaware). The problem here is that the vegetative state can be difficult to distinguish from other conditions of severe disability in which cognitive function is retained in some measure. These include the "minimally conscious state" (MCS) and the "locked-in syndrome" (LIS). With MCS, the patient is wakeful and manifests limited awareness but with variation over time that complicates assessment.[27] In the case of the LIS, affected individuals retain normal cognitive function and sensory perception but with movement generally limited to the eyes on account of severe paralysis, signs of awareness may be difficult to detect.[28]

In the medical literature, misdiagnosis of the vegetative state first surfaced as an incidental finding in a 1991 report from geriatrician Donald Tresch and his colleagues at the Medical College of Wisconsin. While working to identify a study group of patients with PVS from several regional nursing homes, these researchers found on their examinations that eleven of sixty-two subjects (18 percent) bearing the diagnosis had "some awareness of their environment."[29] Two years later, neurologist Nancy Childs from the Healthcare Rehabilitation Center in Austin, Texas, reported a misdiagnosis rate of 37 percent in forty-nine patients referred to

---

25. Multi-Society Task Force on PVS, "Persistent Vegetative State [pt. 1]," 1501 (emphasis added).

26. Jennett, *Vegetative State*, 19.

27. Schnakers and Majerus, "Behavioral Assessment and Diagnosis," 4–5.

28. Schnakers and Majerus, "Behavioral Assessment and Diagnosis," 5.

29. Tresch et al., "Clinical Characteristics of Patients," 930.

PART II | BIOETHICS AND PERSONHOOD

her institution with a diagnosis of coma or PVS.[30] These were not patients believed to be persistently unaware at admission who subsequently recovered consciousness while receiving rehabilitation therapy; rather, they were patients for whom evidence of consciousness was identified within hours or days of arriving at the rehabilitation center, thus discrediting the original diagnosis.[31]

Similar to Childs's experience, clinicians working in the 1990s at London's Royal Hospital for Neurodisability (RHN) reported a high rate of PVS misdiagnosis (43 percent) in a cohort of forty patients admitted over a four-year period (1992–1995).[32] In fifteen of the seventeen misdiagnosed patients (88 percent), cognition was identified within sixteen days of arrival, despite these patients being considered vegetative for an average of twenty-four months prior to admission (a range of six to eighty-two months, with six patients more than one year out from the diagnosis).[33] Almost a decade later, RHN clinicians were still reporting a high rate of misdiagnosis with seventeen of sixty patients (28 percent) referred as persistently vegetative demonstrating awareness on initial examination, and a further ten individuals (for a total of twenty-seven, or 45 percent) evincing cognitive function within four months of arrival.[34] Similarly, researchers with the University of Liège's Coma Science Group reported in 2009 a similar phenomenon with 41 percent of patients admitted with the PVS diagnosis manifesting evidence of cognitive function on early examinations, and, in assessments of another group of patients five years after that, the

---

30. Childs et al., "Accuracy of Diagnosis." Childs and her coauthors speculated that "misdiagnoses in most of these patients was due to the confusion in the terminology used to describe alterations in states of consciousness in the brain-injured." Some cases, however, they attributed to "lack of extended observation for behavioral evidence of cognitive awareness by qualified personnel [at the referring institutions]" ("Accuracy of Diagnosis," 1466).

31. According to Childs et al., "50% (n = 9 of 18) [of the misdiagnoses] were identified within the first day of admission and 78% (n = 14 of 18) by the third day" ("Accuracy of Diagnosis," 1466).

32. Andrews et al., "Misdiagnosis of Vegetative State."

33 Andrews et al., "Misdiagnosis of Vegetative State," 14. Average and range figures calculated from data provided on fourteen of the fifteen patients. Beyond reporting detection of cognition within sixteen days, Andrews was unable to provide specific data on one of the fifteen patients per the request of that individual's relatives.

34. Gill-Thwaites, "Lotteries, Loopholes and Luck," 1321; Gill-Thwaites and Munday, "Sensory Modality Assessment."

number was little improved at 35 percent.[35] Despite abundant reports of the phenomenon in upper-tier medical journals spanning more than two decades, errant diagnosis of the vegetative state in highly debilitated post-comatose patients remains a significant issue.

In considering the problem, RHN's long-time medical director, Keith Andrews, identified several contributory factors. First, the diagnostic effort is, in his judgment, greatly complicated by the fact that PVS is a rare condition. With so few patients, "few clinicians gain the necessary experience for appropriate assessment."[36] Childs made a similar observation and concluded that "diagnosis [of PVS] is applicable only after adequate observation by physicians skilled in neurologic diagnosis."[37] Yet, at least in the RHN experience, the misdiagnoses were generally "made by a neurologist, neurosurgeon, or rehabilitation specialist—all of whom would have been expected to have experience with PVS."[38]

Even those who specialize in treating highly debilitated neurologic patients are not immune from error in diagnosing the vegetative condition. Andrews and his colleagues, who practice in a facility devoted to the care of highly debilitated, post-comatose patients, confess a steep learning curve for the specialists. With more than half of the misdiagnoses detected during the final year of their four-year study, Andrews attributed the increasing detection rate to "the team's *increased sensitivity* owing to the accumulation of experience over several years, coupled with the development of more effective assessment methods."[39] Helen Gill-Thwaites and Ros Munday buttressed Andrew's conclusion as they later reported in 2004 a significant improvement in cognitive detection following implementation at RHN of a more rigorous method for conducting the behavioral evaluation.[40] Similarly, clinical investigators in Buenos Aires reported a few years

---

35. Schnakers et al., "Diagnostic Accuracy"; Stender et al., "Diagnostic Precision."

36. Andrews et al., "Misdiagnosis of Vegetative State," 15.

37. Childs et al., "Accuracy of Diagnosis," 1466.

38. Andrews et al., "Misdiagnosis of Vegetative State," 15.

39. Andrews et al., "Misdiagnosis of Vegetative State," 15 (emphasis added). Andrews reports that ten of the seventeen misdiagnoses were recognized in the final year, four in the third year, one in the second year, and two in the first year. If, in fact, the number and profile of patients admitted to the PVS ward at RHN was stable across the study duration, which Andrews believes to be the case, the data would suggest that the actual misdiagnosis rate may be significantly higher than 43 percent, the figure Andrews reported for the entire four-year duration.

40. Gill-Thwaites and Munday, "Sensory Modality Assessment," 1267.

afterwards developing a patient conditioning technique that led them to identify awareness in four of thirteen patients (31 percent) diagnosed in-house as vegetative on standard examination.[41]

Second, Andrews noted severe patient disabilities as presenting a significant challenge for the diagnostician. As he stated,

> All of the misdiagnosed patients were severely physically disabled, often with contractures [joints fixed in abnormal positions], and were anarthric [unable to speak]. Since demonstration of awareness needs a motor response [e.g., movement of a body part or vocalization] such profound physical disability complicates assessment of awareness.[42]

Disabilities, Andrews further noted, may also include blindness or other severe visual impairment, and in such instances, commonly employed neurologic tests that require the patient to blink the eyes in response to a visual threat or to visually track a specific object are unhelpful and apt to confuse.

In assessing the neurologic patient, Andrews found it critical first to characterize the full extent of disability in order to identify any residual abilities that could function for communication. That effort, he noted, may require many days of observation with extensive physical therapy and even surgery to restore capacity for movement. Recounting an experience with one misdiagnosed patient, Andrews observed,

> We did not identify [the patient's] responses until 25 weeks after admission, though it was obvious from subsequent conversations with him that he had not been vegetative for some time. This patient was admitted with very severe joint contractures which required surgical release and a prolonged physical management programme before he could be seated appropriately in a special seating system. Only when he was satisfactorily seated was it identified that he had a slight shoulder shrug which could be used for communication purposes.[43]

Third, Andrews discovered it is insufficient to rely solely upon the physician's bedside examinations. Rather, what is needed is a "multidisciplinary" effort that makes use of specialists from allied fields. As Andrews described the operation of his clinical ward, "On this unit the level of the patient's awareness is nearly always identified first by the occupational

---

41. Bekinschtein et al., "Classical Conditioning."
42. Andrews et al., "Misdiagnosis of Vegetative State," 15.
43. Andrews et al., "Misdiagnosis of Vegetative State," 14–15.

therapists and then by the clinical psychologist, and only later is communication achieved by other members of the team [the physician included]."[44] That the occupational therapist and not the physician is generally first in Andrews's hospital to identify a PVS misdiagnosis may reflect not only a particular skill set but, perhaps more importantly, greater contact time with the patient. While awareness in the misdiagnosed patient may sometimes be evident within days, it may require weeks, given "the need for [the patient] to accommodate to communicating again, especially through technological aids and after a long period of non-communication."[45] And so, at RHN, the protocol developed for the therapist to devote one hour each day (two thirty-minute sessions) for six weeks to working with the patient, "assess[ing] responses to sensory stimulation and ... identify[ing] the most reliable responses [if any] to command."[46] That amount of time, few, if any, physicians are able to devote to a single patient in a typical hospital setting.

Despite heightened awareness of the issue, misdiagnosis of the vegetative state continues at a high rate, and more recent studies employing sophisticated brain imaging techniques suggest that the real figure may be even higher. In the above-mentioned reports from Tresch, Childs, RHN, and Liège, misdiagnoses were identified on behavioral examination, but beginning with a 2006 report from Adrian Owen at Cambridge University, researchers have come to recognize with the aid of advanced MRI and positron tomographic brain-mapping techniques a subset of wakeful post-comatose patients who are conscious but completely unable to demonstrate any outward signs.[47] In Owen's terminology, these patients are "covertly aware," and in a 2014 paper from Liège's Coma Science Group, the phenomenon was identified in thirteen of forty-one, or 31 percent of patients whom the Liège specialists themselves had diagnosed as vegetative on a thorough behavioral exam.[48]

Responding to these reports, one might suppose the solution a simple one—specifically, that all unresponsive post-comatose patients simply be directed to facilities like those at Liège or RHN for verification of diagnosis. There are, however, very few of these centers in the world and certainly too

44. Andrews et al., "Misdiagnosis of Vegetative State," 15.
45. Andrews et al., "Misdiagnosis of Vegetative State," 15.
46. Andrews et al., "Misdiagnosis of Vegetative State," 13.
47. Owen et al., "Detecting Awareness." See also Cruse et al., "Detecting Awareness"; Owen and Coleman, "Detecting Awareness"; Schnakers et al., "Preserved Covert Cognition."
48. Stender et al., "Diagnostic Precision." Of the thirteen patients judged covertly aware, nine later evidenced behavioral signs of consciousness.

few in the United States to accommodate an estimated thirty-three thousand vegetative patients. As researchers John Whyte and Risa Nakase-Richardson observed in 2013, the reality is that most patients are transferred soon after their injuries to "homes and nursing homes in which they are generally cared for by primary care clinicians with no specialized training in [disorders of consciousness]."[49] Even if avoidable theoretically, the high rate of PVS misdiagnosis seems likely to persist in actual practice.

The "Problem" of Recovery

If the decision to withdraw ANH must rest on the determination of whether or not the post-comatose patient is unconscious, then the high rate of PVS misdiagnosis presents cause for great concern. Further complicating matters, some post-comatose patients declared permanently vegetative will, given enough time, eventually manifest signs of consciousness. These "recoveries" complicate the decision-making process because it is the characterization of a patient's presumed unconscious state as irreversible or permanent that often prompts consideration of withholding ANH. Before permanency is declared, ANH is viewed as right and proper care as it is employed to sustain the patient pending a hoped-for recovery. Once, however, the physician has pronounced the vegetative condition to be irreversible, discussions over whether or not to continue ANH generally ensue.

In an effort to facilitate discussions of care for debilitated post-comatose patients, Jennett and Plum sought to establish a diagnostic category for the most severely affected patients—those who, in their description, "never show evidence of a working mind."[50] Armed with little clinical data, however, they were hesitant at the time to advance in their novel terminology a statement to the effect that there was absolutely no hope of recovery.[51] "'Persistent,'" they concluded, "is safer than '*permanent*' or '*irreversible*.'"[52]

49. Whyte and Nakase-Richardson, "Disorders of Consciousness."

50. Jennett and Plum, "Persistent Vegetative State," 735, 737.

51. Jennett and Plum, "Persistent Vegetative State," 737. As they state, "Exactly how long such a state must persist before it can be confidently declared permanent will have to be determined by careful prospective studies, using the criteria which we have set down here."

52. Jennett and Plum, "Persistent Vegetative State," 735 (emphasis added). By "persistent," then, Jennett and Plum intended to communicate without issuing a definitive prognosis that the patient had been in the vegetative state for a considerable length of time (i.e., a diagnostic statement). Jennett eventually ceased using the term "persistent,"

They were clearly hopeful, however, that subsequent research would deliver the basis for distinguishing post-comatose patients in an "irrecoverable state" of "mindless" existence from those who would go on to recover cognitive function.

Following Jennett and Plum's report in 1972, published clinical data dealing with the issue of cognitive recovery was slow to accrue. Anecdotal reports of recoveries appeared first, but eventually, case series were published, including a contribution from Andrews in 1993 involving eleven patients. These patients, who constituted 24 percent of the forty-three individuals referred to RHN with a PVS diagnosis during its first five years of operation (1987–1991), regained awareness at some point between four months and three years post-injury (a median of five months, with all but one manifesting cognition at ten months or less). None of the patients returned to their pre-injury condition, yet all but one regained the ability to communicate—four verbally. Three patients "became independent in personal care," and four "were eventually able to walk."[53] Regarding final cognitive status, Andrews reported, "All but one of the patients had some degree of cognitive impairment. Two were able to make appropriate decisions about complex matters, four were able to cope in a structured environment, two showed appropriate pleasure reactions to changes in the environment, and two remained profoundly cognitively impaired."

Concerning recovering patients' perceptions of their disabled condition, Andrews reported "Only one patient showed regular distress. . . . Among the other patients there was no evidence that limited recovery was associated with depression or a feeling that a condition of severe disability was worse than non-sentience or death." He continued, "This is a subjective view, but the impression gained was that signs of pleasure were far more common than those of distress." Contrary, then, to assertions that PVS patients "have *permanently* lost consciousness . . . [such that they] *cannot and never* will be able to experience any of the events occurring in the world or

---

preferring to speak only of the "vegetative state" except when intending to convey the prognostic judgment that there is no reasonable hope of recovery, at which point he would use the phrase "permanent vegetative state." While Jennett and other experts in the field prefer this terminological adjustment, the label "persistent vegetative state" remains widely used in both professional and popular treatments of the condition. See Jennett, *Vegetative State*, 4–5.

53. Andrews, "Recovery of Patients," 1598.

in their bodies,"[54] at least some individuals do recover cognition and function sufficient in measure to enable pleasurable experience.

While Andrews's study bore witness to the reality of PVS recovery, its small sample size precluded its use as a resource from which to generate prognostic claims. The MSTF, whose membership included Fred Plum, sought to address that deficiency with a 1994 report that drew from the results of several published case series with a sum total of 754 patients (603 adults and 151 children) rendered in a PVS by acute brain injury. Injuries were categorized as either traumatic (434 adults and 106 children) or nontraumatic (169 adults and 45 children).[55]

In its report, the MSTF made several observations concerning life expectancy and recovery of cognition. Regarding the former, the task force noted a shortened lifespan with an average survival of between two to five years post-injury. While noting individual reports of survival "for more than 17, 37, and 41 years," the MSTF estimated that the probability of living over fifteen years was "less than 1 in 15,000 to 75,000."[56] The most frequently reported cause of death was infection (52 percent of 143 patients for whom such data was available), typically of either the lungs or urinary tract.[57] Mortality rate was also observed to vary according to the type of brain injury with 53 percent of patients with nontraumatic disease dying within twelve months, as compared with 33 percent of patients with traumatic injuries. While subsequent studies have generally affirmed these findings, caution must be exercised in accepting their conclusions. Of particular concern is that the duration of survival may be grossly underestimated in these studies due to a failure to distinguish patients for whom ANH was discontinued from those who died while continuing to be tube-fed.[58]

Concerning cognitive recovery in vegetative patients, the MSTF found that the incidence varied according to the type of injury. In adults and children with traumatic injuries, recovery of consciousness was reported for 52 and 62 percent of patients by twelve months, respectively, whereas with

---

54. Lynn and Childress, "Must Patients Always," 18 (emphasis added).

55. Multi-Society Task Force on PVS, "Persistent Vegetative State [pt. 2]."

56. Multi-Society Task Force on PVS, "Persistent Vegetative State [pt. 2]," 1576.

57. Whether some deaths could have been prevented is unclear from the data. The MSTF did note that "there have been no formal studies of the effect of the level of care on the life expectancy of patients in a persistent vegetative state" (Multi-Society Task Force on PVS, "Persistent Vegetative State [pt. 2]," 1576).

58. For a brief survey of studies published in the decade following the MSTF report, see Jennett, *Vegetative State*, 67–69.

nontraumatic injuries, the respective figures were 15 and 13 percent. Type of injury also influenced the time at which recovery occurred. In the case of nontraumatic injuries, emergence from the vegetative state was reported to have occurred in 11 percent of the 169 patients by three months and 15 percent by six months; no further recoveries were documented after the six-month mark. Conversely, in adult patients with traumatic injuries, 33 percent regained cognitive function by three months, 46 percent by six months, and 52 percent by twelve months; seven additional recoveries (1.6 percent of the 434 patients) were documented to have occurred after twelve months.

In reflecting upon the data, the MSTF concluded the label of "permanent" to be appropriate in describing a vegetative state lasting twelve months or more following a traumatic injury in adults and children but only three months for nontraumatic injury.[59] Although the MSTF admitted it was employing probabilistic judgments, its use of the term "permanent" was at best confusing and at worst misleading, given the simultaneous acknowledgment of recoveries occurring beyond the point at which the MSTF was now drawing the line of permanency.

Compounding the confusion in the MSTF's line of permanency was a methodological misstep in its analysis. Credit goes to disability advocate Chris Borthwick for first drawing attention to the issue two years after MSTF released its report. As Borthwick keenly observed, the MSTF presented the recovery data in the least favorable light as they employed in the denominator of each incidence calculation the total number of patients within the relevant diagnostic subcategory that met the study's inclusion criterion of being vegetative at one month post-injury. "The relevant figure," Borthwick rightly noted, "is not the number who recover in any period as a percentage of the whole but that figure as a percentage of the ones available to recover—i.e., those who had not died or recovered already."[60]

Reanalyzing the data, Borthwick concluded that the actual incidence of cognitive recovery in adults with traumatic injuries after twelve months was 10.6 percent—a figure hardly deserving of the MSTF's characterization of its 1.6 percent calculation as "exceedingly rare."[61] Taking Borthwick's cue,

59. Multi-Society Task Force on PVS, "Persistent Vegetative State [pt. 2]," 1575.
60. Borthwick, "Permanent Vegetative State," 179
61. Multi-Society Task Force on PVS, "Persistent Vegetative State [pt. 2]," 1572, 1574. Per Borthwick, after accounting for patients who had either died or experienced cognitive recovery by the twelve-month mark, the correct denominator for the incidence calculation was 65 and not 434. Working from that figure, he concluded seven recoveries amounts to

we may (using the MSTF data) calculate the incidence of cognitive recovery in adults with nontraumatic injuries beyond the three-month mark to be 6.4 percent (seven recoveries in 110 patients available to recover) and not 4 percent as the MTSF reported. Concerning either figure, however, one might say "infrequent" but certainly not "rare" as per the MSTF.

Since the MSTF's report was published, research dealing with late recovery has been slow to accrue, but three recently published studies suggest that Borthwick was on target. In 2010, clinical researchers in Telese, Italy, reported late recoveries averaging 17.2 months post-trauma in ten of fifty (20 percent) patients that were followed for an average of 25.7 months following admission.[62] Two years later, a multicenter longitudinal analysis with five-year follow-up on thirty-seven patients receiving rehabilitation therapy revealed eight late recoveries—that is, 22 percent—with half of the recoveries occurring more than two years post-trauma.[63] The following year, the Telese researchers reported again on late recovery but with a focus on individuals with nontraumatic injuries.[64] With nine of forty-three (21 percent) of these patients experiencing cognitive recovery beyond the standard (MSTF) cutoff for declaring permanency, the researchers concluded that "late recovery cannot be considered as an exception."

Describing the condition of late-recovered patients, Jennett has observed, "Late recoveries are almost always to very severe disability. Most patients remain totally dependent, some reaching only the minimally conscious state or a little better. Many continue to require tube feeding and are able to communicate only by gesture or coded movements because they cannot speak."[65] In other words, these patients typically are highly debilitated, yet they are nonetheless demonstrably conscious.

10.6 percent (more precisely, the quotient is 10.8 percent, but the difference is insignificant). Even the MSTF's reported incidence of 1.6 percent would seem to merit something more than "exceedingly rare"—"uncommon," perhaps, or even "quite uncommon"—but "exceedingly rare" hardly does justice to a frequency of almost two out of a hundred.

62. Estraneo et al., "Late Recovery." Patients exhibiting late recovery in this study included six with traumatic brain injury, three with anoxic injury, and one with cerebral aneurysm. The range between disease onset and detection of consciousness was fourteen to twenty-eight months.

63. Nakase-Richardson et al., "Longitudinal Outcome of Patients."

64. Estraneo et al., "Predictors of Recovery."

65. Jennett, *Vegetative State*, 67–69.

Medical Fiction?

For Jennett and Plum, the concern of basing treatment decisions for individuals with PVS on indirect assessments of consciousness and slim published evidence constituted no serious obstacle. Imperfect as the clinical knowledge and methods might be, there simply was, they asserted, "no reliable alternative available to the doctor at the bedside" where "decisions have to be made" for patients who, in their view, constituted "the price of reducing mortality from severe brain damage, and enabling many patients to make a reasonable recovery."[66]

While not stating directly the treatment decisions they had in mind, Jennett and Plum's intent seemed nonetheless evident as they concluded, "Certainly the indefinite survival of patients in this [vegetative] state presents a problem with humanitarian and socioeconomic implications which society as a whole will have to consider."[67] Wakeful but unaware patients, it would seem, were marked from the beginning as burdens to be shed, and in less than two decades, that view would come to prevail at the highest level of organized medicine as the AMA advocated ANH withdrawal, with appeal to "the family's emotional suffering and the heavy social and economic costs."[68] An unintended consequence of medical innovation, a drain on family and public resources, and mere biologic residue (organ "collections")—such were the characterizations of patients branded vegetative by experts pressing the narrative of persistent vegetation.

Even as the AMA and MSTF reports projected an aura of complete consensus within the medical community on recognition of PVS as a legitimate diagnosis, such was not the case. There were critics, including psychiatrist Avak Howsepian. In a published critique of the MSTF report, Howsepian took great issue with the claim that all vegetative patients are unconscious.[69] That assertion, he noted, conflates consciousness with awareness and entails the implausible notion that healthy individuals engaged in ordinary dreaming or certain meditative states are unconscious. Dreaming, meditation, sleep walking, and some seizure conditions, Howsepian asserted, all bear witness to a distinction between consciousness and

---

66. Jennett and Plum, "Persistent Vegetative State," 737.

67. Jennett and Plum, "Persistent Vegetative State," 737.

68. Council on Scientific Affairs and Council on Ethical and Judicial Affairs, "Persistent Vegetative State," 426.

69. Howsepian, "1994 Multi-Society Task Force," 4–5.

awareness—a person can be both unaware and conscious at the same time, and this likely includes, he believes, some PVS patients. Although they may be in "total phenomenal darkness," there are good reasons, he insisted, to believe that some "possess a rudimentary form of consciousness—a form so rudimentary . . . that these patients experience neither self-awareness (but only a transient, dim awareness of forceful environmental perceptual stimuli) nor discursive cogitation."[70] Admitting the possibility of a "dim" mental state would, in Howsepian's view, not only signal a more coherent concept of human consciousness, but it may also help explain medical data that fail in some cases of PVS to comport well with the presumption of unconsciousness, including normal or near-normal brain imaging studies, brain wave tracings, and brain function tests.[71]

In rejecting unconsciousness as a criterion for the PVS, Howsepian was not advocating for an expansion of the syndrome to include patients displaying evidence of self-awareness (i.e., patients in either LIS or and MCS). Neither was he seeking to remove patients from the category of PVS. Indeed, no change in PVS patient population numbers would be expected with acceptance of his viewpoint because the "rudimentary" level of consciousness was, he freely admitted, "clinically elusive" (i.e., undetectable by present diagnostic methods).[72] This was no mere academic exercise for Howsepian, however, as he perceived significant ramifications for the clinical management of PVS patients. In particular, he anticipated that acknowledging uncertainty in assessments of the mental status of vegetative patients would promote a higher standard of care for all patients, whether they be conscious or not. As he stated,

> It would not be unreasonable, for example, to expect that patients about whose mental states one is uncertain would be more likely to be treated as if they in fact are, at some level, aware of how they are being treated. One would, in short, predict that such agnosticism

---

70. Howsepian, "1994 Multi-Society Task Force," 6.
71. Howsepian, "1994 Multi-Society Task Force," 8.
72. Howsepian, "1994 Multi-Society Task Force," 6. Howsepian writes, "Now there doesn't appear to me to be any good reasons presently to think that such dimly conscious patients should be properly treated medically any differently from those PVS patients who we suspect are in complete darkness, or that these patients' prognoses would be significantly different, or that their neuropathological disturbances would differ markedly from those PVS patients who are in complete darkness. At least their clinical picture would ex hypothesi be qualitatively identical with the clinical picture of completely unconscious PVS patients."

on the part of PVS patients' caregivers would translate into PVS patient care that is more readily marked by compassion, dignity, and respect.[73]

Even as he critiqued the PVS concept, Howsepian still considered it a valid syndrome. Other critics have been less charitable in their assessments, including Borthwick. Citing both the evidence of a clear predisposition of Jennett et al. towards ceasing ANH and the reportedly high incidences of misdiagnosis and late cognitive recovery, Borthwick characterized the PVS in a 1996 essay as "a biased, partial, circular, and simplistic theoretical construct," and, more succinctly, "medical fiction."[74] Writing eight years later, he remained steadfast as he declared the term "persistent vegetative state" "booby-trapped from the outset"[75] with definitional criteria that functioned "less to discriminate between conditions than . . . to lend scientific authority to judgments previously made on other grounds; that is . . . to give verisimilitude to an otherwise bald and unconvincing narration."[76] Jennett and Plum, he argued, "took a short cut to certainty" as they birthed the PVS concept with "the assumption that future research would . . . confirm their speculation."[77] Research covering more than three decades, Borthwick observed in 2004, neither supported the notion of a uniformly noncognitive state in patients deemed vegetative nor produced the anticipated criteria for declaring permanence in particular cases. Quite the opposite has occurred, he asserted, as research has "established virtually beyond cavil that the diagnosis of persistent vegetative state is liable to considerable error."[78]

In response to the difficulties attending the PVS concept and its clinical application, Borthwick concluded, "We need not only to change the name of persistent vegetative state but to recast its nature completely."[79] Specifically, he believed we ought to approach the vegetative state not as

73. Howsepian, "1994 Multi-Society Task Force," 18.

74. Borthwick, "Permanent Vegetative State," 184.

75 Borthwick and Crossley, "Permanent Vegetative State," 386.

76. Borthwick and Crossley, "Permanent Vegetative State," 381.

77. Borthwick and Crossley, "Permanent Vegetative State," 384–85. Borthwick and Crossley state, "Jennett and Plum believed that it was from time to time desirable to allow such cases [patients declared to be vegetative] to die. . . . This being so, they sought a way for a doctor to be able to say definitively that further treatment would be futile and to have his opinion accepted without any time-wasting arguments; and they took a short cut to certainty."

78. Borthwick and Crossley, "Permanent Vegetative State," 386.

79. Borthwick and Crossley, "Permanent Vegetative State," 388.

a disorder of consciousness but as a condition of severe communicative disability. As he stated,

> Why do we not begin from the standpoint that this [is] a deficit in communication, rather than leaping to a conclusion that there is a deficit in awareness—a conclusion that should only be reached, if at all, when all other explanations have been exhausted? We should in the first instance attempt to remedy communication problems and only then consider whether awareness is irrecoverable.[80]

Beginning with the presumption that we have in the patient declared vegetative an aware though highly disabled person, we would thus understand, Borthwick reasoned, that the place to begin in dealing with these patients is therapy and not a discussion of withdrawing ANH. "Courts should not," he insisted, "accept a prognosis of continuing vegetative state unless the patient has been offered rehabilitation by an expert," and by "expert" he specifically meant "one of the very considerably smaller number of practitioners who had assisted in the recovery re-evaluation of a respectable number of cases."[81] Along those lines, Borthwick identified Andrews and his colleagues at RHN as providing a blueprint for managing patients deemed vegetative—evaluation by a multidisciplinary team of specialists, identification of disabilities that might preclude communication of awareness, regular reassessments that incorporate the latest technology, and extensive therapy aimed at facilitating communication where possible.

By way of analysis, it seems that what Borthwick was really advocating for was a more stringent screening of patients and not so much for a recharacterization of the vegetative syndrome. Neurologists do not move to the conclusion that a patient is in a vegetative state without first determining, correctly or not, that the patient is noncommunicative. In other words, the entry point to a diagnosis of PVS is the observation of patient unresponsiveness, which entails an inability to communicate. If a post-comatose patient is able to communicate on any level, he or she is excluded, by definition, from the category of vegetative. Essentially, Borthwick was simply demanding that physicians withhold judgment on the question of whether a patient is vegetative until the patient has been properly evaluated and given sufficient opportunity to recover, recognizing that once the label of persistent—meaning

---

80. Borthwick and Crossley, "Permanent Vegetative State," 388.
81. Borthwick and Crossley, "Permanent Vegetative State," 388.

permanent—vegetative state is affixed to the patient, the clinical discussion will often shift to a consideration of withdrawing ANH.[82]

With a higher threshold for screening patients put into effect by means of a requirement to provide extensive therapy aimed at identifying and facilitating communicative abilities, more patients may be excluded from the category of vegetative state. There will, however, be patients transitioning out of coma that remain noncommunicative and, more to the general contention, who consistently fail to give any evidence of consciousness. To that point, Andrews and his colleagues reported, "a quarter of those diagnosed as vegetative by the referring team remained vegetative and were almost certainly, from our experience, likely to remain so."[83]

Even, then, as the notion of being "awake but unaware" may turn out to be "medical fiction" in the unfolding narrative of some or even most patients diagnosed as vegetative, there are good reasons to believe that it may very well constitute reality for others. Given, however, the present data concerning misdiagnosis and cognitive recovery, we may agree with Borthwick that projections of certitude to the effect that a particular wakeful, post-comatose patient is, and will remain, unconscious are inappropriate and so too, by extension, the effort to guide treatment decisions solely on such presumption. The most that can be said from the physician's vantage point is that (1) the patient deemed vegetative lacks discernible evidence of consciousness—i.e., is believed to be unconscious on account of a failure to manifest behavioral signs evincing consciousness; and (2) the likelihood of recovering (detectable) conscious activity may indeed be small, though not necessarily nil, if the failure to evince consciousness persists beyond a certain duration.

Families and surrogates whose responsibility it is to decide questions of continued care for a patient declared vegetative would, no doubt, prefer certainty in the diagnostic and prognostic assessments. Pressed for clear-cut answers, or perhaps out of their own convictions regarding course of treatment, physicians may then deliver judgments that project certainty. The overreach is not without consequence as the declaration that the

---

82. Although Borthwick generally avoids in his numerous essays stating his personal view on the ethics of ANH withdrawal, his position emerges in a later writing. With coauthor R. Crossley, Borthwick declares, "It hardly seems fair, for example, that the only circumstance in which a person cannot be killed is if they are able to ask for release. Once having re-established communication, we must show these people that their lives can be made bearable, or we must accept the consequences" (Borthwick and Crossley, "Permanent Vegetative State," 389).

83. Andrews et al., "Misdiagnosis of Vegetative State," 16.

patient is unconscious and will remain so is often a significant factor in decisions to terminate ANH.[84]

However useful or comforting absolute statements concerning the mental status of patients diagnosed as PVS may be to various parties, they are unsupportable by the present medical data. Faced with the challenges of Howsepian, Borthwick, and others, Jennett responded in 2002 with an apparent concession as he stated, "The question of what vegetative patients actually experience is likely to remain a matter of debate for some time."[85] Yet, as he continued on to speak of clinical recovery as a regaining of consciousness, of the lack of awareness as "the crux of the diagnosis of the vegetative state," and of the vegetative state in contrast to a "minimally conscious state," Jennett still communicated the conviction that vegetative patients are unconscious.[86] His response to his critics signalled not a change in the original "wakefulness without awareness" thesis, but, at best, an acknowledgment of the fact that the supportive data he and Plum had anticipated would follow had yet to materialize.

Giving consideration to the more challenged medical picture of PVS and moving also to address the dehumanizing capacity of Jennett and Plum's chosen moniker for this syndrome, a consortium led by Steve Laureys of Liège's Coma Science Group proposed in 2010 a new name—specifically, unresponsive wakefulness syndrome (UWS).[87] Searching the published medical literature from 2010 forward, it appears their efforts have yielded moderate success as the number of publications now slightly favors UWS (sixty-eight) over PVS (forty-nine).[88] Yet, with the terminology of UWS still relatively recent and with so much of the relevant extant literature—medical and ethical—employing only the older term, the present author's practice in presenting the topic is to utilize PVS but with mitigating explanation.

---

84. Andrews et al., "Misdiagnosis of Vegetative State," 13. As Andrews and his colleagues at RHN state, "The diagnosis of the vegetative state can have a major influence on decision-making about the level of care or services provided and may lead to an application being made to the courts for a directive on withdrawal of tube feeding."

85. Jennett, *Vegetative State*, 19.

86. Jennett, *Vegetative State*, 10–11.

87. Laureys et al., "Unresponsive Wakefulness Syndrome."

88. The search utilizing the National Library of Medicine's PubMed database (https://pubmed.ncbi.nlm.nih.gov) was conducted on March 29, 2022, keying separately on the criteria "persistent vegetative state" and "unresponsive wakefulness syndrome."

THE PERMANENT (?) VEGETATIVE (?) STATE

In addressing the ANH-PVS question, ethicists and other commentators routinely assume the narrative of permanent unconsciousness, and for proponents of ANH withdrawal that assumption is critical. These include the solidly pro-life scholar Rakestraw, whose advocacy of the patient-as-dead approach reflected clear desire to honor the sixth commandment ("Thou shall not murder") as he posited homicide as the only alternative—and an unacceptable one at that—to viewing ANH withdrawal as the first stage in proper disposition of mortal remains.[89] Yet, with reported misdiagnosis rates consistently hovering in the 30–40 percent range and with reports of covert awareness suggesting an even higher incidence approaching 50 percent, declaring death by higher-brain criterion in the situation of PVS, for all of its other issues, is from an empirical standpoint a faulty enterprise. To be sure, infallible judgments are not the stuff of clinical medicine, yet it is more than reasonable to balk at a criterion for establishing death—a most important undertaking with huge ramifications—that offers no more certainty than a call of heads on the flip of the coin. And if, adding to such defect, one must also posit a regular occurrence of resurrection from the dead given the data on late cognitive recoveries, it seems little is left to propel the higher-brain criterion forward other than a priori preferences to cease life support.

As presently ascertained, the medical reality is that the vegetative state often is not vegetative and that late cognitive recovery is not so rare an event. Supposing only permanently unconscious persons to be in view—clinging, we could say, to "PVS 1.0"—one merely predicates a disproved situational narrative. It is time—indeed, it is past time—for ethicists addressing the ANH-PVS issue to shed the false narrative and incorporate into their analyses the assumption that any conclusions reached may find application to highly debilitated fellow human beings who, unbeknownst to kin and caregivers, are aware at some level or may become so if ANH were to continue. Given the ubiquity of PVS 1.0 in analyses arguing for the moral permissibility of ANH withdrawal, some might presume that acknowledging the updated narrative ("PVS 2.0") would drive the opposite conclusion—i.e., that ANH must continue. Advocating recognition of PVS 2.0 in analyses and discussions of the ANH-PVS question is this essay's chief concern, but in the remaining space, I shall sketch a position sans the assumption of permanent unconsciousness that argues for the moral

---

89. Rakestraw, "Persistent Vegetative State," 394. As Rakestraw writes, "If we can determine that the PVS individual is dead, then we need not hesitate to withdraw food and water. If on the other hand the patient is alive, we must not take his or her life."

permissibility of foregoing (by proxy) indefinite ANH in the case of PVS in recognition of God's sovereignty over life's terminus.

CONSIDERING THE ANH-PVS QUESTION[90]

> I eagerly expect and hope that I will in no way be ashamed, but will have sufficient courage so that now as always Christ will be exalted in my body, whether by life or by death. (Phil 1:20 NIV)

Few ethicists have written as much on the ANH-PVS issue and with as great a clarity as Lutheran theologian Gilbert Meilaender, a former doctoral student under Ramsey at Princeton. Echoing his mentor's ardent championing of an end-of-life ethics committed to the principle that it is "wrong to aim at death," Meilaender argues that "a decision not to offer [ANH] can enact only one intention: to take the life of the unconscious person . . . [thus violating the] fundamental principle . . . that it is wrong to aim to kill the innocent."[91] Articulated as such, the matter presents as a "one-table" issue keyed on the sixth commandment,[92] but in the analysis below, we shall contend for a "two-table" approach.[93] Contra Meilaender, one may legitimately claim an intention other than aiming at death, and, more to the point, one grounded in the first commandment[94]—specifically, that in declining (by proxy) indefinite ANH, one may truly aim to acknowledge God's sovereignty over human life (and death). In the relation between first

---

90. In what follows, it will become abundantly clear to the reader that the author views belief in God and his sovereignty over life and death as helpful and necessary in dealing effectively with the ANH-PVS issue. Space constraints do not permit a defense of these theological underpinnings, but it is the author's expectation that readers inclined to other viewpoints on fundamental reality may nonetheless benefit in learning how it is that a pro-life Christian can in good conscience work from the most current medical understanding of PVS and conclude moral permissibility for declining indefinite ANH.

91. Meilaender, "On Removing Food," 13.

92. "You shall not murder" (Exod 20:13 NASB).

93. Scripture tells us that God wrote the Ten Commandments on two stone tablets (Exod 34:1). The precise grouping of the commandments on the tablets is not specified in the biblical text, but scholars have long recognized a "theological division" with the first four commandments—those addressing our relationship with God—assigned to a "first table" and the remaining six—those governing dealings between humans—to a "second table."

94. "You shall have no other gods before Me" (Exod 20:3 NASB).

and sixth commandments, the former helps delineate where our responsibility to preserve life ceases in the age of modern medicine.

Letting Die

In applying the sixth commandment to the PVS situation, it is clear that euthanasia—meaning, the intentional ending of the patient's life—is morally out of bounds, regardless of whether the patient has requested it, a doctor recommends it, or the law allows it. Personal freedom, medical opinion, and civil authority do not trump God's commandments. Typically, the appeal will be to compassion and mercy, but most fundamentally, euthanasia is about humans asserting control beyond divinely prescribed boundaries. As Christian ethicist John Jefferson Davis states, "The euthanasia mentality sees man as the lord of his own life."[95] Ironically, the same error drives the polar extreme of medical vitalism which treats lifespan as ultimate. Ramsey identified the connection in *The Patient as Person* as he stated,

> It may be that it is quite natural that in an atheistic and secular age the best morality men can think of is to make an absolute of saving life for yet a bit more spatio-temporal existence.... It may also be that, paradoxically, a secular age is productive of equally powerful currents of thought toward the arbitrary taking of life for the sake of earthly good to come.[96]

Treating life (or the power to extend life) as an absolute (medical vitalism) or presuming the authority to take it without just cause (euthanasia)—with either approach, God's lordship over human life is disrespected.

Aware of these "two opposite extremes," as Ramsey labelled them, pro-life Christian ethicists dealing with end-of-life care strive to stay clear. Meilaender, for example, in arguing against ANH withdrawal, declares, "We are not vitalists," and then explains, "because we do not think that continued life is the only good, . . . we are not obligated to do everything that might be done to keep someone alive."[97] Ethicists contending for the permissibility of ANH withdrawal deal with the other extreme as they fend

---

95. Davis, *Evangelical Ethics*, 201. Similarly, Meilaender comments, "Euthanasia is the ultimate attempt at managing death (and misses the irony that we are attempting to master the very event that announces our lack of mastery)" (Meilaender, "Living Life's End," 20).

96. Ramsey, *Patient as Person*, 1561.

97. Meilaender, "Living Life's End," 17.

off the charge of euthanasia. Christian philosopher Scott Rae, for example, comments, "Some suggest that termination of life support is 'playing God,' ... but that charge is accurate only if [termination of life support] is actually killing a patient, which it is not."[98]

Navigating between the extremes of vitalism and killing, pro-life ethicists routinely invoke the category of "letting die."[99] With passive euthanasia, letting die shares the feature that life-extending treatment is withheld with the expectation that a hastened death will occur. In form and effect, they appear identical, but on account of diverging aims, they are morally distinct. Wrongly, passive euthanasia aims at death—the patient's death is intended, and "pulling the plug" is the chosen means. With letting die, however, the patient's death is foreseen but unintended as a particular moral aim is pursued.[100] Because intentions truly matter in moral assessments, the distinction between letting die and passive euthanasia is real, and so the terms ought not to be used interchangeably. Yet, also because the distinction rests at the level of intention, the two may be difficult to distinguish in practice when data is limited to the externals.[101]

As for the aim of letting die, it is generally claimed that a choice is being made between one kind of life over another, and most often, the appeal is to a life less burdened by treatment.[102] And so, for example, Meilaender contends that for patients with dementia, ANH may be forgone if physical restraints would be required to prevent self-removal of the feeding tube.[103] For patients declared vegetative, however, he rejects the appeal to burdensome treatment on the presumption they are unconscious and thus incapable of suffering. Rae, however, counters that permanently unconscious patients can still be harmed, and as a hypothetical example, he cites

---

98. Rae, *Moral Choices*, 220.

99. Ramsey, *Patient as Person*, 113–64. See also Frame, *Doctrine of Christian Life*, 734–36; VanDrunen, *Bioethics and Christian Life*, 207–11.

100. Ramsey emphasizes that in letting die, we are not omitting care. To the contrary, he notes, "upon ceasing to try to rescue the perishing, one then is free to care for the dying" (Ramsey, *Patient as Person*, 153).

101. For this reason, ethicists defending the category of letting die tend to focus the comparison on overt (active) killing.

102. Ethicists taking this tack include Meilaender, who comments, "Even when care is not useless it may be so burdensome that it should be dispensed with. When that is the case, ... our aim is to relieve the person of a burden, with the foreseen but unintended effect of a hastened death" (Meilaender, "On Removing Food," 17).

103. Sellers and Meilaender, "When to Pull," 48.

a leg amputation performed with no medical benefit in view.[104] Rae also expands the range of burden beyond bodily harm to include violation of a patient's prior wish not to receive ANH. So also David VanDrunen, as he cites "spiritually burdensome" treatment that leaves the patient in a (vegetative) state "in which he is unable to fulfill his religious responsibilities and privileges."[105]

Routinely, secular ethicists deny the distinction between killing and letting die.[106] Dismissing the possibility of a privileged word from above and presuming that we alone are responsible, they see in the distinction nothing more than a quibble over the means by which the patient's death is achieved—omission versus commission. Meeting the secularist on his own turf, the theist working from the "underside"[107] can try pointing to the fact that, with letting die, some other force is at work in bringing about the patient's death, and then argue that the distinction is morally significant. Yet, if in identifying that force, the appeal can be only to nature (i.e., that we allow nature to take its course)—and that truly is all the secularist approach will accommodate—the argument would undercut the whole project of medicine, for what medical intervention does not, in some way, fiddle with nature?

Truly, we may speak of letting die as morally distinct from killing only if there is at work another agent whose responsibility for human life trumps our own, and Scripture clearly indicates we are dealing here with none other than God Almighty.[108] As stated in the book of Deuteronomy, "There is no God besides me. I put to death and I bring to life, I have wounded and I will heal, and no one can deliver out of my hand" (Deut 32:39 NIV). And so, theologian John Frame rightly declares, "We must acknowledge that God is in control of life and death."[109]

---

104. Rae, "Is the Removal," 4.

105. VanDrunen, *Bioethics and Christian Life*, 237.

106. See, e.g., Rachels, "Active and Passive Euthanasia."

107. "Doing Christian ethics . . . from the underside" is how Paul Ramsey described his tactic of articulating Christian moral convictions in philosophical terms. See Ramsey, "Response I," 88; O'Donovan, "Keeping Body and Soul," 38.

108. Truly, there seems little point in avoiding the God factor in discussing the distinction between killing and letting die with secularists, because they understand full well that only if a higher moral agency is at work can the distinction be maintained. See, e.g., Kuhse, *Sanctity-of-Life Doctrine in Medicine*, 31–81.

109. Frame, *Doctrine of Christian Life*, 735.

The proposition that our continued efforts to prolong life may, in some situations, counter God's sovereign decision to bring life to an end presumes not only his providential working in life's final stage, but also the possibility that we may actually resist it to some degree. Death that is instantaneous—what some today would call an "act of God"[110]—affords no chance to resist, but in the era of artificial life support, opportunities may present. Furthermore, since God does not hold us accountable for knowledge accessible only to himself, the condemnation of vitalist medicine also presumes that we can know when God is exercising his prerogative over life's end. This, then, raises the criteriological question—specifically, how can we know when God is exercising this prerogative?

Not Clearly Dying

Ethicists defending the category of letting die generally assert as a chief criterion for its application that the patient be dying. As Meilaender states, "You cannot 'let die' a person who is not dying."[111] Frame agrees as he comments, "When is it right, then, to let someone die? When he is dying."[112] Rightly recognizing the obvious question, he then asks, "What is dying?"

Conceptually, we may in medical contexts think of dying as a process of bodily deterioration with deathward trajectory that is initiated by disease or injury. In some cases, the process may be virtually coincident with death (e.g., massive heart attack, lightning strike), and in others, it may extend over months or even years (e.g., terminal cancer). Exactly when dying gives way to death is a question that has generated much debate in modern times. For much of the history of medicine, death has generally been identified on the basis of what physicians today call a "cardiopulmonary" standard—when breathing and circulation cease, the individual is declared dead. With

---

110. The preference for a sudden death evinces the extent to which the art of dying (*ars moriendi*) has faded from view in modern Christianity. According to Allen Verhey, in prior centuries, "a sudden death was regarded as a bad death, as somehow a little shameful, as if the wrath of God had struck" (Verhey, *Christian Art of Dying*, 12). Verhey goes on to cite numerous downsides to a sudden death, commenting, "Sudden death is not a good way to die, not for the dying person and not for those left to grieve without the opportunity to have said good-bye. It provides no opportunity for dying well and faithfully, no opportunity for speaking and hearing words of faith and community, no opportunity for gestures of affection and reconciliation" (Verhey, *Christian Art of Dying*, 389).

111. Orr and Meilaender, "Ethics & Life's Ending," 37.

112. Frame, *Doctrine of Christian Life*, 735.

the advent of life-sustaining technologies capable of replacing those functions, a movement arose in the late 1960s to update the definition of death, which eventually culminated in the widespread adoption of a "(whole) brain death" standard.[113] In all fifty states now, patients maintained on life support can be declared dead if doctors determine that function in both higher- and lower-brain has irreversibly ceased.

By cardiopulmonary and whole-brain standards, individuals in a PVS are alive and not dead. Whether they should be considered dying, though, is not so straightforward a question. In a printed exchange with Meilaender addressing the ANH-PVS question as the Schiavo affair garnered the national spotlight, physician and medical ethicist Robert Orr raised the issue in stating, "The greatest ethical dilemma surrounding the use or non-use of nutritional support for persons in a PVS arises from the fact that they are not clearly dying."[114] Word order is critical. Orr was not saying these patients are clearly not dying, but that they are not clearly dying, and in an attempt to clarify, he characterized the PVS condition as "lethal in and of itself." Conceding that Orr had indeed identified "a crucial question," but complaining of a lack of "clarity and precision" in the physician's comments, Meilaender responded unequivocally, "Patients in a persistent vegetative state are not dying patients," and on this point he was being consistent, having asserted two decades prior that PVS patients are neither "irretrievably dying" nor even "in the process of dying."[115]

Fleshing out Orr's distinction, we may first note that in some dying patients—the "irretrievably dying," to use Meilaender's term—the pathological insult may be ineradicable and death certain barring a miracle (e.g., end-stage cancer).[116] In those situations, the doctor may proclaim "there is nothing more we can do," and while such may for the patient mark a beginning to dying as an event, from a biological standpoint the resignation serves only to acknowledge the powerlessness of available medical means to inhibit the progression of a lethal process already underway.

In other cases, the pathology may by medical intervention be eliminated and with it the dying process reversed and the threat of death removed (e.g., surgery for a bowel obstruction causing systemic infection and vital organ

---

113. See Ad Hoc Committee of the Harvard Medical School, "Definition of Irreversible Coma"; Henderson, *Death and Donation*, 1–28; Ramsey, *Patient as Person*, 59–112.

114. Orr and Meilaender, "Ethics & Life's Ending," 34.

115. Meilaender, "Confused, Voiceless, Perverse," 139.

116. Meilaender, "Confused, Voiceless, Perverse," 139.

dysfunction). Using Meilaender's terminology, one might describe patients in such scenarios as "retrievably" dying—by curative treatment, the patient is snatched from the path that runs from disease to death. In still other cases, doctors may lack the ability to extricate patients from that path but still have the means to halt the progression towards death—an ineliminable pathology remains but its lethality is restrained by medical intervention. If such occurs before physical demise is clearly evident, it may seem more correct to say only that death is being prevented and so reserve the language of "dying" for patients who bear externally recognizable evidence of physical deterioration. Recognizing, however, that the incurrence of lethal disease or injury is the first stage in the dying process, it may be argued that when via medical intervention death is prevented without eliminating the pathology, the process of dying is only interrupted or suspended. That conclusion would seem even more reasonable in situations where continuous treatment is required to prevent the disease from claiming the patient's life.

With respect to the vegetative condition, ANH resists an ineliminable, lethal pathology that has robbed the patient of certain vital capacities including the ability to prehend food and liquid and also to move them via a coordinated swallow beyond the opening to the airway and into the digestive tract.[117] By delivering water and nutrients directly to the stomach, ANH counters the mortal tug of the patient's disease but it is neither curative nor restorative of lost vital functions—while the patient is sustained by the intervention, the underlying pathology remains much the same as when hemodialysis is employed to keep alive an individual with end-stage kidney disease or when the ventilator is used to maintain a patient bereft of respiratory drive. For these patients, some physiological parameters may normalize under the life support regimen, but there is no release from the lethal pathology that denies them their full complement of vital functions. With each stroke of the ventilator, each pass through the dialysis filter, or each

---

117. According to Jennett, there is some debate among clinicians as to whether patients who meet most criteria for the vegetative state while still retaining the ability to swallow in a coordinated manner sufficient to permit oral feedings should be excluded from the diagnosis. Published data suggests we are dealing here with a minority of patients. Researchers from the Yamaguchi University School of Medicine, for example, reported that in 110 patients classified as vegetative, 26 percent were fed orally (of those, almost 80 percent [22/28] were judged to be in a good or fair nutritional state). Perhaps some of the orally fed patients in this 1977 report were minimally conscious and not truly vegetative (i.e., misdiagnosed), but it may also be that some patients being tube fed were so managed for convenience's sake and not because their swallowing was impaired. See Higashi et al., "Epidemiological Studies"; Jennett, *Vegetative State*, 18.

push of the feeding tube plunger, the patient is pulled lifeward, but as with many patients that no one debates are dying, the individual remains fixed to a course that runs between lethal insult and death. As the effect of each successive pulse of treatment wanes, the trajectory again turns deathward.

Withdrawing Artificial Nutrition and Hydration

On account of their regular and repeated tube feedings, unresponsive, post-comatose patients receiving ANH may not be "clearly dying," but neither are they loosed from the dying process. If treatment is withdrawn, the terminal nature of their pathology will assuredly manifest. Excluding them from the category of letting die, then, suggests the principle "you cannot let die a person who will not die only if you intervene." But that seems to take us in the direction of medical vitalism where the capacity to preserve life serves as its own justification.

Looking to avoid the vitalist error, one might conclude the presence of incurable, naturally lethal pathology is an indication that the divine prerogative over life's terminus is in process. At what point letting die should, if at all, commence, prayerful consideration must be given to the matter of how best to live out the remaining days. There is no reason to suppose that a diagnosis of terminal disease is to be read as an immediate summons from this life. To the contrary, in some situations, God extends "extra" time for purposeful activity. To King Hezekiah, for example, he granted the opportunity to make preparation for his death—"Put your house in order" was the directive (2 Kgs 20:1 NIV). God owes it to no one, but for reasons known only to him, sometimes he provides the dying patient time to order his or her affairs (e.g., reconciling with God, mending relationships, encouraging others, saying good-byes, making provision for spouse and dependents, etc.). Hezekiah took as his first order of business to petition God for a stay of the decree, and God graciously relented. But, whether God extends healing or not—and that, ultimately, is a matter in which he is to be trusted—prayer in time of great distress can be a great blessing as we cast our cares upon "him who is able to do immeasurably more than all we ask or imagine" (Eph 3:20 NIV; cf. 1 Pet 5:7).

When recovery from severe brain injury stalls in a chronic, wakeful, but unresponsive state, continuing ANH for whatever more time is needed to allow others to say good-bye might be justified as a proxy-enabled facilitation of putting one's house in order. Beyond that, the opportunity for ordering affairs would seem passed, and if so, letting die may commence in recognition of God's sovereignty over life's end. That we have the technological capability to extend earthly lifespan does not mean that we should employ it. Truly, given what Scripture tells us about the next life, why would we want to hold back one whom God is pulling to his side, let alone resist God in the process? But neither are we to expedite the process. In letting die, we do not stand in the way and we do not push from behind, but rather, we stand alongside, companying the patient as long as we can with comfort care measures as the process God has ordained for their earthly departure works to completion.[118] Death is not the aim—either as an end in itself or as a means to some other end. Rather, death and the pathologic insult from which it springs are accepted as coming from the hand of God.

For surrogate decision-maker and caregiver facilitating a patient's prior request to forego ANH in the situation of PVS, it is right and proper to grieve but there is no guilt over a death initiated in God's providence truly not by the pulling of a tube but by an ineliminable and lethal pathology. Recognizing that submitting to God's lordship over life is firstly a matter of personal responsibility, it would, however, be morally problematic to withdraw ANH in situations where its continuance has been requested by the patient through prior directive and it is within our power to provide it. For the even tougher cases—specifically, patients never competent or those for whom treatment preferences are unknown—applying the Golden Rule may be the best we can do.

BIBLIOGRAPHY

Ad Hoc Committee of the Harvard Medical School. "A Definition of Irreversible Coma: Report of the Ad Hoc Committee of the Harvard Medical School to Examine the Definition of Brain Death." *Journal of the American Medical Association* 205 (1968) 337–40.

Andrews, Keith. "Recovery of Patients after Four Months or More in the Persistent Vegetative State." *British Medical Journal* 306 (1993) 1597–1600.

Andrews, Keith, et al. "Misdiagnosis of the Vegetative State: Retrospective Study in a Rehabilitation Unit." *British Medical Journal* 313 (1996) 13–16.

Bard, Bernard, and Joseph Fletcher. "The Right to Die." *Atlantic Monthly* 221 (1968) 59–64.

---

118. Presuming the possibility of undetected consciousness, comfort care measures are indicated when facilitating the UWS patient's prior request to withdraw ANH just the same as when ministering to a clearly cognitive individual in extremis.

Bekinschtein, Tristan A., et al. "Classical Conditioning in the Vegetative and Minimally Conscious State." *Nature Neuroscience* 12 (2009) 1343–49.

Borthwick, C. J., and R. Crossley. "Permanent Vegetative State: Usefulness and Limits of a Prognostic Definition." *NeuroRehabilitation* 19 (2004) 381–89.

Borthwick, Christian J. "The Permanent Vegetative State: Ethical Crux, Medical Fiction?" *Issues in Law & Medicine* 12 (1996) 167–85.

Buchanan, Allen E. "The Limits of Proxy Decision-Making." In *Paternalism*, edited by Rolf E. Sartorius, 153–70. Minneapolis: University of Minnesota Press, 1983.

Childs, N. L., et al. "Accuracy of Diagnosis of Persistent Vegetative State." *Neurology* 43 (1993) 1465–67.

Cooper, John W. *Body, Soul, and Life Everlasting: Biblical Anthropology and the Monism-Dualism Debate*. Grand Rapids: Eerdmans, 2000.

Council on Scientific Affairs, and Council on Ethical and Judicial Affairs. "Persistent Vegetative State and the Decision to Withdraw or Withhold Life Support." *Journal of the American Medical Association* 263 (1990) 426–30.

Cruse, Damian, et al. "Detecting Awareness in the Vegetative State: Electroencephalographic Evidence for Attempted Movements to Command." *PLoS One* 7 (2012) e49933.

Davis, John Jefferson. "Concerning the Case of 'Mr. Stevens.'" *Issues in Law & Medicine* 7 (1991) 227–41.

———. *Evangelical Ethics*. 3rd ed. Phillipsburg, NJ: P&R, 2004.

Draper, Heather. "Research and Patients in a Permanent Vegetative State." *Journal of Medical Ethics* 32 (2006) 607.

Drinker, P., and L. A. Shaw. "An Apparatus for the Prolonged Administration of Artificial Respiration: I. A Design for Adults and Children." *Journal of Clinical Investigation* 7 (1929) 229–47.

Estraneo, A., et al. "Late Recovery after Traumatic, Anoxic, or Hemorrhagic Long-Lasting Vegetative State." *Neurology* 75 (2010) 239–45.

Estraneo, Anna, et al. "Predictors of Recovery of Responsiveness in Prolonged Anoxic Vegetative State." *Neurology* 80 (2013) 464–70.

Fletcher, Joseph. "Indicators of Humanhood: A Tentative Profile of Man." *Hastings Center Report* 2 (1972) 1–4.

———. *Morals and Medicine*. Boston: Beacon, 1960.

Fletcher, Joseph F. "Four Indicators of Humanhood: The Enquiry Matures." *Hastings Center Report* 4 (1974) 4–7.

Forte, David F. "Getting Rid of the Vegetables." *First Things* 26 (1992) 13–15.

Frame, John M. *The Doctrine of the Christian Life*. Vol. 3 of *A Theology of Lordship*. Phillipsburg, NJ: P&R, 2008.

Fritz, Zoe. "Can 'Best Interests' Derail the Trolley? Examining Withdrawal of Clinically Assisted Nutrition and Hydration in Patients in the Permanent Vegetative State." *Journal of Medical Ethics* 43 (2017) 450–54.

Gill-Thwaites, Helen. "Lotteries, Loopholes and Luck: Misdiagnosis in the Vegetative State Patient." *Brain Injury* 20 (2006) 1321–28.

Gill-Thwaites, H., and R. Munday. "The Sensory Modality Assessment and Rehabilitation Technique (Smart): A Valid and Reliable Assessment for Vegetative State and Minimally Conscious State Patients." *Brain Injury* 18 (2004) 1255–69.

Henderson, D. Scott. *Death and Donation: Rethinking Brain Death as a Means for Procuring Transplantable Organs*. Eugene, OR: Pickwick, 2011.

Higashi, K., et al. "Epidemiological Studies on Patients with a Persistent Vegetative State." *Journal of Neurology, Neurosurgery, and Psychiatry* 40 (1977) 876–85.

Hoekema, Anthony A. *Created in God's Image*. Grand Rapids: Eerdmans, 1986.

Howsepian, A. A. "The 1994 Multi-Society Task Force Consensus Statement on the Persistent Vegetative State: A Critical Analysis." *Issues in Law & Medicine* 12 (1996) 3–29.

Jennett, B., and F. Plum. "Persistent Vegetative State after Brain Damage: A Syndrome in Search of a Name." *Lancet* 7753 (1972) 734–37.

Jennett, Bryan. *The Vegetative State: Medical Facts, Ethical and Legal Dilemmas*. Cambridge: Cambridge University Press, 2002.

Kuhse, Helga. *The Sanctity-of-Life Doctrine in Medicine: A Critique*. Oxford: Clarendon Press, 1987.

Laureys, Steven, et al. "Unresponsive Wakefulness Syndrome: A New Name for the Vegetative State or Apallic Syndrome." *BMC Medicine* 8 (2010). https://doi.org/10.1186/1741-7015-8-68.

Lindgren, James. "Death by Default." *Law and Contemporary Problems* 56 (1993) 185–254.

Lynn, Joanne, and James F. Childress. "Must Patients Always Be Given Food and Water?" *Hastings Center Report* 13 (1983) 17–21.

Meilaender, Gilbert. "The Confused, the Voiceless, the Perverse: Shall We Give Them Food and Drink?" *Issues in Law & Medicine* 2 (1986) 133–48.

———. "Living Life's End." *First Things* 153 (2005) 17–21.

———. "On Removing Food and Water: Against the Stream." *Hastings Center Report* 14 (1984) 11–13.

Moore, David W. "Three in Four Americans Support Euthanasia." *Gallup Poll Tuesday Briefing* (2005) 98–100.

Moreland, J. P., and Scott B. Rae. *Body & Soul: Human Nature & the Crisis in Ethics*. Downers Grove, IL: IVP Academic, 2000.

Multi-Society Task Force on PVS, The. "Medical Aspects of the Persistent Vegetative State [pt. 1]." *New England Journal of Medicine* 330 (1994) 1499–1508.

———. "Medical Aspects of the Persistent Vegetative State [pt. 2]." *New England Journal of Medicine* 330 (1994) 1572–79.

Nakase-Richardson, Risa, et al. "Longitudinal Outcome of Patients with Disordered Consciousness in the NIDRR TBI Model Systems Programs." *Journal of Neurotrauma* 29 (2012) 59–65.

O'Donovan, Oliver. "Keeping Body and Soul Together." In *Covenants of Life: Contemporary Medical Ethics in Light of the Thought of Paul Ramsey*, edited by Kenneth L. Vaux et al., 35–53. Philosophy and Medicine 77. Boston: Kluwer Academic, 2002.

Orr, Robert D., and Gilbert Meilaender. "Ethics & Life's Ending: An Exchange." *First Things* 145 (2004) 31–38.

Owen, Adrian M., and Martin R. Coleman. "Detecting Awareness in the Vegetative State." *Annals of the New York Academy of Sciences* 1129 (2008) 130–38.

Owen, Adrian M., et al. "Detecting Awareness in the Vegetative State." *Science* 313 (2006) 1402.

Rachels, James. "Active and Passive Euthanasia." *New England Journal of Medicine* 292 (1975) 78–80.

Rae, Scott B. "Is the Removal of Medically Provided Nutrition and Hydration from the Patient in a PVS Ethically Acceptable?" Paper presented at Far West Regional Meeting of the Evangelical Theological Society, Fullerton, CA, Apr. 12, 1991.

———. *Moral Choices: An Introduction to Ethics.* 3rd ed. Grand Rapids: Zondervan, 2009.

———. "Views of Human Nature at the Edges of Life: Personhood and Medical Ethics." In *Christian Perspectives on Being Human: A Multidisciplinary Approach to Integration*, edited by James Porter Moreland and David M. Ciocchi, 235–58. Grand Rapids: Baker, 1993.

Rakestraw, Robert V. "The Persistent Vegetative State and the Withdrawal of Nutrition and Hydration." *Journal of the Evangelical Theological Society* 35 (1992) 389–405.

Ramsey, Paul. *Ethics at the Edges of Life: Medical and Legal Intersections.* New Haven, CT: Yale University Press, 1978.

———. *The Patient as Person: Explorations in Medical Ethics.* New Haven, CT: Yale University Press, 1970.

———. "Response I." In *Covenants of Life: Contemporary Medical Ethics in Light of the Thought of Paul Ramsey*, edited by Kenneth L. Vaux et al., 85–102. Philosophy and Medicine 77. Boston: Kluwer Academic, 2002.

Ravelingien, A., et al. "Proceeding with Clinical Trials of Animal to Human Organ Transplantation: A Way out of the Dilemma." *Journal of Medical Ethics* 30 (2004) 92–98.

Schnakers, Caroline, and Steve Majerus. "Behavioral Assessment and Diagnosis of Disorders of Consciousness." In *Coma and Disorders of Consciousness*, edited by Caroline Schnakers and Steven Laureys, 1–10. London: Springer, 2012.

Schnakers, Caroline, et al. "Diagnostic Accuracy of the Vegetative and Minimally Conscious State: Clinical Consensus versus Standardized Neurobehavioral Assessment." *BMC Neurology* 9 (2009). https://doi.org/10.1186/1471-2377-9-35.

———. "Preserved Covert Cognition in Noncommunicative Patients with Severe Brain Injury?" *Neurorehabilitation and Neural Repair* 29 (2015) 308–17.

Schneiderman, L. J., et al. "Medical Futility: Its Meaning and Ethical Implications." *Annals of Internal Medicine* 112 (1990) 949–54.

Schneiderman, Lawrence J., and Nancy S. Jecker. *Wrong Medicine: Doctors, Patients, and Futile Treatment.* 2nd ed. Baltimore: Johns Hopkins University Press, 2011.

Sellers, Jeff M., and Gilbert Meilaender. "When to Pull a Feeding Tube: Leading Bioethicist Gilbert Meilaender Discusses the Problems of Withdrawing Terri Schiavo's Lifeline." *Christianity Today* 49 (2005) 48–49.

Stender, J., et al. "Diagnostic Precision of Pet Imaging and Functional MRI in Disorders of Consciousness: A Clinical Validation Study." *Lancet* 384 (2014) 514–22.

Tresch, Donald D., et al. "Clinical Characteristics of Patients in the Persistent Vegetative State." *Archives of Internal Medicine* 151 (1991) 930–32.

VanDrunen, David. *Bioethics and the Christian Life: A Guide to Making Difficult Decisions.* Wheaton, IL: Crossway, 2009.

Veatch, Robert. M. "The Impending Collapse of the Whole-Brain Definition of Death." *Hastings Center Report* 23 (1993) 18–24.

Verhey, Allen. *The Christian Art of Dying: Learning from Jesus.* Grand Rapids: Eerdmans, 2011.

Wennberg, Robert N. *Terminal Choices: Euthanasia, Suicide, and the Right to Die.* Grand Rapids: Eerdmans, 1989.

Whyte, John, and Risa Nakase-Richardson. "Disorders of Consciousness: Outcomes, Comorbidities, and Care Needs." *Archives of Physical Medicine and Rehabilitation* 94 (2013) 1851–54.

9

Will Posthumans Be Persons?
Taking the Transhumanist Goal Seriously

Matthew Eppinette

INTRODUCTION

The transhuman movement is actively pursuing the goal of moving beyond current ideas of what it is to be human toward what they see as the next phase of evolution after or beyond human beings. In other words, transhumanists are pursuing becoming posthuman. How are Christians to think about the idea and possibility of the posthuman? Specifically, what are we to make of the personhood of various predicted or imagined forms of posthumanity? In this chapter I will provide an overview of transhumanism, outlining some of its key terms, highlighting several writings that are important to transhumanism, and providing a summary of several key values transhumanists hold. Next, I will highlight a number of themes that commonly recur in transhumanism, and then I will draw attention to some of the leading figures and organizations within transhumanism. The movement is by no means monolithic, so I will attempt to provide some insight as to the various views and subconstituencies within transhumanism. Finally, I will examine posthuman views on personhood and provide an evaluation from a Christian point of view.

WHAT IS TRANSHUMANISM?

The term "transhuman" was coined simply by combining the words "transitional" and "human." At a basic level, transhumanists believe that science and technology are intrinsic aspects of our humanity and should be used in a transformation of the human condition.[1] Most transhumanists trace the origin of the term "transhuman" to a 1927 essay by Julian Huxley (brother of *Brave New World* author Aldous Huxley) in which Huxley suggested transhumanism as the name for "man remaining man, but transcending himself, by realizing new possibilities of and for his human nature."[2] Others trace the origin of the term back to Dante's coinage of *trasumanar* in Paradiso to describe the degree of transformation involved in entering paradise.[3]

The "Transhumanist FAQ," a key transhumanist document that I will discuss in more detail below, defines transhumanism as "a way of thinking about the future that is based on the premise that the human species in its current form does not represent the end of our development but rather a comparatively early phase."[4] The transhumanist organization Humanity+, which hosts the "Transhumanist FAQ" on its website, expands the definition of transhumanism:

1. The intellectual and cultural movement that affirms the possibility and desirability of fundamentally improving the human condition through applied reason, especially by developing and making widely available technologies to eliminate aging and to greatly enhance human intellectual, physical, and psychological capacities.

2. The study of the ramifications, promises, and potential dangers of technologies that will enable us to overcome fundamental human limitations, and the related study of the ethical matters involved in developing and using such technologies.[5]

---

1. Redding, "Can Transhumanism Lead Us."

2. Bostrom, "History of Transhumanist Thought," 6; quoting J. Huxley, *Religion without Revelation*. See also Tirosh-Samuelson, "Engaging Transhumanism," 20; More, "Philosophy of Transhumanism," 8.

3. Cole-Turner, "Going beyond the Human," 151; see also O'Gieblyn, "Ghost in the Cloud."

4. See https://www.humanityplus.org/transhumanist-faq, under "What is transhumanism?"

5. See https://www.humanityplus.org/transhumanist-faq, under "What is transhumanism?"

The transformation of the "human condition" that is in view here is radical. Some even consider it on par with, if not exceeding, the degree of transformation Dante sought to communicate in using the term *trasumanar*. To be clear, the transformation sought is a transformation of both human nature and human being itself.

> Just as we use rational means to improve the human condition and the external world, we can also use such means to improve ourselves, the human organism. In doing so, we are not limited to traditional humanistic methods, such as education and cultural development. We can also use technological means that will eventually enable us to move beyond what some would think of as "human."[6]

Transhumanists, then, are those who are actively looking forward to being involved in or bringing to reality a posthuman era. That is, they anticipate and welcome moving beyond what some would think of as being human at all. As Hava Tirosh-Samuelson points out, the term carries multiple meanings: "Transhumanism . . . denotes the transition from human to posthuman existence as well as activities and attitudes that one is expected to promote in order to bring about the ideal, posthuman future."[7]

To be a posthuman would be as different from a human being as a human being is from an ape.[8] The transformation from human to posthuman will represent both a decisive break with and an advancement beyond humanity as it currently exists. It will be the next evolutionary step after or beyond humanity. A number of possibilities exist for the shape or form that posthumanity might take. It may come about by merging human and machines; it may involve uploading human consciousness into computers, onto computer networks, into robot or synthetic bodies, or some combination of these; or posthumanity may be comprised of artificial intelligence or superintelligence that human beings initiate and by which humans are subsequently surpassed, superseded, and perhaps even eliminated.

Additionally, Zoltan Istvan, who ran for US president in 2016 on the Transhumanist Party ticket, in 2015 developed a "Transhumanist Bill of Rights," which was updated by the party in 2016 and adopted in January 2017.[9] This document attempts to spell out the scope of possible "sen-

---

6. See https://www.humanityplus.org/transhumanist-faq, under "What is transhumanism?"

7. Tirosh-Samuelson, "Transhumanism as Secularist Faith," 716.

8. Bostrom, *Superintelligence*, v.

9. Any future updates will be located on the website of the Transhumanist Party political organization (http://transhumanist-party.org/).

tient entities," human, posthuman, and other, by setting forth seven levels of sentience based on the ability of various beings to successfully achieve "information integration."[10] The document identifies six kinds of sentient beings that would be the bearer of rights under this bill:

1. Human beings, including genetically modified humans
2. Cyborgs
3. Digital intelligences
4. Intellectually enhanced, previously non-sapient animals
5. Any species of plant or animal which has been enhanced to possess the capacity for intelligent thought
6. Other advanced sapient life forms

Notice the ways in which these six kinds of beings add to the abovementioned categories of merging human and machines, uploading human consciousness, and artificial intelligence or superintelligence: animals, plants, and other life forms. The point for now is simply to note the range of possibilities transhumanists imagine regarding possible posthuman life forms.

These transhumanist ideas, of course, do not emerge out of nothing. Nick Bostrom, an Oxford philosopher and cofounder of the World Transhumanist Association, points out that the quest for immortality relayed in the Epic of Gilgamesh is an indicator that human beings have long desired to overcome human limitations, probably for as long as there have been human beings.[11] In addition, the Genesis account of death entering the world demonstrates a desire to understand why death is a part of life. More recently and more directly, transhumanism can be traced to the rise of humanism, particularly "rational humanism, which emphasizes empirical science and critical reason—rather than revelation and religious authority—as ways of learning about the natural world and our place within it, and of providing a grounding for morality."[12]

The development of the theory of evolution allowed us to consider humanity as part of a continuum of development and provided the groundwork that now allows those so inclined to look forward to what the next step or stage of evolutionary development might be. In addition, as humans

---

10. Istvan and US Transhumanist Party, "Transhumanist Bill of Rights," preamble.
11. Bostrom, "History of Transhumanist Thought," 1.
12. Bostrom, "History of Transhumanist Thought," 2.

have moved away from mysticism and religion toward empiricism and science, not only do we gain an understanding of how we have come to be where and as we are, but we are also able to begin developing tools and techniques for taking control of the process of evolution and moving with intentionality and direction toward the next evolutionary step or steps, that is, toward the posthuman.

Works of popular culture, such as novels, films, and television series, both reflect and help to shape ideas of what is desirable, what is possible, and what is probable. Literature professor N. Katherine Hayles points out the important relationship between scientific and nonscientific texts. She writes: "The scientific texts often reveal, as literature cannot, the foundational assumptions that gave theoretical scope and artifactual efficacy to a particular approach. The literary texts often reveal, as scientific work cannot, the complex cultural, social, and representational issues tied up with conceptual shifts and technological innovations."[13]

So then, there is something of an interdependent relationship between science and literature. The latter imagines possibilities that are, often, at least theoretical extensions of the former. Another way of stating it is to say that one of the roles played by literature in general—and science fiction in particular—is to place scientific theories and developments into a narrative that helps make them more intelligible. This provides possibilities for imagining and understanding the ways in which they might affect individuals, families, communities, societies, and even humanity in general.

It should come as little surprise, then, that science fiction has had an influential role in debates around technology, especially works such as Mary Shelley's *Frankenstein*, Aldous Huxley's *Brave New World*, and George Orwell's *Nineteen Eighty-Four*. Hayles points to several works of science fiction she finds to have been significant in shaping cultural, scientific, and technological imaginations: the writings of Philip K. Dick,[14] Bernard Wolfe's *Limbo*, Neal Stephenson's *Snow Crash*, Greg Bear's *Blood Music*, Richard Powers's *Galatea 2.2*, and Cole Perriman's *Terminal Game*. We might add to this list titles such as William Gibson's *Neuromancer*, Richard K. Morgan's *Altered Carbon*, Ernest Cline's *Ready Player One*, and others.

Michael Burdett similarly emphasizes the imagination-shaping power of science fiction as it pertains to ideas around the transhuman and posthuman. He finds that such works may be understood in three broad

---

13 Hayles, *How We Became Posthuman*, 24.
14. See, e.g., Dick, *Do Androids Dream of Electric Sheep?*

categories: "technological adventure and awe," "dystopia and technological enslavement," and "technology and humanity become one."[15] He places in the first category works by Jules Verne, some of H. G. Wells's writings, the pulp version of *Buck Rogers*, and space operas such as the *Star Wars* films. In the second category are works such as the 1927 film *Metropolis*, the *Terminator* films, and the novels *Brave New World* and *Nineteen Eighty-Four*. In the third category are works such as the *Mad Max* films and the televisions shows *Star Trek: The Next Generation*, *Star Trek: Voyager*, and the 2004–2009 version of *Battlestar Galactica*. Ultimately, Burdett finds "the depiction of technology in the future is increasingly coalescing around [the] theme of humanity and technology becoming one."[16] This is consonant with the transhuman movement.

Hayles argues that we are in some ways—many ways, even—already posthuman. She outlines three steps or stages, which are not independent of one another, that have brought us to the present transhuman/posthuman moment. First, information has come to be seen as disembodied, unrelated to and unaffected by the medium in which it is instantiated.[17] Second, "the cyborg was created as a technological artifact and cultural icon."[18] And third, "a historically specific construction called the human is giving way to a different construction called the posthuman."[19] The upshot is: "When information loses its body, equating humans and computers is especially easy, for the materiality in which the thinking mind is instantiated appears incidental to its essential nature."[20] My point here is simply to note the relationship between science, literature, popular and other works of culture, and transhumanism, as well as some of the historical developments that have led to our present situation in which we are able to speak of concepts such as transhumanity and posthumanity.

---

15. Burdett, *Eschatology and Technological Future*, 50–66.

16. Burdett, *Eschatology and Technological Future*, 66.

17. This point is highly contested in philosophy. For an overview of the debate, see Murphy and Brown, *Did My Neurons*, 147–92.

18. Hayles, *How We Became Posthuman*, 2.

19. Hayles, *How We Became Posthuman*, 2.

20. Hayles, *How We Became Posthuman*, 2.

PART II | BIOETHICS AND PERSONHOOD

TRANSHUMANIST DOCUMENTS

Several documents are frequently acknowledged or referenced as key items of transhuman thought and identity. The "Transhumanist Declaration" is an overview statement originally written by an international group of self-described transhumanists in 1998.[21] It has since been modified and refined several times.[22] The version that is current as of this writing appears to have been completed in 2009. It contains eight points that (1) describe humanity as being on the cusp of a new era that will be ushered in by science and technology, (2) point to yet untapped human potential, (3) underscore potential existential risks, (4) call for research investment, (5) highlight the need for risk reduction, (6) stress policymaking that fosters the enhancement of human potential and minimization of existential risk, (7) look toward the possibilities of new forms of sentient life, and (8) emphasize maximal individual autonomous choice.

The "Transhumanist FAQ" is a detailed document covering a broad range of transhumanist ideas in a question and answer format that is familiar on the internet.[23] Other important works on transhuman topics include Bostrom's "Why I Want to Be a Posthuman When I Grow Up," which provides an accessible introduction to and an argument for becoming posthuman. An essay by Verner Vinge, "Technological Singularity," was one of the first pieces to explore the concept of the singularity as it pertains to transhumanism (more on that below).[24] Hans Moravec's *Mind Children: The Future of Robot and Human Intelligence* was an early exploration of artificial/machine intelligence. In *The Engines of Creation: The Coming Era of Nanotechnology*, Eric Drexler brought early attention to the possibilities fostered by nanotechnology. More recently, Ray Kurzweil's *The Age of Spiritual Machines: When Computers Exceed Human Intelligence* and *The*

---

21. Bailey et al., "Transhumanist Declaration."

22. See https://hpluspedia.org/wiki/Transhumanist_Declaration. It is with great reluctance that I include a reference to a wiki-style website, but this is a site internal to the transhumanist movement that is part of one of the leading transhumanist organization's web presence. I believe it accurately reflects the history of the "Transhumanist Declaration."

23. See https://www.humanityplus.org/transhumanist-faq. As of this writing, the current version of the FAQ is 3.0, from 2016. The earliest version available online, via the internet archive, is from 1999 (https://web.archive.org/web/20020213221116/http://www.transhumanism.org/resources/faq.html). Version 2.1, from 2003, is available on Nick Bostrom's website and runs fifty-six pages (https://nickbostrom.com/views/transhumanist.pdf).

24. Vinge, "Technological Singularity," 365.

Singularity Is Near: When Humans Transcend Biology are well known in transhumanist circles, and the latter is even known somewhat outside of transhumanism. Together, these books, book chapters, and articles present a number of the core ideas that transhumanists continue to explore and debate. These debates and explorations take place in several journals, particularly the *Journal of Evolution and Technology*,[25] and in edited volumes such as *H+/-: Transhumanism and its Critics*,[26] as well as in a variety of personal and institutional websites and blogs. As but two examples, see Bostrom's personal website and the website of the Institute for Ethics and Emerging Technologies (IEET).[27]

TRANSHUMANIST THEMES

At one level, the central theme of transhumanism can be summed up as overcoming human limitations and/or enhancing human beings, and it is pictured in the idea (or ideal) of the posthuman. While human enhancement can take many forms, there are recurrent themes or emphases in and around transhumanist discourse regarding the most sought-after enhancements. The "Transhumanist Declaration," for example, identifies four particular aspects of human life transhumanists seek to overcome: "aging, cognitive shortcomings, involuntary suffering, and our confinement to planet Earth," each of which will be discussed briefly below.[28]

Overcoming Aging

Perhaps the most intuitively accessible transhuman theme is simply the desire to live longer. Transhumanists tend to use the language of "overcoming aging," "enhancing longevity," or "radical life extension."[29] The ultimate goal is effective immortality, that is, the ability to avoid "unwanted death."[30] Of course, the idea is not simply to live longer, but to live longer as a healthy person or, as Bostrom puts it, "to radically extend people's active

25. http://jetpress.org.
26. Hansell and Grassie, *H+/-: Transhumanism and Its Critics*.
27. https://nickbostrom.com; https://ieet.org.
28. Bailey et al., "Transhumanist Declaration," point 1.
29. See More, "Philosophy of Transhumanism," 10; More, "Proactionary Principle," 258.
30. Pelletier, "End of Death."

health-spans."[31] Associated with longevity, then, is the eradication of disease and the addition of increased strength, which is also an aspect of overcoming involuntary suffering, which I will discuss below. Many transhumanists are working to stay alive long enough so that they can take advantage of hoped for medical and technological advancements that will counter and reverse the effects of aging.[32] This is known as "longevity escape velocity," the point at which new medical and technological developments each year add more than a year to a person's life.[33] Cryonics plays a role here as well. The idea is that if one's body—or, for some, one's brain—is carefully frozen, it can be stored in such a way that the person can be revived and/or have his or her consciousness uploaded into a computer once the technology to accomplish such things advances sufficiently. Cryonics brings into view both uploading and nanotechnology. The speculation is that nanotechnology will be required to repair any damage incurred by the cryopreservation and thawing processes, to address the underlying cause of death, and/or to rejuvenate cells and tissues. In addition, some speculate that nanotechnology may be important in scanning, uploading, and reconstructing the human brain or human consciousness into computers or onto computer networks.[34]

Overcoming Cognitive Shortcomings

Another common transhuman theme is increased intellectual capacity. This may come about through smart drugs, through brain-computer interfaces, or through scanning and uploading or reconstructing the human brain in ways that allow for "whole brain emulation" and that are "substrate-independent."[35] Already, some use various stimulants such as ordinary caffeine or prescribed drugs such as Modafinil and Adderall as cognition enhancers, aspects of what is known as "cosmetic neurology."[36] In addition, some look to artificial intelligence either to supplement or in some way merge with human intelligence. Others speak of increased ethical capacity

31. Bostrom, "Transhumanist Values," 12.
32. Well-known transhumanist Ray Kurzweil is described as someone "who famously consumes a prodigious daily banquet of dietary supplements and vitamin pills" in his efforts to live indefinitely (O'Connell, *To Be a Machine*, 72).
33. O'Connell, *To Be a Machine*, 180.
34. Bostrom, "History of Transhumanist Thought," 9.
35. Koene, "Uploading to Substrate-Independent Minds"; Merkle, "Uploading."
36. Lyon, "Chess Study Revives Debate"; Chatterjee, "Promise and Predicament."

or "moral enhancement."³⁷ This could come about as an aspect of increased intelligence, through genetic or biochemical enhancement, and/or through artificial intelligence, which may be able to assist humans with taking decisions in the midst of particularly thorny ethical dilemmas.

Overcoming Involuntary Suffering

As mentioned above, alleviating involuntary suffering is in some ways connected to overcoming aging, but it is a considerably larger endeavor than simply that.³⁸ Of course, relief of suffering is also a concern for non-transhumanists, but transhumanists have a distinctive and expansive view of the relief of suffering. The seventh point of the "Transhumanist Declaration" states: "We advocate the well-being of all sentience, including humans, non-human animals, and any future artificial intellects, modified life forms, or other kinds of intelligence to which technological and scientific advance may give rise."³⁹ The elimination of poverty is an important part of transhumanism for some—and certainly an aspect of relieving suffering—and there is a move in some transhuman circles to support universal basic income. The prospects that robots, nanotechnology, and/or artificial intelligence will greatly disrupt human employment provides additional impetus for guaranteed basic income.⁴⁰

Overcoming Confinement to Planet Earth

There seem to be at least two perspectives among transhumanists regarding space exploration. On the one hand, some see it as a natural outgrowth of human capabilities. Human beings have been to the moon; we should go farther.⁴¹ Others feel the need to locate other planets where human beings

37. Savulescu and Persson, "Moral Enhancement."

38. It is not entirely clear to me why the qualifier "involuntary" is used in the Transhumanist Declaration, as there seems to be little discussion of the distinction between involuntary and voluntary suffering in the transhumanist literature. Perhaps the meaning is meant to be obvious: one sometimes willingly takes on a measure of suffering in the course of helping others, enhancing oneself, or for other reasons, and this kind of suffering is not in view.

39. Bailey et al., "Transhumanist Declaration," point 7.

40. Dvorsky, "Better Living through Transhumanism," 62. See also Transhumanist Party, "Constitution."

41. O'Connell, *To Be a Machine*, 18, 34.

may go to live if or when the earth becomes overcrowded or uninhabitable due to disaster, climate change, meteor strike, or some other cause.[42] These, of course, are not mutually exclusive motivations, yet there are at times shades of emphasis in one direction more than in the other. While overcoming confinement to the Earth is listed alongside other priorities in the "Transhumanist Declaration," it seems to receive less attention than the other items, particularly overcoming aging and cognitive shortcomings. Perhaps this is because the need for space exploration is simply less pressing or perhaps it is because of the scale of the task, which until recently was thought to be a nearly exclusive undertaking of national governments. However, SpaceX, Virgin Galactic, and Blue Origin, all private companies, are now actively pursuing space travel and exploration.

Singularity

No mention of the singularity is made in the "Transhumanist Declaration," but it is an important and recurring theme in transhumanism. The idea of the singularity is that a sudden shift is expected to occur when human beings build artificial or machine intelligence that is smarter than human beings and that is capable of building even smarter intelligences.[43] The term "singularity" denotes a point marking a radical change beyond which nothing can at present be known or predicted. The center of a black hole is perhaps the most well-known example of a singularity. Notably, Bostrom points out the fact that not all transhumanists are in agreement about the singularity: "Some see it as a likely scenario, others believe that it is more probable that there will never be any very sudden and dramatic changes as the result of progress in artificial intelligence."[44]

Either of these, the singularity or gradual progress in AI, may lead to "the various human minds on Earth . . . gradually becoming incorporated into a greater Earth-level mind that may be thought of as a 'Global Brain'" that is centered around or centrally controlled by superintelligence(s).[45] Some religious transhumanists have embraced the ideas of Pierre Teilhard de Chardin, who argued that the universe will eventually evolve toward

42. Khazan, "Should We Die?"
43. See https://www.humanityplus.org/transhumanist-faq; Vinge, "Technological Singularity," 365.
44. Bostrom, "History of Transhumanist Thought," 8.
45. Goertzel, "Artificial General Intelligence," 131.

a unified consciousness that he termed the "noosphere." This will involve not only the "networking" of human minds but of human minds and technology. Eventually, everything in the universe will culminate in an Omega Point of God in all and all in God.[46] Transhumanists such as Bostrom, however, reject the reference to any religious or mystical ideas as part of transhumanism calling it "wishful thinking."[47] Transhumanism is for them an entirely material, rational-scientific enterprise. At any rate, as Goertzel points out: "The particulars of this [Global Brain] are yet to unfold, and may be hard for us, as individual humans, to understand as they do."[48]

TRANSHUMAN METAPHYSICS AND ETHICS

It is not simply that transhumanism is for its adherents an entirely material enterprise; according to transhuman metaphysics, all of existence is entirely material.[49] Nothing beyond the tangible, physical world exists, and mechanistic forces explain not only the physical sciences but also human sciences like sociology and psychology.[50] "The human person, for the transhumanist, is best understood as a bundle of molecular and cellular complexes that can be engineered and manipulated."[51] Thus, as Bostrom points out: "If human beings are constituted by matter that obeys the same laws of physics that operate outside us, then it should in principle be possible to learn to manipulate human nature in the same way that we manipulate external objects."[52]

Flowing directly from this metaphysical materialism is the idea that our personal identity is simply the arrangement of the molecules that make up our brains. Ray Kurzweil terms this "patternism," and James Hughes identifies it as "the dominant view among transhumanists in general."[53]

46. Steinhart, "Teilhard de Chardin," 15, 18.
47. Bostrom, "History of Transhuman Thought," 8.
48. Goertzel, "Artificial General Intelligence," 132.
49. Religious versions of transhumanism that would likely be open to transcendent and nonmaterial aspects of reality do exist, but these are relatively minor, outlying groups that do not represent what might be termed mainstream transhumanism. Two examples are the Mormon Transhumanist Association (https://transfigurism.org/) and the Christian Transhumanist Association (https://www.christiantranshumanism.org/).
50. See also Taylor's description of "the immanent frame" (Taylor, *Secular Age*, 539).
51. Miller, *Critiquing Transhumanism*, 119; citing Hoffman, "Transhumanist Materialism," 275.
52. Bostrom, "History of Transhuman Thought," 3.
53. Hughes, "Transhumanism and Personal Identity," 227; citing Kurzweil, *Singularity Is Near*. On the same page, Hughes describes More's "variant of the patternist view."

Hughes's own view is that our idea(s) of the self is/are illusory.[54] Either view is not only compatible with, but important to the desire to upload one's mind or consciousness. The "Transhumanist FAQ" explains: "A widely accepted position is that you survive so long as certain information patterns are conserved, such as your memories, values, attitudes, and emotional dispositions."[55] In other words, "radical changes to the body and brain can occur, but the continuity of the pattern will remain."[56] Note that this is of a piece with Hayles's observation that information has come to be seen as disembodied, unrelated to and unaffected by the medium in which it is instantiated, meaning that now, "equating humans and computers is especially easy, for the materiality in which the thinking mind is instantiated appears incidental to its essential nature."[57] Thus, uploading, duplicating, and backing up the human mind and/or human consciousness all become possible, even if the result is a "distributed identity."[58]

Ted Peters, a liberal theologian who is somewhat sympathetic to transhumanism but who can at times be critical of the movement, argues that evolution, understood as entirely material and mechanistic, is crucial to transhuman metaphysics, psychology, and ethics. Transhumanists see the world evolving to become increasingly complex, and they see human beings as having a psychological desire not simply to survive but to evolve, to move toward or grow into increasing complexity. Peters cites Simon Young's designation of the human "Will to Evolve" as key to understanding human psychology.[59] Concurring, Miller writes: "The normative value shared by transhumanists is the will to evolve, a desire to transcend our biological limitations."[60] Thus, evolution toward transcendence of human limitations becomes the de facto standard by which moral choices are both guided and evaluated.

In a reflection on current trends in transhumanism, Max More finds that when it comes to metaethics, transhumanists take a variety of approaches.

---

54. Hughes, "Transhumanism and Personal Identity," 231.
55. See https://www.humanityplus.org/transhumanist-faq.
56. Miller, *Critiquing Transhumanism*, 122.
57. Hayles, *How We Became Posthuman*, 2.
58. Vita-More, "Aesthetics," 21.
59. Peters, "Transhumanism and Posthuman Future," 149; citing Young, *Designer Evolution*, 183 (capitalization in the original).
60. Miller, *Critiquing Transhumanism*, 143.

However, he finds deontology "uncommon" among transhumanists while "some prominent transhumanists have assumed a consequentialist foundation, in the form of various kinds of utilitarian[ism]."[61] Indeed, transhumanism is highly utilitarian. Tirosh-Samuelson examines transhuman views on the pursuit of human flourishing and happiness and concludes:

> the transhumanist notion [of the pursuit of happiness] is an extension of the hedonic understanding of happiness characteristic of nineteenth-century utilitarianism. Focusing on self-fulfillment, transhumanists do not take seriously the connection between happiness and virtue, which was central to the premodern analysis of human happiness . . . transhumanist discourse has no use for the concept of virtue and the ethos of self-control and character formation that accompany it because it takes happiness to be a product of engineering.[62]

The result is a utilitarianism guided by an overriding principle of acting in accordance with the will to evolve and the pursuit of "complexification."[63]

KEY TRANSHUMANIST FIGURES AND ORGANIZATIONS

As already mentioned, Nick Bostrom is a philosophy professor at the University of Oxford and was in many ways the leader in initiating academic discourse regarding transhumanism.[64] In 1998, he cofounded the World Transhumanist Association and, along with it, an academic journal focused on transhuman and posthuman themes. He has written extensively on transhumanist topics such as human enhancement, existential risk, artificial intelligence, and more.[65] His most recent English-language book as of this writing, *Superintelligence: Paths, Dangers, Strategies*, is a careful look at the dangers of artificial intelligence that reaches a point where it is building machines of increasing intelligence, well beyond what human beings have

---

61. More, "Philosophy of Transhumanism," 13.

62. Tirosh-Samuelson, "Engaging Transhumanism," 38.

63. Peters, "Transhumanism and Posthuman Future," 149; again citing Young, *Designer Evolution*, 202.

64. Khatchadourian, "Doomsday Invention."

65. See https://nickbostrom.com/cv.pdf (accessed Aug. 31, 2017).

a capacity to do or even understand.[66] In addition to his academic appointment, Bostrom serves as director of the Future of Humanity Institute.

Aubrey de Grey is probably the leading and most well-known proponent of radical life extension. He coined the phrase "strategies for engineered negligible senescence" (SENS) and is cofounder of and Chief Science Officer at the SENS Research Foundation.[67] He is also an advocate for the idea of actuarial or longevity escape velocity mentioned above.[68] De Grey has sought to bring his ideas to a popular audience by providing media interviews, giving a TED talk, and appearing on *The Colbert Report*.[69]

Ray Kurzweil is an inventor, computer scientist, and author who is perhaps most well-known for his books *The Age of Spiritual Machines: When Computers Exceed Human Intelligence* and *The Singularity Is Near: When Humans Transcend Biology*. However, Kurzweil's influence extends well beyond his writing. He was cofounder and Chancellor of Singularity University, which focused on the use of "exponential technologies" such as "artificial intelligence, robotics, and digital biology."[70] No longer a university, it is now known as Singularity Group, and focuses on executive leadership training. Kurzweil is a board member of this Singularity Group. In addition, he is director of engineering at Google, where his work focuses on artificial intelligence and its ability to understand natural language.[71] It is worth noting that Alphabet Inc., Google's parent company, is the second largest company in the world by market capitalization and was a significant investor in Singularity University, significant enough that the Google logo appeared in the footer of every page on the Singularity University website.[72] In addition, Alphabet Inc. is the parent company of Calico LLC, a biotech company specifically addressing aging, and DeepMind, a company that specializes in neural networks.[73] The upshot is that through his partnership with Google/Alphabet Inc., Kurzweil has significant financial resources available for the pursuit of goals that are consonant with transhuman aspirations.

66. See also Adams, "Artificial Intelligence."
67. See http://www.sens.org/about/general-faq.
68. Mark O'Connell, *To Be a Machine*, 180.
69. De Grey, "Roadmap to End Aging"; De Grey, "Aubrey de Grey."
70. See https://su.org/about/.
71. Hill, "Exclusive Interview." See also Simonite, "What Is Ray Kurzweil."
72. According to Statista in 2017 (https://www.statista.com/statistics/263264/top-companies-in-the-world-by-market-value/).
73. See https://www.calicolabs.com; https://deepmind.com.

In 2016, Zoltan Istvan, a former journalist, real estate investor, and entrepreneur rose to some measure of notoriety by running for president of the United States representing the newly formed Transhumanist political party.[74] In his platform, he emphasized scientific and biotechnological advancement, particularly developments aimed at "longer lifespans, better health, and higher standards of living."[75] In addition, the Transhumanist Party put forward the previously mentioned "Transhumanist Bill of Rights" that, among other things, sought to: "Lay groundwork for rights for other future advanced sapient beings like conscious robots and cyborgs."[76] The press attention Istvan received was bolstered by his "Immortality Bus," a recreational vehicle with a modified façade that was intended to make it resemble a giant drivable casket.[77] He drove this Immortality Bus on a United States tour from the San Francisco Bay Area across the southwest and southern states to Orlando, Florida, and then from there to Washington, DC. Along the way, he managed to garner coverage from a number of news outlets, including *The New York Times*, *Der Spiegel*, *The Telegraph*, and others.[78] It is worth noting that within transhumanism Istvan was not universally applauded. For example, an anonymous petition entitled "Transhumanists Disavow Zoltan Istvan Candidacy for US Presidency" was posted online during his run.[79] Having not been elected president, Istvan ran as a libertarian candidate for governor of California in 2018.[80] I include him here only because he is, at least in some small way, bringing broader attention to the transhuman movement and raising transhumanist ideas in the minds of the general public.

It is unclear whether Elon Musk considers himself part of the transhumanist movement, but at least two of the projects he has invested in and worked on undoubtedly fit with transhumanist aspirations. The stated goal of SpaceX, where Musk is CEO and lead designer, is "enabling people to live on other planets."[81] In 2016, he launched a company called Neuralink,

---

74. See http://transhumanist-party.org.

75. Istvan, "Transhumanist Party," under "Platform."

76. Istvan, "Transhumanist Party," under "Platform."

77. Istvan, "Immortality Bus."

78. O'Connell, "600 Miles"; Medick, "Und Sie denken"; Jamie Bartlett, "Transhumanists Are on Quest"; Istvan, "Immortality Bus."

79. Cannon, "Transhumanists Disavow Zoltan Istvan."

80. He did not win this election either.

81. See http://www.spacex.com/about.

which is focused on developing a "neural lace" brain-machine interface.[82] In addition, Musk has expressed concern over the potential for artificial intelligence to supersede human beings. On his view, a "high bandwidth interface to the brain will be something that helps achieve a symbiosis between human and machine intelligence and maybe solves the control [of artificial intelligence] problem."[83] Whether or not Musk considers himself a transhumanist, like Kurzweil, he has access to considerable resources to pursue projects that are in accord with transhumanism.

The World Transhumanist Association (WTA) was founded in 1998 by Bostrom and web developer David Pearce at least in part to bring a level of academic respectability to the transhumanist movement. The WTA started *The Journal of Transhumanism* in 1998, and continued publishing it until 2004, when they transferred it to IEET (discussed below).[84] At the same time, the name of the journal was changed to *The Journal of Evolution and Technology*.[85] The World Transhumanist Association was renamed Humanity+ in 2008, in an effort to "make the WTA a more attractive proposition to others who largely agree with its pro-technology emphases."[86] As Humanity+, the organization publishes an online magazine, h+ Magazine, organizes occasional conferences, publishes books, and more.[87] The Humanity+ website hosts the "Transhumanist Declaration" and the "Transhumanist FAQ," which were initially developed in conjunction with the founding of the WTA.

A "techno-progressive" think tank, IEET highlights technological developments geared toward human enhancement. In particular, they focus on developments that come out of the convergence of nanotechnology, biotechnology, information technology, and cognitive science (which are sometimes referred to as NBIC).[88] IEET was founded in 2004 by Bostrom and James Hughes. Bostrom was board chair until 2011, and he remains a senior fellow of the IEET. Hughes is currently executive director of the organization.

82. Statt, "Elon Musk Launches Neuralink."
83. Kharpal, "Elon Musk," para. 7.
84. See http://jetpress.org/history.html.
85. Blackford, "Transhumanism," para. 1.
86. Blackford, "WTA Changes Its Image," para. 2.
87. See http://hplusmagazine.com. For a summary of various projects the organization supports and in which in engages, see https://www.humanityplus.org/projects.
88. See https://ieet.org/index.php/IEET2/about. See also https://ieet.org/research-programs/.

Certainly, there are many other individuals, groups, and organizations that could be included here. Ronald Bailey, science correspondent for *Reason* magazine is influential because of his reporting on scientific and technological developments relevant to transhumanism.[89] Similarly, George Dvorsky, former board chair of IEET, is a contributing editor at *io9*, a website that focuses on the intersection of science, technology, science fiction, and futurism, and that is part of the large Kinja news, culture, and technology online publishing platform, which gives him considerable, popular-level reach.[90] Andy Clark is professor and chair in Logic and Metaphysics at the University of Edinburgh and author of *Supersizing the Mind* and *Natural Born Cyborgs*. The Foresight Institute focuses on nanotechnology in particular.[91] The Lifeboat Foundation is especially attuned to the issue of existential risk.[92]

VARIOUS STRAINS OF TRANSHUMANISM

Writing in 2005, Bostrom described transhumanism as "a loosely defined movement."[93] It is not entirely clear that the movement has become, on the whole, much more well defined in the years since. However, there are a number of identifiable characteristics that form a core of belief and motivation for action for transhumanists. Hank Pellissier, affiliate scholar and former managing director of the IEET, builds on earlier, unpublished work by Bostrom to identify ten categories or strains of transhumanism, each of which emphasizes different aspects of transhuman thought.[94]

Extropianism, one of the earliest transhuman groups, began organizing in the late 1980s. They have a marked optimism about the future and are heavily invested in cryopreservation. The term "extropy" is the opposite of "entropy"; it is meant to indicate progress, energy, improvement, increasing knowledge, and growth.[95] Some extropian enthusiasts take on names that involve wordplay regarding their projections and desires for the future. One example is the founder of the Extropy Institute and CEO of

---

89. See https://reason.com/people/ronald-bailey/articles.
90. See https://kinja.com/georgedvorsky.
91. See https://foresight.org.
92. See https://lifeboat.com/ex/about.
93. Bostrom, "Transhumanist Values," para. 1.
94. Pellissier, "Transhumanism."
95. See also Bostrom, "History of Transhuman Thought," 11–12.

cryopreservation enterprise Alcor Life Extension Foundation, Max More.[96] "Singularitarianism" emphasizes the nearness of the singularity, the role artificial intelligence will play in it, and the need to ensure that the singularity does not spell the end of humanity but instead offers those who are interested the opportunity to become posthuman. Kurzweil is the most prominent singularitarian.[97]

The Hedonistic Imperative combines transhumanist ideas with a hedonistic utilitarianism of maximizing pleasure and minimizing pain. The focus is not only on humanity but also on eliminating suffering for all sentient beings, particularly through genetic engineering and nanotechnology.[98] Democratic transhumanism emphasizes wide access to enhancement technology and puts a high priority on equality and democratic decision-making. James Hughes is a key figure in this sphere. Survivalist transhumanism is perhaps one of the larger strains of transhumanism. The emphasis here is on staying alive long enough to take advantage of coming enhancement technologies (i.e., reaching longevity escape velocity). Libertarian transhumanism, in many ways, cuts across several of the previous strains. Adherents place a high priority on the freedom to make use of or engage in whatever enhancement technologies an individual may desire without government regulation. They cast human enhancement as a civil liberty. Ronald Bailey, science correspondent for *Reason* magazine, is a leading proponent of libertarian transhumanism.

While most transhumanists self-identify as atheists, agnostics, or generally nonreligious, there are a number of transhumanists who see transhumanism as compatible with or even complementary to their beliefs. James Hughes, for example, asserts that "there is no fundamental obstacle to the positive adoption of the Singularity and transhumanist goals of health, longevity, and cognitive enhancement into any faith."[99] Pellissier groups such people under the heading "Religious Transhumanism."[100] As but two examples, Lincoln Cannon founded the Mormon Transhumanist Association

---

96. Max More's wife's name is Natasha Vita-More. Tom Morrow cofounded, with Max More, *Extropy: The Journal of Transhumanist Thought*, which was published from 1989 to 1996. See also Regis, "Meet the Extropians."

97. See also Socrates, "Top 10 Singularitarians." The list includes Isaac Asimov, nineteenth-century writer Samuel Butler, Alan Turing, and Ted Kaczynski (who is better known as the Unabomber).

98. See also the Hedonistic Imperative, https://www.hedweb.com.

99. Hughes, "Politics of Transhumanism," 769.

100. Pellissier, "Transhumanism."

in 2006, and Micah Redding and Christopher Benek founded the Christian Transhumanist Association in 2014.[101]

Cosmopolitan transhumanism emphasizes the global context in which transhuman ideas hope to come to fruition. On this view, human potential will only be fully realized if humanity as a whole is able to unify and cooperate across all boundaries and identities that might divide us, whether national, ethnic, racial, class, or other. The similarly named but distinct strain of "cosmism" sees itself as less dogmatic in its transhumanist views, emphasizing open-mindedness and intellectual humility as keys to advancing toward the posthuman. Anarcho-transhumanism combines transhuman thought with anarchist thought. In particular, it is anti-capitalist and anti-religious. Adherents envision a kind of posthuman networked mind that will eliminate the need for governance.

Two things are worth noting about these categories. First, by no means do they capture all of the various perspectives or groupings that are part of the transhumanist movement. They do, however, capture significant ways of approaching and participating in transhumanism. Second, the above groupings are emphases, not exclusivities. It is likely that most transhumanists see themselves as part of several to many of these strains of transhumanism. Pellissier, for example, views himself as a mix of five of the ten strains: Hedonistic Imperative, survivalist, democratic transhumanist, singularitarian, and extropian.[102]

WHY EXAMINE TRANSHUMANISM?

Views on the goals of and prospects for transhumanism exist on a continuum. At one extreme are people like former transhumanist presidential and gubernatorial candidate Istvan, who has a decidedly idealistic outlook: "In the transhumanist age, we will reach utopia. Crime drops to zero. Poverty will end. Violence will drop. At some point, we become a race of individuals who are pretty nice to each other."[103] At the other extreme are those like Christopher Tollefsen, who argue that the terms "transhuman" and "posthuman" "have no meaning; there is no condition that could be described in either of these ways. All the conditions that receive these names are either (a) impossibilities, (b) deficient human conditions, or (c) amplifications but

---

101. Cannon, "Brief History"; see also https://www.christiantranshumanism.org/history.
102. Pellissier, "Transhumanism."
103. Godwin, "Immortality," para. 45.

not changes of human nature as it already exists."[104] In between these extremes, however, are those who recognize that the technologies that human beings have and are developing are shaping—transitioning, if you will—individuals, families, communities, and indeed humanity itself in various ways. Even if transhumanism itself has not become part of the fabric of our lives, some of the ideas of technological progress toward a better if not wholly utopian future for humanity is undoubtedly a part of our larger cultural narratives.

As for the transhumanist movement specifically, many of their goals—increased longevity, heightened brain power, reduced suffering, improved equality—few would oppose on their face. Of course, there is debate, even within transhumanism, over the means of attaining those goals, how those goals should be ranked against one another, the priority that should be placed on those goals relative to other goals, and the precise shape the full attainment of those goals should take. Ultimately, when we look at the goal of posthumanity, significant questions are raised regarding what is essential about our humanity: What can be changed with respect to our humanity, and what should and what should not be changed? Is the goal of achieving posthumanity a worthy goal? If so, why? If not, why not?

Moreover, much of what might be termed the mainstream of transhumanism is decidedly tilted toward the utopian end of the spectrum. Notice again Istvan's quote: "In the transhumanist age, we will reach utopia. Crime drops to zero. Poverty will end. Violence will drop. At some point, we become a race of individuals who are pretty nice to each other."[105] Such a statement is not at all out of step with the thinking of many, if not most, transhumanists. Such a utopian vision is, ultimately, presenting a soteriology. The overall transhumanist perspective is, at its core, deeply religious. Therefore, I believe it is worth examining and evaluating with seriousness.

TRANSHUMANS, POSTHUMANS, AND PERSONS

As mentioned above, transhumanist metaphysics holds that all of existence is entirely material, and our personal identity exists either as the pattern

---

104. Christopher Tollefsen, in Rubin, "Bioethics and Transhumanism," 3:02. These remarks were made during a panel discussion entitled "Bioethics and the (Trans)Human Future," which was part of a conference entitled "A Worthy Life: Finding Meaning in America," Princeton University, May 22, 2017.

105. Godwin, "Immortality," para. 45.

of information in our brains or it is an illusion. Within this framework, ascribing personhood to a being or entity relies on the capacities a being or entity has. That is to say, according to transhumanism, a person is simply an entity with certain capabilities. Max More writes: "In addressing moral and ethical concerns, transhumanists typically adopt a universal standard based not on membership in the human species but on the qualities of each being. Creatures with similar levels of sapience, sentience, and personhood are accorded similar status no matter whether they are humans, animals, cyborgs, machine intelligences, or aliens."[106] As we will see, the key factors here are sapience and sentience. It is not entirely clear why More included personhood in his list of criteria for moral worth, as it seems to make the logic of his evaluation somewhat circular. That is to say, if the question under consideration is the moral status of a being, i.e., whether the being is a person, then including "level of personhood" in the criteria for deciding makes for an evaluation that includes the expected result as a part of the standard of judgment. Let us therefore set it aside as a criterion for determining personhood, which from a transhuman point of view primarily indicates that an entity has certain capacities and is thus a bearer of rights.

Recall the imagined posthuman possibilities highlighted in the "Transhumanist Bill of Rights":

1. Human beings, including genetically modified humans
2. Cyborgs
3. Digital intelligences
4. Intellectually enhanced, previously non-sapient animals
5. Any species of plant or animal which has been enhanced to possess the capacity for intelligent thought
6. Other advanced sapient life forms

To understand all of these entities as persons, we must introduce the idea of a nonhuman person. Efforts to expand the concept of personhood in this direction are already underway in animal rights and environmentalism. The push for such nonhuman personhood comes from a desire to designate or to increase the rights that an animal or some part of the environment might bear. A case in the state of New York, for example, sought, unsuccessfully, to establish the personhood of an elephant in order to end

---

106. More, "Philosophy of Transhumanism," 13.

its confinement in the Bronx Zoo. A New York appeals court ruled five to two that "writs of habeas corpus only protect the liberty rights of human beings and are not available to animals regardless of their respective level of functional intelligence."[107] In contrast, an Argentinian court ruled in 2014 that an orangutan is indeed a "nonhuman" person.[108] On the environmental front, Mar Menor, a lagoon in Spain, was granted a level of personhood by Spain's Senate. To be clear:

> The new law doesn't regard the lagoon and its watershed as fully human. But the ecosystem now has a legal right to exist, evolve naturally, and be restored. And like a person, it has legal guardians, including a scientific committee, which will give its defenders a new voice.[109]

It is quite likely that we will see similar concepts extended to highly advanced artificial intelligences, both those installed in robots or androids as well as artificial intelligences that exist entirely online.[110] The European Parliament in 2017 adopted a text entitled "Civil Law Rules on Robotics" that seeks to set forth "general principles concerning the development of robotics and artificial intelligence for civil use."[111] Specifically, it called for the setting forth of definitions regarding "cyber physical systems, autonomous systems, smart autonomous robots and their subcategories";[112] establishing a registration system; work toward complementarian rather than replacement systems; and more.

A paper by Ibolya Stefan (professor of law at the University of Miskolc in Hungary, formerly Technical University of Heavy Industry) looks specifically at the issue of personhood and attempts to tease out the essential elements that would be necessary to establish an AI or robot as a

---

107. Mann and Russell, "Habeas Relief Not Applicable," para. 1. Interestingly, the two dissenting judges "each submitted a dissent in which they argue that autonomous beings with substantial cognitive abilities such as the elephant at issue in this case are entitled to the protections that the writ has historically provided" (para. 1), so it is possible that the law will move over time toward recognizing some level of personhood and therefore rights for some animals, at least in some jurisdictions.

108. Lough, "Captive Orangutan."

109. Stokstad, "This Lagoon," para. 3.

110. On the possibility of an AI that exists only online being granted personhood, consider and reflect on the rapidly increasing sophistication of ChatGPT (https://chat.openai.com/) as but one example. Schwitzgebel and Shevlin, "Is It Time."

111. European Parliament, "Civil Law Rules," first heading after "Introduction."

112. European Parliament, "Civil Law Rules," under "General Principles," §1.

person, for example, some level of competency or some set of capacities. Ultimately, Stefan rejects outright the idea of giving legal personhood to AI or robots and suggest that perhaps there is room for something like an "e-personality." Such a move, Stefan admits, would be an imperfect solution because our various legal systems are simply not presently configured in ways that allow them to "cope with these 'artificial creatures.'"[113] Ultimately, "legal personhood [for AI, etc.] would affect each person and even the entire society . . . we need to have a stable legal framework that ensures safety against technology."[114] Such issues raise questions regarding not only what it means to be a person but also what it means to be human and who or what counts as human.[115]

Given the close relationship between personhood and rights, let us return to the "Transhumanist Bill of Rights" for a detailed look at what rights might be in view. First, the bill makes clear what is meant by "sentient entities," those entities that will be the bearers of rights:

> Sentient entities are defined by information-processing capacity such that this term should not apply to non-self-aware lifeforms, like plants and slime molds. Biological processing substrates are referred to as using an "analogue intelligence," whereas purely electronic processing substrates are referred to as "digital intelligence," and processing substrates that utilize quantum effects would be considered "quantum intelligence."[116]

The bill describes eight levels of sentience, beginning with inanimate objects at level 0. Anything demonstrating level 5 or above "information integration" is deemed to have sentience and thus have some rights.

Level 5: Awareness + world model + primarily subconscious self model = sapient or lucid; lucidity means to be meta-aware—that is, to be aware of one's own awareness, aware of abstractions, aware of one's self, and therefore able to actively analyze each of these phenomena. If a given animal is meta-aware to any extent, it can therefore make lucid decisions. Level 5 capabilities include the following:

1. "Sense of self"
2. Complex learned behavior

---

113. Stefan, "Issues of Legal Personhood," 482.
114. Stefan, "Issues of Legal Personhood," 482.
115. Ahmed, "Delinking the 'Human.'"
116. Istvan and US Transhumanist Party, "Transhumanist Bill of Rights," point 6.

3. Ability to predict the future emotional states of the self (to some degree)
4. Ability to make motivational trade-offs

Level 6 adds to the above "dynamic self model + effective control of subconscious," and level 7 is a "singleton" with the "capacity for multiple parallel simulations of multiple world models, enabling cross-domain analysis and novel temporary model generation." Due to the complexity of algorithms involved, level 7 is considered to be "beyond biological capacities."

The "Transhumanist Bill of Rights" assumes that its definition of sentience is sufficient grounding for rights and enumerates twenty-five rights that the sentient beings in levels 5–7 bear. Some of the more interesting rights enumerated include:

- The right "to pursue any and all rights within this document to the degree that they deem desirable—including not at all" (art. 1)
- The rights "of ending involuntary suffering, making personhood improvements, and achieving an indefinite lifespan via science and technology" (art. 4)
- "Involuntary aging shall be classified as a disease" (art. 6)
- "Sentient entities agree to uphold morphological freedom—the right to do with one's physical attributes or intelligence whatever one wants so long as it does not harm others" (art. 10)
- "All sentient entities are entitled to reproductive freedom, including through novel means such as the creation of mind clones, monoparent children, or benevolent artificial general intelligence. All sentient entities also have the right to prevent unauthorized reproduction of themselves in both a physical and a digital context" (art. 12)
- The right "to private internet access," unless in jail or prison (art. 15)
- Universal basic income (art. 19)
- "All nations and their governments will take all reasonable measures to embrace and fund space travel" (art. 23).

Article 25 makes it clear that the authors of this bill view it as an extension of the United Nations' Universal Declaration of Human Rights. It is at least useful to see the place from which the transhumanist movement is starting, even if not all of these enumerated rights seem to be rights at all (e.g., art. 23).

A CHRISTIAN EVALUATION

Transhuman Metaphysics

What are Christians to make of posthumans and persons? Indeed, as the chapter title inquires, will posthumans be persons? To begin, recall Max More's assertion that transhumanism's view on moral standing (i.e., personhood) is "based not on membership in the human species but on the qualities of each being."[117] A Christian perspective on personhood is the opposite of the transhuman view. On a Christian view, persons are members of the human species, all members, irrespective of their qualities or capacities.

The category of e-personality or nonhuman person may come to be, and indeed we are already seeing it develop, as described above. But these entities are not persons in the same way that human beings are persons. Their personhood is markedly different, bearing different rights (and owing different responsibilities and duties) although it is likely such nonhuman personhood would be built upon or related to personhood as we presently understand it applying to human beings. Christians, by contrast, hold that human beings are created in or according to the image of God.[118] No other beings hold this status. Other beings or entities are parts of creation, which humans were given dominion or stewardship over. Therefore, we have no reason to hold that digital intelligences, enhanced animals or plants, or other life forms are or will be persons in the same way that human beings are persons.

This does leave two points of tension. What are we to say about cyborgs and uploaded minds? In an effort to take the transhumanist goal seriously, let us take at face value the claims they make regarding the merging of humans and machines. From this perspective, we might say that as long as a human being is the basis of or at the core of the posthuman entity (e.g., the cyborg or the digitally uploaded mind), the human being is still present, and therefore it is a person. That human being is augmented, enhanced, uploaded, modified—or possibly defaced, depending on how one views the

---

117. More, "Philosophy of Transhumanism," 13.

118. For a robust discussion of the concept of the image of God, see Kilner, *Dignity and Destiny*.

particular change undertaken—but a human person is still at the core of the being as the original being that was augmented, enhanced, etc. Such a view would, it might seem, be compatible with a substance view of personhood, a view that one of this volume's editors has elsewhere defended as in line with the Bible's anthropology.[119] The uploaded or cybernetic entity would, then, at its core, remain a human being, and thus at its core would remain of the same substance.

However, taking claims seriously often involves disagreeing with those claims, and there are good reasons not to take these transhumanist claims at face value. A substance view of personhood is incompatible with the patternism view of personhood, and therefore incompatible with the idea of uploading the human mind or consciousness. By definition, an uploaded mind would move from one substance to another. If such uploading were to become possible, which is far from certain, the uploaded or resulting entity would not be the same person. When it comes to the concept of uploading, continuity of identity is a much-discussed topic within transhumanism. However, Miller believes this to be something of a smokescreen to gain a hearing, concluding that "transhumanists are not ultimately concerned about the persistence of personal identity."[120] Indeed, Natasha Vita-More endorses "a fluid continuity of self over time."[121] Such a view takes the ways in which one naturally changes over time through education and life experience and pushes it to indicate one's identity also changes. This seems to me to be both an overstatement and well out of step with the ways in which we think about ourselves. I am the same person I was twenty and thirty (and more) years ago. My identity has not changed, although certainly, I have grown and (I hope) matured. In light of this, Miller concludes, "Transhumanism's materialist view of the human person and their patternist view of the self are not sufficient to account for personal identity that will persist throughout the trajectory of radical enhancements."[122]

As for whether a cyborg would be a person, perhaps we are best to reserve judgment until we better understand the ways in which living human tissue might be integrated with a computer or machine. Cybernetic beings will exist along a continuum of integration of living tissue and machine.

119. See Rae, "More Than the Sum."
120. Miller, *Critiquing Transhumanism*, 138.
121. Vita-More, "Aesthetics," 21.
122. Miller, *Critiquing Transhumanism*, 137.

Some might argue that a person with an implanted medical device such as a cardiac defibrillator/pacemaker or cochlear implant is in some sense an instance of a cyborg. Certainly, we do not deny that such people are persons or hold that they are nonhuman persons. Of course, transhumanists generally have in mind quite radical merging of human and machine, which could lead to a situation in which the substance of the being is changed (if indeed such a move turns out to be possible, which many doubt). Of course, if the living tissue in a cybernetic being does not come from a human being, it would not be a human person but perhaps could be considered a nonhuman person.

Returning to the concept of uploading the human mind or consciousness, it "is grounded in the functionalistic philosophy of mind, which holds that mental states or cognitive systems are independent of any specific physical instantiation. Mental states are constituted by their causal relationship to other mental states, sensory inputs, and behavioral outputs."[123] Recall again Hayles's observation that the first step toward posthumanism is the separation of information from its instantiated medium."[124] At least two assumptions are at work in such a view.

First, since Hayles is writing about posthumanity, there is an implicit assumption that the real or true essence of a human being is information, and we are right to be skeptical of this idea. The human being, created in the image of God, is a complex, embodied whole. To attempt to separate what we might term the (theoretical) core of information that comprises the true being or the being's identity from the body, is at best a highly theoretical possibility that has yet to be proven. There may be an intuitive sense that the real me is inside of my body and somehow separable from it, but such an idea lacks any empirical evidence at present.

Second is the assumption that information truly does remain the same when instantiated in some other medium, another notion that we are right to doubt. Ultimately, I ask, along with Hayles: "How could anyone think that consciousness in an entirely different medium would remain unchanged, as if it had no connection with embodiment?"[125]

Indeed, such a perspective represents an impoverished view not only of the human person, who is in reality a being created according to the image of God as a complete and unified embodied being, but also of the

123. Miller, *Critiquing Transhumanism*, 133–34.
124. Koene, Uploading to Substrate-Independent Minds.
125 Hayles, *How We Became Posthuman*, 1.

human body. "It would be wrong to assume that materialists hold the body, being 'matter,' is an ultimate good. They irony is that their aim is to be liberated from material embodiment."[126] The human body is not simply an accident, nor is it merely an instrument.[127] The fact of the incarnation—the Second Person of the Triune God dwelling among humanity as both fully God and fully man—gives great emphasis to the status, worth, and uniqueness of human beings and human bodies in God's creation. Of course, transhumanists do not share these convictions. Their view of personhood ultimately falls by its own standards, failing to establish a plausible notion of human personhood and human identity.

Transhuman Ethics

The dominant utilitarianism in transhumanism is, in short, a poor means of doing ethics. A completely unbounded utilitarianism would justify the oppression or even destruction of a few for the good of the many. At present, utilitarian thinking helps give rise to the category of human nonperson. For example, when it comes to the issue of abortion, a large divide exists between those who see personhood as something that emerges or is recognized as a fetus grows and develops on the one hand, and those on the other who believe that each and every human being is a person at each and every stage of his or her development from conception on. For some, then, a very early embryo or a nonviable fetus, is a human nonperson. Hughes is an example of exactly this view. He argues that embryos, early fetuses, and anyone who is permanently unconscious have no rights; they are the property of the family to which they are related.[128] Indeed, he places these human beings on par with plants: family property. Thus embryos, fetuses, and the permanently unconscious may be destroyed for research, convenience, or other reasons. Make no mistake, the results in human history of separating the notion of human and person in this way have always held devastating consequences for those considered to be nonperson humans.

Miller points out what she sees as instability in transhuman ethics and ultimately, a kind of emptiness regarding transhuman ethical discourse. For example, "If morality is grounded in biochemistry and genetics, then Pearce [Hedonistic Imperative] needs to explain what happens to morality after

---

126. Miller, *Critiquing Transhumanism*, 126.
127. Miller, *Critiquing Transhumanism*, 139.
128. Hughes, "Future of Death."

humans transcend their biology."[129] Further, in transhumanism, "rights are not inherent or inalienable, but contingent on whether they confer some advantage to society." Indeed, transhumanist ethics are unstable. De Grey writes: "Morality is not absolute but relative—relative to what one already 'knows' to be 'right.'" Thus, "our moral instinct is self-defining," and subject to change or "evolution."[130] Certainly, there are times when we might, upon some reflection, change our minds regarding whether something is right or wrong, but this is not a change in morality or ethics itself. Rather, it is a realignment of one's views with what one understands to be good, true, and right objectively.

Even with such instability in ethics, Miller points out that "transhumanists still do not hesitate to use moral language such as 'ought' and 'should.'"[131] This should not be surprising given Alasdair MacIntyre's argument that moral discourse today is nothing more than emotivism, wherein "all evaluative judgments and more specifically all moral judgments are *nothing but* expressions of preference, expressions of attitude, or feeling."[132] Even so, we continue to act as if we are making appeals to rational facts and objective standards in our moral discussions. At the risk of overstatement, the overriding standard for transhuman ethics is whether it advances evolution toward complexity. But this misunderstands humanity. We were not created with an overriding imperative to evolve and complexify. While such a statement might seem to be out of step with modern evolutionary biology, the fact is that if complexification is the overriding standard of ethics—and I am asserting that it is in transhumanism—this misrepresents what it means to be truly human. We are in fact interdependent relational beings,[133] created for relationship with God our creator and with each other.

CONCLUSION

In the face of such challenges, how might Christians respond? With respect to technology broadly, Miller recommends a reconsideration of Reinhold Niebuhr's Christian realism, which recognizes the reality of evil in the world, that "progress is not inherently good but ambiguous," and that many

---

129. Miller, *Critiquing Transhumanism*, 130.
130. De Grey, "Curate's Egg," 215.
131. Miller, *Critiquing Transhumanism*, 143.
132. MacIntyre, *After Virtue*, 11–12 (emphasis original).
133. See MacIntyre, *Dependent Rational Animals*; and Snead, *What It Means*.

of the problems we encounter can only finally be solved by God.[134] Similarly, Peters writes: "Despite the benefits or even blessings of computer connections around the world, something at work in the human mind leads to the development of brute and unmitigated destruction. No increase in human intelligence or advance in technology will alter this ever-lurking human proclivity."[135]

Regarding transhuman metaphysics of the human person, Miller argues for a return to Aristotelian metaphysics: "A human being is a single substance that is a composite of body (matter) and soul (form)."[136] Several metaphysical views of the human person compete today, and they may be grouped under the following headings: radical dualism, holistic dualism, nonreductive physicalism, and eliminative/reductive materialism.[137] Of the four, holistic dualism and nonreductive physicalism are often theologically based. The former holds that mind and body are ontologically separable, but functionally and phenomenologically inseparable. Miller's suggested Aristotelian metaphysics, as described, seems to be a version of holistic dualism. Nonreductive physicalism is monistic and contends that human complexity "gives rise to 'higher' human capacities such as morality and spirituality."[138] A rich literature exists on these views, and the particulars need not concern us here beyond the observation that holistic dualism is certainly not compatible with radical enhancements such as uploading the mind or consciousness. Nonreductive physicalism also seems incompatible with the transhuman ambition of uploading the mind, although there may be some who would hold to both as possibilities.[139] In contrast, the patternist view of the human person is a version of radical dualism, sometimes referred to as information/matter duality.[140] While such a view would seem to be compatible with the uploading of the mind, it in fact misunderstands the nature of the human person as an embodied, unified whole.

Some of the things transhumanists believe and long for may seem far-fetched to some readers, as if they are nothing more than the wild

---

134. Miller, *Critiquing Transhumanism*, 147.

135. Peters, "Transhumanism and Posthuman Future," 158.

136. Miller, *Critiquing Transhumanism*, 152.

137 Murphy, "Human Nature," 24–25.

138. Murphy, "Human Nature," 25.

139. For more on holistic dualism, see Cooper, *Body, Soul, Life Everlasting*. For more on nonreductive physicalism, see Brown et al., *Whatever Happened to the Soul?*

140. Hayles, *How We Became Posthuman*, 13.

imaginings of a few. However, the fact is that transhumanism, and many of the assumptions that underlie it, are currently and increasingly operative on at least three levels. First, a great deal of scholarly debate is ongoing regarding the specific aims of transhumanism, the theoretical bases for the claims and desires of transhumanism, and the ways in which such goals might come to be realized. Second, in recent years we have begun seeing both companies and individuals with vast financial resources like Google/Alphabet Inc., Elon Musk, and others direct their monies into a variety of projects, some of which have overtly transhumanist goals in sight and some of which are simply consonant with transhumanist aspirations, ideas, and ideals. Finally, transhumanist ideas are becoming an increasing part of the mainstream of our present cultural imagination or cultural narratives.[141] For these reasons, we should be taking transhumanist goals seriously. In this chapter, I have attempted to do just that with respect to their views on personhood.

BIBLIOGRAPHY

Adams, Tim. "Artificial Intelligence: 'We're Like Children Playing with a Bomb.'" *Guardian*, June 12, 2016. https://www.theguardian.com/technology/2016/jun/12/nick-bostrom-artificial-intelligence-machine.

Ahmed, A. Kayum. "Delinking the 'Human' from Human Rights: Artificial Intelligence and Transhumanism." Open Global Rights, Apr. 10, 2019. https://www.openglobalrights.org/delinking-the-human-from-human-rights-artificial-intelligence-and-transhumanism/.

Bailey, Doug, et al. "Transhumanist Declaration." Humanity+, n.d. http://humanityplus.org/philosophy/transhumanist-declaration/.

Bartlett, Jamie. "Transhumanists Are on a Quest to Discover Eternal Life. Is the citizen science they use the future of technology?" *Telegraph*, Sept. 10, 2015. http://www.telegraph.co.uk/technology/11855952/Transhumanists-are-on-a-quest-to-discover-eternal-life.-Is-the-citizen-science-they-use-the-future-of-technology.html.

Bear, Greg. *Blood Music*. New York: Ace, 1985.

Blackford, Russell. "Transhumanism and *The Journal of Evolution and Technology*." Institute for Ethics and Emerging Technologies, Sept. 28, 2014. https://ieet.org/index.php/IEET2/more/blackford20140928.

———. "WTA Changes Its Image." Metamagician, July 18, 2008. http://metamagician3000.blogspot.com/2008/07/wta-changes-its-image.html.

---

141. "Even if the common person rejects or is repulsed by transhumanism as a contemporary movement, even if this particular movement ultimately dies the death of other forgotten trends that have gone this way in the past, it is part of a much larger cultural imagination which is much more resilient and seems here to stay" (Burdett, *Eschatology and Technological Future*, 47).

Bostrom, Nick. "A History of Transhumanist Thought." *Journal of Evolution and Technology* 14 (2005) 1–25.
———. *Superintelligence: Paths, Dangers, Strategies*. Oxford: Oxford University Press, 2014.
———. "Transhumanist Values." Supplement, *Journal of Philosophical Research* 30 (2005) 3–14.
———. "Why I Want to be a Posthuman When I Grow Up." In *Medical Enhancement and Posthumanity*, edited by Bert Gordijn and Ruth Chadwick, 107–37. International Library of Ethics, Law and Technology 2. New York: Springer, 2008.
Brown, Warren S., et al., eds. *Whatever Happened to the Soul? Scientific and Theological Portraits of Human Nature*. Theology and the Sciences. Minneapolis: Fortress, 1998.
Burdett, Michael S. *Eschatology and the Technological Future*. New York: Routledge, 2015.
Cannon, Lincoln. "Brief History of the Mormon Transhumanist Association." Lincoln Cannon, April 10, 2017; updated Jan. 5, 2021. http://lincoln.metacannon.net/2017/04/a-brief-history-of-mormon-transhumanist.html.
———. "Transhumanists Disavow Zoltan Istvan Candidacy for US Presidency." iPetitions, Sept. 2015. https://www.ipetitions.com/petition/transhumanists-disavow-zoltan-istvan-candidacy.
Chatterjee, Anjan. "The Promise and Predicament of Cosmetic Neurology." *Journal of Medical Ethics* 32 (2006) 110–13.
Clark, Andy. *Natural Born Cyborgs: Minds, Technologies, and the Future of Human Intelligence*. New York: Oxford University Press, 2003.
———. *Supersizing the Mind: Embodiment, Action, and Cognitive Extension*. Philosophy of Mind. New York: Oxford University Press, 2008.
Cline, Ernest. *Ready Player One*. New York: Broadway, 2011.
Cole-Turner, Ronald. "Going beyond the Human: Christians and Other Transhumanists." *Theology and Science* 13 (2015) 150–61.
Cooper, John W. *Body, Soul, and Life Everlasting: Biblical Anthropology and the Monism-Dualism Debate*. Grand Rapids: Eerdmans, 2000.
De Grey, Aubrey. "Aubrey de Grey." *Colbert Report*, Feb. 11, 2008. http://www.cc.com/video-clips/myptag/the-colbert-report-aubrey-de-grey.
———. "The Curate's Egg of Anti-Anti-Aging Bioethics." In *The Transhumanist Reader: Classical and Contemporary Essays on the Science, Technology, and Philosophy of the Human Future*, edited by Max More and Natasha Vita-More, 215–19. Malden, MA: Wiley-Blackwell, 2013.
———. "A Roadmap to End Aging." TED, July 2005. https://www.ted.com/talks/aubrey_de_grey_says_we_can_avoid_aging.
Dick, Philip K. *Do Androids Dream of Electric Sheep?* New York: Del Rey, 1975.
Drexler, Eric. *Engines of Creation: The Coming Era of Nanotechnology*. New York: Doubleday, 1986.
Dvorsky, George. "Better Living through Transhumanism." *Journal of Evolution and Technology* 19 (2008) 62–66.
European Parliament. "Civil Law Rules on Robotics." European Parliament, Feb. 16, 2017. https://www.europarl.europa.eu/doceo/document/TA-8-2017-0051_EN.html.
Gibson, William. *Neuromancer*. New York: Ace, 1984.
Godwin, Richard. "Immortality: Silicon Valley's Latest Obsession Ushers in the Transhumanist Era." *Post Magazine*, Aug. 10, 2017. http://www.scmp.com/

magazines/post-magazine/long-reads/article/2106070/immortality-silicon-valleys-latest-obsession.

Goertzel, Ben. "Artificial General Intelligence and the Future of Humanity." In *The Transhumanist Reader: Classical and Contemporary Essays on the Science, Technology, and Philosophy of the Human Future*, edited by Max More and Natasha Vita-More, 131–37. Malden, MA: Wiley-Blackwell, 2013.

Hansell, Gregory R., and William Grassie, eds. *H+/-: Transhumanism and Its Critics*. Philadelphia: Metanexus Institute, 2011.

Hayles, N. Katherine. *How We Became Posthuman: Virtual Bodies in Cybernetics, Literature, and Informatics*. Chicago: University of Chicago Press, 1999.

Hill, David J. "Exclusive Interview with Ray Kurzweil on Future AI Project at Google." Singularity Hub, Jan. 10, 2013. https://singularityhub.com/2013/01/10/exclusive-interview-with-ray-kurzweil-on-future-ai-project-at-google/.

Hoffman, Steven A. "Transhumanist Materialism: A Critique from Immunoneuropsychology." In *Building Better Humans? Refocusing the Debate on Transhumanism*, edited by Hava Tirosh-Samuelson and Kenneth L. Mossman, 273–302. Beyond Humanism: Trans- and Posthumanism/Jenseits des Humanismus: Trans- und Posthumanismus 3. Frankfurt: Peter Lang, 2012.

Hughes, James J. "The Future of Death: Cryonics and the Telos of Liberal Individualism." *Journal of Evolution and Technology* 6 (2001). https://www.jetpress.org/volume6/death.htm.

———. "The Politics of Transhumanism and the Techno-Millennial Imagination, 1626–2030." *Zygon* 47 (2012) 757–76.

———. "Transhumanism and Personal Identity." In *The Transhumanist Reader: Classical and Contemporary Essays on the Science, Technology, and Philosophy of the Human Future*, edited by Max More and Natasha Vita-More, 227–32. Malden, MA: Wiley-Blackwell, 2013.

Huxley, Aldous. *Brave New World*. New York: Rosetta, 2000.

Huxley, Julian. *Religion without Revelation*. London: Benn, 1927.

Istvan, Zoltan. "The Immortality Bus." Zoltan Istvan, 2015–16. http://zoltanistvan.com/ImmortalityBus.html.

———. "Transhumanist Party." Zoltan Istvan, n.d. http://www.zoltanistvan.com/TranshumanistParty.html.

Istvan, Zoltan, and US Transhumanist Party. "Transhumanist Bill of Rights—Version 2.0." Transhumanist Party, Dec. 14, 2015; updated Jan. 4, 2017. http://transhumanist-party.org/tbr-2/.

Kharpal, Arjun. "Elon Musk: Humans Must Merge with Machines or Become Irrelevant in AI Age." *CNBC*, Feb. 13, 2017. https://www.cnbc.com/2017/02/13/elon-musk-humans-merge-machines-cyborg-artificial-intelligence-robots.html.

Khatchadourian, Raffi. "The Doomsday Invention." *New Yorker*, Nov. 23, 2015. https://www.newyorker.com/magazine/2015/11/23/doomsday-invention-artificial-intelligence-nick-bostrom.

Khazan, Olga. "Should We Die?" *Atlantic*, Feb. 18, 2017. https://www.theatlantic.com/health/archive/2017/02/should-we-die/516357/.

Kilner, John F. *Dignity and Destiny: Humanity in the Image of God*. Grand Rapids: Eerdmans, 2015.

Koene, Randal A. "Uploading to Substrate-Independent Minds." In *The Transhumanist Reader: Classical and Contemporary Essays on the Science, Technology, and Philosophy of the Human Future*, edited by Max More and Natasha Vita-More, 146–56. Malden, MA: Wiley-Blackwell, 2013.

Kurzweil, Ray. *The Age of Spiritual Machines: When Computers Exceed Human Intelligence*. New York: Penguin, 2000.

———. *The Singularity Is Near: When Humans Transcend Biology*. New York: Penguin, 2005.

Lough, Richard. "Captive Orangutan Has Human Right to Freedom, Argentine Court Rules." *Reuters*, Dec. 21, 2014. https://ca.news.yahoo.com/captive-orangutan-human-freedom-argentine-court-rules-203651528.html.

Lyon, Jeff. "Chess Study Revives Debate over Cognition-Enhancing Drugs." *JAMA*, Aug. 16, 2017. http://jamanetwork.com/journals/jama/fullarticle/2649239.

MacIntyre, Alasdair. *After Virtue: A Study in Moral Theory*. 3rd ed. Notre Dame, IN: University of Notre Dame Press, 2007.

———. *Dependent Rational Animals: Why Human Beings Need the Virtues*. Chicago: Open Court, 1999.

Mann, Linton, III, and William T. Russell Jr. "Habeas Relief Not Applicable to Non-Human Animals." Law, July 19, 2022. https://www.law.com/newyorklawjournal/2022/07/19/habeas-relief-not-applicable-to-non-human-animals/?slreturn=20221004153250.

Medick, Veit. "Und Sie denken, Donald Trump sei schräg?" *Spiegel*, Jan. 24, 2016. http://www.spiegel.de/politik/ausland/zoltan-istvan-us-wahlkampf-aus-dem-rollenden-sarg-a-1072645.html.

Merkle, Ralph C. "Uploading." In *The Transhumanist Reader: Classical and Contemporary Essays on the Science, Technology, and Philosophy of the Human Future*, edited by Max More and Natasha Vita-More, 157–65. Malden, MA: Wiley-Blackwell, 2013.

Miller, Julie. *Critiquing Transhumanism: The Human Cost of Pursuing Techno-Utopia*. Phoenix: Public Philosophy, 2022.

Moravec, Hans. *Mind Children: The Future of Robot and Human Intelligence*. Cambridge, MA: Harvard University Press, 1990.

More, Max. "The Philosophy of Transhumanism." In *The Transhumanist Reader: Classical and Contemporary Essays on the Science, Technology, and Philosophy of the Human Future*, edited by Max More and Natasha Vita-More, 3–17. Malden, MA: Wiley-Blackwell, 2013.

———. "The Proactionary Principle." In *The Transhumanist Reader: Classical and Contemporary Essays on the Science, Technology, and Philosophy of the Human Future*, edited by Max More and Natasha Vita-More, 258–67. Malden, MA: Wiley-Blackwell, 2013.

Morgan, Richard K. *Altered Carbon*. New York: Del Rey Ballantine, 2002.

Murphy, Nancey. "Human Nature: Historical, Scientific, and Religious Issues." In *Whatever Happened to the Soul? Scientific and Theological Portraits of Human Nature*, edited by Warren S. Brown et al., 1–30. Theology and the Sciences. Minneapolis: Fortress, 1998.

Murphy, Nancey, and Warren S. Brown. *Did My Neurons Make Me Do It? Philosophical and Neurobiological Perspectives on Moral Responsibility and Free Will*. New York: Oxford, 2007.

O'Connell, Mark. "600 Miles in a Coffin-Shaped Bus, Campaigning against Death Itself." *New York Times*, Feb. 9, 2017. https://www.nytimes.com/2017/02/09/magazine/600-miles-in-a-coffin-shaped-bus-campaigning-against-death-itself.html.

———. *To Be a Machine: Adventures among Cyborgs, Utopians, Hackers, and the Futurists Solving the Modest Problem of Death*. New York: Doubleday, 2017.

O'Gieblyn, Meghan. "Ghost in the Cloud: Transhumanism's Simulation Theology." *n+1* 28 (2017). https://nplusonemag.com/issue-28/essays/ghost-in-the-cloud/.

Orwell, George. *Nineteen Eighty-Four: A Novel*. New York: Harcourt Brace, 1949.

Pelletier, Dick. "End of Death." Institute for Ethics and Emerging Technologies, Jan. 20, 2013. https://ieet.org/index.php/IEET2/more/pelletier20130120.

Pellissier, Hank. "Transhumanism: There Are [at Least] Ten Different Philosophical Categories; Which One(s) Are You?" Institute for Ethics and Emerging Technologies, July 8, 2015. https://ieet.org/index.php/IEET2/more/pellissier20150708.

Perriman, Cole. *Terminal Games*. New York: Bantam, 1994.

Peters, Ted. "Transhumanism and the Posthuman Future: Will Technological Progress Get Us There?" In *H+/-: Transhumanism and Its Critics*, edited by Gregory R. Hansell and William Grassie, 147–75. Philadelphia: Metanexus Institute, 2011.

Powers, Richard. *Galatea 2.2*. New York: Farrar Straus Giroux, 1995.

Rae, Scott B. "More Than the Sum of Its Parts: Philosophical Reflections on Human Personhood." In *Choose Life: Answering Key Claims of Abortion Defenders with Compassion*, edited by Jeanette Hagen Pifer and John K. Goodrich, 99–112. Chicago: Moody, 2022.

Redding, Micah. "Can Transhumanism Lead Us Back to Orthodoxy?" *Christ and Pop Culture* 4 (2016). https://christandpopculture.com/can-transhumanism-lead-us-back-to-orthodoxy/.

Regis, Ed. "Meet the Extropians." *Wired*, Oct. 1, 1994. https://www.wired.com/1994/10/extropians/.

Rubin, Charles. "Bioethics and Transhumanism." *C-Span*, May 23, 2017. https://www.c-span.org/video/?428770-4/bioethics-transhumanism.

Savulescu, Julian, and Ingmar Persson. "Moral Enhancement." *Philosophy Now*, 2012. https://philosophynow.org/issues/91/Moral_Enhancement.

Schwitzgebel, Eric, and Henry Shevlin. "Is It Time to Considering Personhood Right for AI Chatbots?" *Los Angeles Times*, March 5, 2023. https://www.latimes.com/opinion/story/2023-03-05/chatgpt-ai-feelings-consciousness-rights.

Shelley, Mary Wollstonecraft. *Frankenstein: Or, the Modern Prometheus*. Oxford: Oxford University Press, 1980.

Simonite, Tom. "What Is Ray Kurzweil up to at Google? Writing Your Emails." *Wired*, Aug. 2, 2017. https://www.wired.com/story/what-is-ray-kurzweil-up-to-at-google-writing-your-emails/.

Snead, O. Carter. *What It Means to Be Human: The Case for the Body in Public Bioethics*. Cambridge, MA: Harvard University Press, 2022.

Socrates. "Top 10 Singularitarians of All Time." Singularity Weblog, Jan. 23, 2010. https://www.singularityweblog.com/top-10-singularitarians/.

Statt, Nick. "Elon Musk Launches Neuralink, a Venture to Merge the Human Brain with AI." *Verge*, Mar. 27, 2017. https://www.theverge.com/2017/3/27/15077864/elon-musk-neuralink-brain-computer-interface-ai-cyborgs.

Stefan, Ibolya. "Examining the Issues of Legal Personhood of Artificial Intelligence and Robots." *Sectio Juridica et Politica* 38 (2019) 467–86. Doi: 10.32978.sjp.2020.026.

Steinhart, Eric. "Teilhard de Chardin and Transhumanism." *Journal of Evolution and Technology* 20 (2008) 1–22.

Stephenson, Neal. *Snow Crash*. New York: Bantam, 1992.

Sterling, Bruce. "The Transhumanist Bill of Rights Version 2.0." *Wired*, Aug. 21, 2018. https://www.wired.com/beyond-the-beyond/2018/08/transhumanist-bill-rights-version-2-0/.

Stokstad, Erik. "This Lagoon Is Effectively a Person, Says Spanish Law That's Attempting to Save It." *Science*, Sept. 22, 2022, https://www.science.org/content/article/lagoon-effectively-person-says-spanish-law-s-attempting-save-it.

Taylor, Charles. *A Secular Age*. Cambridge, MA: Belknap, 2007.

Tirosh-Samuelson, Hava. "Engaging Transhumanism." In *H+/-: Transhumanism and Its Critics*, edited by Gregory R. Hansell and William Grassie, 19–52. Philadelphia: Metanexus Institute, 2011.

———. "Transhumanism as a Secularist Faith." *Zygon* 47 (2012) 710–34.

Transhumanist Party. "Constitution of the United States Transhumanist Party." Transhumanist Party, Jan. 18–25, 2020; updated Dec. 23–30, 2020. http://transhumanist-party.org/constitution/.

United Nations. "Universal Declaration of Human Rights." United Nations, Dec. 10, 1948. https://www.un.org/en/about-us/universal-declaration-of-human-rights.

Vinge, Vernor. "Technological Singularity." In *The Transhumanist Reader: Classical and Contemporary Essays on the Science, Technology, and Philosophy of the Human Future*, edited by Max More and Natasha Vita-More, 365–75. Malden, MA: Wiley-Blackwell, 2013.

Vita-More, Natasha. "Aesthetics: Bringing the Arts & Design into the Discussion of Transhumanism." In *The Transhumanist Reader: Classical and Contemporary Essays on the Science, Technology, and Philosophy of the Human Future*, edited by Max More and Natasha Vita-More, 18–27. Malden, MA: Wiley-Blackwell, 2013.

Wolfe, Bernard. *Limbo*. New York: Random House, 1952.

Young, Simon. *Designer Evolution: A Transhumanist Manifesto*. Amherst, NY: Prometheus, 2006.

10

On Gene Editing

Luman R. Wing

INTRODUCTION

The recent advent of gene editing, referred to as the CRISPR-Cas9 (clustered regularly interspaced short palindromic repeats–CRISPR-associated protein 9) technology, has astounded the world as one of the greatest technologies for preventing and treating diseases. This remarkable genomic engineering tool has transformed the biomedical industry due to its apparent accuracy, safety, and technical simplicity.[1] Gene editing was first introduced in the 1970s with the development of transgenic mice, which are experimental mice that are bred with unique genes that produce human disease-related conditions such as immunodeficiency or cancers. The challenge with these early studies was the uncertainty as to where the transgenes were inserted in the mouse's genome. A transgene is a gene that has been transferred naturally, or by genetic engineering techniques, from one organism to another. Without having an idea of where the transgene is located in the genome, there may be regions where the transgene could harm the function of other unrelated genes. As gene editing technology

---

1. Doudna and Charpentier, "Genome Editing."

developed, in the 1980s gene editing was applied to embryonic stem cells to produce pluripotent stem cells, which are cells that have the capability of maturing into a variety of cells within the body.

However, even the procedures that were used to transform embryonic stem cells into pluripotent stems cells was technically challenging and inefficient, with only about one in every thousand mature cells being successfully reprogrammed. After a few decades, alternative gene targeting methods were developed, and in 2005 gene editing was coupled with repair methods for correcting disease-related genes. These early studies led to the CRISPR-cas9 technology that was introduced in 2012, which optimized a series of DNA excision-repair enzymes that resulted in a precise method of repairing the broken strands of DNA after the new gene was inserted. The success of CRISPR-cas9 technology is based on the unique enzymes used for inserting a gene into a designated region of the genome or excising a mismatched portion of the DNA that may be damaged, then repairing the new DNA using either of these procedures. As the field of gene editing continued to evolve, by the year 2020, the technology was considered worthy of the Nobel Prize in Chemistry, and it was awarded to Jennifer A. Doudna and Emmanuelle Charpentier.[2]

The CRISPR-Cas9 system has been used in several gene editing clinical studies for the treatment of blood cancers, solid tumors and infectious diseases. While CRISPR-Cas9 technology has received favorable support by the public, there continue to be significant ethical and safety concerns regarding the technology. One of the major safety concerns particularly involved with therapeutic gene editing is a process called insertional mutagenesis, which is when a transgene is inserted into a site in the genome that is off the targeted insertion site. A gene that is inserted into a region of the genome that is off-target may affect other genes resulting in harmful mutations that could lead to tumor formation.

Regulatory agencies have expressed caution regarding this issue, and they have been reluctant to approve gene therapy programs due to the potential for off-target insertional mutagenesis. To address their concerns, the FDA currently requires long-term follow-up evaluations from five to fifteen years for patients who have been receiving gene therapy. The reason for this long duration of observation is due to the uncertainty of where the transgene may also be inserted in the genome. If the transgene is functional at the correct site of insertion, the therapy is generally successful. Yet if

---

2. Doudna and Charpentier, "Genome Editing."

there is any evidence that the transgene has been inserted into off-target regions, the FDA wants to know if the transgene is affecting the function of other genes, particularly if they are the genes related to tumor growth. However, if the off-target insertional mutagenesis occurs in regions of the genome that are not tumor related, and involve the genes related to human behavior, then that will raise bioethical issues such as autonomy and capacities that are worth exploring. Although the science of gene editing has extraordinary therapeutic potential, the uncertainty of the technology remains due to the complexities of genes and genomes.

In addition to the ethical challenges of off-target insertional mutagenesis, are the two types of cells that can be used for human gene editing, namely, somatic (body) cells and germ (reproductive) cells. Depending on which one of these two cell types are used, the consequences of editing the DNA from either cell type differ considerably. Gene editing in somatic cells will last a single lifetime, while editing the DNA from germ cells will affect not only a single lifetime but could also affect several generations.

To address these bioethical issues, this chapter will begin with an overview of the molecular biology of gene editing followed by a discussion of the consequences of how gene editing will affect somatic cells and germ cells. Understanding how gene editing in germ cells could affect the human genome is particularly important due to the profound effects this could have on what it means to be human. Knowing that a human being is identified biologically by a signature sequence of DNA, I will explore how alterations of the human genome could affect certain genes that must be avoided when using gene editing procedures. How will it be possible to avoid these genes when there is uncertainty that a transgene is not sequestered in other regions of the genome due to off-target insertional mutagenesis? If a transgene is wrongfully inserted into a behavioral gene, for example, could it affect the function of the gene, thus resulting in altered behavior? For that matter, does gene editing have the potential to affect biological traits related to personality? This chapter will conclude with a discussion on human dignity, that being human consists of more than a biological system and capacities.

WHAT IS A GENE?

At the core of the study of genetics is the gene, which is a segment of deoxyribonucleic acid (DNA) positioned within the genome that is found within the nucleus of nearly every cell. Genes are essentially biological templates the body uses to make the structural proteins and functional enzymes that are needed to build and maintain tissues and organs. The genetic code is represented by the molecules or bases called guanine (G), cytosine (C), thymine (T), and adenine (A). As DNA is a double-helix molecule, these bases pair up to form a ladderlike structure: G with C and T with A, forming "base pairs" that become the steps of the well-known DNA double helix. Most genes are composed of thousands of base pairs, yet the human genome consists of approximately three billion base pairs, and interestingly, less than 1 percent of these base pairs are actually gene related. The remaining 99 percent of the genome used to be referred to by scientist as "junk" DNA, due to its unusually simple composition in which massive portions of repetitive sequences now understood to be critical for the functional expression of the genes. The emerging science of epigenetics is now at the forefront of gene editing technology, to address how a gene is turned on or off by use of the repetitive sequences of DNA within the genome, as I will discuss in the next section.

Humans have approximately twenty thousand genes dispersed into twenty-three pairs of chromosomes that are found within the nucleus of nearly every cell in the body. Interestingly, only 1.5 percent of our DNA is made up of genes, while 50 percent is made up of repeating sequences and the other 48.5 percent is made up of genes that produce noncoding ribonucleic acid (RNA). The vast amount of DNA regulates the 1.5 percent portion of genes by having them turn on and off in the right cells at the right time.

WHAT IS EPIGENETICS?

The term "epigenetics" is derived from Waddington who defined the term to describe a conceptual solution to a conundrum, a puzzle that arises as a fundamental consideration in developmental biology.[3] The human body is composed of 210 different cell types, and all of the different cells in your body have exactly the same DNA nucleotide sequence, with only a few exceptions in your reproductive and immune systems. Thus, your kidney cells have the exact same DNA as your skin cells and neurons. However, each of the cell types are completely different in terms of the gene products that they produce. How can each cell type have the same DNA, but

---

3. Waddington, *Strategy of the Genes.*

produce such vastly different proteins that form completely different cells? Waddington described this phenomenon with the term "epigenesis" to describe a mechanism that was "above" (*epi-*) the genes that are encoded by the DNA sequence—which is how we currently describe epigenetics.

Essentially, epigenetics is concerned with how the genes function, how genes are read by cells to produce a specific protein. For example, the *MLANA* gene is present in all types of cells but is only "expressed" by the genes in skin cells to produce tyrosine-derived melanin. Epigenetics controls how and where the *MLANA* gene is expressed and in which cell this occurs. Thus, it is by epigenetics that a cell's specialization (e.g., skin cells, blood cell, hair cell, liver cells, etc.) is determined. A fetus develops into a baby based on the genes that are expressed throughout the stages of development (active). The genes that are not necessary during a specific stage of development are silenced (dormant), due to environmental stimuli that can cause genes to be turned "on" or "off." The process by which genes are turned on or off is called gene regulation. Communication molecules from outside of the cell, such as growth factors, have the capability of notifying the cell when to turn a growth gene on or off. Each of these environmental factors can cause chemical modifications to the genes that will turn those genes on or off either immediately or over several generations. Additionally, in certain diseases such as cancer, various genes can be switched from a normal or healthy state to an abnormal or diseased state.

With every gene having "on" and "off" switches, some switches remain on or remain off for extended periods of time, some for an entire lifetime. Genes that are permanently on are mostly structural genes. The genes that are malleable to change include behavioral genes, which can be altered based on environmental conditions. The critical finding in the description of epigenetics is that genes are also controlled from outside the body. Social interactions are a particularly important source of gene regulation.

Different combinations of genes that are expressed, or turned on or off, forms the basis of a unique phenotype. The unique traits of each human being, for example, are based on epigenetics, or the expression of a variety of genes. Although some of epigenetic changes can be inherited and even be transgenerational, interestingly, some epigenetic changes can also be reversible. With changes of expression of twenty-five thousand genes, the number of different combinations of genes being turned on or off could be extraordinary. Conceptually then, if it were possible to map every single cause and effect of the different combinations of genes being expressed, it could be possible to reverse an abnormal/diseased gene's state to a normal/healthy state.

The gene product, or protein, is referred to as the expression of the gene, which is the process by which a cell produces protein molecules from the sequence information in a gene. Thus gene editing may alter gene expression. As I will discuss later in this chapter, there is another editing process by which gene expression can be "tuned" up or down without breaking and repairing DNA. This is known as epigenetic editing.[4] This recent technology may have profound implications as to how to alter the expression of genes without the concerns of insertional mutagenesis. Instead of changing the structure of genes that may need to be altered, a sufficient alteration may be possible by silencing or activating the gene based on environment.

GENE EDITING—METHODS AND LIMITATIONS

Gene editing methods are essentially the introduction of DNA into cells where it can be expressed. Once the DNA is introduced into a cell, it can be inserted or integrated into the DNA of the host cell's genome where it will presumably be expressed in the form of RNA which produces protein. One of the essential molecular tools are meganucleases, which are used to cut the DNA of genes in specific places to allow targeted alterations in the DNA sequence. These massive enzymes have been the standard tools of gene editing for decades until the recent discovery of the CRISPR-Cas9 system which includes two parts, first, the clustered regularly interspaced short palindromic repeat (CRISPR) of RNA, which acts as a guide for genome targeting; and, second, the CRISPR-associated protein 9 (Cas9), which acts as an endonuclease to enable double-stranded breaks.[5]

The CRISPR-RNA molecule is a single guide RNA (sgRNA) that is engineered to specifically target a gene of interest. The only requirement is that the sgRNA recognizes a specific genome region (seventeen to twenty-two base pairs) that is followed by a unique site referred to as 5'-NGG-3' proto-spacer adjacent motif (PAM), which is an essential motif that imparts CRISPR its immunity function (fig. 3). The PAM domain imparts specificity to bind to the PAM sequence and consequently mediates target DNA binding with high specificity. When the endonuclease Cas9 directs DNA

---

4. Holtzman and Gersbach, "Editing the Epigenome."
5. Mali et al., "RNA-Guided Human Genome."

cleavage to create double-stranded breaks, they can be repaired through unique end-joining processes, one of which is a nonhomologous end-joining pathway, which is an error-prone pathway that can result in the creation of insertion-deletions that disrupt the gene. The other end-joining process is a homology-directed repair that occurs in the presence of a donor construct and results in the edited gene. Although this technology was originally developed in bacteria, it has been adapted and has shown to be capable of editing the mammalian genome with high efficiency and selectivity.

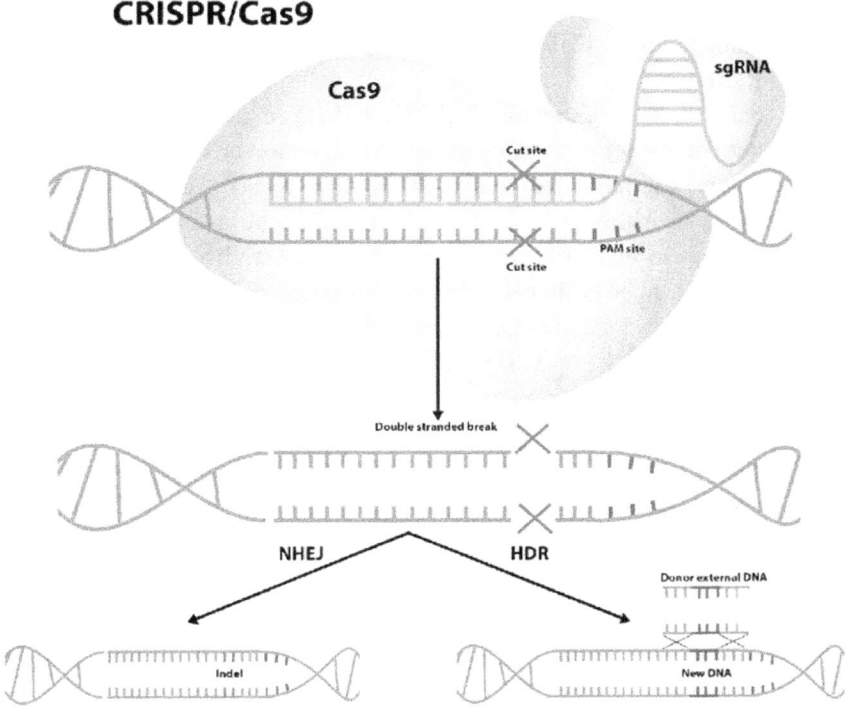

Figure 3—*CRISPR-Cas9 Mediated Gene-Editing Mechanisms*, by Adam Cribbs. A single guide RNA (sgRNA) recognizes a genomic region followed by 5'-NGG-3' PAM sequence, which recruits the Cas9 DNA endonuclease. This introduces a double-stranded break that is repaired by (a) nonhomologous end joining (NHEJ), an error-prone pathway that can result in the creation of insertion-deletions (indels) that can disrupt the gene, or by (b) homology-directed repair (HDR) in the presence of a donor construct.[6]

6. Cribbs and Perera, "Science and Bioethics," 626.

A key feature of the CRISPR system is that single-guide RNA (sgRNA) sequences in CRISPR are paired with Cas9 of other similar nucleases, and they can readily be programmed to edit specific segments of DNA. CRISPR technology is considered the "search and replace" feature that is used to correct errors by slicing out sections of DNA and replacing that removed section with a new, updated sequence of DNA. This allows for the correction of mutant genes which have been the cause of generational genetic diseases.

With early successes in preclinical animal models, the first in-human phase-1 clinical trial was initiated by Carl June from the University of Pennsylvania in 2019.[7] Utilizing an editing strategy of CRISPR/Cas9 edited T-cells in three refractory cancer patients, June found that when three genomic loci were edited, one of which that enhanced antitumor efficiency, engraftment of the engineered T-cells occurred. However, due to the occurrence of some chromosomal translocations, there was concern about these off-target effects. Although this was the first study in humans, the off-target issue continues to be a concern in current clinical studies, and there is a need for patients to be evaluated continuously for several years to minimize the potential limitations of the CRISPR/Cas9 technology.

As introduced above, CRISPR/Cas9 suffers from a major limitation of off-target effects at a rate of around ~50 percent, which has significantly limited the use of gene therapy.[8] Several plausible technological advances are being considered, two of which include optimization of engineered Cas9 enzymes, targeted CRISPR guides, alternative sites for the PAM sequence. Another limitation of CRISPR technology is that the double-stranded breaks created by CRISPR system often leads to apoptosis (cell death) of the cells rather than desired genetic edit, creating further safety concerns regarding the technology.[9] Further concerns include that even with successful on-target edits, they are often accompanied by unintentional deletions of large size and/or complex rearrangements in the genome,[10] which is a major limitation of CRISPR technology that uses double-stranded breaks mechanisms of editing.[11]

7. Stadtmauer et al., "CRISPR-Engineered T Cells."
8. Uddin et al., "CRISPR Gene Therapy."
9. Naeem et al., "Latest Developed Strategies."
10. Lino et al., "Delivering CRISPR."
11. Cullot et al., "CRISPR-Cas9 Genome Editing."

SOMATIC CELL GENOME EDITING

The use of human genome editing to make edits in somatic cells (the cells that comprise an individual body and not the reproductive cells) for purposes of treating genetically inherited diseases is already in clinical trials, as well as FDA-approved therapies. Somatic cells contribute to the various tissues of the body but not to the germline, meaning that, somatic cells are limited to the treated individual and would not be inherited by future generations.

Considerable progress has been made over the past several decades toward clinical applications of somatic cell gene therapy to treat diseases.[12] Gene editing clinical trials were originally conducted in the laboratory, where a patient's blood was collected, the targeted somatic cells were isolated in a petri dish, the genes were edited, and then the modified cells were infused back into the patient. By using this method for treating patients with HIV, for example, the HIV genes in the patient's cells are edited to cut out the sections of DNA that are used to produce the HIV membrane receptors. Without the presence of these receptors on the patient's cells, the HIV virus can no longer gain entry to the cells. This promising procedure is also being evaluated for treating cancer by transforming cells from the immune system, such as T-cells, into cancer-killing cells using gene editing.

With several creative experimental approaches to gene therapy based on the means to add, delete, or modify genes in the somatic cells of living cells or organisms, the prospects for future applications of gene therapy have only started to be realized. However, with the considerable appeal for utilizing gene editing to abolish genetic disorders, challenges to the technology with some gene variants may be either harmful or advantageous depending on the disorder. A prominent example is sickle-cell anemia, which is caused by a variation in one base pair of the hemoglobin gene. Hemoglobin is a protein found in red blood cells that is essential for the transport of oxygen and carbon dioxide throughout the body.

If the sickle hemoglobin variant is inherited from both parents, it causes the hemoglobin protein to aggregate under certain conditions, leading to deformation of the red blood cells into a sickled shape that interferes with blood circulation, causing multiple difficulties and much pain and impairment of the normal tissue functions. When only one parent inherits just one sickle gene variant, it is a rare occurrence to observe signs of

---

12. Cox et al., "Therapeutic Genome Editing."

disease, and these individuals are considered carriers of the sickle-cell gene with the potential of passing it on to their progeny. Interestingly, these carriers are also resistant to the effects on red blood cells caused by the malaria parasite. Apparently, the sickle-cell gene provides a survival advantage in areas where malaria is present, and for that reason, the gene has been selected for and is prevalent in subterranean areas of Africa.

Along with this example are other similar advantaged versus disadvantaged carriers who inherit two disease-associated genes. It is important to note that most human diseases are thought to be affected by genetic variants that occur in multiple genes, with each variant having only a minor effect on disease progression. This finding plays a vital role when considering human genome editing for the treatment of genetically inherited diseases. Most genetically inherited diseases are not the result of single gene—most human diseases are the result of multiple genes. This is an important point when considering altering a gene that may not be disease associated, such as when gene editing has the objective of enhancement, as well as off-target events that may result in conditions far worse than the disorder itself.

As discussed earlier, whether the objective of the gene is to treat a disease (on-target) or if the gene is inserted elsewhere (off-target), both on-target and off-target insertions are ultimately dependent on the expression of the transgene, based on epigenetic factors such as the noncoding regions of the genome. Epigenetic editing can site-specifically control which genes are expressed by affecting the packing and accessibility of cellular DNA at intended gene locations. In contrast to gene editing therapies that involve double-stranded DNA breaks, epigenetic editing therapies can turn on (activate) or turn off (silence) gene expression without changing the DNA sequence. Because they do not break DNA strands, epigenetic editing therapies enable multiple genome locations simultaneously to achieve additive or synergistic effects without chromosomal rearrangement risks that have stymied gene editing therapies. A key advantage of epigenetic editing therapies is that they only seek to adjust the expression levels of a gene and do not require the insertion of a foreign transgene or the permanent removal of a gene that may otherwise serve a secondary function. Of particular interest in this chapter, epigenetic editing may also play a significant role in understanding the expression of behavioral genes due to variations in environment, such as early life adversity and trauma.

HUMAN GERMLINE EDITING

Heritable germline editing, unlike somatic cell gene editing, involves the cells that we pass on to subsequent generations. Cells derived from the reproductive system as well as a fertilized embryo are called germ cells. Editing the genes within a germ cell may offer a potential means of eliminating inherited diseases, particularly with over six thousand single gene-related disorders identified in the human germline. However controversial this may seem, the National Academy of Sciences Committee on Human Gene Editing has indicated that it would be permissible to edit the human genome under certain conditions, yet with caution:

> In light of the technical and social concerns involved, the committee concluded that heritable genome-editing research trials might be permitted, but only following much more research aimed at meeting existing risk/benefit standards for authorizing clinical trials and even then, only for compelling reasons and under strict oversight. It would be essential for this research to be approached with caution, and for it to proceed with broad public input.[13]

The genomes from germ cells are passed on from one generation to the next. Attempts to repair genes within embryonic cells, a procedure referred to as germline editing, have been cautiously endorsed, as stated above, when and if the procedure is considered safe.[14] The reason for this serious caution is that editing the genes in embryos will affect all of the somatic cells of an individual, and the edited genes will also be inherited by future children. The editing of genes in the embryo also raises bioethical issues of therapeutic treatments versus genetic enhancements, where enhancement of genes are primarily for cultural and social purposes, such as eye color or intelligence, instead of for medical therapeutic reasons.

BIOETHICS OF GENE EDITING

In a recent incident that occurred in 2018, He, a professor at the Southern University of Science and Technology in Shenzhen, China, conducted a gene experiment on the DNA of human embryos that was not designed to change the genes of a particular tissue in a single patient, but designed to potentially change the DNA of every cell in the patient, with implications

---

13. National Academies, *Human Genome Editing*, 7.
14. National Academies, "With Stringent Oversight."

for future generations.[15] Essentially, He made the first attempt at germline editing. Although the results from He's embryo editing culminated in the birth of safe and healthy twin girls, the scientific community was outraged by the audacity to edit a gene that did not cause a fatal hereditary disease.

The gene that He selected to edit was a gene that encodes the CCR5 receptor that controls HIV infection. If this gene could be edited, or deleted, then future generations would not be susceptible to HIV infection. Even though this experiment appears to be beneficial to mankind, the way in which He pursued this project was the real reason for accusation of bioethical maleficence by NIH director Francis Collins. The project was conducted without any informed consent process, and most importantly, due to the experimental conditions, there was high probability of off-target effects that could be lethal. The consequence of this challenging situation is a breach in the integrity of the scientific community. Doors to germline editing in early embryos have been opened, and the potential outcome of an off-target insertion of a gene is now a reality. In essence, the human genome is now vulnerable to scientists who believe that editing human embryos may be a gateway to improving humanity. Deleting genes that are unnecessary or even harmful may optimize human beings. Yet as we are finding in molecular biology today, the human genome is vastly more complicated than we ever imagined—we are clearly at the frontier of our understanding of how the human genome functions. Every gene, every repeated sequence, is strategically positioned in the human genome to facilitate the function of how genes are expressed. Altering one gene can have major consequences to other genes. If we continue at this trajectory of altering human embryos, our understanding of what constitutes a human being will be under assault.

What happens if we are able to solve the problem of insertional mutagenesis, having greater accuracy of editing the correct site within the genome, as CRISPR claims to be able to do? Can we assume that if we conquer this issue, we can proceed with editing human embryos, in line with He's experiment? To address these questions, we must first realize that biologists are encountering one of the most extraordinarily complicated systems at the root of gene editing. With very limited knowledge of the efficiency of gene editing, recent findings have demonstrated incomplete editing and inaccurate editing with germ cell gene editing. For example, in a study conducted to understand the role of a particular gene in the development of embryonic stages, Niakan et al. utilized CRISPR to delete a gene

15. Regalado, *Rogue Chinese CRISPR Scientist*.

in human embryos. Following an analysis of the edited embryos, approximately half of the edited embryos had unintended edits. To address the questions above, unintended edits or insertional mutagenesis will continue to be problematic due to the dynamics of cell differentiation in embryonic cell maturation. The results from Niakan's study reinforced the outcome of insertional mutagenesis that led to reproductive abnormalities, including cancer. Niakan and his colleagues concluded from their study, "This is a restraining order for all genome editors to stay the living daylights away from embryo editing."[16] Niakan's paper also sounds the alarm for so-called on-target edits, which can result from edits to the right place in the genome but have unintended consequences.

Kiran Musunuru, a cardiologist at the University of Pennsylvania who uses CRISPR in his lab to research potential heart disease therapies, referred to the unintended consequences of gene editing by stating, "What that means is that you're not just changing the gene you want to change, but you're affecting so much of the DNA around the gene you're trying to edit that you could be inadvertently affecting other genes and causing problems."[17]

The other challenges of unintended editing, as Musunuru alludes to, concern the possibility of whether modified genes will also be affected indefinitely and whether the edited genes will be transferred to future generations with unexpected consequences. Combined with technical limitations and the complexities of biological systems, making precise predictions about the future of an edited genes, gauging potential risks and benefits might be difficult, if not impossible. Thus, the uncertainty resulting from these factors hinders accurate risk-benefit analysis, thereby also complicating the decision-making process. Although heritable genome editing could be considered as a means of preventing the transmission of inherited genetic diseases, many insurmountable challenges await its future.[18]

Even with the dark shadow that has been cast over germ cell gene editing by He, the FDA is moving forward with somatic gene therapies, particularly for the treatment of rare diseases, such as hereditary blindness. Even with the extraordinary potential of the CRISPR technology, there are newer versions of the methods still being developed. Due to the relative ease of conducting CRISPR-cas9 gene editing, ethical concerns arise when

16. Mullin, "Scientists Edited Human Embryos," para. 3.
17. Frosch, "Genome Editing," para. 8.
18. Lin et al., "CRISPR/Cas9 Systems."

considering the potential for biohackers to create hazardous pathogens. With these concerns, as well as the aberrant actions of He mentioned earlier, how do we navigate the treacherous terrain of further abuse of gene editing, particularly the manipulation of human embryos? What may occur if the human genome is altered to the extent that it is no longer officially human? At what point is it decided that the alteration of human genes is only allowed for treating diseases in somatic cells? How much human-directed intervention in nature is appropriate or even permissible? Bioethical questions such as these are currently being debated between social and religious communities.[19]

Although gene editing appears to provide a solution for treating many diseases, the technology is still in its infant stages. Gene editing has many challenges ahead, particularly how to increase the specificity of CRISPR-Cas9 molecules to edit targeted cells. The editing tools may select a certain cell to edit, yet not all of the targeted cells will experience the same effect of the editing as other cell, as Kiran Musunuru described. Another issue is that the editing procedure may occur on only one strand of DNA and not the other. There are currently several major hurdles using gene editing to treat single mutated genetic disorders, such as the single gene mutation that causes sickle cell anemia. Another major challenge is off-target editing, as discussed earlier, when edits are made at the wrong gene. Off-target genetic modifications are frequent, unfortunately, and can alter the function of otherwise intact genes. Multiple studies using early CRISPR-cas9 agents found that greater than 50 percent of RNA-guided endonuclease-induced mutations were not occurring on-target.[20] The off-target effects can confound variables in biological studies leading to potentially misleading and unreproducible results. In the clinical sphere, the major concerns surround the disruption of vital coding regions, leading to genotoxic effects such as cancer.

Finally, the skeptical view is that even if the genome is edited as expected and the desired functional output is achieved at the given time, the complex relationship between genetic information and biological traits (or phenotypes) is not fully understood. Therefore, the biological consequence of editing a gene in germline and/or somatic cells may be unclear and unpredictable, particularly due to the vast complexities of phenotypes. Given the uncertainty regarding how gene expression and modification influence

19. Sandel, *Case against Perfection*.
20. Fu et al., "High-Frequency Off-Target Mutagenesis."

complex biological outcomes, it is difficult to appraise potential risks and benefits. This ambiguity creates a challenge on its own and is one of the sources obscuring efficient ethical deliberation and decision-making.

GENE EDITING AND ENHANCEMENT

The prospect of using gene editing for altering genes to enhance height, gender, eye color, or even intelligence, should be carefully considered before we collectively change social norms.[21] Enhancement has been defined by the National Science Foundation as: "boosting our capabilities beyond the species-typical level or statistically normal range of functioning," "a nontherapeutic intervention intended to improve or extend a human trait," or "improvements in the capacities of existing individuals or future generations."[22]

From these definitions, the NSF stipulated that improving musculature for patients with muscular dystrophy would be restorative, whereas improving musculature for individuals with no known pathology and average capability would be considered enhancement. Although there may be some benefits of individual enhancement, the social stigma that surrounds enhancement applications should be limited to nonheritable somatic gene editing. Heritable gene editing for enhancement of physical and cognitive abilities, such as the embryonic editing of the HIV susceptibility genes in the offspring of He's CRISPR-edited babies described earlier, will permanently alter the human genome. Even if we know that the genes He eliminated may prove to be of benefit to mankind by eradicating susceptibility to HIV, we are still in the infant stages of our understanding of the human genome. What if the genes he eliminated are needed for other genes to function? We must remember that most genes work with other genes to produce a given product. For example, multiple genes work together to produce the proteins that make up eye color, height, and even intelligence. To edit a single gene, it is critical to know if other genes will be adversely affected by this action—which is why the FDA prepared the long-term follow-up guidance for gene editing products. Regulated utilization of CRISPR gene editing must continue to address both the safety and efficacy of the CRISPR/Cas9 technique in treating otherwise untreatable disorders.

---

21. Center for Biologics Evaluation and Research, "Human Gene Therapy Products."
22. Committee on Human Gene Editing, *Human Genome Editing*, 145.

PART II | BIOETHICS AND PERSONHOOD

REGULATORY CHALLENGES OF GENE EDITING

As a regulatory scientist, I have worked closely with the US FDA Center for Biologics Evaluation and Research, which includes the Office of Tissue and Advanced Therapies. This branch of the FDA has a focus on gene editing technologies and recently provided a regulatory guidance document, discussed above, titled "Human Gene Therapy Products Incorporating Human Genome Editing." The FDA recognizes the risks posed by CRISPR technologies, evidenced by their focus on safety and the challenges they have had with regulatory oversight of gene editing products:

> FDA evaluates human gene editing products using a science-based approach weighing the benefits and risks of each product. The benefit-risk profile for each product depends on the proposed indication and patient population, the extent and duration of therapeutic benefit achieved, and the availability of alternative therapeutic options. Some of the specific risks associated with gene editing approaches include off-target editing, unintended consequences of on- and off-target editing, and the unknown long-term effects of on- and off-target editing.[23]

As summarized from their guidance, the FDA concerns reinforce the safety issues discussed throughout this chapter. The unknown long-term effects of on- and off-target editing appear to be insurmountable barriers due to the uncertainty of the fate of the transgene, as described by the FDA in an earlier guidance on long-term follow-up:

> Genome editing, whether ex vivo or in vivo, introduces the risk for delayed adverse effects, due to 1) the permanent nature of change; 2) the potential for off-target genome modifications that can lead to aberrant gene expression, chromosomal translocation, induce malignancies, etc.; 3) the risk for insertional mutagenesis when integrating vectors are used to deliver the genome editing components, and the associated risk of tumorigenicity; and/or 4) the possibility of an immune response to the genome-editing components or the expressed transgene.[24]

Each of these risk factors related to delayed adverse effects will require a sufficient duration of time to see if it is realized. To address the duration of the delayed adverse effects, the FDA has provided further guidance on how

---

23 Center for Biologics Evaluation and Research, "Human Gene Therapy Products," 2.
24. Center for Biologics Evaluation and Research, "Long Term Follow-up," 15.

to conduct of clinical studies that involve gene editing. Prior to enrolling, subjects should be asked to provide voluntary, informed consent to long-term follow-up (LTFU). As discussed, the long-term effects of intended, as well as unintended, editing at on- and off-target loci may be unknown at the time of the gene edited product administration. Therefore, it has been recommended that sponsors conduct LTFU at least fifteen years after the product administration.[25]

Along with the FDA recommendation to follow up with patients for at least fifteen years post-administration of a gene editing product, it is evident that the FDA is concerned with delayed off-target risks with gene editing. Altering genetic material using CRISPR still remains a much debated as well as controversial factor in terms of human utilization. However, a few approvals by FDA lead to the opening of a few clinical trials for gene therapy using CRISPR, described in a prior section, which came after a great deal of review, thorough considerations, and weighing of risk-to-benefit ratio. Current trials in phase 1/2, although very limited, are designed only for patients with severe diseases as cancer or other monogenic debilitating disease, which otherwise remain untreatable. The outcomes from these studies may provide a snapshot as of how safe these tools would be for the less severe cases and how soon they may be implemented as more and more risks associated with the technologies will be discovered and addressed.

GENE EDITING AND NEUROSCIENCE

Gene editing companies that involve central nervous system (CNS) disorders include Editas Medicine and Sangamo Therapeutics. These organizations are addressing disorders such as Alzheimer's disease, amyotrophic lateral sclerosis (ALS), and Huntington's disease.[26] Even in preclinical studies, these organizations are investigating mouse models of epilepsy and autism spectrum disorder genes. Yet, beyond editing CNS genetic disorders, they are investigating whether mutations in neural cells with disordered gene expression can affect specific behaviors. For example, in a study conducted by A. Singh-Taylor at Creighton University (2017), when neonatal rats were weaned under early life stressful conditions, they demonstrated depression-like and anxiety-like behaviors in their brains as adults. These

---

25. Center for Biologics Evaluation and Research, "Long Term Follow-up."
26. Segal, "Grand Challenges."

results were due to the altered neuronal gene expression that occurred in the hypothalamic neurons due to the stressful conditions as neonates.[27]

These findings provided evidence that the genes in the hypothalamic neurons of the neonatal rats were silenced (referred to as epigenetic silencing) in their brains as adults. In another study, Fox et al. (2019) found that reduced *NTRK3* gene expression in the dorsal amygdala of monkeys was associated with increased early-life anxious temperament.[28] However, the anxious disposition could be reversed when the *NTRK3* gene was administered into the amygdala of the monkeys using gene editing technology. These two studies raise questions regarding the extent to which certain behaviors may be controlled by gene or epigenetic editing in neurons of the CNS. If there is a correlation of behavior with gene editing, does this mean that a bad experience can be eliminated using gene editing and/or epigenetic editing? This is where the challenges arise when considering the risk of adverse effects of gene editing, as discussed earlier, particularly how off-target gene modifications could lead to aberrant gene expression. If this occurred in neurons involved in learning and memory, the consequences could potentially affect the phenotype of a biological trait. Whether the gene editing procedure is for the treatment of a disease or enhancement of a desired trait, modifying a gene to change a desired phenotype will require an understanding of the epigenetic factors that affect the expression of the modified gene. Due to the complexities of the biological outcomes that may occur from a single gene modification, gene editing will always be challenged with uncertainties.

SHARING KASS'S CONCERNS

With the revolutionary biological innovation of gene editing technology, there is a responsibility to recognize that this scientific achievement has unforeseen limitations, as observed by Leon Kass, the former chair of the President's Council on Bioethics.[29] Aligned with his concerns regarding current biotechnologies, I wish to reflect on Kass's perspectives on these limitations of modern biology, a science that has carefully defined its conceptual and methodical boundaries. Although biotechnologies, such as gene editing, promise powerful discoveries within its self-determined

27. Singh-Taylor et al., "NRSF-Dependent Epigenetic Mechanisms."
28. Fox et al., "Dorsal Amygdala Neurotrophin-3."
29. Kass, *Life, Liberty and Defense*, 277–97.

boundaries it will never be able to tell us what life is, what is responsible for it, or what it is for.

Although there are many biologists that do not prescribe to these limitations, reductionism and even materialism are insufficient when attempting to explain the nature of the human mind and consciousness. Modern biology is coming to recognize that the diversity of life forms is more than the result of random mutations. This is particularly due to the observation that mutations are only deleterious, that their occurrence does not provide any beneficial function to an organism. Even the recent findings in epigenetics have challenged the orthodoxy of natural selection. Life experiences can effect changes in gene expression, evidenced in heritable genotypes. Yet this alternative view is unlikely to be accepted by modern biologists, as it counters the orthodoxy of modern biology. However, Kass recognizes that there are many current unorthodox scientists, such as John Lennox, emeritus mathematics at Oxford University, who states that "the scientific enterprise itself is validated by God's existence."[30]

Another eminent Oxford molecular biophysicist and theologian, Alistair McGrath, noted for his work in historical, systematic and scientific theology, claims that "within each of us exists the image of God."[31] These two scholars are among thousands, as Kass has discussed, who have followed one of the founding biologists, Aristotle, who emphasized questions of form over matter and wholes over parts, "for whom science was a refined and ever-deepening reflection on the natures and the causes of the beings manifest to us in ordinary experience."[32] Kass explains that there are permanent limitations for the study of life, one of which is that science seeks generalizations, where as living beings are unique. Science seeks to clarify what is obscure, seeks to explain what is perplexing or wondrous. From Kass's experience, current science is overconfident in its ability to treat mystery as simply that which has not yet been understood. To render real mysteries as things incapable of being understood is generally, "to plead guilty to scientific heresy; for this, one gets called a mystic and is encouraged to transfer to the theology department."[33] Can we even look to biology in answering the questions about how we are to live? Kass argues

30. Lennox, *God's Undertaker*, 210.
31. As quoted at https://www.quoteslyfe.com/quote/Within-each-of-us-exists-the-image-359581.
32. Kass, *Life, Liberty and Defense*, 294.
33. Kass, *Life, Liberty and Defense*, 296.

that true biologists recognize that the study of the irreducible complexities of human biology is a science that seeks to understand human nature and human wholeness.

CONCLUSION

Understanding of the extraordinary capabilities of CRISPR-Cas9 technology, medicine has realized a powerful technology that is both preventative and curative of serious illnesses. However, there are serious risks with this technology that have yet to be resolved, namely, the potential for off-target genome modifications that can lead to aberrant gene expression, chromosomal translocation, and malignancies. Even with this cautionary tone, however, gene editing technology will eventually be used to not only alleviate serious illnesses, but also be used to enhance our physical and cognitive abilities.

This chapter has summarized the biology of gene editing, referred to as the CRISPR-Cas9 technology, and has discussed how this technology was originally designed to correct an aberrant gene in order to eliminate the potential of a serious illness.

This chapter detailed the differences between somatic and germ cells and how gene editing technology is becoming a new treatment methodology with the potential for treating and preventing disease, as well as altering traits unrelated to medical needs. This chapter has also addressed how alteration of the human genome, specifically germ cells, may result in unwanted genetic consequences, such as tumor formation. This chapter included a discussion of the bioethical issues related to off-target gene editing and how this could affect the human genome. With the challenges of biological enhancement and other unconventional uses of gene editing, the use of this technology is under scrutiny as to which genes should be edited and if it is for therapeutic purposes or enhancement and how this alteration can affect other genes. Ultimately, this technology may affect humanity beyond our efforts to prevent and treat diseases. With unforeseen limitations, the hope is that true biologists will recognize that the study of human biology, particularly gene editing, will be a science that seeks to understand human nature as well as human wholeness.

BIBLIOGRAPHY

Brokowski, Carolyn, and Mazhar Adli. "CRISPR Ethics: Moral Considerations for Applications of a Powerful Tool." *Journal of Molecular Biology* 431 (2019) 88–101.

Center for Biologics Evaluation and Research. "Human Gene Therapy Products Incorporating Human Genome Editing." FDA, Mar. 2022. Docket number FDA-2021-D-0398. https://www.fda.gov/regulatory-information/search-fda-guidance-documents/human-gene-therapy-products-incorporating-human-genome-editing.

———. "Long Term Follow-up after Administration of Human Gene Therapy Products: Guidance for Industry." FDA, Jan. 2020. Docket number FDA-2018-D-2173. https://www.fda.gov/regulatory-information/search-fda-guidance-documents/long-term-follow-after-administration-human-gene-therapy-products.

Cox, David Benjamin Turitz, et al. "Therapeutic Genome Editing: Prospects and Challenges." *Nature Medicine* 21 (2015) 121–31.

Cribbs, Adam P., and Sumeth M. W. Perera. "Science and Bioethics of CRISPR-Cas9 Gene Editing: An Analysis towards Separating Facts and Fiction." *Yale Journal of Biology and Medicine* 90 (2017) 625–34.

Cullot, Grégoire, et al. "CRISPR-Cas9 Genome Editing Induces Megabase-Scale Chromosomal Truncations." *Nature Communications* 10 (2019) 1136. doi: 10.1038/s41467-019-09006-2.

Doudna, Jennifer A., and Emmanuelle Charpentier. "Genome Editing: The New Frontier of Genome Engineering with CRISPR-Cas9." *Science* 346 (2014) doi: 10.1126/science.1258096.

Evans, John H. *Contested Reproduction: Genetic Technologies, Religion, and Public Debate.* Chicago: University of Chicago Press, 2010.

Fox, Andrew S., et al. "Dorsal Amygdala Neurotrophin-3 Decreases Anxious Temperament in Primates." *Biological Psychiatry* 86 (2019) 881–89. doi: 10.1016/j.biopsych.2019.06.022.

Frosch, Jennifer. "Genome Editing in Human Embryos Has Unintended Side-Effects." PET, June 29, 2020. https://www.progress.org.uk/genome-editing-in-human-embryos-has-unintended-side-effects/.

Fu, Yanfang, et al. "High-Frequency Off-Target Mutagenesis Induced by CRISPR-Cas Nucleases in Human Cells." *Nature Biotechnology* 31 (2013) 822–26. https://www.nature.com/articles/nbt.2623.

Holtzman, Liad, and Charles A. Gersbach. "Editing the Epigenome: Reshaping the Genomic Landscape." *Annual Review of Genomics and Human Genetics* 19 (2018) 43–71.

Kass, Leon. *Life, Liberty and the Defense of Dignity: The Challenge for Bioethics.* New York: Encounter, 2002.

Lennox, John C. *God's Undertaker: Has Science Buried God?* Oxford: Lion, 2011.

Lin, Yanni, et al. "CRISPR/Cas9 Systems Have Off-Target Activity with Insertions or Deletions between Target DNA and Guide RNA Sequences." *Nucleic Acids Research* 42 (2014) 7473–85. https://doi.org/10.1093/nar/gku402.

Lino, Christopher A., et al. "Delivering CRISPR: A Review of the Challenges and Approaches." *Drug Delivery* 25 (2018) 1234–57. doi: 10.1080/10717544.2018.1474964.

Mali, P., et al. "RNA-Guided Human Genome Engineering via Cas9." *Science* 339 (2013) 823–26. https://doi.org/10.1126/science.1232033.

Mullin, Emily. "Scientists Edited Human Embryos in the Lab, and It Was a Disaster." One Zero, June 16, 2020. https://onezero.medium.com/scientists-edited-human-embryos-in-the-lab-and-it-was-a-disaster-9473918d769d.

Naeem, Muhammad, et al. "Latest Developed Strategies to Minimize the Off-Target Effects in CRISPR-Cas-Mediated Genome Editing." *Cells* 9 (2020) E1608. doi: 10.3390/cells9071608.

National Academies of Sciences, Engineering, and Medicine. *Human Genome Editing: Science, Ethics, and Governance.* Washington, DC: National Academies, 2017. https://doi.org/10.17226/24623.

———. "With Stringent Oversight, Heritable Human Genome Editing Could Be Allowed for Serious Conditions." National Academies, Feb. 14, 2017. http://www8.nationalacademies.org/onpinews/newsitem.aspx?RecordID=24623.

Pelligrino, Edmund D. "The Lived Experience of Human Dignity." In *Human Dignity and Bioethics: Essays Commissioned by the President's Council on Bioethics*, 513–40. Washington, DC: Bioethics, 2008.

Regalado, Antonio. "Rogue Chinese CRISPR Scientist Cited US Report as His Green Light." *MIT Technology Review*, Nov. 27, 2018. https://www.technologyreview.com/2018/11/27/1821/rogue-chinese-crispr-scientist-cited-us-report-as-his-green-light/.

Sandel, Michael J. *The Case against Perfection: Ethics in the Age of Genetic Engineering.* London: Belknap, 2009.

Segal, David J. "Grand Challenges in Gene and Epigenetic Editing for Neurological Disease." *Frontiers in Genome Editing* 1 (2019). doi: 10.3389/fgeed.2019.00001.

Singh-Taylor, A., et al. "NRSF-Dependent Epigenetic Mechanisms Contribute to Programming of Stress-Sensitive Neurons by Neonatal Experience, Promoting Resilience." *Molecular Psychiatry* 23 (2018) 648–57. doi: 10.1038/mp.2016.240.

Smith, Christian. *What Is a Person: Rethinking Humanity, Social Life, and the Moral Good from the Person Up.* Chicago: University of Chicago Press, 2010.

Stadtmauer, Edward A., et al. "CRISPR-Engineered T Cells in Patients with Refractory Cancer." *Science* 367 (2020) eaba7365. doi: 10.1126/science.aba7365.

Uddin, Fathema, et al. "CRISPR Gene Therapy: Applications, Limitations, and Implications for the Future." *Frontiers in Oncology* 10 (2020) 1387. doi: 10.3389/fonc.2020.01387.

Urnov, Fyodor D. "Genome Editing B.C. (Before CRISPR): Lasting Lessons from the "Old Testament." *CRISPR Journal* 1 (2018) 34–46. doi: 10.1089/crispr.2018.29007.fyu.

Waddington, C. H. *The Strategy of the Genes.* New York: MacMillan, 1957.

11

In Technology's Shadow
Technological Non-Neutrality and Ethical Considerations Regarding Human Enhancements

E. A. Stevens

INTRODUCTION

Within the field of bioethics, technology is often considered to be neutral. Roughly, this neutral position holds "that technologies are things-in-themselves, isolated objects. . . . Technologies-in-themselves are thought of as simply objects, like so many pieces of junk lying about."[1] Junk here is not intended as a value claim but rather as a claim regarding how technology functions: it lies about waiting for a user to pick it up and use it in one way or another. Subsequently, technologies do not have any causal efficacy within themselves. The assumption which follows from this position is that the user, and at other times the inventor, are the sole means to ensure that a particular technology's use is ethical and even desirable. However, philosophers of technology tend to disagree with this commitment to technological neutrality, claiming instead that technology shapes the user and the world around that user. This matters because a user may believe himself

---

1. Ihde, *Technology and the Lifeworld*, 26–27.

to be fully autonomous from the technology and thus his desires to be fully caused by himself. Yet this may in fact not be the case. The neutral view holds that users or inventors determine a technology's ethical import; the non-neutral view holds that technology influences the user and therefore can change the user enough that the change itself has ethical import. I will attempt to demonstrate within this chapter that technological neutrality is untenable. If it is untenable, the discussion had within bioethics must take non-neutrality into account, especially in relation to enhancements.

When using the word "enhancement," following Giubilini and Sanyal, I mean "biomedical interventions [meant] to improve human capacities, performances, dispositions, and well-being."[2] A therapy, on the other hand, is intended to restore functioning that has been lost. Within this chapter I am assuming that the therapy/enhancement distinction is meaningful. To defend such a claim is beyond the scope of my project. The therapy/enhancement distinction's viability has long been debated,[3] with a definition being far from settled.[4] However, I hold that this is a boundary problem and accordingly am still persuaded that there is a distinction between the two concepts. This can be seen in the starkest examples of both concepts. Technological interventions which result in one's attaining infrared vision or supersonic hearing are clear examples of enhancing an already-existing human capacity, whereas cataract surgery for failing eyesight and cochlear implants are examples of restoring a capacity which has been lost. Though every technological intervention is not so easily delineated, erasing the distinction is a misguided move and only obfuscates the clarity which is needed within the discipline.

This chapter will have three sections. First, I will utilize examples of specific bioethicists who see technology as neutral. This commitment to neutrality results in a user's autonomy factoring heavily into the conversation. Second, I will delineate philosopher of technology Don Ihde's understanding of technological non-neutrality, which culminates in his suggestion that the user is profoundly impacted by technology. Elaborating Ihde's concept of a technosystem will take up the bulk of the second section, for it is within the technosystem that technological non-neutrality is clearly seen. The third and final section is an application of technological non-neutrality towards bioethics discussions surrounding enhancement technologies.

2. Giubilini and Sanyal, "Ethics of Human Enhancement," 233.
3. Parens, "Is Better Always Good?"
4. Gyngell and Selgelid, "Human Enhancement," 111.

TECHNOLOGICAL NEUTRALITY

As previously mentioned, bioethicists tend to view technology as neutral. Andrea Sauchelli, while discussing what he describes as "neo-Luddism," says, "Obviously all technological advancements can be used for the worse."[5] Here, Sauchelli is discussing any views which claim a particular technology is undesirable based on how it is currently changing the world around it. Thus, for Sauchelli, it is foolish to claim any particular technology has shaped the world negatively enough that it should not have been invented. The ability to take any technology currently being used for ill and use it instead for good assumes that the main actor is the human, and that deliberating for particular ends guarantees that those ends are met. The user here stands above and beyond the technology, is not influenced by it, and therefore can deliberate a better use for it.

He also considers the "proper function for which [a technology was] designed" to be part of the ethical consideration.[6] In a subsequent section, I will demonstrate that design does not always ensure how a technology is used and consequently cannot be used constructively to guide the ethical use of a technology. For Sauchelli, however, a technology could be used for ill more easily when not being used as it was designed. Thus, for him, design function has ethical import.

Or, as McGee and Maguire have said in relation to the specific enhancement of brain implants, "Technological innovations as such are neither good nor evil; it is the uses devised for them that create moral implications."[7] This statement is explicit in granting the innovation its moral status based solely on goals, and that no innovation should be considered problematic as such.

Another example from bioethicists Ingmar Persson and Julian Savulsecu goes further to demonstrate how technological neutrality is understood: "It is possible for humankind to improve morally to the extent that the overwhelming powers of action that modern scientific technology affords will be used for the better, all things considered."[8] Persson and Savulescu focus on the possible numerous positive uses of technology. This positive use is not guaranteed. To go further, the focus here is on

5. Sauchelli, "Life Extension," 336.
6. Sauchelli, "Life Extension," 336.
7. McGee and Maguire, "Becoming Borg," abstract.
8. Persson and Savulescu, *Unfit for the Future*, 10–11.

how the technology is being used rather than whether it is shaping society, perceptions, or any other number of things. Many bioenhancements are still within the theoretical phase; however, a good example of a technology changing society is the invention of the typewriter. While a typewriter is not an enhancement, it can still demonstrate the point. Secretaries were dominantly male until the typewriter was invented. Because piano playing was similar to typing, and women were more adept pianists, women adapted quicker than men and eventually displaced male secretaries.[9]

According to Persson and Savulescu, the individuals using the "overwhelming powers of action" will use those powers positively subsequent only to their own moral enhancement.[10] It is worth noting that, within the context Persson and Savulescu are using, any type of moral enhancement is the result of a technological intervention. Thus, technological intervention needs to be used in order to guarantee that subsequently developed technologies are used morally. If technology that is not part of a moral enhancement is used "for the better" by the user of a moral enhancement, it would be an indication that the moral enhancement had enhanced the individual. If the enhanced individual does not use technology "for the better," then they have not succeeded in morally enhancing themselves. Yet again, the consequence of how a technology is used becomes the sole deciding factor regarding ethical import. Moreover, for Persson and Savulescu, a moral enhancement is required for future humans to use technologies morally. Thus, the technology of moral enhancements is itself necessary for other technologies to be used morally. Without moral enhancements, humans will use some technologies wrongly.

Leon Kass is one prominent bioethicist who has argued that technology's influence should be considered within the field of bioethics. Kass considers the "technological project" to turn "all of nature into raw material at human disposal."[11] For him, mastery of nature is problematic when applied to human nature, but not necessarily problematic in itself. However, he considers "the confident pursuit of progress through the mastery of nature, fueled by unbridled technological advance" to be central to an American

---

9. Ihde, *Bodies in Technology*, 97.

10. When using the term "moral enhancement," I mean an intervention which intends to enhance moral behavior and/or moral reflection. To simply alter behavior may or may not be a moral enhancement, depending on how that behavior is altered and how it subsequently interacts with the deliberation of the individual "enhanced."

11. Kass, "Wisdom of Repugnance," 696.

self-identity,[12] which is not problematic in and of itself. In the end, Kass understands technology somewhat differently than other bioethicists, since he does care about how technology has shaped the world. Additionally, he considers particular technologies to be off limits for development based on their intrusion into human bodies.[13] Consequently, he offers a better way forward than is often the case within bioethics, for he is not afraid to say particular technologies should be banned. Unfortunately, his view on the role emotions play within ethical considerations has been given more consideration than his analysis of technology. Considering this, I am hoping to broaden Kass's position on technological non-neutrality and some of his reservations.

As I have demonstrated, the commitment to technological neutrality prevents one from maintaining any technology has so changed the world that its invention was not desirable, for we can always find a better way to use that technology. One such technology, which will be particularly controversial, is the smart phone. Perhaps this technological object should not have been invented because it has resulted in far-reaching changes to the world in which we live. The phenomenon of "smombies"[14] who walk into traffic, thereby resulting in injury or death, is a clear demonstrable negative change to how we relate to the world because of this particular technology. The argument here is not that phones in this instance are being used for unethical ends, for the app being used while the user walks into traffic is of little consequence in this case. Rather, the argument is that smart phones have changed how individuals interact with the world and consequently are not desirable technologies. This is a different type of claim than the type of claim made by someone holding to a neutral view of technology: for them, since smart phones could also be used for good, i.e., they connect people over vast distances, their invention itself is not undesirable. Rather, in this view, we must decide to use smart phones for good and not for ill.

12. Kass, *Life, Liberty and Defense*, 3–4.

13. Cloning is one example Kass is strongly against (Kass, "Wisdom of Repugnance").

14. The term "smombie" is a combination of smart phone and zombie. Roughly, this is used to denote an individual who focuses on their smart phone to the extent that they lose contact with the world around them.

Autonomy as It Relates to Technological Neutrality

Bringing autonomy into this discussion highlights a specific way in which technological neutrality is assumed. The user's autonomy is often taken by bioethicists, especially those who are enthusiastic about enhancements, as what matters morally in relation to specific technologies. The user stands above the technology and decides how the technology is being used and towards what end, which is (as I've previously argued) the morally significant question rather than the question of how the technology and the user are interacting.

The condition of autonomy (sometimes informed consent is added here[15]) is a moral ideal central to an optimistic view of enhancements.[16] Schaefer, Kahane, and Savulescu delineate the numerous accounts of autonomy and how it relates to enhancements. In this case, they point to the difference between a Kantian account of autonomy which "is an aspect of the will: it does not just cause one to act, but is also itself uncaused"[17] and Frankfurt's hierarchical account in which autonomy "is a particular sort of coherence between [first-order and second-order] forms of desires."[18] Schaefer et al. raise the possibility of formulating a new theory of autonomy, but claim this would undermine any further work one would want to do with that theory since it would need to gain credibility prior to being applied to any further reflection.

A more promising approach for Schaefer et al. is to consider two facets that overlap throughout most accounts of autonomy: freedom and self-determination in general, and an individual's ability to reason, deliberate, and evaluate in particular. Freedom and self-determination are often too ambiguous for practical application; thus, one's rational capacity more easily grounds autonomy. This rationality is at a basic level the ability of an individual to understand the current context as well as the options available. Incidentally, if one has false beliefs, one cannot deliberate correctly and thus is not autonomous. If one deliberates via another person's perspective without recognizing it as another's perspective, one is also not

---

15. McGee and Maguire, "Becoming Borg," 299.

16. Indeed, autonomy is considered, along with informed consent, to be "the core ethical concepts of applied ethics and bioethics since the World Medical Association Declaration of Helsinki of 1964" (Korthals, "Naked Emperor," 225).

17. Schaefer et al., "Autonomy and Enhancement," 124.

18. Schaefer et al., "Autonomy and Enhancement," 125.

autonomous.[19] Instead, one is reliant on another individual more than is desirable if one is to be autonomous.

The inverse of rationality can demonstrate how it relates to autonomy: deception can be utilized to hinder an individual's ability to reason and thus also hinders one's autonomy. False beliefs can also hinder that individual's ability to reflect on his own biases and beliefs, which again render him nonautonomous in relation to those particular biases.[20] Pro-enhancement ethicist John Harris is supportive of cognitive enhancement but utilizes autonomy to argue against moral enhancements. For Harris, moral enhancements would lead to the inability to fail in a moral sense, and thus violates autonomy.[21] One must be free to fail if one is to be truly free at all.

Here, I must briefly note that those bioethicists who are skeptical of the desirability of enhancements tend to see autonomy as a weak counter to the types of societal pressures that would influence individuals to select for enhancements.[22] I agree with these concerns. However, it is not only societal pressures that can influence the user of a technology but rather the technology itself.

I do not intend to argue that autonomy as defined by some optimistic bioethicists is not morally relevant. It is. However, by weighing autonomy heavily in regard to biotechnology, it obscures the question of whether a technology could interfere with the rational capacities and desires of the user. If a technology does influence the user in either of these areas, then the user is not fully self-determined as he would be if a technology were a mere neutral tool. In the section that follows, I will turn to look at philosophy of technology and make some basic observations that demonstrate that technology is in fact not a neutral entity.

TECHNOLOGICAL NON-NEUTRALITY

As I have demonstrated, the assumption of technology as neutral impacts how one understands the ethics of any particular technology. However, philosophy of technology, as a discipline, makes the contrary claim that technology is not neutral. Moreover, this claim has been roughly the consensus

---

19. Schaefer et al., "Autonomy and Enhancement," 127.
20. Schaefer et al., "Autonomy and Enhancement," 124–27.
21. Harris, *How to Be Good*, 84–94.
22. This is the underlying thread running through Elliott, *Better Than Well*.

within the discipline since its inception.[23] The technological permeation of our world is seen by some philosophers of technology as problematic, whether it is because of the political shaping done by technology,[24] the drive towards efficiency in all areas of life,[25] or the commodification of things which shouldn't be commodified.[26]

Within this discipline, Don Ihde's work demonstrates that technological objects intrinsically influence or "push" decisions. Ihde is less pessimistic than others, which makes him a fitting philosopher to further nuance the bioethics discourse. Ihde highlights the reciprocal formative influence technological objects have on the user, which, when applied to bioethics discussions, shifts the central considerations.

Don Ihde's Discussion of Technological Non-Neutrality

Ihde states that the non-neutrality of technology in no way implicates technology as harmful. If a technological object is neutral, it is simply an object over which the user has control, even mastery; however, as Ihde sees it, technology reciprocally acts upon the user, thereby removing certain ends as desirable.[27] Thus, the user does not have full control of the technology and therefore cannot always dictate how a technological object will be used. That technology is non-neutral points to the ways in which a technology inclines the individual towards particular ends or particular desires.

For Ihde, inclining is an imposing of a disposition or desire into an individual. It is a highlighting of key aspects, objects, or dispositions within the world or the user to the detriment of other aspects, objects, or dispositions. Those things that are not highlighted to the user fall into the background of the user's perceptions.[28] Naturally, the user has a desire for that which the technology holds out as desirable or visible.

---

23. For one philosopher of technology who does not hold to non-neutrality, see Bunge, "Philosophical Inputs and Outputs."

24. For such a concern, see Winner, *Whale and Reactor*.

25. Postman, *Technopoly*.

26. Borgmann, *Technology and the Character*.

27. Pickering has influenced Ihde's understanding of science and makes a similar argument in Pickering, *Mangle of Practice*. Pickering calls these types of reciprocal actions the "dance of agency."

28. A background is something that is present to the individual, but not necessarily at the fore of her interactions with the world, or even her perceptions. It is similar to how a backdrop works in an old film: it's there, but not the focus, and one usually does not notice it.

Technological non-neutrality influences users in particular ways. I will expound on these in the coming sections: technological milieus (or technosystems) have particular norms or mores, transform experiences, and reduce particular senses of those within the system. To resist such inclinations generated by technology is possible but difficult.

Technosystems

According to Ihde, the milieu of current (Euro-American) society can be described as a technosystem and comes with its own mores and norms. For example, those who, as adolescents, engage in sexual relations are deemed irresponsible if they do not utilize birth control technologies. Within this system, it is no longer acceptable to leave impregnation to chance (or, like in an older time, God's will), but rather impregnation must be controlled as much as possible.[29] Because the system has a way of inclining the individual within it towards certain ends, if those ends are control, then one inclines unintentionally if she believes that birth control has nothing to do with control.

Here it needs to be noted that birth control via technological means has not always been the norm. As Ihde points out, this technological intervention has become the norm over time. Birth control is a simple example from Ihde that can be considered in relation to technologies which have been further developed beyond the control mentioned by Ihde. For example, technologies such as in vitro fertilization (IVF) and genetic testing of embryos are beyond simple birth control techniques. The use of preimplantation genetic diagnosis (PGD) for genetic defects has become a common practice in combination with IVF. If Ihde is correct regarding the trajectories towards control which technology gives, this inclining regarding PGD may in fact go beyond current particular genetic diseases (such as screening against embryos with Huntington's disease) towards the selecting of other features.

The inherent and implicit control which these technologies exert, in other words how they incline the user, has dropped from the foreground into the background. This implicit control has been forgotten, which Ihde claims is often the case. The forgetting of this inclining is problematic in that the user cannot resist these inclinations if need be. Subsequently, PGD, if not removed from its trajectory, will inevitably lead towards further

29. Ihde, *Technology and the Lifeworld*, 179–80.

genetic control of embryos. This does not mean that this trajectory cannot be changed but that it will continue if it is not challenged. Ihde does not state, however, that control is problematic. He simply points towards the elimination of chance (or, the need for control over aspects which previously could not be controlled) as an aspect of technology without discussing its moral weight. Whether this desire for control is negative or positive is a question Ihde circumvents.

The ability to change the trajectory of the technosystem proves Ihde's understanding of a technosystem is different from those who would consider technology to be an absolute aspect of culture. This latter view leads to a deterministic line which is unalterable and self-sustaining (e.g., Ellul and Marcuse).[30] Taken this way, technology would determine the future and also be unchangeable. This is significant for Ihde in that he does not think technology is deterministic in a hard sense. Consequently, he offers a constructive way by which to interact with technology that allows for changing technology's trajectory. To see technology as the only absolute driver of society results in the inability of any individual to impact the future technosystem. This leads to the inevitability a technosystem being all encompassing and dominant. For Ihde, Ellul and Marcuse have an incorrect understanding of technology which easily leads towards a dystopian view (a view which sees technology as necessarily negatively impacting society). On the other hand, utopian views (a view where technology is necessarily positive and leads to massively good outcomes), which also see technology as a cultural absolute, are prevalent but unhelpful.[31]

Unreliable Trajectories

Ihde points out that frequently the intention behind the invention of a technology, and consequently where it aims, are often not met. This leads to the technological trajectory moving away from what was originally intended. Ihde calls the belief that the intention of the inventor matters in the case of a particular technology the "intentional fallacy."[32] The intention of an inventor can never ground a technology into a particular use context. Rather,

---

30. When discussing Ellul and Marcuse, Ihde mentions the following: Ellul, *Technological Society*; Marcuse, *One-Dimensional Man*.

31. Ihde, *Technology and the Lifeworld*, 6–7, 123, 159.

32. Ihde, *Technology and the Lifeworld*, 69.

other users often come along after the invention of a technology and use it for more or less fitting ends. The inventor often has little say over this.

One concrete example of this sideways movement can be seen in a particular invention: the chain saw. The flexible saw was originally invented in the late eighteenth century by two Scottish physicians working independently, John Aitken and James Jeffray. At that time, few solutions were viable in the case of obstructed labor, which results when the mother's pelvis is not large enough to allow the infant's head passage through the birth canal. Only three options were available for obstructed labor: "hysterotomy (cesarean section), which at that time commonly resulted in the death of the mother, embryotomy (craniotomy), which ended the life of the child and pelviotomy (symphysiotomy)."[33] Hysterotomies are now known as cesarean sections, and embryotomies require the doctor to crush the cranium of the infant in utero so that it can be pulled out of the obstructed birth canal. A pelviotomy was a procedure in which the pubic symphysis (a pelvic joint) of the mother would be divided to allow extra room for the infant's head to pass through the birth canal. Pelviotomies were the safest of the procedures available but were not always effective and still often resulted in the death of either the mother, the child, or both. Furthermore, because a scalpel was used, the process often resulted in soft tissue damage surrounding the joint.[34]

Aitken and Jeffray desired to speed up this process and make it safer; thus, they invented a flexible saw. This saw was designed similarly to a watch chain, with teeth added to alter the chain into a saw. A large needle was also added to the end of this saw, allowing it to pass behind the joint and consequently cut from behind the joint. This flexible saw also became useful in other types of bone operations which excised diseased bone tissue. Incidentally, there is little evidence that this flexible saw was in fact used by Jeffray in the case of pelviotomies.

The osteotome, a mechanized version of this flexible saw, was invented by the German physician Bernard Heine in 1830. The flexible saw was passed over a rotating mechanism which was moved via a hand crank. This made the motion of the saw endless as it did not need to be pulled back and forth.[35] Debate persists as to who first applied this mechanized saw in a logging context. In 1861, a saw was designed with a hand crank,

33. Skippen et al., "Chain Saw," 72–73.
34. Hamilton, *Midwifery*, 324–28.
35. Skippen et al., "Chain Saw," 75.

and in 1881, a riding saw was designed which was like a rowing machine.[36] However, in 1906, Samuel J. Bens filed a patent with the US Patent Office for an "endless chain saw" to be used in logging.[37] Although this saw was far too heavy to be practical, it laid the foundation for further alterations. Slow modifications persisted over time, eventually leading to what is now known as the chainsaw.

Ultimately, the chain saw is no longer associated with either surgeries or childbirth. Granted, current chain saws are not identical with the first flexible saws invented, but this does not sever their connection. If flexible saws had not been invented, logging chain saws may also have not been invented. This concrete example shows that a technology which was invented for a particular use can subsequently be used in a radically different way than originally intended. This demonstrates Ihde's view that technology is not always used for the end that was intended. If Ihde is correct, then considering the end for which a specific technology is invented does little to inform the ethics of that technology.

Transformation of Experience

Another aspect of technological non-neutrality is technology's ability to transform one's experience of one's surroundings. Ihde uses the example of a stick with a knife attached to the end which is developed for retrieving bananas. Once one has extended one's body via this instrument, one will from then onward view bananas and their retrieval differently. Since the use of this instrument removed difficulty and effort, efficiency became associated with a technological mediation.[38] Often, a technological instrument is not isomorphic; it does not directly match unmediated experience. A telescope, for example, when mediating the moon, is still somewhat matched to unmediated human perception. A mediation such as infrared imaging technology, however, is no longer isomorphic with previous perception, as it reveals previously unknown phenomena.[39]

Moreover, for Ihde, modern science and modern technology are not synonymous with ancient versions of either science or technology. They

36. Woodcutter, "Why Were Chainsaw [sic] Invented?"
37. US patent 893,897: filed 1906, patented 1908 (https://patents.google.com/patent/US893897A/en).
38. Ihde, *Technics and Praxis*, 54.
39. Ihde, *Technics and Praxis*, 78.

have become inextricably interconnected, with technology being more influential than science. As technological instruments invaded science, a new type of science arose which was dependent on new technologies to continue to grow and develop. For example, a telescope was necessary for Galileo to make the types of discoveries he made. Galileo also realized that the types of discoveries he was making made a new world visible which was previously unknown.[40]

Utilizing this example of Galileo's discoveries, Ihde demonstrates technology's influence within the realm of scientific instrumentation: the scientific world developed into a mostly vision-dominated domain. This development reduced the importance of other human senses into the background: they were relegated to insignificant in constituting a scientific world. Here it is helpful to note that for Ihde, a world is similar to a gestalt, or a full schema by which one views one's surroundings. One's surroundings only make sense and consequently become a coherent whole via this schema.

A technology automatically amplifies particular aspects of this world while reducing others. This reducing relegates some aspects of the world to the background. Once this has happened, those aspects are forgotten.[41] One example is how automobiles change one's understanding of community. Living miles from work and friends is now the norm for those within a technological world. This causes one's community to be spread over vast distances, which has not always been the case. In a walkable community, one constantly interacts with familiar people, even if they are not considered friends. The walkable world is no longer the norm, so one's understanding of community itself has been altered. Once one has forgotten that some aspects of a world have been diminished, those aspects are very difficult to recover. Moreover, one may eventually lose important aspects of the world which could have helped solve problems (medical research, infrastructure, etc.) or promote human flourishing.

Reduction of Senses

A technology may reduce more than particular aspects of a world. It may also lead to the reduction of particular senses within the user. Often, when one is considering a technology, the technology's amplification is the focus, to the extent that it can become a "fascination." However, despite the

40. Ihde, *Instrumental Realism*, 47, 74.
41. Ihde, *Instrumental Realism*, 44–46.

"amplificatory dimension of instrumental technics, phenomenologically it remains the case that the other dimension of instrumental transformation is reductive."[42] Thus, one cannot have the amplification without the reduction. They go together when a technological object is mediating the world.

In the case of an individual in a technologically textured world which is only mediated via visual technology, the individual continues to interact with the world through other senses (taste, touch, etc.). However, this leads to a discontinuity when the technologically mediated visual world is eventually seen as the "real" world. At this point, the world that is not mediated technologically becomes unexciting and thus is slowly reduced from the status it once held.

At this point, the world that is not mediated technologically becomes unexciting and thus is slowly degraded from the status it once held. Additionally, for Ihde, the technological instrument makes visible aspects of the world which were previously unseen and unknown, which leads to an emphasis on microphenomena. The instruments that allow the viewing of such small phenomena thus restrict the viewing of larger phenomena that previously would have been given precedence.

If a user forgets the amplification/reduction symmetry, it is problematic because this transformation inhibits one's ability to interact with the world. Rather than being solely a positive amplification, the technology can easily lead to a reduction. Additionally, this forgetting the possibility of reduction prohibits one from correcting a problem if one needs to be corrected: because one no longer sees the problem and cannot therefore correct it. The reduced background sense is still available to be pulled back into a more direct awareness if one desires, but if it has been so reduced, will one recognize it as available, let alone desire it?

The cultural habit of preferring the visual to all other forms of perception, which is generated by technologies and science, is a type of reduction. Ironically, this "reduction to vision becomes also a reduction of vision."[43] Not all cultures have preferred the visual sense to the other senses. In addition, a second example of scientific preference for the visual can be seen in the scientific reduction of reports to visual data (e.g., Venn diagrams and charts rather than audio aids of the same data). Scientific instrumentation itself is used for this type of visual display and reporting. Thus, the

---

42. Ihde, *Technics and Praxis*, 45.

43. Ihde, *Instrumental Realism*, 47 (emphasis original).

neutrality of the technological mediation within the scientific world, which permeated out towards the world at large, is called into question.[44]

For Ihde, a simple "determinism such that instruments might be thought to embody just any human aim or interest is not adequate. Instruments embody human aims and interests in certain ways, ways in keeping with the necessarily transformational characteristics of the amplification-reduction structure."[45] Thus, technological embodying is not a neutral embodying that can be used however the individual desires. Rather, it transforms one's perceptions, possibly in ways one does not know or perceive. This gives an end to the technology that may not be desired. However, "no technological determinism in the hard sense is adequate either, since technics in its telic dimension provides only a base for inclination rather than determinism in any hard sense."[46] Current decisions regarding the use of any given technology are not determined by the past; thus, the future uses are not set and can be used in more than one way.

As has previously been noted, technology forms an individual's inclinations while leaving the ultimate decisions of how it is used to the individual. But, this inclination gives a trajectory to technology as a whole.[47] This trajectory is established by technology representing one direction as useful rather than another. Because each individual piece of technology informs the individual and guides towards particular ends, technology clears a particular path to follow while allowing for off-path exploration to change the direction. However, Ihde is clear that "one can't rationally control technology. One can enter into the relation and give nudges and inclinations."[48]

APPLYING IHDE'S UNDERSTANDING OF NON-NEUTRALITY TO ENHANCEMENTS

Having shown the problems with the view of technology as neutral, I will now show how the alternative view of non-neutrality matters for a particular question of technology like enhancements. I have attempted to demonstrate that, for Ihde, the user must make decisions regarding the technosystem and its ultimate trajectory. This trajectory often holds out

44. Ihde, *Bodies in Technology*, 37–49.
45. Ihde, *Technics and Praxis*, 48.
46. Ihde, *Technics and Praxis*, 48.
47. Ihde, *Instrumental Realism*, 119.
48. Ihde, *Bodies in Technology*, xix.

particular things as desirable while hiding others. Ihde states that the tracks are not set on which technology must go. The direction is alterable. If we decide we do not like the effect of a particular technology, we can decide to change the direction we are heading with it.

Consequently, before any technology can be challenged, it must be seen clearly. Technological neutrality needs to be rejected in favor of non-neutrality. This will put the user in a better position to refuse the technologies which should be refused as well as notice how her own desires and goals have been influenced by technology. Each of these four aspects of the technosystem can now be applied to enhancements, with good outcomes.

The two main aspects of Ihde's technosystem for our purposes are arguably technology's giving of mores and norms to society and the slow accumulation of control. In this case, John Harris has demonstrated how technology has affected his understanding of moral duty. For him, the progress of medical technology and treatment options imposes on all individuals the moral obligation to participate in medical trials and experiments.[49] This duty is seen through the lens of inevitable medical progress, which Harris hopes will one day give "a better future [to] humanity."[50] This desire for progress has subtly infiltrated Harris's understanding of mores. Whether he finds enhancements to be a moral obligation is a bit more tenuous, though he says not enhancing deprives future generations of particular advantages which we could have given them.[51] To be clear, I hope only to point out that the shift from the claim that one is morally obligated to participate in medical experiments to the claim that one is morally obligated to enhance if given the option is a small one.

The desire for control is also entangled with the technosystem. Enhancements would arguably give the user the perception that she was in greater control of her body itself. This perceived control may at times be correct and other times incorrect, yet the desire itself would be wrapped up with the enhanced body. Additionally, this constant need to enhance and change oneself would likely alienate oneself from one's body. This type of control, as grounded in technological objects, is being offered by the technosystem. Ironically, if a technosystem slowly progresses on the trajectory of enhancements, one would no longer be fully in control, for one must embrace particular enhancements to stay competitive. The control

---

49. Harris, *Enhancing Evolution*, 190.
50. Harris, *How to Be Good*, 54–55.
51. Harris, *Enhancing Evolution*, 139.

an individual has in this trajectory is illusory, for one is forced to accept enhancements which one would not want in other situations.

The unreliable trajectories of technologies are the result of unforeseen consequences. We attempt to predict where a technology will lead, but as Ihde has pointed out, often those predictions are wrong. This tends to be how things end regardless of how much information one has when attempting such predictions. And, as the chainsaw example demonstrates, the one doing the inventing of a new technology cannot predict how that technology will be used. The interaction between the technology, the user, and the greater world shifts numerous factors which cannot possibly be foreseen. Or, as Ihde has put it, the concern here is regarding "unintended consequences, unpredictability, and the introduction of disruptions into an ever growing and more complex system" as well as the "disregard for the materiality of technologies."[52]

In the case of enhancements, the complex system Ihde mentions is not just the technosystem but also the human body. And this is especially the case in relation to invasive interventions that penetrate the body. The body will probably push back on any invasive intervention in ways that are entirely unpredictable. Moreover, the technology itself will behave in ways that aren't predictable. If one is unable to extricate oneself from the technology as often is the case with desired enhancements, then the unforeseen consequences will directly impact the user's body.

Particularly in relation to enhancements, the transformation of experience is exactly the aim of the enhancement. However, when looking at Ihde's example of how one views a banana after having invented a banana retriever,[53] a change becomes apparent. Once one has extended one's body via this instrument, one will from then onward view bananas and their retrieval differently. Since the use of this instrument removed difficulty and effort, efficiency became associated with a technological mediation.[54] Often, a technological instrument is not isomorphic; it does not directly match unmediated experience. Usually when considering some type of physical enhancement, the one wanting the enhancement wants the power which the technology gives. Yet the resulting shift in one's view of the world isn't often also taken into account.

52. Ihde, *Ironic Technics*, 54.

53. For Ihde, a banana retriever is merely a stick with a knife on the end (Ihde, *Technics and Praxis*, 54).

54. Ihde, *Technics and Praxis*, 54.

The enhancement causes the user to lose sight of the world as the mediation changes his interacting with it. Because enhancements would give the user more power, this transformation would be more pronounced than with any current technological mediation. For example, if one could gain the ability to jump fifteen feet in the air, then obstacles become less problematic. One no longer sees his body in relation to objects around him the same way. Even if one cannot see over a ten-foot-high brick wall, he would be able to jump to the top of it. This ability to jump a brick wall would diminish the boundary the wall was intended to enforce. One's experience of the world would necessarily have changed.

Moreover, the user would come to think that walls have always been jumpable. Walls would lose their purpose to this particular user. The danger here would be propounded if the user forgot what his experience of the world was like prior to gaining the ability to jump walls. Ihde does demonstrate that often technology's ability to shape one's experience of the world is forgotten. I would go further to say that the previous experience becomes disdained as "lesser than" after a sufficient amount of time has passed.

The restricting of senses via mediation could become quite problematic when applied to possible bioenhancements. If a technology can effectively reduce particular aspects of the world, even particular senses into the background, then to make that technological intervention permanent will again lead to unexpected consequences. For example, consider an individual who opts for the enhancement of brain-machine interfaces, which are directly implanted into the brain rather than using sensing equipment outside of the brain.[55] Implantation of electrodes can do damage, which has led to the exploration of differing techniques to mitigate such injuries.[56] Elon Musk's startup company, Neuralink, has managed to create a neurochip named the N1 implant. The N1 is designed to be "a fully implantable, cosmetically invisible brain-computer interface to let you control a computer or mobile device anywhere you go."[57] The N1 was intended from the outset to help disabled individuals; however it has also been suggested that this technology may be used to connect individuals to smart homes,[58] as well as "unlock[ing] human potential tomorrow."[59] Consider a user implanting

---

55. Soldozy et al., "Endovascular Stent-Electrode Arrays."
56. Mohammed et al., "Ice Coating."
57. See https://neuralink.com (accessed Jan. 29, 2024).
58. Pisarchik et al., "From Novel Technology."
59. See https://neuralink.com (accessed Jan. 29, 2024).

a future version of the N1 into his brain, which will connect his brain to his phone. He can prompt a search engine for any piece of information which he desires. After some time, he will forget what it was to remember pieces of information because he can ask his phone for that information.

As the speed of phones becomes increasingly faster, the near instant retrieval of information would push the memory of this individual further into the background. Thus, he will have forgotten both what a memory is and that he doesn't have one. It would be a reduction rather than an enhancement precisely because other aspects which were once central to his mind, perhaps even his noetic structure, have been lost without his knowledge. Thus, if one were pressured into opting for a particular enhancement, it is possible that over time, and given the sorts of reduction Ihde has revealed belong to technology, the individual's state would not be improved subsequent to the enhancement. In other words, the technological intervention would not be an enhancement at all; worse, the user who had the enhancement would not know that this was the case.

CONCLUSION

By applying Ihde's insights to contemporary understandings of enhancement technologies, the importance of questioning the assumption of the neutrality of technology has become evident. Because each individual piece of technology informs the individual and guides towards particular ends, technology shifts where the user goes while also allowing the user to change that direction if she so desires. The problem, however, is how much the user's desires are instilled by the technology itself. Yet changing a trajectory instilled by technology must be made by choice[60] and must be affected from within rather than from without such a trajectory. The technosystem tends to be all-encompassing and consequently the changing of the trajectory cannot happen from outside it.

Consequently, the user still has the ultimate ability to shift the overall trajectory of the technosystem and is not entirely determined by that system. Ihde's claim that technosystems are not deterministic separates him from other less optimistic philosophers of technology. Yet the technosystem's ability to shape the individual connects with the previous discussion of autonomy. If one believes that technology is neutral and has no shaping abilities, then one will be more under that technology's influence. Ironically,

---

60. Ihde, *Expanding Hermeneutics*, 156.

those who hold strongly to autonomy as a chief ethical ideal are the least likely to have autonomy from the technologies that they use.

Furthermore, enhancement technologies would situate the user under the sway of that technology more than already-existing technologies because of the invasiveness of enhancements: they cannot be removed at a later time if the user wishes. Often enhancements are seen as additions to one's own body. This is problematic in that technology would itself be the driver of one's ethical deliberation and also may dominate other aspects of one's life. This would happen without the user being aware of it. In the end, one would be unable to extricate oneself from technological desires because enhancement technologies would be ever present, mediating the world. They are not merely neutral objects out in the world but rather have power to change the user and the world. This position of technological non-neutrality must be embraced prior to any ethical considerations of any given enhancements. If this position is not allowed into the discourse, technologies will continue dictating the trajectory taken by the technosystem.

IMPLICATIONS FOR PERSONHOOD

Technological influence can be further elucidated in how we see ourselves as persons. One of the characteristics of technology is that it is always changing, seemingly infinitely malleable while changing the world around us. This malleability can be turned on our own bodies. As a result, embodiment becomes progressively ambiguous. The body's reactions and sometimes even rejection is considered solvable, given enough time.[61]

To be clear, we cannot predict how technologies will be used nor the consequences of using them.[62] Yet, technological neutrality is committed to our ability to control technological development. Moreover, considering control of technological development as a key aspect of ethical decision-making is also a commitment to technological neutrality. For, even if one has control over a particular technology, that technology could still be reciprocally shaping the user in ways which are not obvious to that user.

Genetic manipulation (especially germline manipulation) may result in disastrous new diseases proliferating which we have no way of foreseeing. It reinforces our view of ourselves as mere physical stuff to be mastered and manipulated by our own will. Neurochips may result in migraines, possibly

61. Ren, "Age of Head Transplants."
62. Postman, *Technopoly*, 15.

even the subsequent painful death of the user. Perhaps, depending on which brain region it is installed within, the user will lose empathy or some other vital emotion. It reinforces the view that the human brain is merely an advanced computer and nothing more, which subsequently makes a notion such as whole-brain emulation (or mind uploading, a process by which the human mind would be freed from the biological substrate of the brain and utilize a technological substrate instead) both possible and desirable.

In short: technology both causes unforeseeable consequences and changes how we perceive our personhood. Rather than asking if a technology is being used "for good," it may be a better exercise to at least attempt to foresee how a technology will influence our perception of ourselves as persons, the world around us, or nonhuman animals. Technological mediation will never be inert and consequently will always have influence. If this influence is destructive, it needs to be taken seriously prior to our ability to combat that influence or think ethically about any given innovation. Otherwise, we will simply be held within the sway of technology and never able to fully emerge from its shadow.

BIBLIOGRAPHY

Borgmann, Albert. *Technology and the Character of Contemporary Life: A Philosophical Inquiry*. Chicago: University of Chicago Press, 1984.
Bunge, Mario. "Philosophical Inputs and Outputs of Technology." In *Philosophy of Technology: The Technological Condition; An Anthology*, edited by Robert C. Scharff and Val Dusek, 191–200. 2nd ed. Hoboken, NJ: Wiley Blackwell, 2014.
Elliott, Carl. *Better Than Well: American Medicine Meets the American Dream*. New York: Norton, 2003.
Ellul, Jacques. *The Technological Society*. Translated by John Wilkinson. London: London, 1965.
Giubilini, Alberto, and Sagar Sanyal. "The Ethics of Human Enhancement." *Philosophy Compass* 10 (2015) 233–43.
Gyngell, Chris, and Michael J. Selgelid. "Human Enhancement: Conceptual Clarity and Moral Significance." In *The Ethics of Human Enhancement: Understanding the Debate*, edited by Steve Clarke et al., 111–26. Oxford: Oxford University Press, 2016.
Hamilton, Alexander. *Outlines of the Theory and Practice of Midwifery*. 4th ed. London: Kay, 1796.
Harris, John. *Enhancing Evolution: The Ethical Case for Making Better People*. Princeton, NJ: Princeton University Press, 2010.
———. *How to Be Good: The Possibility of Moral Enhancement*. Oxford: Oxford University Press, 2016.
Ihde, Don. *Bodies in Technology*. Electronic Mediations 5. Minneapolis: University of Minnesota Press, 2001.

———. *Expanding Hermeneutics: Visualism in Science*. Studies in Phenomenology and Existential Philosophy. Northwestern University Press, 1998.

———. *Instrumental Realism: The Interface between Philosophy of Science and Philosophy of Technology*. Indiana Series in the Philosophy of Technology. Bloomington: Indiana University Press, 1991.

———. *Ironic Technics*. Copenhagen: Automatic/VIP, 2008.

———. *Technics and Praxis*. Boston Studies in the Philosophy and History of Science 24. Boston: Dreidel, 1979.

———. *Technology and the Lifeworld: From Garden to Earth*. Indiana Series in the Philosophy of Technology. Bloomington: Indiana University Press, 1990.

Kass, Leon. *Life, Liberty and the Defense of Dignity: The Challenge for Bioethics*. San Francisco: Encounter, 2004.

———. "The Wisdom of Repugnance: Why We Should Ban the Cloning of Humans." *Valparaiso University Law Review* 32 (1998) 679–706.

Korthals, Michiel. "The Naked Emperor." In *The Contingent Nature of Life: Bioethics and Limits of Human Existence*, edited by Marcus Düwell et al., 221–32. International Library of Ethics, Law, and the New Medicine. Dordrecht: Springer Netherlands, 2008.

Marcuse, Herbert. *One-Dimensional Man: Studies in the Ideology of Advanced Industrial Society*. Routledge Classics. New York: Routledge, 2002.

McGee, Ellen M., and Gerald Q. Maguire. "Becoming Borg to Become Immortal: Regulating Brain Implant Technologies." *Cambridge Quarterly of Healthcare Ethics* 16 (2007) 291–302.

Mohammed, Mohsin, et al. "Ice Coating: A New Method of Brain Device Insertion to Mitigate Acute Injuries." *Journal of Neuroscience Methods* 343 (2020). doi: 10.1016/j.jneumeth.2020.108842.

Parens, Erik. "Is Better Always Good?" In *Enhancing Human Traits: Ethical and Social Implications*, edited by Erik Parens, 1–28. Hastings Center Studies in Ethics. Washington DC: Georgetown University Press, 1998.

Persson, Ingmar, and Julian Savulescu. *Unfit for the Future: The Need for Moral Enhancement*. Uehiro Series in Practical Ethics. Oxford University Press, 2012.

Pickering, Andrew. *The Mangle of Practice: Time, Agency, and Science*. Chicago: University of Chicago Press, 1995.

Pisarchik, Alexander N., et al. "From Novel Technology to Novel Applications: Comment on 'An Integrated Brain-Machine Interface Platform with Thousands of Channels' by Elon Musk and Neuralink." *Journal of Medical Internet Research* 21 (2019) e16356. doi: 10.2196/16356.

Postman, Neil. *Technopoly: The Surrender of Culture to Technology*. New York: Random House, 1993.

Ren, Xiao-Ping. "The Age of Head Transplants." *CNS Neuroscience & Therapeutics* 22 (2016) 257–59.

Sauchelli, Andrea. "Life Extension and the Burden of Mortality: Leon Kass versus John Harris." *Journal of Medical Ethics* 40 (2014) 336–40.

Schaefer, G. Owen, et al. "Autonomy and Enhancement." *Neuroethics* 7 (2014) 123–36.

Skippen, M., et al. "The Chain Saw: A Scottish Invention." *Scottish Medical Journal* 49 (2004) 72–75. https://doi.org/10.1177/003693300404900218.

Soldozy, Sauson, et al. "A Systematic Review of Endovascular Stent-Electrode Arrays, a Minimally Invasive Approach to Brain-Machine Interfaces." *Neurosurgical Focus* 49 (2020) E3. doi: 10.3171/2020.4.FOCUS20186.

Winner, Langdon. *The Whale and the Reactor: A Search for Limits in an Age of High Technology*. Chicago: University of Chicago Press, 1988.

Woodcutter. "Why Were Chainsaw [sic] Invented? A Brief History & Evaluation of the Chainsaw." Woodcutter, Oct. 24, 2017; last updated Oct. 26, 2021. https://thewoodcutter.info/history-evaluation-of-the-chainsaw/.

12

Stories from Palliative Care

Michael D. Bacon

INTRODUCTION

There is a surprising amount of internal debate in the world of palliative care about how to talk about what exactly we do. I can't think of another medical specialty with this problem. Nephrologists introduce themselves as kidney doctors, oncologists as cancer doctors, but palliative care physicians? Well, that's a little complicated.

This is partially because hospice and palliative medicine is, counterintuitively, a relatively young field. The American Academy of Hospice Physicians was founded only in 1988, and changed its name to the American Academy of Hospice and Palliative Medicine (AAHPM) only in 1996. Perhaps we are not as good at describing ourselves because we don't have as much practice as other disciplines. Largely, though, palliative care is tough to talk about simply because of the nature of the work. It deals exclusively with serious illnesses, and communication regarding serious illness is notoriously challenging. It must constantly balance tact with clarity, attending to the emotions of all parties while clearly conveying sophisticated information. Overly blunt communication risks causing emotional trauma, while overly vague communication fails to accurately exchange the information required to provide good care.

In our own attempt to be sensitive but direct, our team defines our role this way: "Palliative Care is specialized medical care for people living with a serious illness. This type of care is focused on providing relief from the symptoms and stress of a serious illness. The goal is to improve the quality of life for both the patient and the family."[1]

Symptom management tests the ability of clinicians to put out one fire without starting another. Many chronic illnesses leave patients in intractable pain, treatable only by pain medicine, which itself brings on a host of distressing symptoms ranging from drowsiness, nausea, and constipation to hallucination, delirium, and addiction. Each person responds to pain medications differently, so clinicians must carefully balance and monitor a patient's pain regimen. In some cases, it is simply impossible to alleviate all of a patient's symptoms simultaneously. Patients might need to choose, for example, whether they prefer to alleviate their physical pain or remain alert enough to converse with their loved ones. In addition to managing physical symptoms like pain and nausea, the palliative care team also focuses on the whole person. They address social challenges of serious illness such as emotional distress, isolation from loved ones, and navigating community resources. They also attend to existential concerns, helping patients use spirituality to make sense of the hardships of serious illness and death. In order to create a medical plan which manages all these symptoms effectively and optimizes a patient's quality of life, it is also the role of palliative care to determine what a patient wants out of their medical care.

Clarifying a patient's goals of care is as integral to palliative care as symptom management. Clinicians have these conversations by exploring a patient's values, ensuring the patient has an accurate understanding of their current medical situation, and then reviewing what treatment options are realistically available. With this information, as well as guidance and ongoing support from the team, a patient can set their goals. Some patients with serious illnesses look to their medical treatments to prolong their lives at all costs, even if that means undergoing burdensome treatments and living with a lower quality of life. Other patients prioritize comfort above all else, even if that means deciding not to pursue treatments that could extend their lifespans. Many patients hope to receive aggressive treatments with a plan to eventually shift to comfort-focused treatments if curative therapies

1. See https://www.memorialcare.org/services/palliative-care (accessed Dec. 28, 2023).

prove ineffective. Without understanding what a patient hopes to achieve with their care, we risk offering treatments that run contrary to the wishes of the patient.

In order to manage complex symptoms and explore ever-evolving goals, palliative care teams employ an interdisciplinary approach. Each team is structured slightly differently. For example, I work on a well-staffed inpatient team in an urban, community hospital in the greater Los Angeles area. We currently have three medical providers (one doctor and two nurse practitioners) who manage physical symptoms and lead conversations about complex medical decision-making. We have two clinical social workers who manage psychosocial stressors (issues which strain a patient's mental health or social situation), assess family dynamics, and help patients navigate medical and legal resources and programs. The chaplain on our team provides spiritual and emotional support, facilitates end-of-life rituals, and walks with patients and families through grief and other existential issues. I am also a chaplain, but my role on this team focuses primarily on advance care planning, the practice of preparing patients and families for serious-illness decision-making ahead of time. This includes discussing values and care preferences, selecting healthcare surrogates, and recording these decisions in documents like advance healthcare directives which can be referenced if a patient loses the ability to communicate. Many palliative care teams are smaller, while others may have additional personnel like nurses, pharmacists, case managers, and child life specialists.

This interdisciplinary team works not only to identify an appropriate care plan, but to react to various obstacles which might prevent its implementation. A host of financial, logistical, or social factors can impede patients from getting the care they want. Patients may wait too long before attempting a treatment plan that would have been more effective if it had been attempted earlier, or may simply respond unexpectedly to treatment. Key stakeholders, including family members and other members of the hospital's care team, may even perceive the treatment plan as unethical depending on their own professional backgrounds and personal experiences. For example, a physician might feel that a blood transfusion is medically necessary to save a patient's life, and struggle when that patient declines the transfusion on religious grounds. Or, a patient might believe they are not receiving chemotherapy because their oncologist is discriminating against them, when in fact their oncologist has deemed them too frail to survive the treatment. Palliative care teams are uniquely positioned to observe and engage these sorts of obstacles. As specialists in symptom management, it is our job to stay on top of how distressed a patient is feeling—physically, emotionally, spiritually—in response to a treatment plan. When a patient's quality of life is not meeting their goals, we feel that acutely, and as communication specialists we are able to advocate for a change.

Our hospital is located in one of the most diverse cities in the United States. Our patients, staff, and physicians come from all over the world and bring a wide range of varying cultural, religious, and social practices and beliefs to the table, including beliefs around serious illnesses and care at the end of life. Sometimes these beliefs clash, and when they do, often the palliative care team is consulted to help sort things out. It is my hope that in discussing some of the cases we have encountered over the past few years, I can honor the memories of the patients we've served and the often-unseen work of the staff and clinicians who serve them. I also hope that these stories will provide a closer look at where the rubber of ethics meets the road of patient care.

I will look at common issues and specific case studies through the lenses of the four basic bioethical principles codified by Beauchamp and Childress: beneficence, autonomy, non-maleficence, and justice. All cases and issues discussed here are based on real patients. I have changed names, as well as minor demographic and clinical details in order to protect the privacy of those involved.

Regarding the interaction between theory and practice, the Prussian general Helmuth von Moltke famously wrote that "no battle plan survives first contact with the enemy." No matter how clear a situation may seem from the command post, battlefield adjustments must always be made. I won't go so far as to say, "no bioethical principle survives contact with direct patient care." But it is also my hope that these cases will challenge the reader's ethical convictions as they have challenged mine.

BENEFICENCE

Morality requires not only that we treat persons autonomously and refrain from harming them, but also that we contribute to their welfare.[2]

The most common conflict we encounter is when patients, their families, and their clinicians have different ideas about what is beneficial to the

---

2. Beauchamp and Childress, *Principles of Biomedical Ethics*, 165.

patient. Often, this disagreement surrounds cardiopulmonary resuscitation, more commonly known as CPR. CPR always consists of chest compressions, and can often include administering shocks, ventilation, and medications. CPR is meant to be performed on a patient whose heart has already stopped—someone who is, by the conventional definition, already dead. Conducted properly, CPR is often a miracle. It restores the dead to life. And yet many patients make it known ahead of time that if they were to die, they would not want CPR to be attempted.

CPR is not without its drawbacks. The chest compressions necessary for CPR are extraordinarily violent. When patients receive CPR in a hospital setting, it is not uncommon to see a line of clinicians taking turns delivering these blows, switching off when they become physically exhausted. Broken ribs are common. During CPR, a person often spends an extended period of time without sufficient oxygen reaching their brain. Over half of people who survive CPR suffer some form of brain damage.

Moreover, the success rate of CPR depends largely on the recipients. It is much more effective in young, otherwise healthy individuals (say, a teenaged drowning victim). Hospital inpatients, who are sicker and more frail than the general population, fare worse. Of patients who receive CPR in a hospital setting, only about 17–24 percent survive longer than thirty days.[3] One hospital study found that while 61.2 percent of patients in their hospital initially survive CPR, only about half of those patients live long enough to be discharged.[4] CPR success rates also vary greatly depending on age and other medical comorbidities. If the above thirty-day survival rates for hospital settings seem bleak, consider that the thirty-day survival rate in skilled nursing facilities, where patients tend to be even more medically frail, drops to a mere 1.7 percent.[5] While CPR has the potential for miraculous outcomes, it also carries great risks. Individuals who indicate that they would be willing to receive CPR are willing to risk physical trauma, brain damage, for the increased shot at survival. Other patients deem the risk too great and prefer to forgo the chance at prolonging their life in order to ensure they will not need to undergo the ordeal of CPR.

Patients who decide they never want to receive CPR can make their decision known by changing their code status. Every patient in the hospital is required to have a code status, an indicator that tells the clinical team

---

3. California Coalition for Compassionate Care, *CPR Decision Aid*, 3.
4. Zoch et al., "Short- and Long-Term Survival."
5. California Coalition for Compassionate Care, *CPR Decision Aid*, 3.

what to do if the patient's heart stops. A patient may elect to have their code status read "Do not resuscitate." Many hospitals, seeking to cast a more positive light on this election, have recently begun having these code statuses read, "Do not resuscitate/allow natural death." Patients may also elect a "limited code," where only certain elements of CPR are to be performed. A patient may elect, for example, to decline chest compressions but consent to receive shocks from a defibrillator. Limited codes are generally less effective at resuscitating patients than a full code but help avoid outcomes the patient does not see as beneficial.

Code status conversations must attend to a wide array of cultural and personal baggage. I have had more than one patient tell me they want to receive CPR because "it always works so well on *Grey's Anatomy*." Many others look at a DNR/AND code status as a general surrender and abandonment of care. We constantly reassure patients that electing a DNR/AND code status does not mean they will stop receiving their other treatments, only that if they die naturally, we will not attempt CPR. Other patients tell me how scared they are of CPR and breathe a huge sigh of relief when they learn that they have the right to decline this intervention. CPR is, after all, the default code status if patients do not say otherwise. Many clinicians see rendering CPR as part of their commitment to beneficence and can be suspicious of patients who choose not to receive it.

I remember one young man, Rob, I spoke with in our ICU. Compared to his fellow ICU patients, he was in fairly good health. He was in his thirties and in the ICU only for observation as he recovered from an operation. According to the ICU social worker, he wanted someone to help him complete an advance directive. I introduced myself and began talking to him about his values. He had clearly thought in detail about this. He told me that he was generally willing to undergo any treatment which would potentially prolong his life—intubation, artificial nutrition, invasive surgeries like the one he had just been through. The one thing he could not stomach was CPR. I asked him why, and, tearfully, he told me.

When he was a teenager, his father became seriously ill and was hospitalized. Rob, his mom, and his four siblings were visiting him at bedside when his heart stopped. The nurse called the code team. For the next twenty minutes Rob and his entire family watched staff perform CPR on his father. Although he briefly regained a pulse several times, the code team was unable to resuscitate him permanently. Rob still carried that trauma with him years later. He told me that for him, the most important thing was making sure his own children never went through anything like that, even if he had a relatively good chance of recovery. Rob's values, deeply rooted in his own personal experience, guided him to make a treatment decision. Although many in the ICU initially balked at a patient so young electing to be DNR, once they heard his story, they respected his decision.

While many clinicians feel strongly about CPR being beneficial for young, healthy patients, they can be equally quick to identify CPR as non-beneficial for older and more frail patients. I remember speaking with an elderly gentleman who had requested general information on advance directives. I noticed he came to us with a prehospital DNR form. The patient spoke only Spanish, and the form was in English, so I reviewed it with him to make sure he understood what he was carrying. When I explained what this form meant he seemed confused. He told me a doctor at another facility had instructed him to sign the form because CPR would not help him. I told him that while CPR would likely be painful and had a low chance of success for someone with his age and medical background, it was his right to pursue CPR if he wanted. He confirmed with me that even if there were "one chance in a million," he would want to try anything and everything to spend more time with his family, even if that meant the potential for pain and violence at the end of his life. In his mind, this was the most beneficial thing that could be offered. I alerted his physician, who explained the medical details of CPR in greater detail, and then we assisted him with completing new paperwork that recorded his values.

Whether or not CPR is beneficial depends largely on the goals of the patient. If a terminally ill patient has stated goals of maximizing comfort at all costs, even reduced life expectancy, CPR is not beneficial. If that same patient has stated goals of prolonging life at all costs, and CPR has at least some chance of doing that, it is beneficial. Assuming the patient fully understands the information presented to them, can appreciate the significance of that information as it applies to their situation, can weigh the risks and benefits of the proposed courses of action, and clearly communicate their choice, we are obligated to listen. It is impossible to fully seek a patient's well-being without honoring their autonomy.

AUTONOMY

Personal autonomy is, at minimum, self-rule that is free from both controlling interference by others and from limitations, such as inadequate understanding, that prevent meaningful choice.[6]

Many of the complexities surrounding CPR become even more pronounced when dealing with artificial life support. In the hospital setting, artificial life support includes any artificial intervention that prolongs a person's life beyond the point when they would have otherwise died naturally. Two of the most common forms of artificial life support are mechanical ventilation and artificial nutrition and hydration (ANH). With mechanical ventilation, a machine breathes for a patient who can no longer breathe on their own. ANH provides nutrition and hydration to a patient via feeding tube in situations where they can no longer take food and water by mouth.

These interventions are meant primarily to stabilize patients rather than cure their underlying condition. The hope for someone on artificial life support is that it will buy time for other treatments to work and restore the patient to health. Many times, these treatments are very effective in achieving that goal. If a patient loses the ability to swallow after a stroke, receiving supplemental nutrition through a feeding tube may help that patient stay healthy while speech therapists and other clinicians help the patient learn how to eat again. A patient recovering from a motor vehicle accident may need a ventilator to keep their airway open while their body's natural healing processes occur.

Although artificial life support is very powerful and is instrumental in saving many lives every year, like CPR, it also has many serious risks. These risks become more pronounced the longer these interventions are offered. Long-term mechanical ventilation can increase risk of pneumonia and cause lung damage. It is not uncommon to sedate ventilated patients to mitigate the discomfort of being on a ventilator. Long-term ANH is often associated with increased risks of sepsis, aspiration, diarrhea, pressure sores, skin breakdown, and fluid overload. Both long-term ventilation and ANH are controversial when treating patients suffering from dementia or other cognitive impairments, who often need to be physically or chemically restrained in order to keep them from pulling out their tubes.[7]

---

6. Beauchamp and Childress, *Principles of Biomedical Ethics*, 58.
7. AAHPM Board of Directors, "Statement on Artificial Nutrition."

Long-term life support is also potentially worrisome because it has the potential to keep patients alive indefinitely with a limited quality of life, potentially bedbound, comatose, or totally dependent on the care of others for their activities of daily life. While some find this quality of life acceptable, for others, such an existence is a nightmare. Many patients consider long-term artificial life support in this setting to be above and beyond the scope of normal medical care. These patients would never want to receive these treatments if their physicians did not expect them to wean off life support and resume a somewhat normal life.

One challenge for honoring autonomy when it comes to artificial life support is that patients who are sick enough to need artificial life support are often unable to communicate with their physicians. This is one of the reasons palliative care teams promote the completion of advance directives. Advance directives can be drafted by an individual, filled out using a form at a hospital, or assembled by a lawyer. I have noticed many lawyers in our area include the following statement in advance directives they prepare for their clients:

> I recognize that modern medical technology has made possible the artificial prolongation of my life beyond natural limits. I do not wish to artificially prolong the process of my dying if continued healthcare will not improve my prognosis for recovery and my death is likely to occur within several months, or if I require life support as the result of an irreversible condition, even if that life support might prolong my life for a sustained period. Therefore, I do not want efforts made to prolong my life and I do not want life-sustaining treatment to be provided or continued: (1) if I am in an irreversible coma or persistent vegetative state; or (2) if I am terminally ill and the use of life-sustaining procedures would serve only to artificially delay the moment of my death; (3) or under any other circumstances in which the burdens of treatment outweigh the expected benefits.

In California, physicians are legally bound to honor advance directives with statements like these. And yet, even legal documentation is not always enough to protect a patient's autonomy. Sometimes, physicians with strong paternalistic feelings will override their patient's wishes in order to offer treatments they believe are beneficial, even though the patient has clearly indicated otherwise. This is well illustrated in the case of Mr. Malek, a patient who was referred to our team.

Mr. Malek was chronically ill and living in a skilled nursing facility. His condition was not getting worse, but he depended entirely on artificial life support. He breathed with the assistance of a mechanical ventilator connected to his throat via a tracheostomy and took in nutrition via a feeding tube. He was very weak and relied on assistance from his family or staff at his facility to clean himself, urinate, defecate, and adjust his position to avoid bedsores. Years ago, Mr. Malek had completed an advance directive that included a statement like the one quoted above. His family knew this, and frequently asked Mr. Malek's doctor if they were doing the right thing by continuing artificial life support. The doctor assured them they were. He explained that while Mr. Malek had said he would not want to be on life support if he were dying, he was clearly not dying. As long as he was not dying, there remained, however slim, a possibility of recovery. As for whether the burdens of treatment outweighed the benefits, the doctor reminded the family that if life support were removed Mr. Malek would die, and there could surely be no greater benefit than living. The family was not confrontational and listened to the recommendations of their doctor, even though they suspected what they were witnessing was not what the patient would want.

Eventually, Mr. Malek suffered an infection that required him to come to the hospital. The palliative care team was consulted by a hospitalist to clarify Mr. Malek's goals of care. Clinicians on our team reviewed the patient's advance directive and other records and met with the family. The family again shared that they were worried the patient would not want the treatment he was currently receiving. But, this time, they also shared something else. Although the patient was not able to speak in his current condition, he was occasionally able to write. The family presented a stack of papers, each one with a short sentence or two scrawled on it by Mr. Malek. Our nurse practitioner began flipping through the papers. The first one said, "Kill me." The next one, "Please stop." After that, "This is torture." The stack continued. The family had not shown these papers to Mr. Malek's primary physician because they worried he would simply dismiss the documents like he had already dismissed the patient's advance directive.

By this point, Mr. Malek's condition had deteriorated. He was no longer experiencing the brief moments of lucidly that had enabled him to write his messages to his family. But we did have his messages, as well as a properly executed advance directive that stated Mr. Malek would never want to be kept alive artificially if the burdens of his treatments outweighed the benefits. That moment had clearly arrived. Despite all this evidence, Mr. Malek's primary doctor remained hesitant to withdraw artificial life support and transition Mr. Malek's treatment plan to one which prioritized his comfort. After consulting with other staff at the hospital, the Malek family decided to fire this physician and choose a hospitalist to take over the case. This new provider quickly evaluated the situation, consulted with the palliative team and family, and made arrangements to withdraw life support. Mr. Malek passed away peacefully soon after.

Critics of palliative or comfort focused treatments often worry that physicians will give up on patients too soon or will write off marginalized patients who they don't see as worthy of treatments. But equally worrying are situations where physicians or other parties force patients into receiving life prolonging treatments against their will. Sometimes these motives are nefarious; schemes abound where families keep their loved ones alive only so they continue to receive disability payments on their behalf while Medicare foots the bill for years of mechanical ventilation. But often these motives simply come from members of the care team letting their own values overrule a patient's stated goals.

An oncologist shared with me the story of one of his patients who was expected to live only for a few months. Battling a rare and advanced cancer, this oncologist used his cunning to employ a variety of unique and experimental treatments. He managed to stave off the cancer for five years before his patient eventually succumbed to the disease. Several months after the patient died, the oncologist ran into the patient's widow at a supermarket. He expected to be greeted with praise and admiration. Instead, the widow greeted him with scorn. Confused, he offered, "I'm sorry I couldn't get you more time. Five years was more than many of us ever thought possible."

She replied, "Those five years were the most miserable of our lives. He was so debilitated. I watched the cancer kill him from one side and your treatments kill him from the other. For you it may have been a victory, but for us it was hell."

We never found out why exactly Mr. Malek's doctor was so recalcitrant in refusing to transition to comfort-focused care. It may have been that, like the oncologist, he saw himself as the one battling the patient's sickness and did not want to concede defeat. He may view death as synonymous with failure or may have his own unresolved fear of death that he projects onto his patients. Whatever the case, in his attempt to benefit the patient by prolonging his life, he actually harmed this patient by contradicting his wishes and prolonging his suffering.

NON-MALEFICENCE

Above all, do no harm.

The most basic commitment in medical ethics is the commitment to do no harm. This is what compels military surgeons to treat even enemy prisoners of war. However, even this core commitment can be difficult to carry out in practice.

In some cases, it is not immediately obvious whether a particular intervention is helpful or harmful. Depending on the patient's goals and values, interventions like CPR or artificial life support can be either. Although declining these interventions often means a patient will not live as long, it also spares them the burdensome symptoms. Physicians are generally willing to defer to patients or their surrogates when evaluating the potential benefits of these interventions because the primary goal of declining these interventions is not to shorten the patient's life, but to maximize the patient's quality of life. In avoiding potential physical or emotional harm, shortened survival is a tolerable secondary effect, not the main objective. Alleviating suffering by way of intentionally shortening a patient's life is much more controversial.

Until recently, physician aid in dying (sometimes called physician-assisted suicide) was illegal across the United States. In the 1990s, Dr. Jack Kevorkian was famously tried repeatedly for murder after helping terminally ill patients end their own lives. In 1997, however, Oregon passed legislation allowing doctors to prescribe medication with the intent of ending their patient's life. Several other states followed suit. In 2016 California passed similar legislation called the End of Life Option Act.

In California, the process to apply to end one's own life via the End of Life Option Act is rigorous. To apply, an adult must be of sound mind and have a terminal diagnosis with a life expectancy of six months or less. Patients must make three separate requests for the drug to their primary care physician, who is required to thoroughly explain all other end-of-life options. A second physician must confirm the patient's terminal diagnosis. If there is any doubt about a patient's capacity to make their own medical decisions, a formal mental health evaluation must ensure a patient fully understands their decision and is not being influenced by any underlying mental illnesses. Nobody else may consent to physician aid in dying on a patient's behalf; the patient must sign the consent form on their own and, when the time comes, self-administer the drugs.

Not all patients who apply for physician aid in dying are approved. Mr. Larson was a fiercely independent man in his sixties. He suffered a debilitating stroke and required intubation and artificial nutrition. He had an advance directive that stated he would not want to receive artificial life support if his situation was hopeless. His care team was optimistic about his chances for recovery, so his wife (serving as her husband's healthcare agent) made the decision to continue life support treatments until Mr. Larson was strong enough to eat and breath on his own. Mr. Larson recovered, but not entirely. While he was able to eat and breath without artificial assistance, he needed help to do most everything else. Mr. Larson prided himself on his ability to provide for his family and became despondent after learning he would need their help for simple tasks like getting dressed and using the bathroom. He inquired about the End of Life Option Act but was told he did not qualify as he did not have a terminal diagnosis. He settled for changing his code status to DNR/AND, reasoning that the potential burdens of CPR would not justify the potential benefits of returning to his now limited quality of life. He agreed to work with the rehabilitation staff at the hospital so he could regain some of his strength and was eventually discharged home.

Mr. Larson found it difficult to adapt to his new level of functioning. A few days after his discharge, he walked into his garage and stabbed himself in the heart. His wife found him and immediately called 911. He was rushed to the hospital where he was stabilized and, after weeks in the cardiac ICU, again made a recovery. When he woke up this time, Mr. Larson was irate. During his first admission he had been willing to cooperate with hospital staff, but now he was consistently refusing treatments. He was confrontational with staff and had to be placed in restraints to stop him from pulling out his own IVs. A psychiatrist determined he did not have capacity to make his own medical decisions because he was suffering so intensely from depression. While Mr. Larson had always been ineligible for the End of Life Option Act, this called into question his previous medical decisions as well. He had previously elected to be DNR/AND—was this a valid decision based on his values and a reasonable assessment of his current medical situation, or a manifestation of his suicidality? What should be done if the patient decompensates and requires intubation? Given the patient's advance directive, which had been completed prior to Mr. Larson's initial stroke, Mr. Larson's wife and medical team agreed it would not be appropriate to place the patient on life support again if his condition deteriorated further. They decided to attempt to stabilize the patient's mental health so he could again make his own treatment decisions. Unfortunately, Mr. Larson eventually succumbed to complications of his illness before his depression could be treated and his goals could be readdressed.

Mr. Larson's tragic story hopefully illustrates that great care is taken when deciding who can exercise the End of Life Option Act. Although Mr. Larson wanted to end his own life, he was not terminally ill, and his decision was likely influenced by an acute mental health crisis. The intent of the End of Life Option Act is not to provide access to suicide for anyone who is unhappy with their current quality of life, but to help terminally ill patients who have made their peace avoid needless and otherwise unavoidable suffering.

One such patient was Ms. Guzman. By the time Ms. Guzman's cancer was discovered, it had spread all over her body, including a large mass on her tongue. There were no curative options. Doctors did offer Ms. Guzman palliative treatments which could help control her symptoms and improve her quality of life. As the mass on Ms. Guzman's tongue grew, it began to interfere with her breathing. Doctors removed her tongue entirely in a procedure called a major glossectomy. Despite her grim prognosis and functional limitations, Ms. Guzman made it her mission to continue to live as normally as possible for as long as possible. For months she continued her work as a medical scheduler; when she lost her tongue, her employer reassigned her to work as a transcriptionist, a position where she could continue to work but no longer had to speak directly with patients.

Ms. Guzman's cancer continued to spread. Doctors eventually needed to remove a tumor in her neck that was threatening her airway. This time, there was a complication. The wound developed necrotizing fasciitis, a bacterial infection which eats away at soft tissue. Due to the wound's location, standard treatments like amputation and debridement were impossible, and the infection did not respond to antibiotics. Seeing that the infection was eating towards Ms. Guzman's carotid artery, doctors placed protective stents. The bacteria continued to progress, however, until parts of Ms. Guzman's stents were visible to the naked eye. She could no longer go to work because of her neck wound. Not only was her cancer expected to kill her within months, but it was only a matter of time before her spreading neck wound would cause a carotid blowout, meaning she would spend her final moments hemorrhaging from her neck or face. Understandably terrified, she asked about the End of Life Option Act. Her process seemed straightforward; she was clearly terminally ill, and there was no doubt as to her decision-making capacity. Her only barrier was a physiological one: because she no longer had a tongue, she could not self-ingest the aid-in-dying drugs. Physicians contemplated asking Ms. Guzman to administer the drugs through her feeding tube, but unfortunately the law mandated the drug must be taken orally. The medical team frantically searched for alternatives. Eventually they proposed palliative sedation.

AAHPM defines palliative sedation as the "intentional lowering of awareness towards, and including, unconsciousness for patients with severe and refractory symptoms." In other words, it is the practice of managing severe symptoms by sedating a patient to the point where they are no longer aware of them. It is often temporary, used only as long as the patient's symptoms are expected to continue. Ms. Guzman, however, wanted her sedation to be permanent. She wanted her physicians to sedate her, keep her comfortable, and discontinue all ANH. After careful discussion between Ms. Guzman, her family, her oncologist, the hospital bioethics committee, and the palliative care team, the plan was approved. She walked onto the hospital ward under her own power. Her family and closest friends visited her at bedside to say goodbye. Our chaplain led a prayer. The medical team sedated her, and she fell asleep. Per Ms. Guzman's instructions, she was not given any artificial nutrition or hydration. Her family members rotated sitting vigil at the bedside until she died three days later.

Non-maleficence requires providers not to do harm to their patients. In Ms. Guzman's case, the combination of sedation and non-provision of ANH was carried out in order to hasten her death. For many years, bringing about the death of your own patient was unequivocally seen as doing harm. But what were the alternatives for Ms. Guzman? To tell her that she must see things through to the end? To deny her a comfortable, controlled death on a hospital bed, and force her to bleed out at some unknown point in the days ahead? Would that not also have harmed her and her family?

Physician aid in dying is still highly controversial, even in the palliative care community. AAHPM holds a neutral position on the issue, stating it is still too early to understand all the implications of physician aid in dying becoming part of routine medical care. When weighing the risks and benefits of further legalization of physician aid in dying, we would do well to remember patients like Mr. Larson and Ms. Guzman.

JUSTICE

The dead cannot cry out for justice. It is a duty of the living to do so for them.[8]

It is tempting to evaluate all patient care questions on a case-by-case basis. Published standards of care sometimes seem inflexible and unreasonable to clinicians at the bedside. I have frequently found myself advocating for exceptions to hospital policy in order to better serve the needs of a patient who, to me, seemed unfairly restricted by well-meaning but poorly informed regulatory guidelines. The hazard in an increasingly subjective ethical approach, however, is that it provides a greater opportunity for clinician bias (implicit and otherwise) to impact the care a patient receives.

Historically, the American healthcare system has failed to provide truly equitable care to its patients. A recent study revealed many physicians incorrectly believe that Black patients have a higher pain tolerance than White patients, a belief that contributes to chronic mismanagement of pain in Black patients.[9] Another recent study noted that Black patients at one urban medical center were more than twice as likely as White patients to contain negative descriptors like "agitated" and "not compliant" in their medical record.[10] This very real and present bias—combined with a long and well-documented history of nonconsensual medical experimentation on people of color in the United States—has (justifiably) led to a distrust of the medical system, which then makes patients experiencing discrimination "more likely to delay care, less likely to receive recommended chronic disease screening, and less likely to follow their physician's recommendations."[11] Victims of bias in healthcare are less likely to get the care they need, leading to less favorable outcomes than other patients. The COVID-19 pandemic laid this fact bare. In Los Angeles County, where my team works, the age-adjusted COVID-19 mortality rate for non-Latino White residents was 171 per 100,000. For Black residents, it was 301 per 100,000. For Latinos, the rate soared to 444 per 100,000.[12] The root causes of this disparity are diverse. In addition to bias in provision of treatment, social factors like poverty, unstable housing, precarious employment, and

---

8. Bujold, *Diplomatic Immunity*, 60.
9. Hoffman et al., "Racial Bias."
10. Sun et al., "Negative Patient Descriptors," 207.
11. Sun et al., "Negative Patient Descriptors," 203.
12. Per http://publichealth.lacounty.gov/media/Coronavirus/data/# (accessed Mar. 12, 2022).

low insurance coverage all contributed to worse COVID-19 outcomes.[13] Health challenges simply do not impact everyone equally.

This inequality did not just manifest in different mortality rates. In order to protect patients and staff from COVID-19 infection, our hospital implemented a number of safety measures. These included mandating wear of certain personal protective equipment on campus, conducting health screenings of all employees, and limiting patient visitation. By far our least popular safety measure was our restriction on patient visitation. During lulls, inpatients were permitted as many as two visitors at a time as long as they met certain screening criteria. During the peak of the pandemic, however, visitation was almost entirely suspended. Exceptions were few and far between, and were supposed to be extended only for patients who were actively dying or were unable to make their own treatment decisions. Most hospital staff took these restrictions very seriously. When the father of one of our nursing directors was hospitalized, she refrained from visiting him because she did not think it would be fair to the other patients on her unit. Although the burden of being hospitalized with little to no visitation was a heavy one, she felt it important that she not receive any special treatment just because she worked at the hospital.

That being said, many family members did request exceptions to come visit their loved ones in the hospital. While clinicians refused most of these exemptions, some were granted. Exceptions tended to be granted to patients who were most persistent, persuasive, and knew how to speak the language of the healthcare system. This often meant that wealthier, better educated families were able to secure exceptions, while poorer families or those who spoke English as a second or third language were less successful. One family in particular was able to routinely visit a patient to walk with him during his physical therapy sessions. They had convinced the staff that the patient absolutely needed them to be present for emotional support. While this would have been a perfectly normal part of any other admission, during the pandemic it was a luxury that other patients were not granted. Staff members who had reluctantly yet dutifully denied their own ailing patients similar exceptions were frustrated. These exceptions were also impossible to hide from other patients, as most rooms in our hospital hold more than one bed. Lonely patients demanded explanations for why this family was allowed to visit but their own family members were asked to wait outside. Many felt they were being discriminated against. By granting this exception

---

13. Allen et al., *COVID-19 and Social Determinants*, 2–7.

to the visitation policy, staff may have alleviated the emotional suffering of a single patient, but exacerbated feelings of animosity and perceptions of discrimination in others.

Early in the pandemic, our hospital worried that visitation might not be the only resource in short supply. As we watched other hospitals around the country struggle with shortages of staff and equipment, we grappled with the possibility that we would not be able to treat all our patients equally because we simply would not be able to treat all our patients. Normal responses to mass casualty situations were not available in a global pandemic. We could not divert patients to or request staff from other facilities because they would be just as impacted as we were. When the federal government mobilized medical personnel from the National Guard and Army Reserve to provide added clinical support to civilian medical centers, they found many guardsmen and reservists (including myself) were already working at the very hospitals we were meant to relieve. Clinicians brainstormed ideas for how to maximize the resources we had on hand. Proposals included everything from having patients share ventilators to waiving state-mandated nurse to patient ratios, which did occur. Creativity aside, we had to consider the very real possibility that we would have to ration care.

In situations like this some sort of order must be established. Traditional triage generally seeks to maximize resources by differentiating between those patients who will probably die even if they receive treatment, those who can survive without treatment, and those who will likely live if they are treated but may die if they are not.[14] Resources are first allocated for the last group since that is where they would save the most lives. Any surplus resources may be given to the other groups as able.

COVID-19 presented unique challenges to this system. Since it was such a new disease, it was difficult to anticipate exactly how it would impact any given patient. This made triage difficult. Early in the pandemic, we observed that generally a patient's age, body composition, and existing medical history impacted how well they handled the infection. But we had no idea about specifics. If we were trying to judge whether a healthy sixty-five-year-old or a nineteen-year-old with asthma would be more likely to survive COVID-19, we simply did not know. COVID-19 also took a remarkably long time to develop in patients. It might take two weeks from infection for symptoms to manifest in a patient, a further two weeks before that patient was hospitalized, another two weeks before they required

---

14. Kipnis, "Triage and Ethics."

intensive care, and another two weeks before they died. Unlike battlefield triage, it was impossible to accurately predict how severe a certain case of COVID-19 would be.

Knowing that traditional triage methods may not be effective, hospital leaders brainstormed alternatives. We worried about what we would do if two (or more) patients needed mechanical ventilation, but there was only one ventilator available. We worried even more about what we would do if a patient who seemed treatable needed a ventilator, but they were all being used by patients who had slimmer chances of survival. We considered a "first come, first served" system. The situation was so dire at the time, we also thought seriously about prioritizing patients with medical training or other valuable skills who could potentially rejoin the fight against COVID-19 after their recovery. Hospital leaders settled on what they called a comparison of life experiences. If the decision had to be made to save one of two patients, priority would be given to the patient who had had fewer key "life experiences" like marrying, parenting children, or graduating college. The idea was to give as many people as possible an opportunity to live a full, meaningful life.

The system was imperfect. It inherently discriminated against older patients. The weighing of life experiences itself was subjective. How would we compare the life experience of someone who had dedicated themselves entirely to their career with someone who had raised a large family but never worked? What if one had traveled the world while the other had never left Los Angeles, but was a beloved community leader here? In seeking a system to protect ourselves from subjectivity, we may have simply deferred our subjectivity until later in the decision-making process.

Thankfully, we never had to put this imperfect system to the test. Our hospital capacity was stretched to the absolute limit—at one point, two-thirds of our patients were infected with COVID-19. When our ICUs filled up, we set up makeshift wards in vacant recovery rooms. When our morgue filled up, we rented refrigerated box trucks. When our emergency room filled up, the military put up tents in the parking lot. Nurses cared for more patients at a single time than they ever had before. We had to turn away patients with nonemergency situations or previously scheduled elective procedures, but we never had to refuse someone life-saving care. Not all hospitals across the country were so lucky.

CONCLUSION

In the face of the resource scarcity posed by the pandemic, palliative care teams across the country collaborated on a conversation guide for bedside clinicians. It was meant to support clinicians who might not typically have serious illness conversations. The guide contained general tips about addressing common questions and concerns related to COVID-19. It guided users through how to break bad news to patients and families and tactfully explain the dying process. The most sobering sections, though, covered how to tell someone there were not enough resources available to take care of them. If ICUs were full, and clinicians were talking with a patient who knew they would die without ICU level care, the guide recommended reading the following statement: "Your situation does not meet criteria for the ICU right now. The hospital is using special rules about the ICU because we are trying to use our resources in a way that is fair for everyone. If this were a year ago, we might be making a different decision. This is an extraordinary time. I wish I had more resources."[15]

There is no satisfying way to hear that you are going to die. That there are no resources to save you, or that those resources are being allocated to someone with a supposed better chance at survival. But I think the above statement is as good as any. It is direct without being unnecessarily macabre. It explains that there is a universal standard being applied to everyone, and that that standard is (or at least tries to be) founded in equity. It acknowledges that standards change over time. It lands on a note of empathy: I wish things were different.

It embodies the core of how palliative care clinicians practice. They enter situations where it may be impossible to honor all the core principles of biomedical ethics. Seriously ill patients may lack autonomy because they are too sick to speak. They may be victims of great injustice, saddled with cancer after doing everything right. Physicians may not be able to offer treatments they believe to be beneficial if a patient's disease is simply untreatable. In fact, they may be placed in a position where whatever they do will cause some harm and be forced to choose the lesser evil. And yet even in seemingly "unwinnable" situations, we can seek to honor those whom the principles are meant to protect: our patients. Instead of puzzles to be solved, we must commit to care for patients as persons with intrinsic value, regardless of their background or present situation.

15. VitalTalk, "COVID Ready Communication Playbook," 7.

Empathy and accountability must be the touchstones of this commitment. We must never forget that questions of right and wrong have real consequences that mediate how we encounter and alleviate the suffering of others. Mistakes are inevitable, but we must see these mistakes not as ammunition with which to fight those with whom we disagree, but as information we can use to shape more compassionate, patient centric standards and practices. As new information comes to light and new stories are told, we must continue to ensure we integrate these experiences into our ethic, lest we repeat the same mistakes again and again.

Let us never lose sight of our responsibility to patients. May we remain committed to this process of continued improvement, seeking feedback from patients, colleagues, and anyone with a story to tell, open to being reoriented when our moral compass is shifted too strongly by our past or our prejudices. In doing so, we honor not only those who have shaped us in some small way by allowing us to participate in their care, but the stories and experiences of patients across the healthcare system.

Although it is impossible to be entirely impartial, we can and ought to strive to meet our patients where they are, grounded in empathy, honestly seeking their well-being within the framework of a compassionate ethic of care designed for their good.

BIBLIOGRAPHY

AAHPM Board of Directors. "Statement on Artificial Nutrition and Hydration Near the End of Life." AAHPM, Sept. 13, 2013. http://aahpm.org/positions/anh.

Allen, Jessica, et al. *COVID-19 and the Social Determinants of Health and Health Equity: Evidence Brief.* Geneva: World Health Organization, 2021. https://www.instituteofhealthequity.org/resources-reports/covid-19-the-social-determinants-of-health-and-health-equity---who-evidence-brief/equity-covid-19-and-the-social-determinants-of-health-sdh.pdf.

Beauchamp, Tom L., and James F. Childress. *Principles of Biomedical Ethics.* 4th ed. Oxford: Oxford University Press, 2001.

Bujold, Lois McMaster. *Diplomatic Immunity.* Wake Forest, NC: Baen, 2002.

California Coalition for Compassionate Care. *CPR Decision Aid.* Sacramento: CCCC, 2018.

Hoffman, Kelly M., et al. "Racial Bias in Pain Assessment and Treatment Recommendations, and False Beliefs about Biological Differences between Blacks and Whites." *Proceedings of the National Academy of Sciences of the United States of America* 113 (2016) 4296–301.

Kipnis, Ken. "Triage and Ethics." *Virtual Mentor* 4 (2002) 19–21. doi: 10.1001/virtualmentor.2002.4.1.puhl1-0201.

Sun, Michael, et al. "Negative Patient Descriptors: Documenting Racial Bias in the Electronic Health Record." *Health Affairs* 41 (2022) 203–11. https://doi.org/10.1377/hlthaff.2021.01423.

VitalTalk. "COVID Ready Communication Playbook." VitalTalk, n.d. https://www.vitaltalk.org/wp-content/uploads/VitalTalk_COVID_English.pdf.

Zoch, Thomas W., et al. "Short- and Long-Term Survival after Cardiopulmonary Resuscitation." *Archives of Internal Medicine* 160 (2000) 1969–73. doi:10.1001/archinte.160.13.1969.

Index

a priori truths, 74
a posteriori truths, 74
abstract concepts, 16
abortion, 3, 8, 46, 156, 157, 199, 203–6, 207, 212, 284
and infanticide, 203–8
accidental change, 62
actual person, 27–28, 30–32, 34. *See also* potential person
agency, 127, 128, 130, 131, 141, 144, 146, 247
amnesia, 127, 137
amnesiac, 174
Andrews, Keith, 228–30, 233, 240–242
applied ethics, 1, 149, 200, 320
Aristotelian, 16, 17, 109, 110, 112, 133, 150, 161, 167, 311, 176
Aristotelianism, 64
Aristotelian tradition, 3, 152
Aristotelian constituent ontology, 81
Aristotelian metaphysics, 3, 112, 119, 286
Aristotelian-Thomistic metaphysics 119
Aristotelian-Thomistic hylomorphic ontology, 6, 95, 109, 110, 112, 119
Aristotelian-Thomistic framework, 5, 93
Neo-Thomistic hylomorphism, 109, 115
Thomistic perspective, 119
Aristotelian-Thomistic human ontology, 119
artificial intelligence, 258, 259, 264–66, 269, 270, 272, 274, 278
digital intelligence 279
artificial persons, 172. *See also* robotic persons, social persons
Aquinas, Thomas, 109–11, 113, 116, 119, 150
autonomy, 3, 10, 39, 43, 144, 145, 213, 215, 217, 295, 316, 320, 321, 333, 334, 341, 344, 345, 346, 357

Bayesian, 56
Bealer, George, 5, 49, 66, 72–78, 95
beneficence, 46, 341, 343
Berkeley's immaterialist ontology, 57
Berkeley's idealism, 58, 59
bioethics, 1–5, 7, 8, 10, 15–16, 35, 38, 46, 96, 149, 155–56, 199–200, 202, 214, 218, 220–21, 310, 315–16, 318–19, 322, 352
bioethics of gene editing, 303–7
biological naturalism 133
biomedical ethics 357
biomedical issues 2
blindsight 127, 137, 138
Boole, George, 161–62
Borthwick, Chris, 235, 236, 239, 240–242
Borthwick, Chris and Rosemary Crossley, 239, 241

INDEX

Bostrom, Nick, 257–59, 263, 264, 266, 267, 269, 270, 272, 273
brain imaging, 226, 231, 238
brain-alone hypothesis, 127, 130, 131, 133, 136, 138, 140, 141, 143, 145
 brain alone, 126, 129
brain's electromagnetic field, 134–36
Brown, Warren S., 115, 200, 261, 286

Cajal, Santiago Ramón y, 113
capacity, 20, 119, 141
 actual, 173
 unactualized, 204, 69
 cognitive, 222
 for consciousness, 119, 226
 intellectual, 264
Cartesian substance dualism, 127, 135, 141, 146, 201. *See also* non-Cartesian substance dualism
categorial concepts, 74
Chalmers, David, 89, 95, 115, 131, 133, 138
Chisholm, Roderick, 56, 66
Churchland, Patricia, 6, 126, 127–34, 136–39, 141, 143–46, 201
classical logic, 159–62. *See also* logical relations
CPR, 342–45, 349, 350
cognitive enhancement, 321, 274
comatose, 224, 346. *See also* post-comatose patients
consequentialist ethics, 3. *See also* utilitarianism
concept of personhood, 19–22, 277
conceiving, 65–66, 208
conceivability arguments, 132
consciousness, 5, 6, 20, 24, 31, 49, 55, 58, 76, 79, 80, 81, 93–99, 101, 102–9, 112–15, 117–19, 126–41, 143, 144, 146 157, 171, 177, 187, 201, 202, 225, 226, 228, 231–34, 236–38, 241, 242, 252, 258, 259, 264, 268, 283, 286, 311
COVID-19, 353–57
CRISPR-CAS9, 10, 293, 294, 298–300, 304–9, 312

crosspeople, 8, 182, 183, 185, 187–91, 194, 202. *See also* subpeople
cryonics, 264
cyborg, 261, 281–83

debtor's paradox, 18, 19, 40, 42, 43, 200
de dicto knowledge, 67, 79, 80, 81. See also *de re* knowledge
default mode network, 106, 107, 108
Dennett, Daniel, 7, 153, 156–58, 161, 162, 164–67, 170–75, 177, 201
de re knowledge, 79, 80, 85. See also *de dicto* knowledge
Descartes, René, 57, 131
descriptive persons, 36, 38, 41, 42, 43
descriptive personhood, 22–24, 35, 37
detecting consciousness, 5, 94–98, 109, 118, 119
diachronic personal identity, 63
disorders of consciousness, 94, 98, 99–101, 104, 232, 240
disembodied intermediate state, 52, 55
 disembodied, 84, 261, 268
 disembodied existence, 88
 self-embodied, 56
 embodied person, 69, 75, 77
 embodied subjects, 138
dispositions, 7, 32, 35, 68, 69, 77, 111, 153, 167–69, 172–76, 268, 316, 322
DNA, 206, 294–303, 305, 306; see also RNA
Dobbs, 203
dualism, 6, 59, 86, 126, 127, 130, 132–34, 136, 137, 140, 141, 143, 146, 201. *See also* substance dualism; property dualism
dualist field theory, 134–36
 dorsal attention network, 106, 107,
 electromagnetic, 134, 136,
 emergent subject hypothesis, 141, 143
 dualist intuitions, 60, 65, 86, 87, 88

eidetic/categorial intuitions, 81, 83, 85
embryos, 34, 199, 202, 203, 206, 208–13, 284, 303–6, 323, 324

end of life, 2, 8, 46, 199, 202, 204, 215, 217, 223, 244, 245, 340, 341, 349, 350
end of life option act, 351, 352
Epic of Gilgamesh, 259
epigenetics, 296, 297, 311
ethical problems, 2, 3, 4
ethics, 1, 5, 7–8, 15, 35–36, 38, 40–46, 52, 181, 185, 194, 200, 202–23, 268, 284–85, 321, 341
euthanasia, 2, 3, 8, 156, 215, 216, 217, 245, 246
    physician-assisted suicide, 8, 156, 215, 349
European Parliament, 278
explanatory gap, 132, 133
external relation, 82

Feinberg, Joel, 21, 22, 24, 25, 26, 34, 35, 37
fetus, 158, 173, 203–8, 212, 284, 297
first-order capacity, 173. See also second order capacity
first-person knowledge, 171
    first-person or *de se* beliefs, 186
    first-person thoughts, 186–87
    first-person point of view, 49, 201
Fletcher, Joseph, 205, 222, 252
folk ontology, 60, 87
free will, 46, 126, 130, 144–46, 201
    hard determinism, 144
    soft determinism, 144, 145
    indeterminism, 144, 145
    libertarianism, 144
    self-determined, 130, 144
    self-determinism, 144
functionalist approach, 170–72
fuzzy boundaries, 165–67

generous ontology, 7, 8, 181–85, 190–94, 202
gene, 293–312
    gene editing, 8, 10, 211, 213, 214, 293–96, 298, 301–10, 312
    proto-spacer adjacent motif, 298
genetic testing, 8, 211–13, 323

preimplantation genetic diagnosis, 212, 323
global neural workspace theory, 105
God 55, 65, 70, 111, 132, 134, 150, 151, 154, 216, 222, 244, 246–48, 251, 252, 267, 281, 283–86, 311
Goetz, Stewart, 84, 85
germline editing, 303–4

hard problem of consciousness, 95
    easy problem of consciousness, 131
Harris, John, 321, 330
Hasker, William, 84, 115, 133
hedonistic utilitarianism, 274
    hedonistic imperative, 274, 275, 284
Heil, John, 7, 152, 153, 167–69
Heiddeger, Martin, 16
holistic dualism, 286
Howsepian, Avak, 237–39, 242
Hughes, James, 267, 268, 272, 274, 284
human organism, 8, 38, 39, 155, 194, 202, 258
    living/biological organism, 119
    human being/living organism, 155
human persons, 3, 4, 5, 6, 8, 15, 16, 19, 50–55, 89, 111, 113, 115, 155, 172, 173, 175, 176, 200, 205, 211–13, 215, 218
human nature, 10, 109, 110, 111, 112, 115, 226, 257, 258, 267, 276, 312, 318
human enhancement, 263, 269, 272, 274
Hume, David, 36, 81, 112, 129
Husserl, Edmund, 5, 60, 61, 70, 71, 79–83, 85, 86
    epistemology, 79
    ontology, 81, 82
    mereology, 82
Huxley, Aldous, 257
Huxley, Julian, 257
hylomorphism, 109, 110, 115

identity theory, 94
identity, 16, 18, 23, 27, 62, 63, 64, 74, 80, 94, 115, 132, 154, 184, 185, 188190, 191, 193, 262, 268, 282, 283, 284

identity relation, 63
identity overtime, 154, 184, 185, 188, 190, 193
Ihde, Don, 10, 315, 318, 322–24, 326–33
indexicals, 77, 78
inductive argument, 56
infanticide, 3, 8, 21, 208
informative rigid designators, 58, 89. *See also* rigid designators
information, 261, 268, 277, 279, 283, 286, 298, 306, 331, 333, 338
information processing, 137–38, 279
    neural information processing, 145
immortality, 154, 259, 263, 271, 275, 276
inseparable part, 82. *See* also separable part
integrated information theory, 105
    theory's prediction, 98
    information integration, 259, 279
internal relation, 50, 82
intelligent person, 154
intrinsic relation, 50
intrinsic value, 50–53, 57, 89, 201, 357
intuitions, 60, 66, 72, 73, 75–77, 83, 86–88
    dualist intuitions, 60, 65, 86, 87, 88
Istvan, Zoltan, 258, 271
IVF, 209–12, 323

Jackson, Frank, 89, 174
Jennett, Bryan and Fred Plum, 9, 220, 221, 223–26, 232, 233, 237, 239, 242
Jennett, Bryan, 233, 236, 239, 242, 250
justice 353–56

Kant, Immanuel, 16
    deontology, 39
    autonomy, 320
    ethics, 1
Kaplan, David, 78
Kass, Leon, 1, 310, 311, 318, 319
Kim, Jaegwon, 64, 84, 85, 95, 170
knowledge arguments 132
Kripke, Saul, 73, 88
Kurzweil, Ray, 264, 267, 270, 272, 274

Levine, Joseph, 132
Lewis, David, 34, 182, 183, 191
Lindemann, Hilde, 207, 208
limitations, 162–63
    competing interpretations, 161–62
Locke, John, 19, 22, 24, 27, 154–56, 158, 175, 183, 193
    Lockeanism, 155, 186
locked-in syndrome, 102, 227
logical relations, 160–61
Lowe, E. J., 3, 115, 133, 135, 152, 153, 154, 155, 156, 174, 177

Madell, Geoffrey, 71, 58
Marmodoro, Anna, 112
Martin, C. B., 7, 153, 168, 169, 177, 201
Massimini, Marcello, 101, 104
McGrath, Alistair, 311
medical ethics, 1, 9, 220, 223, 349
Meditations, 57
Meilaender, Gilbert, 223, 244–46, 248, 249
mental causation, 95, 141, 143
    neural causation, 143
    top-down causation, 144, 145
    downward causation, 129
    causal chains, 69, 70, 71, 72
mental types, 76
mental tokens, 76
mental properties, 82, 85, 86, 94, 126, 133, 183–85
Merricks, Trenton, 59–63, 65, 77
meta-aware, 279
metaphysics, 4, 5, 7, 8, 15–19, 35–38, 40–46, 114, 153, 155, 156, 172, 181, 194, 199–202, 218
metaphysical truths, 36, 35, 38, 42
    descriptive, 37–40
    ethical, 35, 36, 42
    normative, 38–40
meta-ontology, 3
methodological objection, 36, 42, 43, 45
Mill, John Stewart, 39, 37
Miller, Julie, 268, 282, 283, 284–86
mind-body powers model, 5, 6, 95–98, 105, 108, 109, 112–19, 202

INDEX

minimally conscious state, 99, 100, 101, 227, 236, 242
misdiagnosis, 227–29, 231, 232, 239, 241, 243
modal and grounding argument, 51–56
modal argument, 5, 49, 57–59, 60, 74, 75, 77, 84, 85, 86, 87, 88, 89
modal knowledge, 65–70, 73, 75–79, 81, 83, 84, 87–89
  modal epistemology, 5, 65, 66, 67, 69, 72, 73, 74, 75, 82, 86, 87
modal intuitions, 60, 61, 65, 73, 83, 88, 89
modal dualism, 84
moral enhancement, 265, 318
moral realism, 1, 2
moral irrealism, 1, 2
moral properties, 39
Moreland, J. P., 109, 119, 134, 156, 201, 223, 208
More, Max, 268, 274, 277, 281
multiple realization, 131
multi-track powers ontology, 173
multi-track powers model, 169, 172, 174
multi-track dispositions model, 173, 174
Murphy, Nancey, 200, 261, 286
Musk, Elon, 271, 272, 287

nanotechnology, 262, 264, 265, 272–74
naturalistic concepts, 74
naturalistic dualism, 133, 136, 141
natural kinds, 69, 74
naturalist ontology, 77
neural correlates of consciousness, 5, 95, 97, 105
  neural correlates, 114
neural dependence, 6, 137–38, 127, 128, 130, 133, 134, 135, 136, 137, 138
neurobiological theory, 98, 105, 109
neuron, 113
neuroplasticity, 141, 142. *See also* subject-direct neuroplasticity
neuroscience, 6, 96, 114, 126, 127, 131, 146, 201, 309
non-Cartesian substance dualism, 141. *See also* dualism
non-maleficence, 46, 341, 349, 352

bioethical maleficence, 304
non-reductive physicalism, 286
normative persons, 36, 37
normative personhood, 22–24, 35–37
Nozick, Robert, 40
numerical identity, 185
  numerical identity over time, 190

objects, 18, 53, 61, 62, 63, 64, 67, 71, 73, 75, 79, 80, 81, 83- 86, 150, 161, 167, 175, 177, 267, 279, 315, 322, 330, , 332, 334,
objects of formal ontology, 81
O'Connor, Timothy, 5, 67–70
Oderberg, David, 3, 109, 156, 173
Olson, Eric, 7, 8, 150, 155, 202
ontology, 1, 3, 83, 151, 204, 208
ontology of human personhood, 1, 4
ontology of persons, 3, 4
ontological questions, 3, 6
ontological objection, 36, 37

pain, 20, 39, 76, 99, 131, 170, 171, 225, 301, 339, 344, 353
palliative care, 10, 11, 216, 338–41, 346, 347, 352, 357
  team and family, 348
  treatment, 351
  sedation, 352
Parfit, Derek, 166, 190
parthood, 64, 65
persons, 2, 3, 6, 7, 19–21, 26, 30, 32, 34, 36, 37, 38, 39, 41, 42, 45, 46, 51, 52 126, 137, 150, 151, 154, 155, 157–62, 163–65, 172, 175, 176, 200, 201, 202, 205–9, 211–18, 243, 249, 256, 276, 277, 281, 283, 334, 335, 341, 357
  physical persons, 55
  non-physical persons, 55
personal identity, 7, 8, 63, 154, 155, 193, 200, 202, 203, 209, 267, 268, 276, 282. *See also* identity
person-making properties, 4, 15, 19, 20, 23, 24, 34, 165, 176
person-stages, 8, 183, 184, 187, 192–94, 202

365

persistence of persons, 20
persistent vegetative state, 9, 99, 184, 215, 220, 221, 224–26, 232, 233–35, 239, 242, 243, 249, 346. *See also* vegetative state
    artificial nutrition and hydration, 221, 345
    central nervous system, 225, 309
phase sortal 26, 27, 28–35. *See also* substance sortal
physicalist ontology, 6, 96
physicalist intuition, 86, 87
physicality, 50–56, 62
physical body, 51–56, 58, 60, 61, 84, 110, 111, 154
physicalism, 5, 6, 50, 53–56, 59, 61, 65, 84, 88, 94–97, 109, 110, 119, 127, 132, 134, 135, 200, 201
    standard physicalism, 50, 54
physical properties, 84, 114
Plato, 181
post-comatose patients, 229, 231, 232, 233, 240, 241, 251
    comatose patient, 46, 174
posthuman, 9, 10, 256, 258, 259, 260–263, 269, 274, 275, 277, 281
possible world, 51, 52, 53, 54, 60, 61
potential persons, 20, 21, 26, 28, 29
predicate logic, 159, 163
proprioception, 128
proper constituent, 62
property dualism, 49, 65, 85, 134
psychological continuity, 8, 155, 190, 192, 194, 202
Puccetti, Roland, 150, 173
Putnam, Hilary, 71, 131
powers ontology, 7, 153, 174–77, 201, 205

qualia, 132, 133, 144–46
quality of life, 11, 51, 99, 221, 339, 341, 346, 349, 350, 351
quantum, 145, 279
quantification theory, 163. *See also* predicate logic
    quantification, 163–65
Quine, W. V. O., 3, 182

Rae, Scott, 8, 156, 223, 246, 247, 282
radical dualism, 286
rational intuition(s), 65, 66, 67, 70, 73, 75, 79
Rawls, John, 44
Rea, Michael, 18
reflective equilibrium, 36, 44, 45, 68
rigid designators, 58, 61, 85, 89. *See also* informative rigid designators
reproductive techniques, 2
reproductive technologies, 8, 208–10, 211
RNA, 296, 298–300, 306; see also DNA
robotic persons, 172. *See also* potential persons, social persons
robots, 146, 150, 172, 265, 271, 278, 279
Roe v Wade, 203–4

Savulescu, Julian, and Nick, Bostrom, 2
Schaefer, G. Owen, 320, 321
Schopenhauer, Arthur, 16
Searle, John, 95, 133
second-order capacity, 173. *See also* first-order capacity
    second-order introduction, 71
    first-order and second-order forms of desires, 320
self, 6, 49, 59, 65, 85, 106, 115, 126, 127, 130, 137, 138, 142, 143, 146, 201, 224, 268, 279, 280, 282
self-awareness, 20, 108, 126, 127, 128, 187, 238,
    conscious awareness, 80, 93, 101, 216
    direct awareness, 72, 75, 80, 81, 84, 85, 86, 328
    intuitive awareness, 85, 86, 89,
self-concept, 20, 154, 157, 158, 176
self-identity, 63, 319. *See also* personal identity, identity
self-knowledge, 81
self-consciousness, 150, 157, 158, 174, 176, 183
sentient entities, 279–80
separable part, 82
simple view, 63

Singer, Peter, 2, 3, 7, 21, 153, 156–59, 161, 162, 164–66, 171–74, 177, 201, 204, 205, 217
singularity, 262, 266, 267, 270, 274
social persons, 172
somatic cell, 295, 301, 303, 306
soul, 5, 49, 50–58, 63, 110–13, 115, 119, 126–29, 131, 133, 134, 136–38, 200–203, 208, 226, 286
spatial relations, 82
spiritual substance, 49, 58, 201
split-brain, 60, 128, 138
split-mind, 128
Stefan, Matthias, 278, 279
Strawson, Galen, 135, 154
Strawson, Peter, 155
subject-direct neuroplasticity, 141–43. See also neuroplasticity
   agent directed, 137, 138
substance sortals, 27–29, 34, 156
substance dualism, 5, 49, 57, 65, 127, 135, 141, 146, 201, 203
   Generic substance dualism, 5, 49
subpeople, 7, 182–86, 188, 189, 202. See also crosspeople
supervenience, 94, 95
square of personhood opposition, 159, 160
Swinburne, Richard, 50, 84, 89

Taliaferro, Charles, 84, 85, 86
technology, 10, 118, 213, 214, 240, 257, 260–262, 264, 267, 272, 273, 279, 280, 285, 286, 293–95, 298–300, 306, 312, 315–35, 346
   biotechnology, 2, 3, 8, 211, 213, 272, 321
   enhancement biotechnology, 2
   enhancement technologies, 10, 214, 274, 316, 333, 334
   Institute for Ethics and Emerging Technologies, 263
   medical technology, 204, 207, 330, 346
   technology ethics, 1
   technosystem, 316, 323, 324, 329–31, 333, 334

temporal circuits hypothesis, 98, 105–8, 115–17
temporal parts, 7, 182, 191, 202
therapy, 142, 228, 230, 236, 240, 241, 294, 300, 301, 309, 316, 354
   constraint-induced movement, therapy 142
   germline therapy, 214
   gene therapy, 294, 300, 301, 307, 308, 309
   somatic gene therapy, 301
theory of justice, 44. See also justice
Thomson, Judith Jarvis, 3, 206, 207
transhumanism, 9, 150, 256–59, 261–63, 265–69, 271–77, 281–87
   transhumanist bill, 258, 259, 271, 277, 279, 280
   transhumanist ethics, 284–85
   transhuman metaphysics, 267, 268, 276, 281, 286
   World Transhumanist Association, 259, 269, 272
truthmaker, 67, 68
Tooley, Michael, 7, 153, 156–59, 161, 162, 164–75, 177, 201, 204, 205
Tononi, Giulio, 101, 102, 103, 104, 105
two-dimensional semantics, 89
two notions of a person, 154, 175

unconsciousness, 6, 102, 118, 139, 223, 238, 243, 352
   anesthetic-induced unconsciousness, 6, 139
   permanent unconsciousness, 223, 243, 284
   conscious and unconscious, 96, 97, 108, 115, 126
unconscious, 9, 30, 31, 99, 101, 102, 105, 107, 108, 118, 139, 220, 223, 224, 225, 227, 232, 237, 238, 241, 242, 244, 246
unified consciousness, 140, 267
unresponsive person(s), 5, 93, 104, 117, 118
utilitarianism, 39, 188, 200, 269, 274, 284

Van Inwagen, Peter, 3, 16–18, 38, 86–88, 150
vegetative state, 9, 99, 184, 215, 220, 221, 222, 224–27, 229, 231–33, 235, 237, 239, 240–243, 247, 250; see also persistent vegetative state

wakeful state, 224, 225
wakefulness, 9, 99, 224, 225, 242,
Warren, Mary Ann, 19, 20, 22, 201, 205

Wiggins, David, 27, 30, 34, 35, 156
Wittgenstein, Ludwig, 151
Wolf, Naomi, 207

Yolton, John, 55
Young, Simon, 268, 269

Zimmerman, Dean, 59, 150
zombie world, 52, 132, 319